Applied Linguistics in Action

Applied Linguistics in Action: A Reader presents students with an applied linguistics framework for the analysis of real-world problems in which language is a central issue. The reader allows students to develop both the theoretical and empirical skills crucial to an understanding of language teaching and other language-related professional practices.

Part One brings together seven key discussions of the nature and direction of contemporary applied linguistics, relating theory and description of language in use to educational and other professional contexts. Issues include the politics of applied linguistics, its responses to globalisation, and its relation to social theory.

While the discussions in Part One are largely theoretical, Part Two, through abridged versions of thirteen case studies, demonstrates at a much more practical level how general principles formulated in Part One can be applied to a range of specific real-world problems. While the majority of studies are from educational settings, the breadth of current applied linguistic enquiry is illustrated by others relating to legal forensics, literary analysis, translation, language therapy, lexicography, and workplace communication.

The editors' introductions, both to the volume as a whole and to each individual part, guide the student through the difficult transition from general discussion to specific application, highlighting the most significant issues, and helping the student to see the relevance of both general theory and specific applications to the needs of their own studies, and their professional practice beyond.

Applied Linguistics in Action: A Reader is essential reading for advanced level undergraduates and postgraduates on applied linguistics, English language, and TESOL/TEFL courses.

Guy Cook is Professor of Language and Education at The Open University. His books include *Genetically Modified Language* (2004), *Applied Linguistics* (2003) and *The Discourse of Advertising* (2001).

Sarah North is a Senior Lecturer in Applied Language Studies at The Open University. Recent publications include *Exploring English Grammar* (2009) and chapters in *A Companion to English Language Studies* (2010) and *Language and Literacy: Functional Approaches* (2006).

This reader, along with the companion volume *Applied Linguistics Methods: A Reader*, form part of *Investigating Language in Action* (E854), a course belonging to the Open University MA in Education programme.

The Open University Masters in Education

The Open University Masters in Education is now firmly established as the most popular postgraduate degree for education professionals in Europe, with over 3,000 students registered each year. It is designed particularly for those with experience of teaching, the advisory service, educational administration or allied fields. The Masters in Education (Applied Linguistics) is of particular relevance to teachers of English or educators who are interested in exploring the role of language in education. Successful study on the MA entitles students to apply for entry into the Open University Doctorate in Education programme.

Details of this and other Open University courses can be obtained from the Student Registration and Enquiry Service, The Open University, PO Box 197, Milton Keynes MK7 6BJ, United Kingdom: Telephone +44 (0) 845 300 6090, e-mail general-enquiries@open.ac.uk.

Alternatively, you may wish to visit the Open University website at www.open.ac.uk, where you can learn more about the wide range of courses and packs offered at all levels by The Open University.

Applied Linguistics in Action

A Reader

Edited by

Guy Cook and Sarah North

LONDON AND NEW YORK

The Open University
Walton Hall
Milton Keynes
MK7 6AA
United Kingdom
www.open.ac.uk

First published 2010
by Routledge
2 Park Square, Milton Park, Abingdon, Oxon OX14 4RN

Simultaneously published in the USA and Canada
by Routledge
270 Madison Ave, New York, NY 10016

Routledge is an imprint of the Taylor & Francis Group, an informa business

Typeset in Perpetua and Bell Gothic by
Florence Production Ltd, Stoodleigh, Devon
Printed and bound in Great Britain by
CPI Antony Rowe, Chippenham, Wiltshire

British Library Cataloguing in Publication data
A catalogue record for this book is available from the British Library

Library of Congress Cataloging in Publication Data
Applied linguistics in action : a reader / edited by Guy Cook and Sarah North.
   p. cm.
1. Applied linguistics. 2. English language—Social aspects. I. Cook, Guy
(Guy W. D.). II. North, Sarah, Dr.
P129.A67 2009
418—dc22   2009002009

ISBN 10: 0–415–54546–3 (hbk)
ISBN 10: 0–415–54547–1 (pbk)

ISBN 13: 978–0–415–54546–4 (hbk)
ISBN 13: 978–0–415–54547–1 (pbk)

Contents

Illustrations

Figures

Tables

Acknowledgements

The editors and publishers would like to thank the following for kind permission to use copyright material:

Brumfit, C.J. and Oxford University Press for 'Language, linguistics, and education', in *Individual Freedom in Language Teaching*, pp. 3–19, 2001.

Crystal, David and Cambridge University Press for Chapter 1 'Why a global language?' in *English as a Global Language*, 2003.

Dijkstra, Bourgeois, Petrie, Burgio, Allen-Burge and Taylor and Francis for 'My recaller is on vacation: discourse analysis of nursing-home residents with dementia', in *Discourse Processes*, 33 (1), 2002.

Easton Ellis, B. and Alfred A. Knopf, a division of Random House, for an extract from *Lunar Park*, pp. 107–8, 2005.

Fabrício, B., Santos, D. and Palgrave Macmillan for '(Re-) locating TEFL: the (re-) framing process as a collaborative locus for change', in J. Edge (ed.) *(Re-) Locating TESOL in an Age of Empire*, pp. 65–83, 2006.

Hurry, J., Nunes, T., Bryant, P., Pretzlik, U., Parker, M., Curno, T., Midgley, L. and Taylor and Francis for 'Transforming research on morphology into teacher practice', *Research Papers in Education*, 20 (2), 197–206, 2005.

Jasso-Aguilar, R. and Cambridge University Press for 'Sources, methods and triangulation in needs analysis: a critical perspective in a case study of Waikiki hotel maids', in M. Long (ed.) *Second Language Needs Analysis*, pp. 127–58, 2005.

Jenkins, J. and Oxford University Press for 'A sociolinguistically based, empirically researched pronunciation syllabus for English as an international language', in *Applied Linguistics*, 23 (1), 83–103, 2002.

Jieun Lee and Oxford University Press for 'Interpreting inexplicit language during courtroom examination', in *Applied Linguistics*, 30 (1), 2009.

Myers, G. and Oxford University Press for 'Applied linguists and institutions of opinion', in *Applied Linguistics*, 26 (4), 527–45, 2005.

O'Keeffe, A., McCarthy, M., Carter, R. and Cambridge University Press for 'Idioms in everyday use and in language teaching', in *From Corpus to Classroom: Language use and language teaching*, pp. 80–94, 2007.

Oztalk: University of Technology, Sydney, Macquarie University Australian English Database for an extract from their database.

Pennycook, A. and Cambridge University Press for 'English in the world/the world in English', in J.W. Tollefson (ed.) *Power and Inequality in Language Education*, pp. 34–58, 1995.

Prodromou, L. and Cambridge University Press for 'Bumping into creative idiomaticity', in *English Today*, 89 (23/1), 14–24, 2007.

Rampton, B. and Multilingual Matters for 'Continuity and change in views of society in applied linguistics', in H. Trappes-Lomax (ed.) *Change and Continuity in Applied Linguistics*, pp. 97–114, 2000.

Rosa, E.A. and Dunlop, R.E. and Oxford University Press for 'Poll Trends: Nuclear Power: Three decades of public opinion', in *Public Opinion Quarterly*, 58: 295–325.

Sealey, A., Carter, B. and Continuum International Book Publishing Ltd for 'Making connections: some key issues in social theory and applied linguistics', in *Applied Linguistics as a Social Science*, pp. 17–33, 2004.

Steedman, C. and Virago for Figure 1.2, in *The Tidy House*, pp. 213–14, 1982.

Thornbury, S., Slade, D. and Cambridge University Press for 'The grammar of conversation', in *Conversation: From description to pedagogy*, pp. 73–86, 90–6 and 100–3, 2006.

Waterton, C., Wynne, B. and Sage for 'Can focus groups access community views?' in Kitzinger, J. (ed) *Developing Focus Group Research*, pp. 12–43, 1999.

Widdowson, H.G. and the Copyright Clearance Centre for 'The ownership of English', in *TESOL Quarterly*, 28 (2), 377–89, 1994.

Widdowson, H.G. and Oxford University Press for 'The theory of practice', in *Defining Issues in English Language Teaching*, pp. 1–15, 2003.

Wray, A., Staczek, J.J. and Equinox for 'One word or two? Psycholinguistic and sociolinguistic interpretations of meaning in a civil court case', in *Speech, Language and the Law*, 12 (1): 1–18, 2005.

Every effort has been made to trace copyright holders but this may not have been possible in all cases. Any omissions brought to the attention of the publisher will be remedied in future editions.

Introduction

Guy Cook and Sarah North

This book is a reader in applied linguistics. There has been a good deal of debate about the scope and nature of applied linguistics. Recently however, a certain degree of consensus seems to have been achieved, that applied linguistics is concerned with:

> The theoretical and empirical investigation of real-world problems in which language is a central issue.
>
> (Brumfit 1995: 27)

This useful and concise definition of the field is now both widely accepted and widely quoted, and informs the thinking behind this volume and its companion. As a broad definition it has a number of distinct advantages. It differentiates applied linguistics from other branches of linguistics by foregrounding its orientation towards language-related problems, and it implies – though it does not explicitly say this – that work in applied linguistics can have some impact upon those problems, potentially influencing how decisions are made about them. It is also general enough to encompass the many disparate activities and areas of enquiry that call themselves applied linguistics, and it can unite approaches to language which are different, even incompatible. However, it also necessarily leaves many questions open and unanswered. Which theories are best suited to applied linguistic investigation? What empirical methods should be used? How are problems to be identified? Which problems should the applied linguist investigate? After these problems have been investigated, what action might be taken to impact upon them? What is the relation between theorising, empirical investigation, and action?

The aim of this volume and its companion is to present the reader with a variety of answers to these questions through a selection of writings. This first volume focuses in particular on the questions: Which theories? and Which real world problems? The companion volume, *Applied Linguistics Methods: A Reader* (Coffin *et al.* 2009) addresses the methodologies for empirical investigation (and of course the theories behind them), considering three which are both widely used and particularly well suited to applied linguistic enquiry, namely systemic functional linguistics, linguistic ethnography and critical discourse analysis.

In this present volume then, the emphasis is upon theory and practice, and the complex relation between the two, with a general movement from the most general and theoretical perspectives towards more practical examination of specific problems, although a neat division between theory and practice is – as the first chapter points out – neither possible nor desirable. **Part 1** presents a selection of influential reflections upon the nature of the discipline, and the particular relation between theory and practice that lies at its heart. These discussions also consider the ways in which applied linguistics relates to and draws upon other disciplines, and its position within the changing intellectual and political landscape around it. **Part 2** presents a variety of reactions to the growth of English as an international language. This is a key factor in any consideration of contemporary real-world language-related problems, and for this reason has been given a section of its own. **Part 3** complements the largely theoretical perspectives of Parts 1 and 2, by presenting a series of investigations into specific real-world problems. These give some indication of the scope and variety of applied linguistic activity today, treating not only problems related to language teaching and learning – the longest-established area of applied linguistic enquiry – but also law, interpreting, language disorders, the workplace, and opinion polling.

This sounds neat – but things are never so straightforward, especially where real-world contexts are concerned. Consider more closely for example this notion of 'real-world problems in which language is a central issue'. This is potentially so large a category that it threatens to disable any discipline which proposes to tackle all such problems and maintain any kind of identity and coherence. As Greg Myers observes in Part 3 of this volume:

> It is hard to think of any 'real-world' problems – from global warming, to refugees to genetic counselling to outsourced call centres to AIDS/HIV to military intelligence – that do not have a crucial component of language use. Almost every 'real-world problem' confronting humanity involves 'language [as] a central issue'.
>
> (Myers 2005)

We need then some way of delimiting activity.

Traditionally applied linguistics has favoured one particular set of problems; that of how best to teach an additional language. (In practice the scope has been even narrower, as the language investigated with relation to these questions was predominantly English.)

So close was this association that in the words of Pit Corder, one of the founders of the discipline:

Of all the areas of applied linguistics, none has shown the effects of linguistic findings, principles and techniques more than foreign language teaching – so much so that the term 'applied linguistics' is often taken as being synonymous with that task.

(Corder 1973: cover notes)

Taking a slightly different route but reaching the same conclusion, Alan Davies (1999) has argued reductively that applied linguistics is what applied linguists do, and that this is overwhelmingly the investigation of language teaching and learning. This characterisation of the field is widespread and tenacious. Many other recent reference books and introductions take a very similar line (e.g. Johnson and Johnson 1998; Kaplan 2002; Schmitt 2002). The *Longman Dictionary of Applied Linguistics* for example (Richards *et al.* 2002) defines the scope of the discipline both broadly and narrowly, but significantly gives the narrow definition first:

1 the study of second and foreign language learning and teaching;

relegating to second place a definition more in keeping with Brumfit's, and more in keeping with the broad approach in this volume;

2 the study of language and linguistics in relation to practical problems such as lexicography, translation, speech pathology, etc.

Although language teaching and learning is still undoubtedly the major area of enquiry, and is for this reason addressed by the majority of the chapters in this volume, the discipline has in recent years branched out into new areas. In the course of that expansion it has developed new methodologies and theories, and encountered new disciplines and theories, all of which have fed back fruitfully into the core area of language teaching and learning. So it is not that new areas of enquiry are replacing an old one, but rather that the discipline as a whole is expanding, with the original area of study remaining as strong and dynamic as ever, enriched and complemented by its new companions.

These new areas of applied linguistics are neither the limitless list envisaged by Myers, nor the strangely truncated one of Richards *et al.*, which ends so abruptly and mysteriously with 'etc.' after only three examples. In practice a number of quite precise new areas have emerged as major focuses of applied linguistic enquiry and are now covered in the discipline's major journals (*Applied Linguistics* and *The International Journal of Applied Linguistics*) and in presentations at its major conferences. Some of these are relatively new, such as forensic linguistics (the deployment of knowledge about language in criminal and other legal investigations), the study of workplace communication or of public communication. Others, such as clinical linguistics, deaf linguistics, language planning, language testing, lexicography, literary stylistics, and translation studies, have a separate and independent identity. Although these have long, well-established histories – often much longer than applied linguistics – and must therefore be embraced with respect and a due sense of their independence and authority, they all primarily address real-world language-related problems, and fall therefore within the rubric of the discipline as Brumfit defined it.

But problem identification, whether in the core areas of language teaching and learning, or in any other, is not just a simple matter of listing areas and then locating within them ready-made problems. For if it were only this, then applied linguistics would be merely responsive, a kind of trouble-shooting service industry which can be called in to provide a quick fix. It is much more than this, problematising areas where practice has been taken for granted, and reformulating long-standing problems in new and exciting ways. The chapters in this volume show how this can be done, and it is our conviction that the reader will find in this volume and its companion a rich view of the main themes of applied linguistics today.

References

Brumfit, C.J. (1995) 'Teacher professionalism and research', in G. Cook and B. Seidlhofer (eds) *Principle and Practice in Applied Linguistics*. Oxford: Oxford University Press.

Coffin, C., Lillis, T. and O'Halloran, K. (2009) *Applied Linguistics Methods*. London: Routledge.

Corder, S.P. (1973) *Introducing Applied Linguistics*. Harmondsworth: Penguin.

Davies, A. (1999) *An Introduction to Applied Linguistics*. Edinburgh: Edinburgh University Press.

Johnson, K. and Johnson, H. (eds) (1998) *The Encyclopaedic Dictionary of Applied Linguistics*. Oxford: Blackwell.

Kaplan, R.B. (2002) *The Oxford Handbook of Applied Linguistics*. New York/Oxford: Oxford University Press.

Myers, G. (2005) 'Applied linguistics and institutions of opinion', *Applied Linguistics* 26 (4): 527–45. (Also in this volume, pp. 257–73.)

Richards, J., Platt, J. and Weber, H. (2002) *The Longman Dictionary of Language Teaching and Applied Linguistics*. London: Longman.

Schmitt, N. (2002) *An Introduction to Applied Linguistics*. London: Arnold.

PART ONE

Applied linguistics in theory

Guy Cook and Sarah North

Introduction to Part One

In our general introduction we have adopted Brumfit's characterisation of applied linguistics as a discipline addressing problems in which language is a central issue. The four chapters in this first part, though they may not refer or subscribe directly to this view, nevertheless treat important matters that arise from it. Of key concern is the relation between theory and practice, and consideration of how the abstractions and idealisations of academic enquiry into language (i.e. linguistics) are relevant or can be made relevant as *applied* linguistics in the world of professional practice, and, conversely, how they may be changed and enriched through their encounter with practitioners.

Related to this concern, and inevitably arising from it, is the issue of inter-disciplinarity. For if disciplinary identity has been traditionally seen as a matter of abstracting from the real world to deal only with certain aspects of the object of enquiry, then it is hard to see how a mode of enquiry which defines itself by its capacity to understand real-world problems, can maintain such a level of abstraction. Applied linguistics cannot of its nature remain within an ivory tower where disciplinary identity can be easily preserved, but must rather get its hands dirty by entering and engaging with the real-world problems that it purports to examine, and in which it has some pretensions to intervene. Addressing real-world problems will only have validity if they can be treated in the round. To isolate certain features as though they were the only factors in the problem is not only to simplify but also to distort. If, for example, one wants to understand the impact of a certain approach to teaching or language acquisition, one cannot do so convincingly by isolating the 'input' and the 'output' (as teacher and student language have been reductively called) from factors affecting student motivation, the personality of the teacher, the social and language groups to which the students belong, the cultural traditions in which the lesson takes place and countless other factors besides. This immediately takes us beyond 'linguistics' into an ever-expanding encounter with other modes of enquiry: economic, historical, political and psychological. But if this is the case what happens to the identity of applied linguistics as a separate area of enquiry? Does it not simply evaporate into a mixture of every approach? If it is an intersection of disciplines, of which linguistics is but one equal partner among many, how can it have a disciplinary identity of its own?

The first chapter in this section, Henry Widdowson's 'The Theory of Practice', addresses these difficult problems directly and subtly. The argument avoids simplistic extremes, neither arguing that theory from an academically defined area of enquiry should be imposed upon practice, nor that practical experience and the professional wisdom derived from it somehow invalidate and undermine the authority of academic enquiry. Indeed, Widdowson queries the basis of the popular distinction between theory and practice, pointing out that so-called professional wisdom is itself a kind of theorising. His argument is that disciplinary enquiry is inevitably partial, necessarily involving abstraction and idealisation, considering some aspects of its object and disregarding others – but it is valid nevertheless. However, applied linguistics is not in his view automatically and unproblematically relevant to real-world issues, nor the only relevant source of insight. It needs to be made so, through what Widdowson refers to as a process of mediation. This is not to deny the relevance of other disciplines and the contributions they can make, or the importance of knowledge of practitioners, but to see applied linguistics as one independent and specific area of insight among others. Conversely, in his vision of the discipline, applied linguistics should be treated as an autonomous area. Its enquiries are not to be measured only by their usefulness, nor dictated by the demands of practitioners and policy makers, but should make their own independent contribution to understanding of language-related problems. Applied linguistics 'does not impose a way of thinking but points out things which might be worth thinking about'.

In the next chapter, 'Language, Linguistics, and Education', Christopher Brumfit addresses similar territory to Widdowson, but with a more specific orientation towards education and in particular teacher training. He begins with the wry observation that language and education are areas on which everybody claims expertise, and that this makes the job of the researcher into both particularly difficult. Like Widdowson, he too sees the task of applied linguistics as one of mediation rather than imposition, and academic theory and practical experience as equal but independent contributors to understanding of the language-related problems of education. Theories cannot tell us everything, least of all how to teach. But they do have a contribution to make. Conversely, there are aspects of research whose worth is not to be measured only by their practical applications. 'Understanding does not necessarily require change to follow'. Though Brumfit, like Widdowson, is committed to the disciplinary integrity of applied linguistics, this chapter touches upon a number of related disciplines – anthropology, social psychology, sociolinguistics – and is in itself interdisciplinary in that it deals with the intersection of education (as an academic field of enquiry) and applied linguistics.

The next two chapters are somewhat different in their perspective, less troubled by the issue of preserving disciplinary identity, more concerned with how to understand the changes to enquiry which follow from changes in the world around applied linguistics, and to present a more positive view of methodologies which may benefit from an expansion of disciplinary and philosophical purview.

Ben Rampton's 'Continuity and Change in Views of Society in Applied Linguistics' seeks to examine how the disciplinary activity of applied linguistics has been affected by changes in the general intellectual currents around it. He considers four views – conservative, liberal-pluralist, Marxist, post-modern – presenting these and their implications for views of culture, language, research, philosophy, politics and intervention, in a useful tabular summary. In the discussion around this summary, he tackles in particular what a post-modernist approach has meant in practice for applied linguistics research. In contrast to older liberal and leftist views, in which social and linguistic action and identity is explained and described from the perspective of the larger social systems they exemplify, this new post-modernist approach conveys a 'sense that we "assemble" ourselves from a plethora of changing options, deciding what is right and wrong for ourselves'. For better or for worse – and Rampton is not suggesting either – this subtle shift of perspective has had an enormous influence on recent applied linguistic research, leading to a more localised and less judgemental perspective, without appeal to the 'grand narratives' favoured by earlier research.

In the last chapter of this section, 'Making Connections' by Alison Sealey and Bob Carter, the notion of interdisciplinary enquiry is realised in a particularly clear and lucid presentation of the principles and practice of contemporary applied linguistics, where insights from other disciplines – and in particular social theory – are brought to bear upon actual enquiry. Recent work on language and language analysis is integrated with this social perspective to allow a rich palette of approaches, each of which is briefly characterised by Sealey and Carter, including sociolinguistics, ethnography, discourse analysis and critical discourse analysis, and language ecology. There is a sense here of regained calm and order, as though the traumatic and defensive introspection and self-examination of the first three chapters has been absorbed by a developing discipline, and can emerge as a powerful set of tools for an engagement with real-world problems in ways and on terms which are suited to contemporary needs.

Chapter 1
_____

Henry Widdowson

The theory of practice

[. . .]

To theorize about language teaching is to subject common-sense assumptions to critical reflection. You may, as a result, reject or accept them, but either way, you will have some rational basis for your decision. Thought of in this way, theory is not remote from practical experience but a way of making sense of it.

But if theory is so beneficial and indeed so crucial to good practice, as I am claiming it is, why, one must wonder, is it treated with such distrust, not to say disdain, in the language teaching profession, even by those (indeed, it seems, especially by those) who insist that teachers should be 'reflective practitioners'? One reason is that it is associated with the academic discipline of linguistics, and this is seen to be an abstruse field of enquiry at several removes from the reality of the language classroom. Furthermore, in perverse defiance of this obvious limitation, there are claims by people calling themselves applied linguists that this arcane discipline can nevertheless yield insights of practical pedagogic relevance. What makes matters worse is that applied linguists, exploiting the prestige of the discipline they seem to serve, assume an air of superior wisdom and impose these insights unilaterally on an all too deferential teaching profession. In short, as Thornbury has recently put it, language teaching is 'at risk of being hi-jacked by men in white coats' (Thornbury 2001: 403).

This suspicion and resentment of theory are widespread, and misconceived. The misconception is grounded in a misunderstanding of linguistics and its relationship

Edited extract from: Widdowson, H.G. 'The theory of practice', in *Defining Issues in English Language Teaching*, Oxford University Press, pp. 1–15, 2003.

with applied linguistics, and of the nature of theory itself. In respect to the last of these, it is interesting to note that even those who are strident in their opposition to theory are not averse to making theoretical claims themselves. Consider the following text, which appears as a general preface to a series of resource books for English teachers.

A letter from the Series Editors

Dear Teacher,
This series of teachers' resource books has developed from Pilgrims' involvement in running courses for learners of English and for teachers and teacher trainers. Our aim is to pass on ideas, techniques and practical activities which we know work in the classroom . . .

(Lindstromberg and Rinvolucri 1990)

This Preface is couched in the form of a letter, a device designed to reduce the usual formal distance between author and reader. But authority is nevertheless retained in this first paragraph by the presentation of credentials: the series is underwritten by extensive experience running courses at this persuasively named institution *Pilgrims*, not only for learners of English, but also for teachers and teacher trainers too. And the use of the plural of course carries the implication of generality. But we need to ask *which* learners, *which* teachers, *which* teacher trainers are being referred to here, and the extent to which it is reasonable to suppose that they are representative of *all* learners, teachers, teacher trainers. The implication of generality is carried over into the second paragraph. The use of the definite article is significant here: *the* classroom, that is to say, the generic classroom. The assumption appears to be that what works in one classroom will be generalizable to all others.

In short, the authors are extrapolating from what has happened in their particular classrooms with particular groups of learners and teachers and are, in effect, making a global claim for a local experience, backed up by the persuasive assertion of authority: they *know* what works. So although the authors talk about things working in actual practice, what they are doing is abstracting from this actuality and making a theoretical statement about how things work in general. Furthermore, we might note, it looks as if the authors are transmitting their influence unilaterally: they are passing on ideas and practices which bear the mark of their authority. There is no suggestion that these need to be critically examined and their relevance worked out in consideration of local conditions, which will in many cases be completely different from those which obtain in the classrooms from which these generalities have been derived. Knowing how things have worked in particular circumstances is thus taken as know-how in general. What we seem to have here is, in effect, the assertion of theoretical authority disguised as practical down-to-earth advice based on an appeal to illusory shared experience.

To point this out is not to say that one cannot or should not infer general methodological principles from particular practices but only that we need to recognize that in doing so we are making theoretical claims; it is misleading to suggest otherwise. Furthermore, we need to exercise a little caution in making such claims, recognize that they may be based on limited empirical evidence, and resist the temptation to transmit them as the truth. And this applies to *any* theoretical statement, whether it comes from linguists, educationists, teachers, teacher trainers, and whether it comes covertly in the guise of practical down-to-earth advice, or overtly in the idiom of an academic discipline.

Theory is concerned with the abstraction of generalities from particulars (which is why the statement we have just been considering is a theoretical one in spite of appearances). As such it is bound to disregard certain differences in order to establish commonalities. Theory then allows us to identify something as an instance of a more general category of things, and this requires us to ignore other features which are incidental and not categorial. But the essential point to note is that theory is always, and inevitably, *partial*. The abstractions of theory can never match up with the actualities of experience. When theory is referred to practice, it is bound to get caught up in the complexities of the real world from which it has been abstracted. The question always is: how can theory, no matter how global its claims, be interpreted so as to be relevant to local circumstances?

There is a well-entrenched belief among many in the language teaching profession that theory is necessarily opposed to practice. It is ironical that this belief is so often encouraged by those who themselves make theoretical pronouncements about how and what to teach in classrooms under the guise of practical advice. But there is no opposition between theory and practice, and to set them up against each other is, wilfully or not, to misrepresent the nature of both. Instead of setting up a pointless polarity and dismissing the relevance of theory out of hand, what we need to do is explore how it can be *made* relevant and turned to practical advantage. And this is where applied linguistics comes in.

Another persistent belief in some language teaching circles is that not only is theory *opposed* to practice, but is *imposed* upon it by so-called applied linguists who, by a process of transmission, seek to apply linguistic ideas and findings directly and unilaterally into language pedagogy. Such a belief is based on a misconception about the nature of applied linguistics, which is aided and abetted by its very name.

For applied linguistics as it relates to language education does not just take linguistics and apply it. To see why this is so, we need to be clear about the nature of linguistics as a disciplinary enquiry, and the extent to which it is applicable to the concerns of everyday life, including those of the practising teacher.

Linguistics makes statements about language in general or languages in particular, but these statements are necessarily abstractions from the actuality of language as experienced by its users. From their different theoretical perspectives or positions linguists will map out language in different ways, giving prominence to some aspects (deemed to be essential) at the expense of others (deemed to be incidental). All models of linguistic theory, and the descriptions based on them, will be inevitably partial and limited in scope. Of course linguists will always find grounds to prefer one to another and claim validity for their own; and, like everything else, linguistic ideas and attitudes are subject to changing fashion. What needs to be recognized is that what linguists represent is a particular version of reality, abstracted and analysed out of the data of actually occurring language. Such representations are necessarily remote from everyday experience, and from the immediate awareness of ordinary language users.

In some people's minds, of course, this is just what is wrong with them, and when looking at the complex algebraic formulations of generative grammar, one might be inclined to agree. But the remoteness and partiality of linguistic descriptions does not invalidate them. On the contrary, such descriptions are revealing precisely *because* they are partial and informed by a particular perspective. If linguistics could provide us with representations of experienced language, it would be of no interest whatever. Linguistic accounts of language only have a point to the extent that they are detached from, and different from, the way language is experienced in the real world.

And this particular version of linguistic reality needs a means of expression that is correspondingly at a remove from the way actual language users talk about their language. It has been suggested that linguists, and other academics, deliberately develop a specialist terminology to keep ordinary people in the dark and sustain the mystery, and the mastery, of their intellectual authority. Edward Said in his Reith lectures some years ago made this observation:

> Each intellectual, book editor and author, military strategist and international lawyer, speaks and deals in a language that has become specialized and usable by other members of the same field, specialist experts addressing other specialist experts in a lingua franca largely unintelligible to unspecialized people.
>
> (Said 1994)

But fields of enquiry are necessarily delimited and plotted by their specialist terminology. It is, of course, true that specialist terminology, in common with any other uses of language, can also serve to exercise power, to sustain group solidarity, and exclude outsiders. But this does not warrant condemning it as a kind of conspiracy to corner specialist knowledge, and sustain superiority by keeping ordinary people in a state of exploitable ignorance. For specialist terminology can also have the entirely legitimate use of expressing conceptual distinctions which define different ways of thinking. And it is not just intellectuals, military strategists, lawyers, or linguists, who develop specialist modes of expression. Everybody does it. Said does it himself. All communities do it because all communities develop distinctive ways of talking about things from their own sociocultural perspective. In this sense there *are* no unspecialized people but only people who are specialized in different modes of thought associated with different uses of language which are bound to be, in some degree, unintelligible to others. And if you are an outsider, one of the others, you call it jargon.

The point to be made, then, is that the linguist's representations are not replications of language as it occurs in the real world – the terminology they use, their metalanguage, will be correspondingly remote from everyday usage. What linguists do is to formulate their own version of linguistic reality *on* their own terms and *in* their own terms.

But what good are they, then, to people who live in the real world? What use can they possibly be to people like language teachers and learners who have to come to terms with realities which linguists, it would seem, have conveniently distanced themselves from? The answer is, I think, that these representations can be used as frames of reference for taking bearings on such realities from a fresh perspective.

This involves a process of mediation whereby the linguist's abstract version of reality is referred back to the actualities of the language classroom. And this essentially is what applied linguistics seeks to do.

In this view, applied linguistics is not a matter of the application but the appropriation of linguistics for educational purposes. Its aim is to enquire into what aspects of linguistic enquiry can be made relevant to an understanding of what goes on in language classrooms. And this cannot be a unilateral process, for relevance is obviously conditional on particular pedagogic circumstances. And these circumstances are obviously affected by educational as well as linguistic considerations. Language teachers are teachers, and what they teach is not just a language but a subject on the school curriculum.

Mediation, then, involves neither opposition nor imposition, but the realization of interdependency: practice makes reference to theory only to the extent that theory has relevance to practice. Not everybody would see things in this way, of course. John Sinclair, for example, is sceptical of the idea of mediation:

> Applied linguists, I have the impression, see themselves as mediators between the abstract and heady realms of linguistic theory and the humdrum practical side of language teaching.
>
> (Sinclair 1998: 84)

But from my own point of view, it is entirely correct that applied linguists should see themselves as mediators. From the perspective of outsiders, linguistic theory may indeed be a heady realm, and language teaching humdrum practice. And this is just the kind of difficulty that mediation has to deal with by showing that what is commonly dismissed as heady and abstruse can also be interpreted as providing a legitimate intellectual perspective, and that this can be relevantly related to language teaching to make it more meaningful and less humdrum. Without mediation, the heady just remains heady, the humdrum, humdrum.

Mediation as I have described it here is a way of making linguistics useful, and this, I have argued, is made necessary by the very abstract nature of linguistic enquiry. But what if we make it less abstract? What if we build usefulness into the design of the enquiry and instead of going to the bother of making theories useful, just make useful theories instead? We could then cut out the mediating middleman. This would appear to be the position that Labov takes. He first expresses the view that linguistics, far from dealing with abstractions, should be involved in the facts of the real world.

> A sober look at the world around us shows that matters of importance are matters of fact. There are some very large matters of fact: the origin of the universe, the direction of continental drift, the evolution of the human species. There are also specific matters of fact: the innocence or guilt of a particular individual. These are the questions to answer if we would achieve our fullest potential as thinking beings.
>
> (Labov 1988: 182)

I do not myself feel competent to judge the factuality of the origin of the universe and the evolution of species, but my own sober look at the world around us shows that matters of fact are frequently extremely elusive because they are essentially relative. And this is especially the case with specific ones. People have a way of constructing their own facts to suit themselves, figments of their particular sociocultural values and beliefs, and this is surely particularly true of such matters as innocence and guilt. These are not facts: they are value judgements. To treat them as facts is to subscribe to one set of values and disregard others. You may believe you have good moral reasons for doing this, but that is another matter. There are, of course, certain things about the world we live in we can be fairly sure about, and which we can reasonably call factual: population statistics, for example, gross national product, the Dow Jones index. But these are hardly matters which applied linguistics is likely to influence. The kind of issues we are confronted with are not matters of fact of this kind but matters of opinion, attitude, prejudice, point of view. These are the important things which determine the way people think and act. But they are not matters of *fact*. They are matters of *perspective*. And it is for just this reason that mediation of some kind is called for: to see how far these different perspectives, these different fixes people take on the world, can be related, and perhaps reconciled.

As Thomas Gradgrind discovered to his cost in Dickens' *Hard Times*, one should be wary of being too fixated on facts, particularly in educational matters. Not infrequently they turn out to be projections of prejudice. 'Everybody knows that . . .' but what everybody knows is a social construct; a matter not of fact but convenient belief sanctioned by a particular community. Common sense is always communal sense. So it would be unwise to take such facts as given in advance and then design a theory to account for them. For the theory will then simply confirm partiality, and sustain beliefs without substantiating them. And yet Labov does seem to be speaking in favour of devising theories to fit the preconceived facts. He goes on:

> General theory is useful, and the more general the theory the more useful it is, just as any tool is more useful if it can be used for more jobs. But it is still the application of the theory that determines its value. A very general theory can be thought of as a missile that attains considerable altitude, and so it has much greater range than other missiles. But the value of any missile depends on whether it hits the target.
>
> (Labov 1988: 182)

Useful theory, a tool for doing jobs, hitting the target: all this sounds very down-to-earth, even humdrum – certainly no heady realms here. And yet, the missile analogy is a misleading one, and a disturbing one as well. For how can you be so certain in advance what targets you want to hit? What if the targets change, as they are prone to do, so that your fixation on certain particular targets makes it impossible to aim at others? And, crucially, who decides on what is a target and what is not? Missile makers have no say in the matter – they just follow orders, and theory makers would presumably do the same. But whose orders? On this account, theorists would design theories defined as useful for hitting targets determined by all manner of motives: the dictates of commercial profit, perhaps, or political expediency, or whatever. Make me an economic theory which I can use to justify the ruthless exploitation of market forces. Make me a social theory which I can use to justify racism, genocide, ethnic cleansing. Of course, people who talk about useful theories are thinking of benevolent uses. But equally theories can, and have been, made to measure to match malevolent designs as well.

The application of a theory determines its value, says Labov. Well that, it seems to me, depends on what you mean by value. If you mean its practical use, that is one thing. If you mean its theoretical validity, that is surely quite a different matter. Einstein's theory of relativity turned out to be extremely useful for the construction of the atom bomb. But I doubt if anybody would seriously propose that the validity of the theory was in any way determined by the dropping of the bomb in 1945. That, we can agree, was a pretty large matter of fact. But what, we might ask, of the more specific 'facts' of guilt and innocence in this case? These are not so easy to decide.

Increasingly these days, academics are called upon to justify what they are doing in the name of usefulness. The idea of scholarship itself sometimes seems anachronistic and quaint, and intellectual enquiry for its own sake is something we feel calls for some kind of apology. In such a climate, notions like reality, factuality, usefulness sound particularly appealing: they can be invoked in the cause of accountability, and to counter the charge that linguistics is an elitist academic discipline, an abstract and heady realm remote from the everyday world. But this populist appeal is suspect, and can, I think, undermine the integrity of academic enquiry. Linguistics as such only exists by virtue of its specialization as a disciplinary discourse in its own right, and only has validity to the extent that it presents reality on its own intellectual authority and in its own specialist terms. If it starts producing theories and descriptions to specification and their validity is measured by their utility value, then its authority, it seems to me, is bound to be compromised. This does not mean that linguists should set out to be deliberately useless. Nor does it mean that particular problems in the world should not stimulate enquiry; rather, the course of enquiry should not be determined in advance to come up with expedient solutions. To my mind, then, it is not within the brief of linguists to make useful theories. On the contrary, as soon as they start doing that, they lose their scholarly independence and with it their value to the non-scholarly world. This value depends not on making useful theories but on making theories useful. But this is not within the linguists' brief either. For it requires a distancing from their disciplinary perspective and the recognition of its possible relationship with others. This is what I mean by mediation. So the linguist, qua linguist, is not in a position to judge what use might be made of linguistic theory and description. Their usefulness potential is for others to realize. One linguist at least has recognized this well enough. I refer to Chomsky, and his often-cited comments to the effect that he is sceptical about the significance for pedagogy of insights from psychology and linguistics.

> Furthermore, I am, frankly, rather sceptical about the significance, for the teaching of languages, of such insights and understanding as have been attained in linguistics and psychology.
>
> (Chomsky 1966/71: 152–3)

Chomsky's comments, however, were made in an address to the Northeast Conference on the Teaching of Foreign Languages, and his scepticism is prefaced by an explicit disclaimer to any expertise in language pedagogy. He recognizes that the significance he refers to, and is sceptical about, is not actually for him to decide, and later in the lecture from which these comments come, he makes the following (rather less often cited) remarks:

> It is possible – even likely – that principles of psychology and linguistics, and research in these disciplines, may supply insights useful to the language teacher. But this must be demonstrated, and cannot be presumed. It is the language teacher himself who must validate or refute any specific proposal. There is very little in psychology or linguistics that he can accept on faith.
>
> (Chomsky 1966/71: 155)

What Chomsky is talking about here is not the applications but implications of his linguistics and these, as he makes clear, it is not his business to work out. It is not the business of any linguist, for no matter how close they may seem to come to terms with reality, they can only come to terms with reality on their *own* terms. The domains and discourses of linguistics and of such practical activities as language teaching remain as distinct as ever. And Chomsky's comments are as relevant now as they were then.

The usefulness of insights that linguistics supplies must be demonstrated. But a little close analysis of Chomsky's text will reveal a difficulty or two. Note the passive and the deleted agent. The usefulness must be demonstrated. But who is it that does the demonstrating? Who is to be the agent? The teacher. But how do teachers recognize these insights in the first place? Linguists, as I have already said, develop their own specialist discourses to suit their own disciplinary perspective on language, and so they should. So whatever insights might be forthcoming cannot simply be *supplied*, retailed from one discourse to another. For one thing, as Edward Said points out, the insights will be couched in an idiom 'largely unintelligible to unspecialised people'. And language teachers are unspecialized as far as linguistics is concerned. So we need a third party, a mediating agent whose role is to make these insights intelligible in ways in which their usefulness can be demonstrated.

So linguistic insights for the purposes of the language teacher are created by mediation. But, equally, so is the usefulness. Applied linguistics is often said to be concerned with the investigation of real-world problems in which language is implicated. But this seems to suggest that problems, like insights, are somehow already there as well-defined entities, that somebody in the real world supplies a problem, the linguist supplies an insight and the applied linguist matches them up. But things are not like that. To begin with, problems are perceived and formulated in culturally marked ways; in other words, they belong to particular discourses. So it is likely that they will need to be reformulated so as to make them amenable to investigation. It may indeed be the case that what people identify as a problem is simply the symptom of another one that they are not aware of. In a sense then, investigation, which of its nature belongs to a discourse other than that of the problem, will necessarily reformulate it, and change it into something else, which in turn may create problems that were not perceived at all in the first place. So just as linguistic insights are a function of the mediation, so are the problems they are related to. The process brings together two discourses or versions of reality and this requires an adjustment of fit whereby an area of convergence is created, compounded of elements of both discourses but belonging exclusively to neither.

Since the area of convergence belongs to neither discourse, proponents of both are likely to be somewhat ambivalent about it. Thus language teachers, for example, may, and indeed often do, think of it as an unwanted, and unwarranted, intrusion on their domain. And it is true that there are times when it is: when we get linguistics applied, as distinct from applied linguistics, the process whereby linguistic findings are foisted on pedagogy on just the presumption of relevance that Chomsky warns us against. Conversely, linguists may feel that the area of convergence is a misrepresentation that distorts their discipline. Applied linguists thus find themselves in an anomalous position, in a no-man's land they have made for themselves, and not infrequently under fire from both sides. They could withdraw from the middle ground, of course, and leave the two sides of language teaching and linguistics to get on with their own business without reference to each other. After all, it is the meddling of applied linguistics, one might argue, that has created the conditions of conflict in the first place. But since the business of both sides is with language, there should surely be *some* common ground, some areas of convergence to be explored.

Mediation, then, as I have described it, seeks to identify insights from the linguistic disciplines of potential relevance to the language subject. Its purpose is to stimulate the theorizing process whereby teachers assume the role of reflective practitioners. But it cannot replace that process, nor can it establish relevance in advance, for that clearly must take the local teaching/learning context into account. There has been much emphasis on the importance of acknowledging the legitimacy of language teachers' own 'cognitions', their own structures of knowledge and ways of thinking (Woods 1996). Nothing I have said about applied linguistic mediation denies that legitimacy. On the contrary, it is these cognitions that constitute the pedagogic discourse that insights from linguistic discourse need to be reconciled with for relevance to be realized. There are, however, two points to be made about such cognitions. Firstly, it would obviously be a mistake to suppose that they are general to all teachers. As with the generic reference to classrooms mentioned earlier, talking about teachers has a down-to-earth appeal, and the danger is that it might be taken as carrying of itself a guarantee of practicality. But we should recognize that such ideas can be just as theoretical as any that come from linguistics, and need just as much to be validated as relevant by reference to local conditions. Teachers' cognitions – which teachers?

Secondly, the recognition of the importance of teacher cognitions, even giving them priority, does not surely preclude the possibility that they might be extended, modified, even changed out of all recognition by influences from outside, including appropriately mediated linguistic insights. There has sometimes been the suggestion that taking account of teacher cognitions is an *alternative* to applied linguistics, in that it is an encouragement of self-realization rather than an imposition of transmitted ideas. But as I have argued, applied linguistics (as distinct from linguistics applied) is not such an imposition, but a way of encouraging theorizing, in which the teachers' own thinking would be necessarily involved. There is no reason why teachers should be deprived of the opportunity to develop their cognitions with reference to other ideas, and it is surely the purpose of teacher education to provide such an opportunity.

Applied linguistics, as conceived of here, is, then, a mediating process which explores ways in which the concerns of linguistics as a discipline can be relevantly related to those of the language subject. There are two features of this process which it is important to stress. In the first place, in this view of applied linguistics, it is indeed linguistics that is taken as the disciplinary point of reference. Though not linguistics applied, it is linguistics mediated. And the mediation is not across disciplines, different academic discourses, but across the divide between the disciplinary domains of detached enquiry and that of practical experienced reality, between expertise and experience. The very nature of the problem being addressed is, of course, likely to involve taking bearings from other disciplines as well. But if applied linguists were required to have expertise across the whole range of potentially relevant academic disciplines, they would be in no position to say anything at all. Applied linguistics is routinely referred to as interdisciplinary, as if this were its distinguishing feature. Though this may lend it a certain academic prestige, it is, to my mind, misleading. The interdisciplinary expertise that is evident in most of the work that is carried out in its name is, not surprisingly, very limited indeed. It seems to me preferable to accept that what we are doing in applied linguistics is exploring the relevance of *linguistics* (bearing in mind that this itself covers a wide range of interdisciplinary enquiry) and to recognize that what we have to say is therefore necessarily partial and provisional. We are pointing things out from a particular and necessarily limited point of view.

The second essential feature of applied linguistic mediation is that the process is necessarily a critical one in that it involves following through the implications, and questioning the validity of accepted ideas. What is applied in applied linguistics is a kind of positive and enquiring scepticism which seeks not so much to provide solutions as to propose how problems might be reformulated. I should make it clear, however, that when I say that mediation is necessarily critical, I am not using that term in the more specific, politically committed sense that is assigned to it in work in linguistics and sociology, and taken up in Pennycook (2001). For Pennycook, the kind of mediation I am proposing here amounts to what he calls 'liberal ostrichism', in that it ridiculously fails to engage with, or even recognize, the social injustice that lies at the heart of the problems it addresses. To counteract the bland complacency to the world's evils that such ostrichism implies, Pennycook proposes a critical applied linguistics which not only seeks to expose inequality and prejudice but is politically committed to their eradication. His book is a manifesto for an applied linguistics with a mission, with a cause, or, as he puts it 'with an attitude'. As will be readily imagined, I have some reservations about the Pennycook position. In the first place, mediation does not, as he appears to suppose, imply any indifference to moral or political issues. The work of many a so-called ostrich has been informed and inspired by the belief in social justice without feeling it necessary to give it the label 'critical' and put it on polemical display. And, more crucially, without imposing it unilaterally as a preconceived doctrine. What Pennycook seems to be proposing is that no matter how locally particular a problem might be, it must be cast in the same ideological image and subjected to the same process of sociopolitical interpretation. This is politics applied. Now, of course, the cause of social justice that Pennycook proclaims is one that everybody, overtly and in principle, would espouse. But it is interpreted in local practice in many different sociopolitical ways, some of which may seem to be at some variance with this principle. And what if the cause is not so worthy? We come to the same issue as was discussed earlier in this chapter in relation to Labov's proposal for devising useful theories. So long as Pennycook is on the side of the angels, all is well. But what if his mission is malevolent, or even well meaning but misconceived? Promoting an applied linguistics with an attitude may not be a very wise thing to do. It all depends on the attitude.

The applied linguistics that informs the kind of enquiry I undertake does not impose a way of thinking, but points things out that might be worth thinking about. Pointing out leaves open the question of what action might be appropriately taken, and is in this respect different from recommendation. There is a moment in Robert Bolt's play *A Man for All Seasons*, which nicely illustrates the difference. Richard Rich has been pleading with Sir Thomas More to employ him. More, not trusting him, refuses. A subsequent exchange with the Duke of Norfolk runs as follows:

MORE: Oh, your grace, here is a young man desperate for employment. Something in the clerical line.
NORFOLK: Well, if you recommend him . . .
MORE: Oh, I don't recommend him; but I point him out.

There is no shortage of people recommending what language teachers should do, whether they call themselves methodologists, teacher trainers, or applied linguists, whether they base their recommendations on practical experience, empirical evidence, or theoretical expertise. But they are in no position to recommend particular courses of action though they can, of course, point out possibilities it might be profitable to explore.

References

Chomsky, N. (1966) 'Linguistic theory', in R.G. Mead (ed.) *Language Teaching: Broader Contexts*. Northeast Conference on the Teaching of Modern Languages: Reports of the Working Committees. New York: MLA Materials Center. Reprinted in J.P.B. Allen and P. van Buren (eds) (1971) *Chomsky: Selected Readings*. Oxford: Oxford University Press.

Labov, W. (1988) 'The judicial testing of linguistic theory', in D. Tannen (ed.) *Linguistics in Context: Connecting Observation and Understanding*. Norwood, NJ: Ablex.

Lindstromberg, S. and Rinvolucri, M. (1990) *Introduction to Pilgrims Longman Resource Books*. London: Longman.

Pennycook, A. (2001) *Critical Applied Linguistics: A Critical Introduction*. Mahwah, NJ: Erlbaum.

Said, E. (1994) *Representations of the Intellectual. The 1993 Reith Lectures*. New York: Pantheon Books.

Sinclair, J.M. (1998) 'Large corpus research and foreign language teaching', in R. Beaugrande, M. Grosman and B. Seidlhofer (eds) *Language Policy and Language Education in Emerging Nations*. Stamford, CT: Ablex.

Thornbury, S. (2001) 'Lighten up. A reply to Angeles Clemente', *ELT Journal* 55 (4).

Woods, D. (1996) *Teacher Cognitions in Language Teaching*. Cambridge: Cambridge University Press.

Chapter 2

Christopher Brumfit

Language, linguistics, and education

[. . .]

Academic studies and educational practice

'Language' and 'education' share two disadvantages that many other areas of study avoid: they are both too familiar. We all use language, and many of us have strong views about it; we have all been educated, and we all have strong views about that. Expertise confronts experience, and experts have a difficult task defending their own expertise against others' perceived experience.

Yet language is full of puzzles that experience alone cannot solve, and one of the greatest of these is the exact relationship between speech, writing, and the whole educational process. For a start, language operates on many levels and with many functions simultaneously, so that the relationship is always complex.

[. . .]

Much has been written on the relationships between language and learning, but for every generalization we attempt to make in our textbooks and our teaching, there will be thousands of individuals using language for their own purposes, with their own devices and methods, confounding our general and abstract pronouncements with their own precise and concrete instances. As in any exploration centred on human beings, the fact of our individual self-consciousness destabilizes the response

Edited extracts from: Brumfit, C.J. 'Language, linguistics, and education', in *Individual Freedom in Language Teaching*, Oxford University Press, pp. 3–19, 2001.

and confuses the questioner. Each unexpected example makes us ask whether we have interpreted our own practice accurately or completely, and each time we do that our certainty is undermined. Certainty becomes the enemy of truth.

The risks that are being hinted at here can be more explicitly illustrated by considering the relationship between any descriptive discipline and a social and institutionalized practice such as education. Education is specifically concerned with intervention by one part of society in the lives of others. Such intervention is meant to be positive rather than negative, and safeguards of various kinds are provided to ensure that unsatisfactory intervention is avoided. But the mechanisms for intervening and the mechanisms for safeguarding are themselves part of the process of education, and have to be taken into account when the relationship between research and practice is examined.

As a field of study, 'education' tries to improve the quality of education provision in two related ways. First, the attempt to understand processes of education, in general and in particular, is needed both as part of our need to understand our environment and in order to inform discussion of educational policy. When it works successfully, this activity should lead – though often indirectly and after a long time lag – to more sensitive policy making at local and national levels, and to improved methods of teaching particular areas of the curriculum. Second, the attempt to develop appropriate teaching procedures, through experimentation with new materials and techniques and arising out of dissatisfaction with the old ones, leads simultaneously to criticism of current models of learning and teaching and to greater support for the teaching profession in its task within the educational system. Thus development, enquiry, improvement, and critique operate simultaneously and interactively.

This is of course an idealized picture, though it is difficult to see how we can afford to be content with much less. And, indeed, it does seem to be a realizable ideal, as long as researchers, teachers, advisers, materials writers and other practitioners can interchange roles, collaborate, and have effective administrative support for such close relationships. These are practical needs, but they should not obscure the epistemological difficulties also associated with achievement of such integration.

A rich and complex area of human activity such as education cannot be treated as if understanding and explanation suffice to cause desirable change. Indeed, the current state of schooling, at any time in any country, is never the result of careful planning and coherent policy: too many parents, teachers, learners and administrators subvert plans by a mixture of idealism, effort, divergent views about aims, laziness, incompetence and exciting but unpredictable innovation. For the past 20 years Britain has been going through a period of centralization and control, but schools, teachers, and classrooms still differ markedly, not just in quality of learning experience, but in different types of excellence and creativity. We have to note, though, that the complex task of understanding any aspect of education can in principle be separated from the task of implementing change. Understanding does not necessarily require change to follow. What is crucial is the mediation process, by which understanding from a variety of relevant disciplines is integrated to the needs of particular teachers and administrators in particular positions in particular schools, so that creativity can be maintained.

Some recent controversies in language teaching illustrate the problems in integrating research and teaching. There is, for example, a strong research tradition in second language acquisition studies which maintains that learners of foreign languages acquire much of the linguistic system in predictable ways. Studies of learners in different sets of conditions have suggested that generalizations can be made about the order in which certain language forms tend to appear, and such studies have resulted in substantial debate on their implications for linguistic theory and pedagogic practice (Davies *et al.* 1984; Mitchell and Myles 1998). But the usefulness of such studies can easily be exaggerated. Observations about the tendencies of learners can give us a general orientation for discussions of teaching; they cannot tell us how to teach specific groups of learners in any detail. This is because we have no way of knowing the relevance of such studies to particular learners until we know the conditions determining who is where on the scale being used: a collective tendency, however well attested, tells us nothing about the potential behaviour of an individual learner. Similarly, advocates of 'telling' pupils in English classes about, for example, the English writing system (Stubbs 1986: 229) or of listing objectives for teaching English (HMI 1984) are oversimplifying the implications of such apparent reliance on a transmission model of learning. Not only is the direct transmission model concerned with only one half of the activity, the teacher's, but even if the transmission model is desired, the teaching profession needs to understand why it is a better model than alternatives. Matching research to human practice is only simple in the minds of tyrants. But that is not because it cannot be done; rather, it is because the complexity and creativity of human behaviour makes 'simple' answers valid only at a high level of generality. Specific behaviour may operate within these generalizations, but a long process of discussion and interpretation, and of trial and error, provides the only means of avoiding mismatches between general statements and particular interventions in individual lives. Because of this, it is probably more honest to talk about the 'implications' of theory and research for practice than the 'applications'. Theory and research have to be digested by teachers, administrators, and policy makers and converted to something which works in their particular institutions, and with the people who teach and study in them. And this applies equally to other areas where language studies impinge on education. But to justify this argument, it will be necessary to summarize current views on the contexts of language use.

Language and its uses

'Language' has always been an object of interest to scholars outside linguistics itself. Literary theorists and literary critics, philosophers, psychologists, sociologists and anthropologists have all persistently concerned themselves with language. What is remarkable has been the degree of consensus over the nature of language that has emerged in education from a diverse range of theoretical perspectives initially established in the 1960s and 1970s. While linguistics has in some traditions moved away from language located in the world towards increasingly abstract cognitive models, educational linguists, and others concerned with areas traditionally regarded as applied linguistics, have found themselves turning more towards the other language-interested disciplines. Indeed, it sometimes appears as if serious research into contextualized language activity is prevented from developing by the dominance of linguistic research concerned with idealizations which remove language from any systematic relationship with users or their purposes.

But other traditions within linguistics have fed the movement towards more socially sensitive language awareness. As descriptive linguists have concerned themselves with meaning, and moved into discourse analysis and pragmatics, so their interests have intersected with the concerns of researchers from other disciplines. Attempts deriving from anthropology to analyse speech events in relation to factors such as participant roles, settings, and topics (Hymes 1967) began the systematization of the interplay between language and social environment. At the same time, sociolinguistic studies demonstrated the ways in which syntactic or phonological rules may be observably adjusted according to the status or social position of users (Labov 1972).

These studies were essentially descriptive in intention. Social psychologists, however, provided the beginnings of accounts of the motivation of such systematic changes. Giles (1977) has suggested that there is a clear disposition to converge on the language of interlocutors where there is goodwill, and to diverge where there is antagonism. A number of studies in areas of ethnic or cultural conflict (for example Wales, Belgium, and Canada) showed that negative relations with outsiders cause speakers unconsciously to increase the dialect features of their locality away from the metropolitan mode to the local, while positive relations with outsiders promote a decrease of such localization. Such evidence is compatible with Grice's conversational maxims (Grice 1975) which are based on the view that a prime function of conversation is to facilitate communication as effectively as possible. To this end, features which might cause confusion in communication will be reduced wherever there is a desire for effective communication. At the same time, we should note that such features may be increased where the intention is to obscure rather than to clarify. There is evidence that children perceive language markers very early (Day (1982) demonstrated that by the age of three they have clear in- and out-group perceptions based on the speech of those they hear), and Reid (1978) and Romaine (1984) produced data which indicates that adolescents have very definite ideas about the social significance of different language forms. Thus language behaviour combines perceptions of group membership and identity with judgements about the degree of communication to strive for.

Such studies reinforce our awareness of the sensitivity and variability of language. The range of associations which may be acquired by any specific symbol available to us is immense, and these associations may be private or public. All families have their own private associations, as well as a certain number of vocabulary items peculiar to themselves. These associations may become highly wrought artefacts and spill over into literature and the public domain, as with the juvenile writings of the Brontës, or Isherwood's early fantasies. Equally, they may remain private and intensely local in range. But the potential scope for interaction between the private and the public is infinite. Every utterance has an internal and an external history, and the speaker or writer will only be aware of a small part of either of these. Because the overlap in experience of a particular language item or language event is incomplete for each speaker and listener, misunderstanding, or legitimate alternative interpretation, is constantly possible. And constellations of personal experience build up into ideologies, patterns of belief that underlie whole modes of human activity, binding the behaviour patterns of groups who identify themselves as cultures – physicists or stamp collectors, educationalists or readers of Kafka, Jehovah's Witnesses or structuralists, undertakers or ministry officials or bakers. There is no group too important or too trivial to bond linguistically and form a temporary culture, with its own characteristic linguistic forms and its own (for the moment) shared assumptions.

It is important to emphasize the variety (and the frequent superficiality) of our linguistic and cultural associations, because there is a strong tendency to see both language and culture as relatively solid and unnegotiable, and the relations between them as fixed. Yet education above all other social forces is concerned with establishing the mutability of culture and the languages that reflect and contribute to it. We have to operate within the linguistic system we receive, otherwise we shall not communicate. But we are never its prisoner, and learning to transcend our current language to perceive and contribute to future communicative and conceptual capacities is the self-educational task for each of us. To make sense of this process, we have to try to locate language in some of its rich context.

Language in the classroom

Let me try to illustrate this principle with a simple example. Steedman (1982) devoted a whole book to a remarkable analysis of a collaborative story produced by three eight-year-old primary school girls. The passage quoted in Figure 2.1 is in fact the sole interpolation by a fourth girl into the lengthy, and eventually incomplete story.

Steedman comments about this episode:

> When the girls worked together in writing, they operated by a model of social life that demonstrated to them more cohesion and co-operation between women than it did between men. There were pressures on the boys to act aggressively and to display their conflict with each other, though the girls too were usually told to hit back. When Lisa, who joined the three writers of 'The Tidy House' after several days of diplomatic approaches, wrote a portion of the text, she had the character Jamie tell her nine-year-old son Carl to fight back in the playground. This scene echoed many conversations with all the children throughout the year in which they would patiently explain to me, yet again, that whilst the school's most stringently enforced rule forbade fighting, they had been told by their parents to hit back . . . The passage by Lisa mirrored her own, very recent experience. She had had two close friends, Carla and Melissa. They had gone to nursery school together, walked back and forth together, sat together and played in the streets together through five long years. The arrival of Lindie in the spring had destroyed the balance of this old friendship. Admitted back into the fold towards the end of the week, the constraints of the plot that Lisa was faced with and the gender of the child character she had to write about meant that there was no alternative but to write of herself as Carl, the boy.

(Steedman 1982: 136–7)

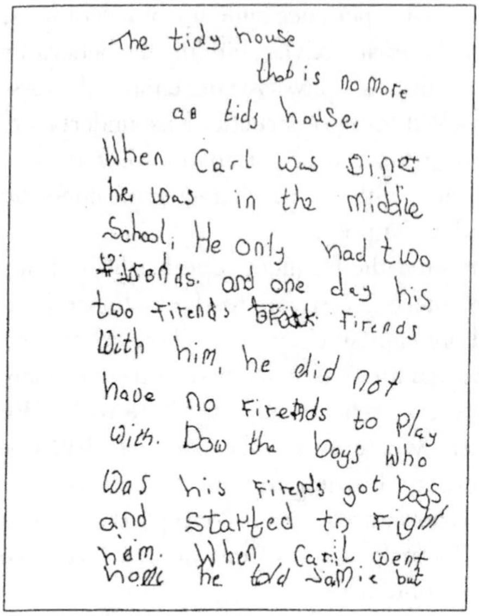

The tidy house
that is no more
as kids house.
When Carl was dine
he was in the middle
School, He only had two
Firends. and one day his
too firends black firends
With him, he did not
have no firends to play
With. Now the boys Who
Was his firends got boys
and started to fight
ham. When Caril went
home he told Jamie but

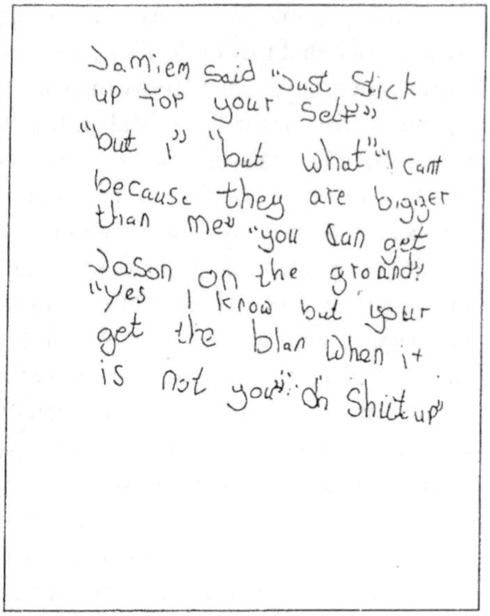

Jamiem said "Just stick
up for your self"
"but I" "but what" "I cant
because they are bigger
than me" "you can get
Jason on the groand"
"yes I know but your
get the blan When it
is not your" "oh Shut up"

Figure 2.1 Carolyn Steedman: The Tidy House 1982: 213–14.
London: Virago

The point is not whether this was in some sense 'the true' account of what motivated the writing; rather it is that some similar account to this had to be true. Writing of this kind is necessarily reflecting a complex of personal and conventional attributes which must be recognized and responded to (but which may not be precisely identified) by any primary teacher, or indeed in another sense by any reader. For the writer, the conventions of school writing, of children's literature, and of parental expectations all converge in this one short episode in addition to the conventions demanded by the existing lengthy text which was already available. This was simultaneously a public and a private act, as imaginative writing often is. But it functions as part of a cumulative educational process: to assign it an exact and isolated role would be like asking the exact role of each blade of grass in a field. Yet few people would wish to deny that the role of such writing in the process of personal development is important.

If we are to make sense of language use in education, then, the interpretation of meaning is at least as important as the recognition of form. Yet the interpretation of meaning will never be an objective activity, for meaning depends not only on the context and the conventions appropriately deployed to match the context, but also on the interpretations of those who read or listen, and the intentions of those who speak. It is widely recognized that together we make our meanings, but less widely accepted that we cannot be fully aware of the meanings that we make. Language users operate rather like action painters drawing their colours from a moving palette, and spraying them back at it: we take our meanings from the language, but by the time we are ready to return them, the language has subtly shifted. None of us speaks the same language twice, any more than we drive exactly the same route twice. Using language is changing language.

Such recognition of language as necessarily in flux, reflecting the movement and life of the minds that use it, enables us to see language activity in the education system as a process of working, not just a product of learning. Developments in second language acquisition research make it difficult to see the learning even of foreign languages as distinct from the process of language use: learning is using and using is learning (see, from different perspectives, Stevick 1976; Krashen 1981; Brumfit 1984). Of course, there are also formal activities associated with the learning – people learn vocabulary lists off by heart more than is commonly acknowledged – but these activities are preliminary to the language learning process itself, for only when the language items are fused into active meaning systems by the process of use, is the language system developing for the learner's own purposes. We may learn the tokens of language formally, but we learn the system by using it through reading or writing, or conversing.

Learning new concepts and developing new capacities are thus frequently realized through the development of new language, and the development of new language must be realized through the development of meaning. Other systems than language may of course perform similar functions, but in literate societies especially, links between education and literacy are so close that language will remain the dominant code for the foreseeable future. Even a world dependent on the Internet cannot replace language with images that are independent of language.

Language policy

So far, we have been concerned mainly with language in the general educational process. Some commentators, indeed, have come close to arguing that the general educational process is essentially a matter of playing the appropriate language games. Hirst, for example, associated the development of concepts with 'the symbols of our common languages' (Hirst 1974: 83) so that education may become the interplay between (1) the appropriate language forms that we are socialized to produce by schooling, and (2) the ideas that emerge from the context which language both creates and responds to. [. . .] it begins to make sense to demand certain minimum language 'rights' for all learners in state education.

A minimum requirement for all learners would be: (1) development of mother tongue or dialect; (2) development of competence of a range of styles of English for educational, work-based, social and public-life purposes; (3) development of knowledge of the nature of language in a multilingual society, including basic acquaintance with some languages from the total range of those available in education or in the local community; (4) development of a fairly extensive practical competence in at least one language other than their own (Brumfit 1986, 1995).

[. . .]

Many teachers will find themselves engaged in work with multilingual classes, and an awareness of children's and adults' capacities to cope with language issues is a necessary prerequisite to successful teaching.

[. . .]

Language in teacher education

For teachers of ESOL (English for Speakers of Other Languages) language has always been a significant element in professional preparation. [. . .] [L]anguage activity is divided in teacher education across a range of possible courses, none of which has language as a prime focus and none of which is obliged to deal with language at all. Nor, indeed, can we say that teachers typically receive high-level training in language work. A survey I conducted for the National Congress on Languages in Education, which involved sending a detailed questionnaire to nearly 150 institutions concerned with teacher education in the UK, including all state training institutions, revealed [. . .] that we could not by any means guarantee that all teachers would have any explicit awareness of the nature of the language that is so important in their classrooms. Nor did surveys of the knowledge of language of undergraduates or teachers in training suggest that these figures conceal widespread understanding rather than ignorance (Bloor 1986).

> [. . .]

But there is another perhaps slightly more contentious dimension to this story, for in Britain language has customarily been the concern of English teachers. [. . .] Some degree courses do include some work on language; many do not include anything on contemporary linguistics, sociolinguistics, or psycholinguistics, to mention only three areas of direct relevance to the classroom. Nor, indeed does 'linguistics' have a good name with English teachers (though to what extent that reflects an out-of-date model of what linguistics, and especially applied linguistics is, to what extent it reflects the failures of undergraduate linguistics courses to convince students of the excitement and relevance of the discipline, and to what extent it is simply fear of a scientific approach, is difficult to determine: probably there are elements of all three). But the fact remains that the prime teachers of 'language' in our schools frequently, perhaps usually, have had no specific knowledge of this field at all.

The difficulty is that this leaves a camouflaged trap. We have qualified 'English' teachers, they are concerned with 'language', therefore we have qualified 'language teachers', is the false syllogism. What we in fact have is an incapacity to provide sensitivity about language as a social instrument, except at an amateur level. I doubt whether this can be said about any other major area of the curriculum. Even one-year, full-time postgraduate courses are few and far between, and of course the weight of the profession lies heavily with those who are understandably committed to the three years of full-time literary or cultural study that has provided them with the academic basis for their English teaching as their undergraduate degree. It is difficult to see how the necessary expertise for basic work in this area can be achieved by less than the equivalent of one year's full-time study at either undergraduate or postgraduate level. And if the study of language (whether it is described as 'language' or as 'linguistics') is to be recognizably the medium we are all aware of in our daily lives, it needs to be based on the broad view of the function of language that I am outlining here.

Yet it is important to see that this is not a conflict between 'arid science and humane creativity', to quote one English teacher in a discussion group I was in at a conference. Language work in education has to recognize the potential impact of literature, the need to write for personal pleasure, and language as a means of personal identity. [. . .]

To experience language without imaginative response is to impoverish it, but so too is to experience language without intellectual rigour. Language is in fact the cheapest scientific data available to schools, and pupils, in my experience, invariably enjoy thinking about it, as a socially significant system and as an abstract system alike, if the teacher is committed, knowledgeable, and enthusiastic.

I have tried to argue, then, that language is intimately bound up with the process of education, at all levels, and that teachers and administrators need to be sensitive to this and informed about the way language operates in society. I have also argued, in passing, that explicit language responsibilities require a policy for all learners about what they are entitled to expect, and that all teachers require some knowledge of language, and teachers of English, particularly (though of other languages too) require specific work on language if they are not to mislead the public about their own expertise.

[. . .]

References

Bloor, T. (1986) 'What do language students know about grammar?' *British Journal of Language Teaching* 24 (3): 157–60.

Brumfit, C.J. (1984) *Communicative Methodology in Language Teaching*. Cambridge: Cambridge University Press.

Brumfit, C.J. (1986) 'Towards a language policy for multilingual secondary schools'. Keynote lecture at CILT/European Community Pilot Project Seminar, University of London Institute of Education, September 1986. Published in J. Geach (ed.) 1989: 7–19.

Brumfit, C.J. (1995) *Language Education in the National Curriculum*. Oxford: Blackwell.

Davies, A., Criper, C. and Howatt, A.P.R. (eds) (1984) *Interlanguage*. Edinburgh: Edinburgh University Press.

Day, R.R. (1982) 'Children's attitudes towards language', in E.B. Ryan and H. Giles (eds). 1982: 116–31.

Giles, H. (ed.) (1977) *Language, Ethnicity, and Intergroup Relations*. London: Academic Press.

Grice, H. (1975) 'Logic and conversation', in P. Cole and J. Morgan (eds) 1975: 41–59.

Hirst, P. (1974) *Knowledge and the Curriculum*. London: Routledge and Kegan Paul.

HMI (1984) *English 15–16*. London: HMSO.

Hymes, D. (1967) 'Models of the interaction of language and social setting', *Journal of Social Issues* 23 (2): 9–28.

Krashen, S. (1981) *Second Language Acquisition and Second Language Learning*. Oxford: Pergamon Press.

Labov, W. (1972) *Sociolinguistic Patterns*. Philadelphia, PA: University of Pennsylvania Press.

Mitchell, R.F. and Myles, F. (1998) *Second Language Learning Theories*. London: Edward Arnold.

Reid, E. (1978) 'Social and stylistic variation in the speech of children: some evidence from Edinburgh', in P. Trudgill (ed.) 158–75.

Romaine, S. (1984) *The Language of Children and Adolescents*. Oxford: Basil Blackwell.

Steedman, C. (1982) *The Tidy House*. London: Virago.

Stevick, E.W. (1976) *Memory, Meaning and Method*. Rowley, MA: Newbury House.

Stubbs, M.W. (1986) *Educational Linguistics*. Oxford: Basil Blackwell.

Chapter 3

Ben Rampton

Continuity and change in views of society in applied linguistics

[. . .]

The interface between 'tradition' and 'modernity' has been enormously formative for the social sciences. According to Giddens:

> sociology has its origins in the coming of modernity – in the dissolution of the traditional world and the consolidation of the modern . . . With the arrival of industrialism, the transfer of millions of people from rural communities to cities, the progressive development of mass democracy, and other quite fundamental institutional changes, the new world was savagely wrenched away from the old . . . Sociology was born of the attempt to track [this] . . ., but until well into the twentieth century was itself rather too strongly stamped by the context of its own origins.
>
> (1990: 15–16)

I cannot comment on how fair this is to sociology, but it certainly makes sense if one looks at anglophone sociolinguistics from the 1960s.

Starting with the seminal conference at Yeshiva in 1966, one of the central missions of sociolinguistics was to make modern institutions, especially schools, more hospitable to socially and ethnically diverse populations – populations which, in one way or another, were generally thought to be non-modern. In the process, debates about the relationship between children and schools threw up a huge array of dichotomies, and these ranged across:

Edited extracts from: Rampton, B. 'Continuity and change in views of society in applied linguistics', in H. Trappes-Lomax (ed.) *Change and Continuity in Applied Linguistics*, Multilingual Matters, pp. 97–114, 2000.

- *modes of expression*, which were supposed to be either vernacular or standard, oral or literate, concrete or abstract, implicit or explicit, narrative or argumentative, metaphorical or rational, contextualised or decontextualised, particularistic or universalistic, etc.
- *types of social organisation*, where it was home vs. school, close networks vs. open networks, homogeneous vs. heterogeneous, solidarity- vs. status-based, mechanical vs. organic, etc.
- *social categories*: host–migrant, white–black, majority–minority, male–female, middle-class/working-class.

Sociolinguists often devoted very considerable energy to contesting these polarities and the long collocational chains that they tended to form – chains which would counterpose particularistic vernacular oral narrative in traditional close working-class networks to literate, universalistic argument within the status-oriented modern middle-class. But whether they were for or against, whether or not they were trying to uncouple associations like these or to reverse the idea that it was a question of better vs. worse, dichotomous thinking of this kind had a very deep hold in the 1960s, 1970s and 1980s, serving as a central battleground in the work of scholars such as Labov, Hymes, Bernstein, Wells, Heath and Cummins. Indeed, there is a sense in which the arguments look like modernity's struggle to define itself through a process of contrast and comparison, and quite a few of the terms recurring in the sociolinguistic debate – 'decontextualisation' and 'universalistic' for example – resonate with the philosophical underpinnings of liberal modernity. (For fuller discussion, see Rampton, 1999.)

Admittedly, much of the specificity of the work of particular scholars is lost when they are grouped together within a particular historical and epistemic juncture in this manner, and so I would like to go one step further and suggest that, on the whole, there was a very strong current of romanticism in sociolinguistics. Looking back at this period, Bernstein talks about the dominance of a model of competence which saw everyone as 'inherently competent, . . . [as] active and creative in the construction of valid worlds', 'announced . . . the universal democracy of acquisition', 'celebrated . . . everyday oral language' and was suspicious of 'official socialisers' (Bernstein, 1996: Chapters 3 and 7). In line with this, a great deal of work in sociolinguistics declared itself opposed to the narrow prejudices of policymakers and popular opinion, and argued instead that subordinate and marginal groups had an authenticity and integrity of their own. In fact, though, it was very hard to challenge modernity's cornerstone values, or to do more than rehabilitate modernity's others along modernist lines. The main strategy in this advocacy was to try to show that the behaviour of these non-standard groups was systematic and coherent – it was justifiable, in other words, in terms of the rational values of system and coherence that modernity rated most highly – much higher, for example, than sanctity or splendour.

Indeed at this point we enter a rather general critique of linguistics itself – a critique that perhaps gets its most succinct and powerful expression in Pratt's 1987 paper 'Linguistic Utopias'. Pratt connects a commitment to system-in-grammar and coherence-in-discourse to the notion that language competence is shaped through a process of socialisation to consensual norms, and she calls this cluster of ideas 'the linguistics of community'. Yes, right from the start, sociolinguists took issue with Chomsky's idealisation about the homogeneous speech community, and language diversity and variation were obviously an article of faith. But even so, the belief was that this diversity was describably structured, and whenever they met it, the sociolinguist's strongest instinct was to root out what they supposed was an orderliness and uniformity beneath the surface, an orderliness laid down in the early years of community belonging. One can see this in the variationist's quest for the vernacular; in research on code-mixing and code-switching, where the emphasis was on systematic patterns established within relatively stable bilingual in-groups; and in work on cross-cultural conflict and misunderstanding, where the problem was attributed to the gap between integrated cultural and linguistic systems. As Pratt says, 'when social division and hierarchy [*were*] studied, the linguist's choice [was] often to imagine separate speech communities with their own boundaries, sovereignty, and authenticity, . . . giv[ing] rise to linguistics that seeks to capture identity, but not the relationality of social differentiation' (1987: 56, 59, 61).

What would the alternative be? To address this, it is worth now turning to the new historical and epistemic problematic that is coming to replace the tradition/modernity juncture.

Sociolinguistics at the Modernity/Postmodernity Interface

In a paper entitled 'A sociological theory of postmodernity', Zygmunt Bauman (1992: 187–205) summarises a number of major differences between classical sociology and the late-modern perspectives that are becoming increasingly influential. A number of these differences are by now fairly familiar, but for the sake of what I would like to say later it is worth flagging up one or two.

Whereas modernist sociology saw 'society' and other collective entities as unified and integrated totalities, there is a feeling now that that idea was rather uncomfortably based on an idealisation of the nation state, and that, instead, 'the reality to be modelled is . . . much more fluid, heterogeneous and under-patterned than anything sociologists have tried to grasp intellectually in the past' (Bauman, 1992: 65). In terms of human behaviour and development, classical ideas about our actions gaining significance from their function in the social system give way to the view that what we do plays a major role in shaping the habitats we live in, and far from being socialised into the norms of a social group whose monitoring subsequently keeps us morally in line, there is much more of a sense that we 'assemble' ourselves from a plethora of changing options, deciding what is right and wrong for ourselves. Methodologically, social science gives up its dreams of being a legislator, a 'healer of prejudices' and an 'umpire of truth', and instead, the best it can do is operate as a translator and interpreter.

[. . .]

There have been some broadly comparable shifts in the view of ethnicity. It is no longer enough to see ethnicity as either cultural inheritance or as the strategic/political accentuation of inheritance – it is also necessary to reckon with the ways in which ethnic forms, products and symbols are marketised and disseminated as desirable commodities, life-style options and aesthetic objects. All in all, whether it is age- or ethnicity-based, belonging to a group now seems a great deal less clear, less permanent and less omni-relevant than it did 15 years ago. We are now much more conscious that community membership doesn't just happen to a person, but that much of it is created in the here-and-now. And, as it becomes harder to think of communities as separate sociocultural blocs, it becomes necessary to reconceptualise the politics that dominated debates about language and culture for much of this century. This is what Table 3.1 attempts to chart, and in the last column on the right, there is a potted resume of some of the key characteristics of the perspective that Bauman discusses.

There are two points to make about this table. First, if one takes, for example, the ideas along the right hand side, they are obviously rather broad and general. They could be loosely linked to names like Berger and Luckman, Giddens, Hall, Bourdieu, Foucault, etc., but I would not claim a spotless pedigree for them and that is really the point. What they signify is not so much a substantive theory, consisting of claims open to empirical refutation, as what Brumfit (1997) calls a new *Zeitgeist*, and what others might describe as a new ontology, a new set of non-refutable, metaphysical presuppositions about the fundamental qualities and forces at work in the phenomena and processes being studied (see Cohen, 1987: 275–80).

The second point to clarify about the chart is that, in spite of the left to right movement, it would be a mistake to interpret it as the final triumph of post-modernism. To different degrees in different quarters, all four of these perspectives are alive and well, and in fact it is because of *unresolved* conflicts of perspective that I spoke of the *junctures* of tradition-and-modernity and modernity-and-post-modernity. It is sometimes imagined that any even half-favourable mention of post- or late-modernity means the abandonment of all commitment to scientific method, but that is a grossly unwarranted inference: the sociolinguistics that I refer to puts a great deal of emphasis on being logical, empirical, careful, sceptical and systematic, and more generally I would certainly say that such qualities are important for the discovery, analysis and reporting of phenomena beyond our ordinary imagining. The difference is, though, that people are now probably much more sensitive to the limitations of their methods, and they are also more aware of the historical specificity of the traditions they are working in.

[. . .]

Applied Linguistics in Late Modernity

It is probably worth admitting straightaway that if one follows the romantic model of competence that Bernstein attributes to sociolinguistics and many other social sciences in the 1960s, 1970s and 1980s – if one is committed to 'the universal democracy of acquisition' where everyone is inherently competent and official socialisers are suspect – then the applied linguistics of language teaching doesn't look terribly appealing. Admittedly, there is some alignment with this competence model in ideas about the integrity, autonomy and authenticity of language learner language in interlanguage theory, and communicative language teaching also looks in the same direction. Even so, my guess is that much of the tension in the 1960s, 1970s, and 1980s between ELT/EFL on the one hand and English mother-tongue

Table 3.1 Four orientations to cultural diversity

Interpretation of linguistic diversity:	I Diversity as deficit	II Diversity as difference	III Not diversity, domination	IV Deficit, difference & domination as discourse
View of culture:	Culture as elite canon/standard.	Cultures as sets of values, beliefs & behaviours.	Culture as reflection of socio-economic relations.	Culture as the processes & resources involved in situated, dialogical sense-making.
Approach to language:	Prescriptivism: norms & standards to be followed.	Descriptivism: system & authenticity of non-standard forms.	Determinism: language either subordinate to, or a distraction from, structures of political & economic domination.	Social constructionism: reality extensively constructed through institutional discourse & discursive interaction.
View of research:	Neutral, objective, informative.	Neutral, objective, advocate.	Part of apparatus of hegemony; scientific imperialism.	Either regime of truth/discipline, or empowering, giving voice to subjugated knowledge.
Descriptive concerns/focus:	The canon. The Other lacks culture & knowledge.	The Other's autonomy & integrity.	Self & Other in larger system.	Global & national discourses, diaspora & multi-local sites.
Philosophical & political emphasis:	Superiority of 'Us'. 'Them' at fault.	Relativism. Cultures incommensurable: 'we' can't say 'them' at fault.	Power. Capitalist oppression. Resistance through the unity of oppressed groups.	Power, difference & contingency. 'Them' resists, or sees things differently.
Assumption about the world:	Universals & grand narratives: development/modernisation/global markets. subplots.	Grand narratives maybe, but celebration of the subplots.	Universals & grand narratives: imperialism/dependency.	Universals & grand narratives disclaimed.
Intervention strategy:	Assimilation	Multiculturalism	Anti-racism/anti-imperialism	Anti-essentialism
Typical politics:	Conservatism	Liberal pluralism	Marxism	Post-modernism

teaching on the other can be explained in terms of major differences in the extent to which they could commit themselves professionally to the competence model that Bernstein describes. It is also likely that the competence model has been one of the main factors that has made modern foreign language education seem so uninspiring to sociolinguists. Certainly, if one looks through [the journal] *Language in Society* or any number of introductory sociolinguistics textbooks, it is hard to find even a passing reference to instructed foreign languages, and if you're principally committed to rehabilitating rich but repressed community knowledges, it's not difficult to see why.

What happens, though, when the humanities and social sciences turn to new topics and there is a growth of interest in cultural flows, in boundaries and margins rather than centres, and in uncertainty and ambivalence? What happens if the climate of the times changes, competence models lose their intuitive appeal, and instead, discussion turns to the political economy of language, to the uneven production, circulation and distribution of symbolic and cultural resources, to ideology, exclusion, legitimation and resistance? What happens if anti-essentialism moves in, and we start to wonder whether feelings of group belonging aren't themselves socially constructed in the here-and-now? The answer, of course, is that the applied linguistics of other-language teaching-and-learning starts to look a bit different. It is hard to think of any other area of language study which is as centrally concerned with fluidity, marginality and transition, with what people can't do with language and with how they get by with what they can, and whatever your flavour – whether it's interstate agents or postcolonial flaneurs, whether it's Quirk, Kachru, Phillipson or Pennycook – there is longstanding involvement with globalisation and the management of transnational communication.

In fact, that is not the only way in which new directions in sociolinguistics turn out to be a traditional staple for language-teaching applied linguistics. Far from being the distinctive product of late modern experience, reflexivity and self-consciousness about language have been constitutive features of foreign language education since time immemorial, and coming very often out of language teaching itself (unlike their colleagues in modernist sociolinguistics), applied linguists have never been properly socialised into doctrines about language research being ethically neutral and 'linguistics being descriptive, not prescriptive' (cf. Cameron 1994: 21).

I am not suggesting that the applied linguistics of language teaching has been a coherent academic programme, guided by the ideas of radical linguistic thinkers like Le Page and Tabouret-Keller or Harris. Obviously, the concerns and engagements of language-teaching applied linguistics are very large, diffuse and amorphous and, in my view anyway, there is still really quite a lot that could do with conceptual refitting. But just as clearly, though, there is much more involved here than a family of hillbillies waking up to find that they're sitting on an oil-field.

If one rereads, for example, Criper and Widdowson's 1975 paper on 'Sociolinguistics and language teaching' in the *Edinburgh Course in Applied Linguistics*, one sees a much sharper understanding of idealisation as a situated strategy, and of the limits of sociolinguistic generalisation, than anything to be found in introductory sociolinguistics textbooks. This is a line that Widdowson worked out more explicitly in his papers on models and fictions (1984), and a little later on it is matched by Brumfit's (1984) argument that, as well as 'knowledge that' and 'knowledge how', there is 'knowledge of what it is to . . .' – '"knowledge of what it is to be a language teacher" has a legitimate claim to be considered in methodological discussion'. Applied linguistics worked out its rejection of naive descriptivism quite a long time ago, at a time when naive descriptivism still dominated orthodox sociolinguistics, and it was not simply abandoning it for some kind of crude back-to-basics prescriptivism.

My guess is that one half of this epistemological reflexivity came from talking to sceptical teachers working on real-world language problems, and that the other came from applied linguistics' precarious position in the academy and its need both to differentiate and justify itself to linguists. But whatever the sources, from the mid-1970s on, scholars such as Widdowson, Brumfit and Strevens were reflecting on positional knowledge, interdisciplinarity and the 'real world' in ways that anticipate a good deal of what is being said today. And indeed, in my view, it was neither an accident nor a revolution that made BAAL Annual Meetings such an important arena for some of the most celebrated recent developments in British sociolinguistics. In terms of international profile, both critical discourse analysis and the new literacy studies stand out in British sociolinguistics; my impression is that from the late 1980s onwards, much of the debate around this work went on at BAAL annual meetings (much more, for example, than at the Sociolinguistics Symposia); and my contention is that, in spite of any regrets he now might express, the critical reflexivity of someone like Widdowson did a great deal to open the ground for it.

Overall, then, I would suggest that the applied linguistics of language teaching stands to gain a good deal from the epistemic shifts I described earlier, and that after years of trying to fight for respectability and inclusion in the academic mainstream, there are a number of ways in which it is really rather well-positioned at the juncture between modernity and postmodernity.

[. . .]

References

Bakhtin, M. (1984) *Problems in Dostoevsky's Poetics*. Minneapolis, MN: University of Minnesota Press.

Bauman, Z. (1992) *Intimations of Post-modernity*. London: Routledge.

Bernstein, B. (1996) 'Sociolinguistics: a personal view', in *Pedagogy, Symbolic Control and Identity* (pp. 147–56). London: Taylor & Francis.

Brumfit, C. (1984) *Communicative Methodology in Language Teaching*. Cambridge: Cambridge University Press.

Brumfit, C. (1997) 'Theoretical practice: applied linguistics as pure and practical science', *AILA Review*.

Cameron, D. (1994) 'Putting our theory into practice', in D. Graddol and J. Swann (eds) *Evaluating Language* (pp. 15–23). Clevedon: BAAL/Multilingual Matters.

Clifford, J. (1992) 'Traveling cultures', in L. Grossberg, C. Nelson and P. Treichler (eds) *Cultural Studies* (pp. 96–116). London: Routledge.

Cohen, I. (1987) 'Structuration theory', in A. Giddens and J. Turner (eds) *Social Theory Today* (pp. 273–308). Oxford: Polity.

Collins, J. (1998) *Understanding Tolowa Histories: Western Hegemonies and Native American Responses*. London: Routledge.

Criper, C. and Widdowson, H. (1975) 'Sociolinguistics and language teaching', in J. Allen and S. Pit Corder (eds) *Papers in Applied Linguistics: Edinburgh Course in Applied Linguistics* (Vol. 2) (pp. 155–217). Oxford: Oxford University Press.

Fairclough, N. (1992) *Discourse and Social Change*. Oxford: Polity.

Giddens, A. (1990) *Social Theory and Modern Sociology*. Oxford: Polity.

Goodwin, M.H. (1990) *He Said She Said*. Bloomington, IN: Indiana University Press.

Gumperz, J. (1982) *Discourse Strategies*. Cambridge: Cambridge University Press.

Harris, R. (1981) *The Language Myth*. London: Duckworth.

Heller, M. (1999) *Linguistic Minorities and Modernity*. London: Longman.

Kachru, B. (ed.) (1982) *The Other Tongue*. Oxford: Pergamon.

LePage, R. and Tabouret-Keller, A. (1985) *Acts of Identity*. Cambridge: Cambridge University Press.

McDermott, R. (1988) 'Inarticulateness', in D. Tannen (ed.) *Linguistics in Context: Connecting Observation and Understanding* (pp. 37–68). Norwood, NJ: Ablex.

Pennycook, A. (1994) *The Cultural Politics of English as an International Language*. London: Longman.

Phillipson, R. (1992) *Linguistic Imperialism*. Oxford: Oxford University Press.

Pratt, M.L. (1987) 'Linguistic utopias', in N. Fabb *et al.* (eds) *The Linguistics of Writing* (pp. 48–66). Manchester: Manchester University Press.

Quirk, R. (1990) 'Language varieties and standard language', *English Today* 21: 3–10.

Rampton, B. (1999) 'Deutsch in inner London and the animation of an instructed foreign language', *Journal of Sociolinguistics* 3 (4).

Rampton, B. (2001) 'Crosstalk, language crossing and cross-disciplinarity in sociolinguistics', in N. Coupland, C. Candlin and S. Sarangi (eds) *Sociolinguistics and Social Theory*. London: Longman.

Rampton, B. (2003) 'Speech community', in J. Verschueren, J-O Ostman, J. Blommaert and C. Bulcaen (eds) *Handbook of Pragmatics*. Amsterdam: John Benjamins.

Widdowson, H. (1984) 'Applied linguistics: the pursuit of relevance' and 'Models and fictions', in *Explorations in Applied Linguistics 2* (pp. 7–20 and 21–7). Oxford: Oxford University Press.

Chapter 4

Alison Sealey and Bob Carter

Making connections
Some key issues in applied linguistics

[. . .]

It is traditional in introductions to applied linguistics to begin with linguistics and then explain what is applied about it. For example, Carter (1993) indicates that '. . . applied linguistics is the application of linguistic theories, descriptions and methods to the solution of language problems which have arisen in a range of human, cultural and social contexts' (p.3). If 'linguistics reifies "language"', asks Brumfit (1997: 90), 'what does applied linguistics reify? More than just language – "language practices"'. What applied linguists do could be considered a definition of what the discipline is (Davies 1999), so, since (on strict quantitative measures) by far the majority of its work is concerned with foreign language teaching, this is what it is perceived to be by many. But this overlooks a great deal. Cook (2003: 8), for example, lists a significant number of areas that 'fall within our definition of applied linguistics and are claimed as areas of enquiry by organizations and journals concerned with the discipline'. This list includes the following three main areas and their sub-categories: Language and education: first language education, additional language education (subdivided into second and foreign language education), clinical linguistics, language testing; Language, work and law: workplace communication, language planning, forensic linguistics; Language, information and effect: literary stylistics, critical discourse analysis, translation and interpretation, information design, lexicography. From this broader perspective, applied linguistics may be redefined

Edited extracts from: Sealey, A. and Carter, B. 'Making connections: some key issues in social theory and applied linguistics', in *Applied Linguistics as a Social Science*, Continuum, pp. 17–33, 2004.

as 'problem-based researching into communication-mediated issues in social life' (Candlin pers. comm.). In such explorations, applied linguistics draws on a range of communication-interested disciplines and tools. Linguistics features among these, but certainly not to the exclusion of the others; indeed our claim that applied linguistics needs to be understood as a social science exemplifies the fact that descriptions of language and languages alone are inadequate to account for language-related practices and the problems associated with these. Thus 'applied linguistics' is a somewhat problematic label, but one that is convenient and has become established despite its problems.

What then are the core issues with which applied linguistics is concerned? Obviously, language itself is one key area of enquiry; the motivated practice of human agents as they use language is another; and the nature of the structured social contexts within which people seek to pursue their interests – where language is usually a medium for doing so, and is sometimes also an objective of those interests – is a third. In this part of the chapter, we sketch out some of the ways in which applied linguists have contributed to our understanding of these overlapping dimensions of language in social life, influenced as they are by a range of disciplinary perspectives. The division of topics into these three sections is necessarily somewhat arbitrary, since the social theoretical position we advance takes account of the *interplay* between the different domains, or strata, of the social world. However, we start with those topics which are most closely linked to language itself, move on to those concerned with situated practices, and conclude with an outline of some of the wider social issues to which applied linguistics makes a contribution.

Applied linguistics and descriptions of language

What does it mean to describe 'language'? What does such a description need to include? 'Language' may be conceptualized variously as a form of human behaviour, sounds in the air and marks on the page, a system of symbolic communication, an innate cognitive competence; and the answers to these questions may depend on who is asking them and why: the researcher recording the characteristics of a nearly-extinct language is likely to need different kinds of information from that required by the minister devising the language policy of a newly independent territory, or a language teacher, or a translator and so on. For some of these purposes applied linguistics draws on linguistics, especially when what the applied linguist needs to do is to give some account of the properties of a language, for example in the context of courses for the teachers of language learners or of children learning literacy. It might be assumed that the descriptions of the properties of languages which linguistics has made available would be ideal for such purposes, but this does not always turn out to be so, partly because the aims of the two enterprises are far from identical.

Linguistics is sometimes referred to as 'autonomous' linguistics, a phrase which signals its concern with the formal system of language as independent from other disciplines (Crystal 1991). The goal of linguistic enquiry, in this tradition (which is associated particularly with Chomsky), is the abstraction from the ubiquitous and polymorphous phenomenon which is language, towards greater understanding of the universals of the human mind. Describing a language is synonymous with 'describing part of the minds' of its speakers (Salkie 2001: 107, 110). The data of speakers' actual behaviour (their 'performance'), in this context, 'are disregarded . . . because they are of little theoretical interest: they do not provide reliable evidence for the essential nature of human language' (Widdowson 1996: 70). A summary statement of this essential nature, of what is common to human languages, is provided by Pinker (1999: 92): 'the ingredients of language are a list of memorized words, each an arbitrary pairing between a sound and a meaning, and a set of productive rules that assemble words into combinations'. Units such as individual sounds, which are normally meaningless on their own, are elements in a combinatorial system. The finite number of elements – such as the distinct sounds which contrast with each other in any one language – can combine to generate exponentially larger numbers of units of meaning. According to the Chomskyan tradition, human beings, endowed as they are with linguistic 'competence', are genetically programmed to be able to process language – any language – and what is of interest is the interface between language and mind.

The area of second language acquisition provides one overlap between the concerns of autonomous linguists and those of applied linguists. Some would claim, with Gregg (1993), that the basic focus of this research is 'L2 competence, in the Chomskyan sense of the term: How do L2 learners acquire competence in a second language? or, Why do learners not acquire the same competence as native speakers of the L2?' (p. 278). However, the more 'applied' this interest is, and the more pressing the need not just to investigate these questions but to actually teach particular learners, the greater the priority given to speakers' linguistic *performance*. Applied linguistics thus necessarily concerns itself with language *behaviour*, with speaking, listening, reading and writing. As conceived within theoretical – or autonomous – linguistics, such behaviour involves those features of language which are 'secondary . . ., incidental, and peripheral' in contrast to those which are 'essential and primary' (Widdowson 1996: 24–5).

The question of how far the study of language should involve attention to empirical evidence will be revisited in this and subsequent chapters, but at this point it may be useful, particularly for those readers who are less familiar with the linguistic disciplines, to provide a very basic, and necessarily greatly simplified, outline of what is thought to be involved in human linguistic competence.

Integrationist and functionalist accounts of language

The most thoroughgoing rejection of the separation of linguistic form from social function is perhaps that articulated by Harris and his associates. Harris (2001) draws a distinction between 'autonomists' – those who believe language is a set of verbal tools, and communication just the use to which those tools happen to be put – and 'non-autonomists', those who believe language *is* communication. He defines himself as an 'integrationist', and thus among those who take 'the most radical position' (p.131) on this issue. Integrationists see the extrapolation from individual cases to general rules as illegitimate, because language is a negotiated protocol between individuals which varies with each negotiation. (Other interpretations of integrationism also challenge mentalist versions of linguistics, though from slightly different positions. See, for example, Lieb 2002.)

Another approach which denies a distinction between language 'competence' (the abstract mental capacity, or potential, to deploy language) and 'performance' (the realization of this capacity in actual utterances) is defined as 'functional', associated particularly with Halliday, who proposes that 'language is as it is because of what it has to do' (Halliday 1978: 19), and that the way to understand language is to start from the principle that 'the linguistic system is a sociolinguistic system' (ibid.: 72). There is considerable integration, in Halliday's system, of the uses to which language is put and the patterns of its grammar and vocabulary. The functions of language include not only the communication of ideas (the 'ideational' function), and the organization of texts themselves (the 'textual' function) but also the participation in communicative acts, enabling human beings 'to take on roles and to express and understand feelings, attitude and judgements' (Bloor and Bloor 1995: 9). The descriptive system which has developed from this perspective on language as practice includes categories and labels such as 'Actor', 'Goal' and 'Process' which signal a concern with meaning, including interpersonal meaning. Rather than seeing the sentence as the largest unit of analysis, and sentences as composed of aggregations of smaller units, this perspective posits the text as 'the basic unit of the semantic process' (ibid.: 107). For Hallidayan functionalists, it is more useful to see text as *encoded in* sentences rather than *composed of* them, and the emphasis on understanding what language is is much more inter- than intra-individual. As Chouliaraki and Fairclough (1999: 140) express it, 'the social is built into the grammatical tissue of language'.

In this approach there is a shift of emphasis from the invisible workings of the individual mind towards the empirically observable behaviour of the language user. Many applied linguists would argue that this is more useful to them than the formalist approach to language description associated with Chomsky. As Carter (1993) puts it:

> There is a primary focus on language in use rather than on language as an abstract system and the models of analysis developed within functional linguistics are therefore of particular use for the analyses of naturally occurring spoken and written texts, often those produced within educational contexts.
>
> (p. 31)

A concern with empirical evidence of language-users' behaviour underpins another development in language description, whereby researchers have developed large, electronically stored 'corpora': 'collection[s] of pieces of language, selected and ordered according to explicit linguistic criteria in order to be used as a sample of the language' (Sinclair 1996 in Aston and Burnard 1998). A key objection made by corpus linguists to traditional descriptions is the weight placed by the latter on the intuition of the native speaker of a language, a procedure which Sinclair (1991) likens to 'that of the physical sciences some 250 years ago' (p.1). Corpus linguistics uses the computer to store and to search very large quantities of language data which have been produced for actual communicative purposes by (usually) large numbers of speakers and/or writers. The corpus known as the Bank of English, for example, includes over 400 million words of running text drawn from newspapers, magazines, fiction and non-fiction books, brochures, leaflets, reports and letters, as well as transcripts of everyday conversations, meetings, discussions and radio programmes.

The software used to investigate a corpus allows the identification of recurring patterns; in particular, *concordancing* programs identify the contexts within which particular linguistic items, such as a specific word or group of words, occur. *Collocations* are patterns of co-occurrence of words – 'You shall know a word by the company it keeps', wrote Firth (1957: 11, cited in Stubbs 1996) – and corpus investigations have identified some facts about such patterns which had not been identified by earlier methods of analysis. Corpus linguists have found reason from their research to challenge the adequacy of traditional grammatical categories. They argue that corpus evidence points to a different kind of classification, of 'patterns' functioning differently from the paradigm/syntagm matrix described above. Again, communicative function is foregrounded:

> As communicators we do not proceed by selecting syntactic structures and independently choosing lexical items to slot into them. Instead we have concepts to convey and communicative choices to make which require central lexical items, and these choices find themselves syntactic structures in which they can be said comfortably and grammatically.
>
> (Francis 1995 in Hunston and Francis 2000: 31)

Applied linguistics and human practice

As we have argued, within applied linguistics, concerns about what people do with language make it difficult to be satisfied with accounts which confine language, and descriptions of language, to internalized mental rules. In this section, we consider some ways in which language is researched less as a set of rules and more as a human practice, and highlight some applied linguistic activities which are conducted from this perspective.

Language corpora and applied linguistics

Although it has generated much useful information for the enterprise of language description, the original impetus for the development of a corpus like the Bank of English was pedagogic, so that reference books for language learners, such as grammars and dictionaries, could be based on evidence rather than intuition. Those involved in syllabus design can, if they wish, make decisions about when to introduce certain items based on their relative frequency, or can teach words as they appear in their most typical contexts (Nattinger and DeCarrico 1992). The ambition of many learners to sound 'authentic' may be aided by this kind of approach. Other areas of applied linguistic activity which are supported by corpora of various kinds (including parallel corpora in different languages) include for example translation, stylistics and forensic linguistics (Hunston 2002).

Discourse analysis and applied linguistics

Another area of research in which applied linguists are active is the analysis of discourse, where the aim is not so much the identification of the patterns and systems that constitute a language as the use of that language for specific communicative purposes. The term 'discourse analysis' carries a number of different meanings, and those who practise it operate within a range of disciplines, from the more sociological to the more linguistic. Work more strongly associated with the former tends to explore how 'discursive practices [may be] constitutive of knowledge', while that linked with the latter has been termed 'textually oriented discourse analysis' (Fairclough 1993: 38).

Insights from both orientations, though more usually the latter, are 'applied' in language teaching, where learners need to be familiar not only with sentence-level constructions but also with the larger patterns which characterize a wide range of text types and social interactions. For discussions of different methods and models of discourse analysis in respect of their usefulness to teachers and students of (English as a) foreign language, see, for example, Cook 1989, McCarthy 1991, McCarthy and Carter 1994. The different genres into which discourse can be subdivided have also been explored in applied linguistics, and research continues into how different text types may be classified, and how the discourse of particular kinds of practice, particularly academic practice, is constituted and learned.

Sociologists may well be more familiar with the approaches to discourse analysis which have developed out of ethnomethodology, with its interest in how people produce and interpret conversation. The seminal theorists associated with this kind of conversation analysis (CA) include Garfinkel, Sacks, Schegloff and Jefferson. These conversation analysts have sought to identify, for example, the ways in which speakers open and close conversations, and how turns and transitions between speakers are managed within fractions of a second. Some applied linguists have sought to explore how the findings of CA may be utilized in pedagogic contexts (e.g. Seedhouse 2005; Wong 2002), while Firth (1996) uses a CA approach to look at intercultural encounters, analysing interactions in English between non-native speakers.

Sociocultural and ecological theories in applied linguistics

Many applied linguists whose work involves them in the field of additional language learning have developed ways of thinking about the process which draw on ideas, from disciplines such as psychology and education, where learning is conceived of as significantly inter- as well as intra-individual. '[S]pecifically human forms of mental activity are not processes that occur invisibly inside someone's head but are instead the activity of socio-historically constituted people engaged in the historically situated activity of living' (Dunn and Lantolf 1998: 427). Particularly influential here is the work of Vygotsky and his sociocultural theory of mind, which has been taken up by a number of applied linguists – see, for example, Lantolf 2000, Lantolf and Pavlenko 1995, Smagorinsky 2001.

A further development in culturally situated accounts of language use and language learning, to which some of the same researchers have contributed, makes use of the metaphor of ecology. Rejecting the implications of likening language learning either to the input–output process associated with machines and computers, or to the linear acculturation process associated with a period of apprenticeship, ecological approaches invoke a concept of language learning as 'a nonlinear, relational human activity, co-constructed between humans and their environment, contingent upon their position in space and history, and a site of struggle for the control of power and cultural memory' (Kramsch 2002: 5).

This much more global view of what applied linguists are interested in takes us beyond applicable descriptions of language itself, and accounts of language learning and use as intersubjective practices. We consider a selection of the ways in which the discipline intersects with the study of social institutions and issues of power.

Applied linguistics and social contexts

It has been claimed that 'social processes, sociology, anthropology, and media studies recently seem to have replaced pedagogy, linguistics, and psychology as the major preoccupations in British applied linguistics' (Rampton 1995: 233). This may be something of an overstatement, given in particular the size of the continuing enterprise of language teaching in which applied linguists are involved. However, there are many areas where the discipline overlaps with those social sciences whose focus is on more macro phenomena, and we touch on some of them here.

Critical discourse analysis

While applied linguistics contributes to the description of communicative practices partly through its work in discourse analysis, some of its theorists and researchers are committed to analyses which not only describe 'what is', but also enquire into 'how it has come to be, and what it might become, on the basis of which people may be able to make and remake their lives' (Chouliaraki and Fairclough 1999: 4). For example, a virtual research group concerned with 'language in the new capitalism' is interested in 'the language and meaning of contemporary capitalism, and the links between economic, social and linguistic change in the contemporary world', in the belief that 'a better understanding of how language figures in the new capitalism . . . increases our capacity to question and critique it, and to change it' (LNC 2003). The 'critical linguists' and, later, 'critical discourse analysts' who have used the analysis of language practices to illuminate issues of power and inequality include, for example, Chouliaraki and Fairclough (1999), Fairclough (1989, 1995, 2001), Fowler et al. (1979) and Kress (1985). Among their data are texts produced by institutions, such as universities, government departments or commercial corporations, the output of news media (both print and broadcast) as well as the discourse of political speeches, and there is, again, a particular affinity between the systemic functional description of language associated with Halliday (see above) and the enterprise of exploring large-scale political issues through the analysis of language (see particularly Chouliaraki and Fairclough 1999).

The methods available to corpus linguists are also drawn on in studies of social and cultural values. According to Teubert (1999), corpus linguistics 'is based on the concept that language is a fundamentally social phenomenon, which can be observed and described first and foremost in the empirical data readily available, that is, in communication acts'. Corpus linguists have explored cultural preoccupations in their data, such as various examples of specific lexical items being repeatedly found with other words that have one kind of connotation rather than another, leading Stubbs (1996) to propose that the analytic methods made possible by these methods could enhance new versions of the kind of social commentary carried out by Raymond Williams in his *Keywords* (1976), and he provides examples here and in Stubbs 2001.

In the previous section we highlighted the link between discourse analysis with an applied linguistic provenance and the conversation analysis conducted by sociologists. The critical discourse analyst Billig (1999a, 1999b) has attacked traditional conversation analysis on the grounds that it 'conveys an essentially non critical view of the social world', but there are many analysts who use the CA approach to explore the role of talk in the constitution and maintenance of asymmetrical social relationships, particularly in institutional discourse. For example, the collection edited by Drew and Heritage (1993) reports on the interactions between professionals and 'clients' in a wide variety of settings, including doctor–patient consultations, legal hearings, news interviews, visits by health visitors, psychiatric interviews, and calls to the emergency services. Contributors include sociologists and applied linguists, some of whom are well-known for developing the branch of the discipline which has drawn particularly on anthropological and ethnographic methodologies.

Ethnography and applied linguistics

If mentalist accounts of language are criticized by applied linguists for their inadequacy in describing language practices, and conversation analysis attracts criticism for its failure to deal with social conflict, corpus linguists have been criticized for taking language data out of the context of its production (Widdowson 2000), and some applied linguists who are committed to the detailed study of language practices eschew the analysis of decontextualized corpus data in favour of research methods developed by anthropologists and ethnographers. In the 1970s, Hymes described an approach to language description (partly as a reaction against Chomsky) which he termed 'an ethnography of speaking', by which he meant 'a description that is a theory – a theory of speech as a system of cultural behaviour' (Hymes 1974: 89), and since then a number of scholars have conducted detailed studies in diverse social settings of various 'speech communities', looking at the range of language choices open to speakers and the ways in which variation is patterned. Examples of such studies are found in Gumperz (1982), whose introduction claims that 'communication cannot be studied in isolation; it must be analyzed in terms of its effect on people's lives. We must focus on what communication does: how it constrains evaluation and decision making, not merely how it is structured' (p.1). Gumperz and his associates have long been involved in the close observation of the ways in which different social identities and different language practices can lead to miscommunication among individuals and groups (see, for example, Roberts *et al.* 1992; Roberts and Sarangi 1999), and one practical effect of such work has been the involvement of applied linguists as consultants to companies and organizations seeking to ameliorate problems in communication, such as those of doctors in training or between managers and their workforces. The British Association of Applied Linguistics recently established a special interest group to foster developments in contemporary theories and practices in linguistic ethnography, and their research involves areas such as literacy practices, institutional discourse, urban heteroglossia, multilingualism and children's home and school learning. The study of 'intercultural communication' has also benefited from some ethnographic studies, as advocated by Blommaert (1998, 2001), with an increasing interest in using ethnographic approaches also in the *teaching* of languages and 'intercultural competence' (see Byram and Fleming 1998; LARA 2003).

Sociolinguistics

The contributions of researchers such as Hymes and Gumperz span approaches which appeal to both applied linguistics and sociolinguistics. The latter sub-discipline is quite broad in scope, but it is basically concerned with exploring how people use language differently in different social contexts. Practitioners whose interest is predominantly in language description, particularly language change, often use a quantitative approach in the measurement of linguistic variables, and 'correlating linguistic variation as the dependent variable with the independent variables such as linguistic environment, style or social categories is the primary empirical task of sociolinguistics' (Chambers 1995: 17). For others, the legitimate concerns of sociolinguistics are deemed to extend to issues which are elsewhere delineated as 'the sociology of language', while there is also a great deal of potential common ground between this broader interpretation of 'sociolinguistics' and the broader interpretations of 'applied linguistics'. The most inclusive definitions of either discipline may make the distinction between the two effectively redundant. To give just one example here, a widely publicized controversy was sparked in the late 1990s by the decision of the Oakland School Board in California to recognize 'Ebonics' as 'the primary language of African American children'. Sociolinguists who have studied the detail of phonological, lexical and grammatical variations between varieties of English spoken by black and white Americans suddenly found themselves in the media spotlight (Rickford 1999). The extremely heated debate concerned *both* the status and characteristics of a language variety *and* the political and pedagogic issues of what language and literacy teaching practice should be.

Forensic linguistics

It is an indication of just what a crucial role language plays in social life that being – or indeed failing to be – the author of a particular text or utterance can result in severe punishment. Forensic linguistic enquiry scrutinizes language such as statements allegedly made by an accused person or witness, the assessed work of students suspected of plagiarism, suicide notes apparently written shortly before death, threatening letters or telephone calls and disputed police interview records. Methods of analysis include linguistic and statistical measures to establish authorship and whether texts have been altered, and phonetic procedures used to aid 'earwitness' testimony in voice lineups. A number of applied linguists have acted as expert witnesses in court cases, demonstrating once again the range of activity covered by this discipline.

As people's language behaviour comes under ever-increasing scrutiny, the informed accounts provided by applied linguistics of linguistic *performance* as well as *competence* is likely to continue to be in demand.

Responding to social problems with applied linguistics

The foregoing discussion has provided an indication of some of the areas of social life in which applied linguists are active. As we have noted, the realm of education sees a significant proportion of this activity, and this extends from research into how the individual learner – including learners who may have some clinical condition affecting language interpretation or production – processes spoken language or written text, through analyses of what goes on in language and literacy classrooms, and on to questions about the global influence of specific languages, notably English, as education systems all over the world are involved in decision-making about which languages are to be taught in their schools. We have also illustrated how the language of social interactions and institutions from a much wider range of contexts than education is not only analysed but also subject to suggested alterations as a result of some of the projects in which applied linguists are involved. Commercial institutions, workplaces, media texts, family conversations, intercultural encounters, hospitals and emergency services: all of these sites have been investigated in the course of applied linguistic research.

References

Aston, G. and Burnard, L. (1998) *The BNC Handbook: Exploring the British National Corpus with SARA*. Edinburgh: Edinburgh University Press.

Billig, M. (1999a) 'Whose terms? Whose ordinariness? Rhetoric and ideology in Conversation Analysis', *Discourse and Society* 10 (4): 543–58.

Billig, M. (1999b) 'Conversation analysis and the claims of naivety', *Discourse and Society* 10 (4): 572–7.

Blommaert, J. (1998) 'Different approaches to intercultural communication: a critical survey'. Paper presented at *Lernen und Arbeiten in einer international vernetzten und multikulturellen Gesellschaft*, Expertentagung Universität Bremen, Institut für Projektmanagement und Wirtschaftsinformatik.

Blommaert, J. (2001) 'Ethnography as counter-hegemony: remarks on epistemology and method'. Paper presented at the *International Literacy Conference*, Cape Town.

Bloor, T. and Bloor, M. (1995) *The Functional Analysis of English: A Hallidayan Approach*. London: Arnold.

Brumfit, C. (1997) 'How applied linguistics is the same as any other science', *International Journal of Applied Linguistics* 7 (1): 86–94.

Byram, M. and Fleming, M. (eds) (1998) *Language Learning in Intercultural Perspective*. Cambridge: Cambridge University Press.

Carter, R. (1993) *Introducing Applied Linguistics*. London: Penguin Books.

Chambers, J.K. (1995) *Sociolinguistic Theory: Linguistic Variation and its Social Significance*. Oxford: Blackwell.

Chouliaraki, L. and Fairclough, N. (1999) *Discourse in Late Modernity: Rethinking Critical Discourse Analysis*. Edinburgh: Edinburgh University Press.

Cook, G. (1989) *Discourse*. Oxford: Oxford University Press.

Cook, G. (2003) *Applied Linguistics*. Oxford: Oxford University Press.

Crystal, D. (1991) *A Dictionary of Linguistics and Phonetics*. Oxford: Blackwell.

Davies, A. (1999) *An Introduction to Applied Linguistics: From Practice to Theory*. Edinburgh: Edinburgh University Press.

Drew, P. and Heritage, J. (eds) (1993) *Talk at Work: Interaction in Institutional Settings*. Cambridge: Cambridge University Press.

Dunn, W.E. and Lantolf, J.P. (1998) 'Vygotsky's Zone of Proximal Development and Krashen's *i + 1*: incommensurable constructs; incommensurable theories', *Language Learning* 48 (3): 411–42.

Fairclough, N. (1989) *Language and Power*. London: Longman.

Fairclough, N. (1993) *Discourse and Social Change*. Cambridge: Polity Press in association with Blackwells.

Fairclough, N. (1995) *Critical Discourse Analysis: Papers in the Critical Study of Language*. London: Longman.

Fairclough, N. (2001) 'The discourse of New Labour: critical discourse analysis', in M. Wetherell, S. Taylor and S.J. Yates (eds) *Discourse as Data: A Guide for Analysis* (pp. 229–66). London and Milton Keynes: Open University and Sage.

Firth, A. (1996) 'The discursive accomplishment of normality: on 'lingua franca' English and conversation analysis', *Journal of Pragmatics* 26: 237–59.

Fowler, R., Hodge, B., Kress, G. and Trew, T. (1979) *Language and Control*. London: Routledge and Kegan Paul.

Gregg, K. (1993) 'Taking explanation seriously; or, let a couple of flowers bloom', *Applied Linguistics* 14 (3): 276–94.

Gumperz, J.J. (ed.) (1982) *Language and Social Identity*. Cambridge: Cambridge University Press.

Halliday, M.A.K. (1978) *Language as Social Semiotic*. London: Edward Arnold.

Harris, R. (2001) 'Linguistics after Saussure', in P. Cobley (ed.) *Semiotics and Linguistics* (pp. 118–33). London: Routledge.

Hunston, S. (2002) *Corpora in Applied Linguistics*. Cambridge: Cambridge University Press.

Hunston, S. and Francis, G. (2000) *Pattern Grammar: A Corpus-driven Approach to the Lexical Grammar of English*. Amsterdam: John Benjamins.

Hymes, D. (1974) *Foundations in Sociolinguistics: An Ethnographic Approach*. London: Tavistock Publications.

Kramsch, C. (2002) Introduction: 'How can we tell the dancer from the dance?', in C. Kramsch (ed.) *Language Acquisition and Language Socialization: Ecological Perspectives* (pp. 1–30). London and New York: Continuum.

Kress, G. (1985) *Linguistic Processes in Sociocultural Practice*. Oxford: Oxford University Press.

Lantolf, J.P. (ed.) (2000) *Sociocultural Theory and Second Language Learning*. Oxford: Oxford University Press.

Lantolf, J.P. and Pavlenko, A. (1995) 'Sociocultural theory and second language acquisition', *Annual Review of Applied Linguistics* 15: 108–24.

LARA (Learning and Residence Abroad) (2003) http://lara.fdtl.ac.uk/lara/ethno.html (accessed 16 July 2003).

Lieb, H.-H. (2002) *Basic Characteristics of Integrational Linguistics: A Brief Summary*. http://camelot.germanistik.fu-berlin.de/il/+en/basic-en.html (accessed 28 December 2002).

LNC (Language in the New Capitalism) (2003) www.cddc.vt.edu/host/lnc/LNC.htm (accessed 16 July 2003).

McCarthy, M. (1991) *Discourse Analysis for Language Teachers*. Cambridge: Cambridge University Press.

McCarthy, M. and Carter, R. (1994) *Language as Discourse: Perspectives for Language Teaching*. Harlow: Longman.

Nattinger, J.R. and DeCarrico, J.S. (1992) *Lexical Phrases and Language Teaching*. Oxford: Oxford University Press.

Pinker, S. (1999) *Words and Rules: The Ingredients of Language*. London: Phoenix.

Rampton, B. (1995) 'Politics and change in research in applied linguistics', *Applied Linguistics* 16 (2): 233–56.

Rickford, J.R. (1999) 'The Ebonics controversy in my backyard: a sociolinguist's experiences and reflections', *Journal of Sociolinguistics* 3 (2): 267–75.

Roberts, C., Davies, E. and Jupp, T. (1992) *Language and Discrimination: A Study of Communication in Multi-ethnic Workplaces*. London: Longman.

Roberts, C.J. and Sarangi, S. (eds) (1999) *Talk, Work and Institutional Order: Discourse in Medical, Mediation and Management Settings*. Berlin: Mouton de Gruyter.

Salkie, R. (2001) 'The Chomskyan revolutions', in P. Cobley (ed.) *Semiotics and Linguistics* (pp. 105–17). London: Routledge.

Seedhouse, P. (2005) *The Interactional Architecture of the Language Classroom: A Conversation Analysis Perspective*. Oxford: Blackwell.

Sinclair, J. (1991) *Corpus, Concordance, Collocation*. Oxford: Oxford University Press.

Smagorinsky, P. (2001) 'Rethinking protocol analysis from a cultural perspective', *Annual Review of Applied Linguistics* 21: 233–45.

Stubbs, M. (1996) *Text and Corpus Analysis*. Oxford: Blackwell.

Stubbs, M. (2001) *Words and Phrases: Corpus Studies of Lexical Semantics*. Oxford: Blackwell.

Teubert, W. (1999) 'Corpus linguistics – a partisan view', *International Journal of Corpus Linguistics* 5 (1), http://tractor.bham.ac.uk/ijcl/teubert_cl.html (accessed 28 December 2002).

Widdowson, H.G. (1996) *Linguistics*. Oxford: Oxford University Press.

Widdowson, H.G. (2000) 'On the limitations of linguistics applied', *Applied Linguistics* 21 (1): 3–25.

Williams, R. (1976) *Keywords: A Vocabulary of Culture and Society*. London: Fontana.

Wong, J. (2002) 'Applying conversation analysis in applied linguistics: evaluating English as a second language textbook dialogue', *International Review of Applied Linguistics* 40 (1): 37–60.

PART TWO

English in the world

Guy Cook and Sarah North

Introduction to Part Two

The linguistic landscape of the world has changed dramatically in recent decades, accelerated by globalisation, new communication technologies and mass migration. English is now known and used so widely that it can legitimately be described as a global language. At the same time other languages which were formerly used for international communications are now employed less and less for this purpose, and the world's smallest languages are disappearing at an alarming rate. Consequently there is concern about the effects of these changes upon the cultural heritage and identity for speakers of languages other than English. The situation affects almost all language-related problems which the applied linguist is likely to consider, and it is for this reason that we have devoted a section of this reader to it.

We begin with a chapter by David Crystal 'Why a Global Language?' in which he both describes the current situation of English in the world, and evaluates the consequences of what he unequivocally judges to be its status as the global language. This is a balanced but optimistic view which considers both the advantages of a global language in facilitating communication and augmenting opportunities for all its speakers, but also recognises potential threats to diversity and identity. Unashamed to be identified as a 'liberal idealist' he takes issue with those who see the spread of English as either a threat to other languages, or a cause of their decline, arguing that it is possible for a global language to coexist non-detrimentally with others.

Whereas Crystal is concerned with the impact or possible impact of English on other languages in the world, the next chapter, 'The Ownership of English' by Henry Widdowson, deals with the impact of its spread upon the English language itself, and in particular upon the pretensions of the English-speaking nations, and of English native speakers, to treat it as something which they own, telling others how it should be used. Just as control of it necessarily passed from Britain to its former colonies, allowing for the creation of alternative standard forms – notably in the USA – so now, he argues, this ownership must be recognised as passing on again to all those who use the English language in the contemporary world. The consequences of this position are enormous, especially for language teaching and learning where – if it is accepted – the measure of what counts as an acceptable model and goal for the English learner also changes considerably.

While Crystal and Widdowson, though treating different consequences of the spread of English, may be seen as broadly compatible in their outlook, the next chapter by Alastair Pennycook takes a very different view. (Crystal has indeed already referred to Pennycook's critique of his own position as 'naive liberal idealism' and a 'liberal laissez-faire attitude'.) The main point of disagreement here is not the description of the spread of English, but rather an assessment of the desirability of that spread, and a very different assessment of the relation between the ascendancy of English and the fate of other languages. Although Pennycook agrees that the growth of English is not the only reason for the retreat of other languages, he does see it as a major cause, and one to be resisted rather than welcomed or allowed.

The first three authors, despite their differences, have in common that they all remain at a level of generality and abstraction. The next chapters are more specific in their analysis of the consequences of the spread of English. Fabrício and Santos nicely provide a bridge from the general to the specific by framing their consideration of one particular situation – attitudes to English expressed by Brazilian school students – within a more general consideration of attitudes towards the use of English in the Brazilian education system, and its use in the world in general.

In the last chapter, Jennifer Jenkins takes a much more specific task, which may be related to the implications of the chapter by Widdowson. For if English no longer belongs to native speakers in the way that has traditionally been considered, then there is room for a new non-native speaker model of the language. Jenkins focus is on a model of English – 'English as a lingua franca' – in which teachability and learnability are paramount, and success is to be measured by international intelligibility, rather than approximation to native-speaker identity.

The careful reader will notice a number of shared allusions and cross references running throughout these five chapters. Crystal takes issue with Pennycook, and vice versa. In the course of their arguments, Pennycook and Widdowson both invoke the reflections of Nigerian writer Chinua Achebe, though with rather different conclusions. Fabrício and Santos make use of Pennycook's position, but refer critically to advocacy of English as a lingua franca, such as Jenkins', for being too concerned with the utilitarian functions of language, and too little with its ecological role in promoting and preserving identity and power. In short, those engaged in the debates around the implications of the spread of English, are well aware of others' positions, and what we hope will emerge from this selection of chapters is an insight into the developing thinking on what all agree is a crucial topic for applied linguistic research: the effects of the globalisation of English on all aspects of language use, function and learning.

Chapter 5

David Crystal

Why a global language?

[. . .]

What is a global language?

A language achieves a genuinely global status when it develops a special role that is recognized in every country. This might seem like stating the obvious, but it is not, for the notion of 'special role' has many facets. Such a role will be most evident in countries where large numbers of the people speak the language as a mother tongue – in the case of English, this would mean the USA, Canada, Britain, Ireland, Australia, New Zealand, South Africa, several Caribbean countries and a sprinkling of other territories. However, no language has ever been spoken by a mother-tongue majority in more than a few countries (Spanish leads, in this respect, in some twenty countries, chiefly in Latin America), so mother-tongue use by itself cannot give a language global status. To achieve such a status, a language has to be taken up by other countries around the world. They must decide to give it a special place within their communities, even though they may have few (or no) mother-tongue speakers.

There are two main ways in which this can be done. Firstly, a language can be made the official language of a country, to be used as a medium of communication in such domains as government, the law courts, the media, and the educational system. To get on in these societies, it is essential to master the official language as

Edited extracts from: Crystal, David, Chapter 1 'Why a global language?' in *English as a Global Language*, Cambridge University Press, 2003.

early in life as possible. Such a language is often described as a 'second language', because it is seen as a complement to a person's mother tongue, or 'first language'. The role of an official language is today best illustrated by English, which now has some kind of special status in over seventy countries, such as Ghana, Nigeria, India, Singapore and Vanuatu. This is far more than the status achieved by any other language – though French, German, Spanish, Russian and Arabic are among those which have also developed a considerable official use. New political decisions on the matter continue to be made: for example, Rwanda gave English official status in 1996.

Secondly, a language can be made a priority in a country's foreign language teaching, even though this language has no official status. It becomes the language which children are most likely to be taught when they arrive in school, and the one most available to adults who – for whatever reason – never learned it, or learned it badly, in their early educational years. Russian, for example, held privileged status for many years among the countries of the former Soviet Union. Mandarin Chinese continues to play an important role in South-east Asia. English is now the language most widely taught as a foreign language – in over 100 countries, such as China, Russia, Germany, Spain, Egypt and Brazil – and in most of these countries it is emerging as the chief foreign language to be encountered in schools, often displacing another language in the process. In 1996, for example, English replaced French as the chief foreign language in schools in Algeria (a former French colony).

In reflecting on these observations, it is important to note that there are several ways in which a language can be official. It may be the sole official language of a country, or it may share this status with other languages. And it may have a 'semi-official' status, being used only in certain domains, or taking second place to other languages while still performing certain offical roles. Many countries formally acknowledge a language's status in their constitution (e.g. India); some make no special mention of it (e.g. Britain). In certain countries, the question of whether the special status should be legally recognized is a source of considerable controversy – notably, in the USA.

Similarly, there is great variation in the reasons for choosing a particular language as a favoured foreign language: they include historical tradition, political expediency, and the desire for commercial, cultural or technological contact. Also, even when chosen, the 'presence' of the language can vary greatly, depending on the extent to which a government or foreign-aid agency is prepared to give adequate financial support to a language-teaching policy. In a well-supported environment, resources will be devoted to helping people have access to the language and learn it, through the media, libraries, schools, and institutes of higher education. There will be an increase in the number and quality of teachers able to teach the language. Books, tapes, computers, telecommunication systems and all kinds of teaching materials will be increasingly available. In many countries, however, lack of government support, or a shortage of foreign aid, has hindered the achievement of language-teaching goals.

Distinctions such as those between 'first'-, 'second'- and 'foreign'-language status are useful, but we must be careful not to give them a simplistic interpretation. In particular, it is important to avoid interpreting the distinction between 'second' and 'foreign' language use as a difference in fluency or ability. Although we might expect people from a country where English has some sort of official status to be more competent in the language than those where it has none, simply on grounds of greater exposure, it turns out that this is not always so. We should note, for example, the very high levels of fluency demonstrated by a wide range of speakers from the Scandinavian countries and the Netherlands. But we must also beware introducing too sharp a distinction between first language speakers and the others, especially in a world where children are being born to parents who communicate with each other through a lingua franca learned as a foreign language. In the Emirates a few years ago, for example, I met a couple – a German oil industrialist and a Malaysian – who had courted through their only common language, English, and decided to bring up their child with English as the primary language of the home. So here is a baby learning English as a foreign language as its mother tongue. There are now many such cases around the world, and they raise a question over the contribution that these babies will one day make to the language, once they grow up to be important people, for their intuitions about English will inevitably be different from those of traditional native speakers.

These points add to the complexity of the present-day world English situation, but they do not alter the fundamental point. Because of the three-pronged development – of first language, second language, and foreign language speakers – it is inevitable that a global language will eventually come to be used by more people than any other language. English has already reached this stage. About a quarter of the world's population is already fluent or competent in English, and this figure is steadily growing – in the early 2000s that means around 1.5 billion people. No other language can match this growth. Even Chinese, found in eight different spoken languages, but unified by a common writing system, is known to 'only' some 1.1 billion.

What makes a global language?

Why a language becomes a global language has little to do with the number of people who speak it. It is much more to do with who those speakers are. Latin became an international language throughout the Roman Empire, but this was not because the Romans were more numerous than the peoples they subjugated. They were simply more powerful. And later, when Roman military power declined, Latin remained for a millennium as the international language of education, thanks to a different sort of power – the ecclesiastical power of Roman Catholicism.

There is the closest of links between language dominance and economic, technological, and cultural power, too, and this relationship will become increasingly clear as the history of English is told. Without a strong power-base, of what-ever kind, no language can make progress as an international medium of communica-tion. Language has no independent existence, living in some sort of mystical space apart from the people who speak it. Language exists only in the brains and mouths and ears and hands and eyes of its users. When they succeed, on the international stage, their language succeeds. When they fail, their language fails.

This point may seem obvious, but it needs to be made at the outset, because over the years many popular and misleading beliefs have grown up about why a language should become internationally successful. It is quite common to hear people claim that a language is a paragon, on account of its perceived aesthetic qualities, clarity of expression, literary power, or religious standing. Hebrew, Greek, Latin, Arabic and French are among those which at various times have been lauded in such terms, and English is no exception. It is often suggested, for example, that there must be something inherently beautiful or logical about the structure of English, in order to explain why it is now so widely used. 'It has less grammar than other languages', some have suggested. 'English doesn't have a lot of endings on its words, nor do we have to remember the difference between masculine, feminine, and neuter gender, so it must be easier to learn'. In 1848, a reviewer in the British periodical *The Athenaeum* wrote:

> In its easiness of grammatical construction, in its paucity of inflection, in its almost total disregard of the distinctions of gender excepting those of nature, in the simplicity and precision of its terminations and auxiliary verbs, not less than in the majesty, vigour and copiousness of its expression, our mother-tongue seems well adapted by *organization* to become the language of the world.

Such arguments are misconceived. Latin was once a major international language, despite its many inflectional endings and gender differences. French, too, has been such a language, despite its nouns being masculine or feminine; and so – at different times and places – have the heavily inflected Greek, Arabic, Spanish and Russian. Ease of learning has nothing to do with it. Children of all cultures learn to talk over more or less the same period of time, regardless of the differences in the grammar of their languages. And as for the notion that English has 'no grammar' – a claim that is risible to anyone who has ever had to learn it as a foreign language – the point can be dismissed by a glance at any of the large twentieth-century reference grammars. The *Comprehensive Grammar of the English Language*, for example, contains 1,800 pages and some 3,500 points requiring grammatical exposition.

This is not to deny that a language may have certain properties which make it internationally appealing. For example, learners sometimes comment on the 'familiarity' of English vocabulary, deriving from the way English has over the centuries borrowed thousands of new words from the languages with which it has been in contact. The 'welcome' given to foreign vocabulary places English in contrast to some languages (notably, French) which have tried to keep it out, and gives it a cosmopolitan character which many see as an advantage for a global language. From a lexical point of view, English is in fact far more a Romance than a Germanic language. And there have been comments made about other structural aspects, too, such as the absence in English grammar of a system of coding social class differences, which can make the language appear more 'democratic' to those who speak a language (e.g. Javanese) that does express an intricate system of class relationships. But these supposed traits of appeal are incidental, and need to be weighed against linguistic features which would seem to be internationally much less desirable – notably, in the case of English, the accumulated irregularities of its spelling system.

A language does not become a global language because of its intrinsic structural properties, or because of the size of its vocabulary, or because it has been a vehicle of a great literature in the past, or because it was once associated with a great culture or religion. These are all factors which can motivate someone to learn a language, of course, but none of them alone, or in combination, can ensure a language's world spread. Indeed, such factors cannot even guarantee survival as a living language – as is clear from the case of Latin, learned today as a classical language by only a scholarly and religious few. Correspondingly, inconvenient structural properties (such as awkward spelling) do not stop a language achieving international status either.

A language has traditionally become an international language for one chief reason: the power of its people – especially their political and military power. The explanation is the same throughout history. Why did Greek become a language of international communication in the Middle East over 2,000 years ago? Not because of the intellects of Plato and Aristotle: the answer lies in the swords and spears wielded by the armies of Alexander the Great. Why did Latin become known throughout Europe? Ask the legions of the Roman Empire. Why did Arabic come to be spoken so widely across northern Africa and the Middle East? Follow the spread of Islam, carried along by the force of the Moorish armies from the eighth century. Why did Spanish, Portuguese and French find their way into the Americas, Africa and the Far East? Study the colonial policies of the Renaissance kings and queens, and the way these policies were ruthlessly implemented by armies and navies all over the known world. The history of a global language can be traced through the successful expeditions of its soldier/sailor speakers. And English has been no exception.

But international language dominance is not solely the result of military might. It may take a militarily powerful nation to establish a language, but it takes an economically powerful one to maintain and expand it. This has always been the case, but it became a particularly critical factor in the nineteenth and twentieth centuries, with economic developments beginning to operate on a global scale, supported by the new communication technologies – telegraph, telephone, radio – and fostering the emergence of massive multinational organizations. The growth of competitive industry and business brought an explosion of international marketing and advertising. The power of the press reached unprecedented levels, soon to be surpassed by the broadcasting media, with their ability to cross national boundaries with electromagnetic ease. Technology, chiefly in the form of movies and records, fuelled new mass-entertainment industries which had a worldwide impact. The drive to make progress in science and technology fostered an international intellectual and research environment which gave scholarship and further education a high profile.

Any language at the centre of such an explosion of international activity would suddenly have found itself with a global status. And English was apparently 'in the right place at the right time' (p. 78). By the beginning of the nineteenth century, Britain had become the world's leading industrial and trading country. By the end of the century, the population of the USA (then approaching 100 million) was larger than that of any of the countries of western Europe, and its economy was the most productive and the fastest growing in the world. British political imperialism had sent English around the globe, during the nineteenth century, so that it was a language 'on which the sun never sets' (Quirk 1985: 1). During the twentieth century, this world presence was maintained and promoted almost single-handedly through the economic supremacy of the new American superpower. Economics replaced politics as the chief driving force. And the language behind the US dollar was English.

Why do we need a global language?

Translation has played a central (though often unrecognized) role in human interaction for thousands of years. When monarchs or ambassadors met on the international stage, there would invariably be interpreters present. But there are limits to what can be done in this way. The more a community is linguistically mixed, the less it can rely on individuals to ensure communication between different groups. In communities where only two or three languages are in contact, bilingualism (or trilingualism) is a possible solution, for most young children can acquire more than one language with unselfconscious ease. But in communities where there are many languages in contact, as in much of Africa and South-east Asia, such a natural solution does not readily apply.

The problem has traditionally been solved by finding a language to act as a lingua franca, or 'common language'. Sometimes, when communities begin to trade with each other, they communicate by adopting a simplified language, known as a *pidgin*, which combines elements of their different languages (Todd 1984). Many such pidgin languages survive today in territories which formerly belonged to the European colonial nations, and act as lingua francas; for example, West African Pidgin English is used extensively between several ethnic groups along the West African coast. Sometimes an indigenous language emerges as a lingua franca – usually the language of the most powerful ethnic group in the area, as in the case of Mandarin Chinese. The other groups then learn this language with varying success, and thus become to some degree bilingual. But most often, a language is accepted from outside the community, such as English or French, because of the political, economic or religious influence of a foreign power.

The geographical extent to which a lingua franca can be used is entirely governed by political factors. Many lingua francas extend over quite small domains – between a few ethnic groups in one part of a single country, or linking the trading populations of just a few countries, as in the West African case. By contrast, Latin was a lingua franca throughout the whole of the Roman Empire – at least, at the level of government (very few 'ordinary' people in the subjugated domains would have spoken much Latin). And in modern times Swahili, Arabic, Spanish, French, English, Hindi, Portuguese and several other languages have developed a major international role as a lingua franca, in limited areas of the world.

The prospect that a lingua franca might be needed for the *whole* world is something which has emerged strongly only in the twentieth century, and since the 1950s in particular. The chief international forum for political communication – the United Nations – dates only from 1945. Since then, many international bodies have come into being, such as the World Bank (also 1945), UNESCO and UNICEF (both 1946), the World Health Organization (1948) and the International Atomic Energy Agency (1957). Never before have so many countries (around 190, in the case of some UN bodies) been represented in single meeting-places. At a more restricted level, multinational regional or political groupings have come into being, such as the Commonwealth and the European Union. The pressure to adopt a single lingua franca, to facilitate communication in such contexts, is considerable, the alternative being expensive and impracticable multi-way translation facilities.

Usually a small number of languages have been designated official languages for an organization's activities: for example, the UN was established with five official languages – English, French, Spanish, Russian and Chinese. There is now a widespread view that it makes sense to try to reduce the numbers of languages involved in world bodies, if only to cut down on the vast amount of interpretation/translation and clerical work required. Half the budget of an international organization can easily get swallowed up in translation costs. But trimming a translation budget is never easy, as obviously no country likes the thought of its language being given a reduced international standing. Language choice is always one of the most sensitive issues facing a planning committee. The common situation is one where a committee does not have to be involved – where all the participants at an international meeting automatically use a single language, as a utilitarian measure (a 'working language'), because it is one which they have all come to learn for separate reasons. This situation seems to be slowly becoming a reality in meetings around the world, as general competence in English grows.

The need for a global language is particularly appreciated by the international academic and business communities, and it is here that the adoption of a single lingua franca is most in evidence, both in lecture-rooms and board-rooms, as well as in thousands of individual contacts being made daily all over the globe. A conversation over the Internet between academic physicists in Sweden, Italy, and India is at present practicable only if a common language is available. A situation where a Japanese company director arranges to meet German and Saudi Arabian contacts in a Singapore hotel to plan a multi-national deal would not be impossible, if each plugged in to a three-way translation support system, but it would be far more complicated than the alternative, which is for each to make use of the same language.

As these examples suggest, the growth in international contacts has been largely the result of two separate developments. The physicists would not be talking so conveniently to each other at all without the technology of modern communication. And the business contacts would be unable to meet so easily in Singapore without the technology of air transportation. The availability of both these facilities in the twentieth century, more than anything else, provided the circumstances needed for a global language to grow.

People have, in short, become more mobile, both physically and electronically. Annual airline statistics show that steadily increasing numbers are finding the motivation as well as the means to transport themselves physically around the globe, and sales of faxes, modems, and personal computers show an even greater increase in those prepared to send their ideas in words and images electronically. It is now possible, using electronic mail, to copy a message to hundreds of locations all over the world virtually simultaneously. It is just as easy for me to send a message from my house in the small town of Holyhead, North Wales, to a friend in Washington as it is to get the same message to someone living just a few streets away from me. In fact, it is probably easier. That is why people so often talk, these days, of the 'global village'.

These trends would be taking place, presumably, if only a handful of countries were talking to each other. What has been so impressive about the developments which have taken place since the 1950s is that they have affected, to a greater or lesser extent, every country in the world, and that so many countries have come to be involved. There is no nation now which does not have some level of accessibility using telephone, radio, television, and air transport, though facilities such as fax, electronic mail and the Internet are much less widely available.

The scale and recency of the development has to be appreciated. In 1945, the United Nations began life with fifty-one member states. By 1956 this had risen to eighty members. But the independence movements which began at that time led to a massive increase in the number of new nations during the next decade, and this process continued steadily into the 1990s, following the collapse of the USSR. There were 190 member states in 2002 – nearly four times as many as there were fifty years ago. And the trend may not yet be over, given the growth of so many regional nationalistic movements worldwide.

There are no precedents in human history for what happens to languages, in such circumstances of rapid change. There has never been a time when so many nations were needing to talk to each other so much. There has never been a time when so many people wished to travel to so many places. There has never been such a strain placed on the conventional resources of translating and interpreting. Never has the need for more widespread bilingualism been greater, to ease the burden placed on the professional few. And never has there been a more urgent need for a global language.

What are the dangers of a global language?

The benefits which would flow from the existence of a global language are considerable; but several commentators have pointed to possible risks (Crystal 2000). Perhaps a global language will cultivate an elite monolingual linguistic class, more complacent and dismissive in their attitudes towards other languages. Perhaps those who have such a language at their disposal – and especially those who have it as a mother tongue – will be more able to think and work quickly in it, and to manipulate it to their own advantage at the expense of those who do not have it, thus maintaining in a linguistic guise the chasm between rich and poor. Perhaps the presence of a global language will make people lazy about learning other languages, or reduce their opportunities to do so. Perhaps a global language will hasten the disappearance of minority languages, or – the ultimate threat – make *all* other languages unnecessary. 'A person needs only one language to talk to someone else', it is sometimes argued, 'and once a world language is in place, other languages will simply die away'. Linked with all this is the unpalatable face of linguistic triumphalism – the danger that some people will celebrate one language's success at the expense of others.

It is important to face up to these fears, and to recognize that they are widely held. There is no shortage of mother-tongue English speakers who believe in an evolutionary view of language ('let the fittest survive, and if the fittest happens to be English, then so be it') or who refer to the present global status of the language as a 'happy accident'. There are many who think that all language learning is a waste of time. And many more who see nothing wrong with the vision that a world with just one language in it would be a very good thing. For some, such a world would be one of unity and peace, with all misunderstanding washed away – a widely expressed hope underlying the movements in support of a universal artificial language (such as Esperanto). For others, such a world would be a desirable return to the 'innocence' that must have been present among human beings in the days before the Tower of Babel (Eco 1995).

It is difficult to deal with anxieties which are so speculative, or, in the absence of evidence, to determine whether anything can be done to reduce or eliminate them. The last point can be quite briefly dismissed: the use of a single language by a community is no guarantee of social harmony or mutual understanding, as has been repeatedly seen in world history (e.g. the American Civil War, the Spanish Civil War, the Vietnam War, former Yugoslavia, contemporary Northern Ireland); nor does the presence of more than one language within a community necessitate civil strife, as seen in several successful examples of peaceful multilingual coexistence (e.g. Finland, Singapore, Switzerland). The other points, however, need to be taken more slowly, to appreciate the alternative perspective. The arguments are each illustrated with reference to English – but the same arguments would apply whatever language was in the running for global status.

• *Linguistic power* Will those who speak a global language as a mother tongue automatically be in a position of power compared with those who have to learn it as an official or foreign language? The risk is certainly real. It is possible, for example, that scientists who do not have English as a mother tongue will take longer to assimilate reports in English compared with their mother-tongue colleagues, and will as a consequence have less time to carry out their own creative work. It is possible that people who write up their research in languages other than English will have their work ignored by the international community. It is possible that senior managers who do not have English as a mother tongue, and who find themselves working for English language companies in such parts of the world as Europe or Africa, could find themselves at a disadvantage compared with their mother-tongue colleagues, especially when meetings involve the use of informal speech. There is already anecdotal evidence to suggest that these things happen.

However, if proper attention is paid to the question of language learning, the problem of disadvantage dramatically diminishes. If a global language is taught early enough, from the time that children begin their full-time education, and if it is maintained continuously and resourced well, the kind of linguistic competence which emerges in due course is a real and powerful bilingualism, indistinguishable from that found in any speaker who has encountered the language since birth. These are enormous 'ifs', with costly financial implications, and it is therefore not surprising that this kind of control is currently achieved by only a minority of non-native learners of any language; but the fact that it is achievable (as evidenced repeatedly by English speakers from such countries as Denmark, Sweden and the Netherlands) indicates that there is nothing inevitable about the disadvantage scenario.

It is worth reflecting, at this point, on the notion that children are born ready for bilingualism. Some two-thirds of the children on earth grow up in a bilingual environment, and develop competence in it. There is a naturalness with which they assimilate another language, once they are regularly exposed to it, which is the envy of adults. It is an ability which seems to die away as children reach their teens, and much academic debate has been devoted to the question of why this should be (the question of 'critical periods') (De Houwer 1995; Baker and Prys Jones 1998). There is however widespread agreement that, if we want to take the task of foreign language learning seriously, one of the key principles is 'the earlier the better'. And when that task is taken seriously, with reference to the acquisition of a global language, the elitism argument evaporates.

• *Linguistic complacency* Will a global language eliminate the motivation for adults to learn other languages? Here too the problem is real enough. Clear signs of linguistic complacency, common observation suggests, are already present in the archetypal British or American tourist who travels the world assuming that everyone speaks English, and that it is somehow the fault of the local people if they do not. The stereotype of an English tourist repeatedly asking a foreign waiter for tea in a loud 'read my lips' voice is too near the reality to be comfortable. There seems already to be a genuine, widespread lack of motivation to learn other languages, fuelled partly by lack of money and opportunity, but also by lack of interest, and this might well be fostered by the increasing presence of English as a global language.

It is important to appreciate that we are dealing here with questions of attitude or state of mind rather than questions of ability – though it is the latter which is often cited as the explanation. 'I'm no good at languages' is probably the most widely heard apology for not making any effort at all to acquire even a basic knowledge of a new language. Commonly, this self-denigration derives from an unsatisfactory language learning experience in school: the speaker is perhaps remembering a poor result in school examinations – which may reflect no more than an unsuccessful teaching approach or a not unusual breakdown in teacher–adolescent relationships. 'I never got on with my French teacher' is another typical comment. But this does not stop people going on to generalize that 'the British (or the Americans, etc.) are not very good at learning languages'.

These days, there are clear signs of growing awareness, within English-speaking communities, of the need to break away from the traditional monolingual bias (European Commission 2002). In economically hard-pressed times, success in boosting exports and attracting foreign investment can depend on subtle factors, and sensitivity to the language spoken by a country's potential foreign partners is known to be particularly influential (Coulmas 1992). At least at the levels of business and industry, many firms have begun to make fresh efforts in this direction. But at grass-roots tourist level, too, there are signs of a growing respect for other cultures, and a greater readiness to engage in language learning. Language attitudes are changing all the time, and more and more people are discovering, to their great delight, that they are not at all bad at picking up a foreign language.

In particular, statements from influential politicians and administrators are beginning to be made which are helping to foster a fresh climate of opinion about the importance of language learning. A good example is an address given in 1996 by the former secretary-general of the Commonwealth, Sir Sridath Ramphal. His title, 'World language: opportunities, challenges, responsibilities', itself contains a corrective to triumphalist thinking, and his text repeatedly argues against it (Ramphal 1996).

It is all too easy to make your way in the world linguistically with English as your mother tongue . . . We become lazy about learning other languages . . . We all have to make a greater effort. English may be the world language; but it is not the world's only language and if we are to be good global neighbours we shall have to be less condescending to the languages of the world – more assiduous in cultivating acquaintance with them.

It remains to be seen whether such affirmations of good will have long-term effect. In the meantime, it is salutary to read some of the comparative statistics about foreign language learning. For example, a European Business Survey by Grant Thornton reported in 1996 that 90 per cent of businesses in Belgium, the Netherlands, Luxembourg and Greece had an executive able to negotiate in another language, whereas only 38 per cent of British companies had someone who could do so. In 2002 the figures remained high for most European countries in the survey, but had fallen to 29 per cent in Britain (Grant Thornton 2002). The UK-based Centre for Information on Language Teaching and Research found that a third of British exporters miss opportunities because of poor language skills (CILT 2002). And English-monolingual companies are increasingly encountering language difficulties as they try to expand in those areas of the world thought to have greatest prospects of growth, such as East Asia, South America, and Eastern Europe – areas where English has traditionally had a relatively low presence. The issues are beginning to be addressed – for example, many Australian schools now teach Japanese as the first foreign language, and both the USA and UK are now paying more attention to Spanish (which, in terms of mother-tongue use, is growing more rapidly than English) – but we are still a long way from a world where the economic and other arguments have universally persuaded the English-speaking nations to renounce their linguistic insularity.

• *Linguistic death* Will the emergence of a global language hasten the disappearance of minority languages and cause widespread language death? To answer this question, we must first establish a general perspective. The processes of language domination and loss have been known throughout linguistic history, and exist independently of the emergence of a global language. No one knows how many languages have died since humans became able to speak, but it must be thousands. In many of these cases, the death has been caused by an ethnic group coming to be assimilated within a more dominant society, and adopting its language. The situation continues today, though the matter is being discussed with increasing urgency because of the unprecedented rate at which indigenous languages are being lost, especially in North America, Brazil, Australia, Indonesia and parts of Africa. At least 50 per cent of the world's 6,000 or so living languages will die out within the next century (Crystal 2000).

This is indeed an intellectual and social tragedy. When a language dies, so much is lost. Especially in languages which have never been written down, or which have been written down only recently, language is the repository of the history of a people. It is their identity. Oral testimony, in the form of sagas, folktales, songs, rituals, proverbs, and many other practices, provides us with a unique view of our world and a unique canon of literature. It is their legacy to the rest of humanity. Once lost, it can never be recaptured. The argument is similar to that used in relation to the conservation of species and the environment. The documentation and – where practicable – conservation of languages is also a priority, and it was good to see in the 1990s a number of international organizations being formed with the declared aim of recording for posterity as many endangered languages as possible (Crystal 2000).

However, the emergence of any one language as global has only a limited causal relationship to this unhappy state of affairs. Whether Sorbian survives in Germany or Galician in Spain has to do with the local political and economic history of those countries, and with the regional dominance of German and Spanish respectively, and bears no immediate relationship to the standing of German or Spanish on the world stage. Nor is it easy to see how the arrival of English as a global language could directly influence the future of these or many other minority languages. An effect is likely only in those areas where English has itself come to be the dominant first language, such as in North America, Australia and the Celtic parts of the British Isles. The early history of language contact in these areas was indeed one of conquest and assimilation, and the effects on indigenous languages were disastrous. But in more recent times, the emergence of English as a truly global language has, if anything, had the reverse effect – stimulating a stronger response in support of a local language than might otherwise have been the case. Times have changed. Movements for language rights (alongside civil rights in general) have played an important part in several countries, such as in relation to the Maori in New Zealand, the Aboriginal languages of Australia, the Indian languages of Canada and the USA, and some of the Celtic languages. Although often too late, in certain instances the decline of a language has been slowed, and occasionally (as in the case of Welsh) halted.

The existence of vigorous movements in support of linguistic minorities, commonly associated with nationalism, illustrates an important truth about the nature of language in general. The need for mutual intelligibility, which is part of the argument in favour of a global language, is only one side of the story. The other side is the need for identity – and people tend to underestimate the role of identity when they express anxieties about language injury and death. Language is a major means (some would say the chief means) of showing where we belong, and of distinguishing one social group from another, and all over the world we can see evidence of linguistic divergence rather than convergence. For decades, many people in the countries of former Yugoslavia made use of a common language, Serbo-Croatian. But since the civil wars of the early 1990s, the Serbs have referred to their language as Serbian, the Bosnians to theirs as Bosnian, and the Croats to theirs as Croatian, with each community drawing attention to the linguistic features which are distinctive. A similar situation exists in Scandinavia, where Swedish, Norwegian and Danish are largely mutually intelligible, but are none the less considered to be different languages.

Arguments about the need for national or cultural identity are often seen as being opposed to those about the need for mutual intelligibility. But this is misleading. It is perfectly possible to develop a situation in which intelligibility and identity happily co-exist. This situation is the familiar one of bilingualism – but a bilingualism where one of the languages within a speaker is the global language, providing access to the world community, and the other is a well-resourced regional language, providing access to a local community. The two functions can be seen as complementary, responding to different needs. And it is because the functions are so different that a world of linguistic diversity can in principle continue to exist in a world united by a common language.

None of this is to deny that the emergence of a global language can influence the structure of other languages – especially by providing a fresh source of loan-words for use by these other languages. Such influences can be welcomed (in which case, people talk about their language being 'varied' and 'enriched') or opposed (in which case, the metaphors are those of 'injury' and 'death'). For example, in recent years, one of the healthiest languages, French, has tried to protect itself by law against what is widely perceived to be the malign influence of English: in official contexts, it is now illegal to use an English word where a French word already exists, even though the usage may have widespread popular support (e.g. *computer* for *ordinateur*). Purist commentators from several other countries have also expressed concern at the way in which English vocabulary – especially that of American English – has come to permeate their high streets and TV programmes. The arguments are carried on with great emotional force. Even though only a tiny part of the lexicon is ever affected in this way, that is enough to arouse the wrath of the prophets of doom (they usually forget the fact that English itself, over the centuries, has borrowed thousands of words from other languages, and constructed thousands more from the elements of other languages – including *computer*, incidentally, which derives from Latin, the mother-language of French) (Serjeantson 1935; Crystal 1995; Görlach 2002).

The relationship between the global spread of English and its impact on other languages attracted increasing debate during the 1990s. The fact that it is possible to show a correlation between the rate of English adoption and the demise of minority languages has led some observers to reassert the conclusion that there is a simple causal link between the two phenomena, ignoring the fact that there has been a similar loss of linguistic diversity in parts of the world where English has not had a history of significant presence, such as Latin America, Russia and China. A more deep-rooted process of globalization seems to be at work today, transcending individual language situations. Anachronistic views of linguistic imperialism, which see as important only the power asymmetry between the former colonial nations and the nations of the 'third world', are hopelessly inadequate as an explanation of linguistic realities (Phillipson 1992; Pennycook 1994). They especially ignore the fact that 'first world' countries with strong languages seem to be under just as much pressure to adopt English, and that some of the harshest attacks on English have come from countries which have no such colonial legacy. When dominant languages feel they are being dominated, something much bigger than a simplistic conception of power relations must be involved (Lysandrou and Lysandrou 2003; Brenzinger 1998; Crystal 2000; Mufwene 2001, 2002)

These other factors, which include the recognition of global interdependence, the desire to have a voice in world affairs, and the value of multilingualism in attracting trade markets, all support the adoption of a functionalist account of English, where the language is seen as a valuable instrument enabling people to achieve particular goals. Local languages continue to perform an important set of functions (chiefly, the expression of local identity) and English is seen as the primary means of achieving a global presence. The approach recognizes the legacy of colonialism, as a matter of historical fact, but the emphasis is now on discontinuities, away from power and towards functional specialization (Fishman *et al.* 1996). It is a model which sees English playing a central role in empowering the subjugated and marginalized, and eroding the division between the 'haves' and the 'have nots'.

Those who argue for this position have been dismissed as displaying 'naive liberal idealism' and adopting a 'liberal laissez-faire attitude' (Pennycook 2001). Rather, it is the linguistic imperialism position which is naive, disregarding the complex realities of a world in which a historical conception of power relations has to be seen alongside an emerging set of empowering relationships in which English has a new functional role, no longer associated with the political authority it once held.

If working towards the above goal is idealism, then I am happy to be an idealist; however, it is by no means laissez-faire, given the amount of time, energy and money which have been devoted in recent years to language revitalization and related matters. Admittedly, the progress which has been made is tiny compared with the disastrous effects of globalization on global diversity. But to place all the blame on English, and to ignore the more fundamental economic issues that are involved, is, as two recent commentators have put it, 'to attack the wrong target, to indulge in linguistic luddism' (Lysandrou and Lysandrou 2003). Solutions are more likely to come from the domain of economic policy, not language policy. As Lysandrou and Lysandrou conclude:

> If English can facilitate the process of universal dispossession and loss, so can it be turned round and made to facilitate the contrary process of universal empowerment and gain.

[. . .]

A critical era

It is impossible to make confident predictions about the emergence of a global language. There are no precedents for this kind of linguistic growth, other than on a much smaller scale. And the speed with which a global language scenario has arisen is truly remarkable. Within little more than a generation, we have moved from a situation where a world language was a theoretical possibility to one where it is an evident reality.

No government has yet found it possible to plan confidently, in such circumstances. Languages of identity need to be maintained. Access to the emerging global language – widely perceived as a language of opportunity and empowerment – needs to be guaranteed. Both principles demand massive resources. The irony is that the issue is approaching a climax at a time when the world financial climate can least afford it.

Fundamental decisions about priorities have to be made. Those making the decisions need to bear in mind that we may well be approaching a critical moment in human linguistic history. It is possible that a global language will emerge only once. Certainly, as we have seen, after such a language comes to be established it would take a revolution of world-shattering proportions to replace it. And in due course, the last quarter of the twentieth century will be seen as a critical time in the emergence of this global language.

All the signs suggest that this global language will be English. But there is still some way to go before a global lingua franca becomes a universal reality. Despite the remarkable growth in the use of English, at least two-thirds of the world population do not yet use it. In certain parts of the world, English has still a very limited presence. And in some countries, increased resources are being devoted to maintaining the role of other languages (such as the use of French in several countries of Africa). Notwithstanding the general world trend, there are many linguistic confrontations still to be resolved.

Governments who wish to play their part in influencing the world's linguistic future should therefore ponder carefully, as they make political decisions and allocate resources for language planning. Now, more than at any time in linguistic history, they need to adopt long-term views, and to plan ahead – whether their interests are to promote English or to develop the use of other languages in their community (or, of course, both). If they miss this linguistic boat, there may be no other.

References

Baker, Colin and Prys Jones, Sylvia (1998) *Encyclopedia of Bilingualism and Bilingual Education*. Clevedon: Multilingual Matters.

Brenzinger, Matthias (ed.) (1998) *Endangered Languages in Africa*. Cologne: Rüdiger Köper.

CILT (Centre for Information on Language Teaching and Research) (2002) *Speaking up for Languages*. London: CILT.

Coulmas, Florian (1992) *Language and Economy*. Oxford: Blackwell.

Crystal, David (1995) *The Cambridge Encyclopedia of the English Language*. Cambridge: Cambridge University Press.

Crystal, David (2000) *Language Death*. Cambridge: Cambridge University Press.

De Houwer, Annick (1995) 'Bilingual language acquisition', in Paul Fletcher and Brian MacWhinney (eds) *The Handbook of Child Language* (pp. 219–50). Oxford: Blackwell.

Eco, Umberto (1995) *The Search for the Perfect Language*. Oxford: Blackwell.

European Commission (2002) *European Year of Languages 2001: Some Highlights*. Brussels: European Commission, Language Policy Unit.

Fishman, Joshua A., Conrad, Andrew and Rubal-Lopez, Alma (eds) (1996) *Post-imperial English*. Berlin and New York: Mouton de Gruyter.

Görlach, Manfred (ed.) (2002) *English in Europe*. Oxford: Oxford University Press.

Grant Thornton (2002) *European Business Survey*. London: Grant Thornton.

Lysandrou, Photis and Lysandrou, Yvonne (2003) 'Global English and proregression: understanding English language spread in the contemporary era', *Economy and Society* 32 (2): 207–33.

Mufwene, Salikoko S. (2001) *The Ecology of Language Evolution*. Cambridge: Cambridge University Press.

Mufwene, Salikoko (2002) 'Colonization, globalization, and the future of languages in the twenty-first century'. Translated paper based on a contribution to a UNESCO debate, Paris, September 2001.

Pennycook, Alistair (1994) *The Cultural Politics of English as an International Language*. London: Longman.

Pennycook, Alistair (2001) *Critical Applied Linguistics*. New York: Erlbaum.

Phillipson, Robert (1992) *Linguistic Imperialism*. Oxford: Oxford University Press.

Quirk, Randolph (1985) 'The English language in a global context', in Randolph Quirk and H.G. Widdowson (eds) *English in the World* (pp. 1–6). Cambridge: Cambridge University Press.

Ramphal, Sridath (1996) 'World language: opportunities, challenges, responsibilities'. Paper given at the World Members' Conference of the English-Speaking Union, Harrogate, UK.

Serjeantson, Mary (1935) *A History of Foreign Words in English*. London: Routledge and Kegan Paul.

Todd, Loreto (1984) *Modern Englishes: Pidgins and Creoles*. Oxford: Blackwell.

Chapter 6

Henry Widdowson

The ownership of English

At a time when territorial disputes and matters of ownership and identity are so prominent in the affairs of the world in general, it is perhaps appropriate to raise the question of how we stake out our own territory as English teachers in delimiting and designing our world. And to ask who does the designing and on what authority.

To start with, who determines the demarcation of the subject itself? We are teaching English and the general assumption is that our purpose is to develop in students a proficiency which approximates as closely as possible to that of native speakers. But who are these native speakers?

One answer might be: the English. And why not? A modest proposal surely. England is where the language originated and this is where the English (for the most part) live. The language and the people are bound together by both morphology and history. So they can legitimately lay claim to this linguistic territory. It belongs to them. And they are the custodians. If you want real or proper English, this is where it is to be found, preserved, and listed like a property of the National Trust.

Of course English, of a kind, is found elsewhere as well, still spreading, a luxuriant growth from imperial seed. Seeded among other people but not ceded to them. At least not completely. For the English still cling tenaciously to their property and try to protect it from abuse. Let us acknowledge (let us concede) that there are other kinds of English, offshoots and outgrowths, but they are not real or proper English, not the genuine article.

Edited version of: Widdowson, H.G. 'The ownership of English', in *TESOL Quarterly* 28 (2): 377–89, Copyright Clearance Centre, 1994.

As an analogy, consider a certain kind of beverage. There are all kinds of cola, but only one which is the real thing. Or, further afield, an analogy from the French. They have, until just recently, successfully denied others the right to use the appellation *Champagne* for any wine that does not come from the region of that name where Dom Perignon first invented it. There may be all kinds of derivative versions elsewhere, excellent no doubt in their way, but they are not real or proper Champagne, even though loose talk may refer to them as such. Similarly, there is real English, Anglais réal, Royal English, Queen's English, or (for those unsympathetic to the monarchy) Oxford English. The vintage language.

I do not imagine that such a view would gain much support. The response is more likely to be outrage. You cannot be serious. Well, not entirely, it is true. As I have expressed it, in somewhat extravagant terms, this position is one which very few people would associate themselves with. It is reactionary, arrogant, totally unacceptable. And the argument is patently absurd. Perhaps as I have expressed it. But then why is it absurd? The particular associations of England, Queen and country, and Colonel Blimp which I have invoked to demonstrate the argument also in some respects disguise it. If we now remove the position from these associations and strip the argument down to its essential tenets, is it so readily dismissed? Is it indeed so uncommon after all? I want to suggest that the ideas and attitudes which I have just presented in burlesque are still very much with us in a different and less obvious guise.

To return briefly to Champagne. One argument frequently advanced for being protective of its good name has to do with quality assurance. The label is a guarantee of quality. If any Tom, Jane or Harry producing fizzy wine is free to use it, there can be no quality control. Recently an English firm won a court case enabling it to put the name Champagne on bottles containing a nonalcoholic beverage made from elderflowers. Elderflowers! The Champagne lobby was outraged. Here, they said, was the thin end of the wedge. Before long the label would be appearing on bottles all over the place containing concoctions of all kinds calling themselves Champagne, and so laying claim to its quality. The appellation would not be *controllée*. Standards were at stake. There can only be one. This is it. Be wary of variant products of lower quality.

And the same point is frequently made about English. In this case, you cannot, of course, preserve exclusive use of the name and indeed it would work against your interests to do so, but you can seek to preserve standards by implying that there is an exclusive quality in your own brand of English, aptly called standard English. What is this quality, then? What are these standards?

The usual answer is: quality of clear communication and standards of intelligibility. With standard English, it is argued, these are assured. If the language disperses into different forms, a myriad of Englishes, then it ceases to serve as a means of inter-national communication; in which case the point of learning it largely disappears. As the language spreads, there are bound to be changes out on the periphery; so much can be conceded. But these changes must be seen not only as peripheral but as radial also and traceable back to the stable centre of the standard. If this centre does not hold, things fall apart, mere anarchy is loosed upon the world. Back to Babel.

In itself, this argument sounds plausible and it is difficult to refute. But for all that, there is something about it which is suspect. Let us replay it again. Standard

English promotes the cause of international communication, so we must maintain the central stability of the standard as the common linguistic frame of reference.

To begin with, who are we? Obviously the promoters of standard English must themselves have standard English at their disposal. But to maintain it is another matter. This presupposes authority. And this authority is claimed by those who possess the language by primogeniture and due of birth, as Shakespeare puts it. In other words, the native speakers. They do not have to be English, of course, that would be too restrictive a condition, and one it would (to say the least) be tactless to propose, but they have to be to the language born. Not all native speakers, you understand. In fact, come to think of it, not most native speakers, for the majority of those who are to the language born speak nonstandard English and have themselves to be instructed in the standard at school. We cannot have any Tom, Jane and Harry claiming authority, for Tom, Jane and Harry are likely to be speakers of some dialect or other. So the authority to maintain the standard language is not consequent on a natural native-speaker endowment. It is claimed by a minority of people who have the power to impose it. The custodians of standard English are self-elected members of a rather exclusive club.

Now it is important to be clear that in saying this I am not arguing against standard English. You can accept the argument for language maintenance, as indeed I do, without accepting the authority that claims the right to maintain it. It is, I think, very generally assumed that a particular subset of educated native speakers in England, or New England, or wherever, have the natural entitlement to custody of the language, that the preservation of its integrity is in their hands: their right and their responsibility. It is this which I wish to question. Not in any spirit of radical rebellion against authority as such but because I think such questioning raises a number of crucial issues about the learning and teaching of the language.

Consideration of who the custodians are leads logically on to a consideration of what it is exactly that is in their custody. What is standard English? The usual way of defining it is in reference to its grammar and lexis: it is a variety, a kind of superposed dialect which is socially sanctioned for institutional use and therefore particularly well suited to written communication. In its spoken form it can be manifested by any accent. So it is generally conceded that standard English has no distinctive phonology. The same concession is not, however, extended to its graphology. On the contrary, it is deviant spelling which, in Britain at least, is most frequently singled out for condemnation. There is something of a contradiction here. If standard English is defined as a distinctive grammatical and lexical system which can be substantially realized in different ways, then what does spelling have to do with it? It is true that some spelling has a grammatical function (like the 's which distinguishes the possessive from the plural) but most of it does not. If you are going to ignore phonological variation, then, to be consistent, you should surely ignore graphological variation as well and overlook variations in spelling as a kind of written accent.

The reason it is not overlooked, I think, is that standard English, unlike other dialects, is essentially a written variety and mainly designed for institutional purposes (education, administration, business, etc.). Its spoken version is secondary, and typically used by those who control these institutions. This means that although it may not matter how it is spoken, it emphatically does matter how it is written.

Furthermore, because writing, as a more durable medium, is used to express and establish institutional values, deviations from orthographic conventions undermine in some degree the institutions which they serve. They can be seen as evidence of social instability: a sign of things beginning to fall apart. So it is not surprising that those who have a vested interest in maintaining these institutions should be so vexed by bad spelling. It is not that it greatly interferes with communication: it is usually not difficult to identify words through their unorthodox appearance. What seems to be more crucial is that good spelling represents conformity to convention and so serves to maintain institutional stability.

Similar points can be made about grammatical features. Because language has built-in redundancy, grammatical conformity is actually not particularly crucial for many kinds of communicative transaction. What we generally do in the interpretative process is actually to edit grammar out of the text, referring lexis directly to context, using lexical items as indexical clues to meaning. We edit grammar back in when we need it for fine tuning. If the reason for insisting on standard English is because it guarantees effective communication, then the emphasis should logically be on vocabulary rather than grammar. But the champions of standard English do not see it in this way: on the contrary, they focus attention on grammatical abuse. Why should this be so? There are, I think, two reasons.

Firstly, it is precisely because grammar is so often redundant in communicative transactions that it takes on another significance, namely that of expressing social identity. The mastery of a particular grammatical system, especially perhaps those features which are redundant, marks you as a member of the community which has developed that system for its own social purposes. Conversely, of course, those who are unable to master the system are excluded from the community. They do not belong. In short, grammar is a sort of shibboleth.

So when the custodians of standard English complain about the ungrammatical language of the populace, they are in effect indicating that the perpetrators are outsiders, nonmembers of the community. The only way they can become members, and so benefit from the privileges of membership, is to learn standard English, and these privileges include, of course, access to the institutions which the community controls. Standard English is an entry condition and the custodians of it the gatekeepers. You can, of course, persist in your nonstandard ways if you choose, but then do not be surprised to find yourself marginalized, perpetually kept out on the periphery. What you say will be less readily attended to, assigned less importance, if it is not expressed in the grammatically approved manner. And if you express yourself in writing that is both ungrammatical and badly spelled, you are not likely to be taken very seriously.

Standard English, then, is not simply a means of communication but the symbolic possession of a particular community, expressive of its identity, its conventions, and values. As such it needs to be carefully preserved, for to undermine standard English is to undermine what it stands for: the security of this community and its institutions. Thus, it tends to be the communal rather than the communicative features of standard English that are most jealously protected: its grammar and spelling.

I do not wish to imply that this communal function is to be deplored. Languages of every variety have this dual character: they provide the means for communication and at the same time express a sense of community, represent the stability of its conventions and values, in short its culture. All communities possess and protect their languages. The question is which community, and which culture, have a rightful claim to ownership of standard English? For standard English is no longer the preserve of a group of people living in an offshore European island, or even of larger groups living in continents elsewhere. It is an international language. As such it serves a whole range of different communities and their institutional purposes and these transcend traditional communal and cultural boundaries. I am referring to the business community, for example, and the community of researchers and scholars in science and technology and other disciplines. Standard English, especially in its written form, is their language. It provides for effective communication, but at the same time it establishes the status and stability of the institutional conventions which define these international activities. These activities develop their own conventions of thought and procedure, customs and codes of practice; in short, they in effect create their own cultures, their own standards. And obviously for the maintenance of standards it is helpful, to say the least, to have a standard language at your disposal. But you do not need native speakers to tell you what it is.

And indeed in one crucial respect, the native speaker is irrelevant. What I have in mind here is vocabulary. I said earlier that the custodians of standard English tend to emphasize its grammatical rather than its lexical features. I have suggested that one reason for this is that grammar is symbolic of communal solidarity. "Ungrammatical" expressions mark people as nonmembers. What you then do is to coax or coerce them somehow into conformity if you want to make them members (generally through education) or make them powerless on the periphery if you don't. So much for grammar. What then of lexis.

It is said that standard English is a variety, a kind of dialect, in that it is defined by its lexis and grammar. In fact, when you come to look for it, standard lexis is very elusive. It is my belief that it does not actually exist. And on reflection it is hard to see how it could exist. To begin with, the notion of standard implies stability, a relatively fixed point of reference. So if I invent a word, for example, it is not, by definition, standard. But people are inventing words all the time to express new ideas and attitudes, to adjust to their changing world. It is this indeed which demonstrates the essential dynamism of the language without which it would wither away. So it is that different groups of users will develop specialist vocabularies, suited to their needs but incomprehensible to others. When I look at my daily newspaper, I find innumerable words from the terminology of technology, law, financial affairs, and so on which I simply do not understand. They may claim to be English, but they are Greek to me. Are they standard English? One way of deciding might be to consult a standard reference work, namely a learners' dictionary. But most of these words of restricted technical use do not appear. This is because, reasonably enough, the dictionary only contains words of wide range and common occurrence. If this is the way standard is to be defined, then these words of restricted use do not count by definition. Yet they are real enough, and indeed can be said to represent the reality of English as an international language. For the reason why English is international is because its vocabulary has diversified to serve a range of institutional uses.

As I indicated earlier, the custodians of standard English express the fear that if there is diversity, things will fall apart and the language will divide up into mutually unintelligible varieties. But things in a sense have already fallen apart. The varieties of English used for international communication in science, finance, commerce, and so on are mutually unintelligible. As far as lexis is concerned, their communicative viability depends on the development of separate standards, and this means that their communication is largely closed off from the world outside.

The point then is that if English is to retain its vitality and its capability for continual adjustment, it cannot be confined within a standard lexis. And this seems to be implicitly accepted as far as particular domains of use are concerned. Nobody, I think, says that the abstruse terms used by physicists or stockbrokers are nonstandard English. It is generally accepted that communities or secondary cultures which are defined by shared professional concerns should be granted rights of ownership and allowed to fashion the language to meet their needs, their specific purposes indeed. And these purposes, we should note again, are twofold: they are communicative in that they meet the needs of in-group transactions, and they are communal in that they define the identity of the group itself.

The same tolerance is not extended so readily to primary cultures and communities, where the language is used in the conduct of everyday social life. Lexical innovation here, equally motivated by communicative and communal requirement, is generally dismissed as deviant or dialectal. Take, for example, the two words *depone* and *prepone*. The first is a technical legal term and therefore highly respectable. The second *prepone* is not. It is an Indian English word of very general currency, coined to contrast with *postpone*. To postpone an event means to put it back, to prepone an event is to bring it forward. The coinage exploits the morphology of English in an entirely regular way. It is apt. But it is also quaint. An odd Indian excrescence: obviously nonstandard. And yet there is clearly nothing deviant in the derivational process itself, and indeed we can see it at work in the formation of the related words *predate* and *postdate*. But these are sanctioned as entirely ordinary, proper, standard English words. What, then, is the difference? The difference lies in the origin of the word. *Prepone* is coined by a nonnative-speaking community, so it is not really a proper English word. It is not pukka. And of course the word *pukka* is itself only pukka because the British adopted it.

Where are we then? When we consider the question of standard English what we find, in effect, is double standards. The very idea of a standard implies stability, and this can only be fixed in reference to the past. But language is of its nature unstable. It is essentially protean in nature, adapting its shape to suit changing circumstances. It would otherwise lose its vitality and its communicative and communal value. This is generally acknowledged in the case of specialist domains of use but is not acknowledged in the case of everyday social uses of the language. So it is that a word like *depone* is approved and a word like *prepone* is not.

But the basic principle of dynamic adaptation is the same in both cases. And in both cases the users of the language exploit its protean potential and fashion it to their need, thereby demonstrating a high degree of linguistic capability. In both cases the innovation indicates that the language has been learned, not just as a set of fixed conventions to conform to, but as an adaptable resource for making meaning. And making meaning which you can call your own. This, surely, is a crucial condition. You are proficient in a language to the extent that you possess it, make it your own, bend it to your will, assert yourself through it rather than simply submit to the dictates of its form. It is a familiar experience to find oneself saying things in a foreign language because you can say them rather than because they express what you want to say. You feel you are going through the motions, and somebody else's motions at that. You are speaking the language but not speaking your mind. Real proficiency is when you are able to take possession of the language, turn it to your advantage, and make it real for you. This is what mastery means. So in a way, proficiency only comes with nonconformity, when you can take the initiative and strike out on your own. Consider these remarks of the Nigerian writer, Chinua Achebe (1975):

> I feel that the English language will be able to carry the weight of my African experience. . . . But it will have to be a new English, still in communion with its ancestral home but altered to suit its new African surroundings.
>
> (p. 62)

Achebe is a novelist, and he is talking here about creative writing. But what he says clearly has wider relevance and applies to varieties of English elsewhere. The point is that all uses of language are creative in the sense that they draw on linguistic resources to express different perceptions of reality. English is called upon to carry the weight of all kinds of experience, much of it very remote indeed from its ancestral home. The new English which Achebe refers to is locally developed, and although it must necessarily be related to, and so in communion with, its ancestral origins in the past, it owes no allegiance to any descendants of this ancestry in the present.

And this point applies to all other new Englishes which have been created to carry the weight of different experience in different surroundings, whether they are related to specialist domains of use or to the contexts of everyday life. They are all examples of the entirely normal and necessary process of adaptation, a process which obviously depends on nonconformity to existing conventions or standards. For these have been established elsewhere by other people as appropriate to quite different circumstances. The fact that these people can claim direct descent from the founding fathers has nothing to do with it. How English develops in the world is no business whatever of native speakers in England, the United States, or anywhere else. They have no say in the matter, no right to intervene or pass judgement. They are irrelevant. The very fact that English is an international language means that no nation can have custody over it. To grant such custody of the language is necessarily to arrest its development and so undermine its international status. It is a matter of considerable pride and satisfaction for native speakers of English that their language is an international means of communication. But the point is that it is only international to the extent that it is not their language. It is not a possession which they lease out to others, while still retaining the freehold. Other people actually own it.

As soon as you accept that English serves the communicative and communal needs of different communities, it follows logically that it must be diverse. An international language has to be an independent language. It does not follow logically, however, that the language will disperse into mutually unintelligible varieties. For it will naturally stabilize into standard form to the extent required to meet the needs of the communities concerned. Thus it is clearly vital to the interests of the international community of, for example, scientists or business people, whatever their primary language, that they should preserve a common standard of English in order to keep up standards of communicative effectiveness. English could not otherwise serve their purposes. It needs no native speaker to tell them that. Furthermore, this natural tendency towards standardization will be reinforced by the extending of networks of interaction through developments in telecommunications and information technology. For there is little point in opening up such amazing new transmission systems if what you transmit makes no sense at the other end. The availability of these new channels calls for the maintenance of a common code. And these are therefore likely to have greater influence on stabilizing the language than the pronouncements of native speakers.

The essential point is that a standard English, like other varieties of language, develops endo-normatively, by a continuing process of self-regulation, as appropriate to different conditions of use. It is not fixed by exo-normative fiat from outside: not fixed, therefore, by native speakers. They have no special say in the matter, in spite of their claims to ownership of real English as associated with their own particular cultural contexts of use.

And yet there is no doubt that native speakers of English are deferred to in our profession. What they say is invested with both authenticity and authority. The two are closely related, and a consideration of their relationship brings us to certain central issues in language pedagogy. An example follows.

Over recent years, we have heard persuasive voices insisting that the English presented in the classroom should be authentic, naturally occurring language, not produced for instructional purposes. Generally, what this means, of course, is language naturally occurring as communication in native-speaker contexts of use, or rather those selected contexts where standard English is the norm: real newspaper reports, for example, real magazine articles, real advertisements, cooking recipes, horoscopes and what have you. Now the obvious point about this naturally occurring language is that, inevitably, it is recipient designed and so culturally loaded. It follows that access to its meaning is limited to those insiders who share its cultural presuppositions and a sense of its idiomatic nuance. Those who do not, the outsiders, cannot ratify its authenticity. In other words, the language is only authentic in the original conditions of its use, it cannot be in the classroom. The authenticity is nontransferable. And to the extent that students cannot therefore engage with the language, they cannot make it their own. It may be real language, but it is not real to them. It does not relate to their world but to a remote one they have to find out about by consulting a dictionary of culture. It may be that eventually students will wish to acquire the cultural knowledge and the idiomatic fluency which enable them to engage authentically with the language use of a particular native-speaking community by adopting their identity in some degree, but there seems no sensible reason for insisting on them trying to do this in the process of language learning. On the contrary, it would seem that language for learning does need to be specially designed for pedagogic purposes so that it can be made real in the context of the students' own world.

The importance of getting students engaged with the language, cognitively, affectively, personally, is widely accepted as established wisdom. Let the learners be autonomous (at least up to a point), allow them to make the language their own, let them identify with it, let not the teacher impose authority upon them in the form of an alien pattern of behaviour. Very well. But this injunction is totally at variance with the insistence on authentic language, which is an imposition of another authority, namely that of native-speaker patterns of cultural behaviour. If natural language learning depends on asserting some ownership over the language, this cannot be promoted by means of language which is authentic only because it belongs to somebody else and expresses somebody else's identity. A pedagogy which combines authenticity of use with autonomy of learning is a contradiction. You cannot have it both ways.

The notion of authenticity, then, privileges native-speaker use (inappropriately, I have argued) as the proper language for learning. But it also, of course, privileges the native-speaker teachers of the language. For they, of course, have acquired the language and culture as an integrated experience and have a feel for its nuances and idiomatic identity which the nonnative speaker cannot claim to have. Indeed, native speakers alone can be the arbiters of what is authentic since authenticity can only be determined by insiders. So if you give authenticity primacy as a pedagogic principle, you inevitably grant privileged status to native-speaker teachers, and you defer to them not only in respect to competence in the language but also in respect to competence in language teaching. They become the custodians and arbiters not only of proper English but of proper pedagogy as well.

But what if you shift the emphasis away from contexts of use to contexts of learning, and consider how the language is to be specially designed to engage the student's reality and activate the learning process? The special advantage of native-speaker teachers disappears. Now, on the contrary, it is nonnative-speaker teachers who come into their own. For the context of learning, contrived within the classroom setting, has to be informed in some degree by the attitudes, beliefs, values and so on of the students' cultural world. And in respect to this world, of course, it is the native-speaker teacher who is the outsider. To the extent that the design of instruction depends on a familiarity with the student reality which English is to engage with, or on the particular sociocultural situations in which teaching and learning take place, then nonnative teachers have a clear and, indeed, decisive advantage.

In short, the native-speaker teacher is in a better position to know what is appropriate in contexts of language use, and so to define possible target objectives. Granted. But it is the nonnative-speaker teacher who is in a better position to know what is appropriate in the contexts of language learning which need to be set up to achieve such objectives. And that, generally speaking, is not granted. Instead what we find is that native-speaker expertise is assumed to extend to the teaching of the language. They not only have a patent on proper English, but on proper ways of teaching it as well.

So it is that the approaches to pedagogy which are generally promoted as proper are those which are appropriate to contexts of instruction in which native-speaker teachers operate. And their prestige, of course, exerts a powerful influence so that teachers in other contexts are persuaded to conform and to believe that if the approaches do not fit, it is their fault.

So it is that native speakers write textbooks and teachers' books, make pronouncements and recommendations, and bring to remote and hitherto benighted places the good news about real English and good teaching to lighten their darkness.

Real English: their English. Good teaching: their teaching. But both are contextually limited by cultural factors. Their English is that which is associated with the communicative and communal needs of their community, and these may have little relevance for those learning English as an international language.

And their teaching is suited to particular contexts of instruction which in many respects are quite different from those which obtain in the world at large. Consider, for example, a language school in England, with English as the ambient language outside the classroom, the students well off and well motivated, but quite different in linguistic and cultural background both from each other, and from the teacher. In such a context it is, of course, necessary to focus on what can be established as a common denominator. Everybody is here in England, for example, and everybody is human. And so you devise an approach to teaching which combines authenticity with an appeal to universal natural learning and humanistic response. This is an example of appropriate pedagogy: such an approach is necessary and of course it works in these local conditions. Highly commendable. But it is exclusive in that it excludes possibilities which might be particularly appropriate elsewhere – translation, for example. The problem is when an absolute virtue is made of local necessity by claims of global validity, when it is assumed that if the approach works here it ought to work, or made to work, everywhere else. This is a denial of diversity.

For of course there is no reason why it should work elsewhere where quite different conditions obtain. It is difficult to resist the conclusion that such an approach, which makes a virtue of necessity, is only privileged because of the authority vested in the teachers by virtue of their native-speaker status. This is not to say that it may not offer ideas worth pondering, but then these ideas have to be analysed out of the approach and their relevance evaluated in reference to other contexts. You should not assume, with bland arrogance, that your way of teaching English, or your way of using English, carries a general guarantee of quality. To put the point briefly: English and English teaching are proper to the extent that they are appropriate, not to the extent that they are appropriated.

TESOL has recently made public its opposition to discrimination against the nonnative teacher, as a matter of sociopolitical principle. This is obviously to be welcomed. But if it is to be more than a token gesture, such a move needs to be supported by an enquiry into the nature of the subject we are teaching, what constitutes an appropriate approach, what kinds of competence is required of teachers – in other words an enquiry into matters of pedagogic principle which bring sociopolitical concerns and professional standards into alignment.

References

Achebe, C. (1975) 'The African writer and the English language', in *Morning Yet on Creation Day*. London: Heinemann.

Chapter 7

Alastair Pennycook

English in the world/
the world in English

[. . .]

What I would like to explore in this chapter is the *worldliness* (cf. Said 1983) of English. I want to maintain the ambiguity of this term – worldliness in the sense of being in the world and worldliness in the sense of being global – and to argue that English is inextricably bound up with the world: English is in the world and the world is in English. Following Said's (1983: 35) question as to whether there is a way to deal fairly with a text without either on the one hand reducing it to its worldly circumstances or on the other leaving it as a hermetic textual cosmos, I want to ask how we can understand the relationship between the English language and its position in the world in such a way that neither reduces it to a simple correspondence with its worldly circumstances nor refuses this relationship by considering language to be a hermetic structural system unconnected to social, cultural and political concerns.

This chapter, therefore, will seek to draw relations between global inequalities and the English language. I will also be trying to work out ways of thinking about this relationship that avoid the pitfalls of structuralist determinism. I think it is of great importance in looking at questions of language, power and inequality that we examine very carefully the critical frameworks we employ. In the next sections I shall review the predominant paradigm of writing on English as an International Language (EIL) before discussing more critical work that has raised numerous questions about the global spread of English. This will be followed by a discussion of . . . how we can conceptualize the question of the world being in English, and also of how opposition to the power of English and western discourses can be formed.

From: Pennycook, A. 'English in the world/the world in English', in J.W. Tollefson (ed.) *Power and Inequality in Language Education*, Cambridge University Press, pp. 34–58, 1995.

The predominant paradigm

Otto Jespersen ([1938] 1968) estimated speakers of English to have numbered 4 million in 1500, 6 million in 1600, 8.5 million in 1700, between 20 and 40 million in 1800, and between 116 and 123 million in 1900. . . . Today, rough agreement can be found on figures that put the total number of speakers of English at between 700 million and 1 billion. This figure can be divided into three roughly equal groups: native speakers of English, speakers of English as a second (or intranational) language, and speakers of English as a foreign (or international) language. It is this last group that is the hardest to estimate but clearly the fastest-growing section of world speakers of English.

    [. . .]

There seems to be fairly broad agreement on the reasons for and the implications of this spread. Although perhaps not all would agree with Hindmarsh's (1978) bland optimism that "the world has opted for English, and the world knows what it wants, what will satisfy its needs" (p. 42), this view is nevertheless not too distant from the predominant view. Although few today would overtly cling to the common nineteenth-century arguments that England and the English language were superior and thus intrinsically worthy of their growing pre-eminence, the spread of English is today commonly justified by recourse to a functionalist perspective, which stresses choice and the usefulness of English, and suggests that the global spread of English is natural (although its spread was initiated by colonialism, since then it has been an accidental by-product of global forces), neutral (unlike other, local languages, English is unconnected to cultural and political issues), and beneficial (people can only benefit by gaining access to English and the world it opens up). Platt *et al.* (1984), for example, introducing the question of the "new Englishes", deal with the spread of English thus: "Many of the New Nations which were once British colonies have realised the importance of English not only as a language of commerce, science and technology but also as an international language of communication" (p. 1). Similarly, Kachru (1986: 8–9) argues that:

> English does have one clear advantage, attitudinally and linguistically: it has acquired a *neutrality* in a linguistic context where native languages, dialects, and styles sometimes have acquired undesirable connotations. . . . It was originally the foreign (alien) ruler's language, but that drawback is often overshadowed by what it can do for its users. True, English is associated with a small and elite group; but it is in their role that the *neutrality* of a language becomes vital.

He goes on to suggest that "whatever the reasons for the earlier spread of English, we should now consider it a positive development in the twentieth-century world context" (p. 51).

The main issue of debate is whether efforts should be made to maintain a central standard of English or whether the different varieties of English should be acknowledged as legitimate forms in their own right. The popular view, according to Crystal (1988), is that "while all mother-tongue speakers inevitably feel a modicum of pride (and relief) that it is their language which is succeeding, there is also an element of concern, as they see what happens to the language as it spreads around the world. . . . Changes are perceived as instances of deterioration in standards" (p. 10). . . . In academic circles, the two leading figures in this debate have been Kachru (e.g. 1985) and Quirk (e.g. 1985), the former arguing, for example, that "native speakers of this language seem to have lost the exclusive prerogative to control its standardization" (p. 30), and the latter maintaining, for example, that "the existence of standards . . . is an endemic feature of our mortal condition and that people feel alienated and disorientated if a standard seems to be missing in any of these areas" (pp. 5–6).

Apart from some work on the sociological and social psychological implications of the spread of English (see Fishman *et al.* 1977), which has also suggested that English is a neutral tool of international communication, the principal focus of work on EIL has been on questions of standards or on descriptions of varieties of English. The key issues, then, as represented in Kachru's important edited volume, *The Other Tongue: English Across Cultures*, are questions of models, standards, and intelligibility (e.g., Kachru 1982a, 1982b; Nelson 1982), and descriptions of the new forms of English: Nigerian English (Bamgbose 1982), Kenyan English (Zuengler 1982), Singapore English (Richards 1982), and so on.

The view that the spread of English is natural, neutral and beneficial also seems to hold sway for many people more directly involved in English language teaching. Naysmith (1987) suggests that there is a "cosy, rather self-satisfied assumption prevalent at successive national and international conferences that ELT [English Language Teaching] is somehow a 'good' thing, a positive force by its very nature in the search for international peace and understanding" (p. 3). With the extent of the debate on the role of English in the world being between a conservative view on standards and a more liberal pluralist concept of variety, and with the primary concerns being those of intelligibility and description, most people in English language teaching have been poorly served by academic work that fails to address a far more diverse range of questions that might encourage a reassessment of our role as teachers of English in the world. It is to some of the critical work that has sought to address these issues that I shall turn in the next section.

Critical views on English in the world

What I think is sorely lacking from the predominant paradigm of investigation into English as an international language is a broad range of social, historical, cultural and political relationships. There is a failure to problematize the notion of choice and an assumption that individuals and countries are somehow free of economic, political and ideological constraints; there is a lack of historical analysis that would raise many more questions about the supposed naturalness of the spread of English during both the colonial and neo-colonial eras; there is a view of language that suggests that it can be free of cultural and political influences and therefore neutral. . . .

As I have argued elsewhere (Pennycook 1989a, 1990), this divorce of language from broader questions has had major implications for teaching practice and research.

[. . .]

English language teachers have been poorly served by the limited analysis of EIL provided by mainstream applied linguistics. There has been little opportunity to speculate on questions other than structural varieties of English. As Phillipson (1988) suggests, the "professional training of ELT people concentrates on linguistics, psychology and education in a restricted sense. It pays little attention to international relations, development studies, theories of culture or intercultural contact, or the politics or sociology of language or education" (p. 348). . . .

Cooke (1988) has described English as a Trojan horse, arguing that it is a language of imperialism and of particular class interests. Both he and Judd (1983) draw attention to the moral and political implications of English teaching around the globe in terms of the threat it poses to indigenous languages and the role it plays as a gatekeeper to better jobs in many societies. First of all then, English poses a threat to other languages. This is what Day (1980, 1985) has called linguistic genocide. In his study of the gradual replacement of Chamorro in Guam and the North Marianas, Day (1985) concludes pessimistically that "as long as the Marianas remain under the control of the United States, the English language will continue to replace Chamorro until there are no native speakers left. This has been American policy and practice elsewhere, and there is no reason to believe that Guam and the North Marianas will be an exception" (p. 180). Although this may seem to be an extreme case, we should nevertheless acknowledge the widespread threat that English presents. If it is not posing such a threat to first languages, as a universal second language it is constantly replacing other languages in daily use and school curricula. In bilingual or multilingual societies, for example, the prevalence of English can easily lead to the disregarding of one or more other languages.

The second major issue raised here is the extent to which English functions as a gatekeeper to positions of prestige in society. With English taking up such an important position in many educational systems around the world, it has become one of the most powerful means of inclusion into or exclusion from further education, employment, or social positions. In many countries, particularly former colonies of Britain, small English-speaking elites have continued the same policies of the former colonizers, using access to English language education as a crucial distributor of social prestige and wealth. Ngugi (1985) describes his experiences in Kenya, where not only was his native language proscribed with humiliating punishments (similar punishments and proscriptions were also the norm in schools for Canada's Aboriginal peoples) but English became "*the* main determinant of a child's progress up the ladder of formal education" (p. 115):

> [N]obody could go on to wear the undergraduate red gown, no matter how brilliantly they had performed in all the papers in all other subjects, unless they had a *credit* (not even a simple pass!) in English. Thus the most coveted place in the pyramid and in the system was only available to holders of an English-language credit card. English was the official vehicle and the magic formula to colonial elitedom.

[. . .]

The extent to which English is involved in the political, educational, social and economic life of a country is clearly a result of both the historical legacy of colonialism and of the varying success of countries since independence in warding off the threats of neo-colonialism. The different roles of English and Swahili in Kenya and Tanzania, for example, need to be seen with respect to both their colonial pasts and the different educational and development policies in the two countries (Zuengler 1985). In Tanzania, Swahili has become widely used as the national and official language due in no small part to Nyerere's insistence on "education for self-reliance", a policy that emphasized the need for each stage of schooling to be complete in itself and to prepare Tanzanians to participate in the socialist development of the country. In Kenya, by contrast, although Swahili is also the official national language, English remains the dominant language of Kenya's economic and legal spheres as it is the dominant language of much schooling, especially in Nairobi, within an educational system that has sought more to prepare an elite few for higher education than to educate a citizenry capable of maintaining a policy of socialist self-reliance.

If English thus operates as a major means by which social, political and economic inequalities are maintained within many countries, it also plays a significant role as a gatekeeper for movement between countries, especially for refugees hoping to move to the English-speaking countries. In his extensive studies of the English language programmes in the Southeast Asian refugee processing centres, Tollefson (1988, 1989) has suggested that they "continue to limit refugees' improvement in English language proficiency, capacity for cultural adaptation and preemployment skills, thereby contributing to the covert goal of ensuring that most refugees will only be able to compete effectively for minimum-wage employment" (1988: 39). These programmes then, although ostensibly providing immigrants with English language education to prepare them for their immigration to the United States, serve as centres for the preparation of a workforce to suit the US economy. They are constantly oriented towards the Americanization of immigrants, a process that assumes that American society has little or nothing to learn from immigrants' cultures and that "immigrants' primary civic responsibility is to transform themselves by adopting that society's dominant values, attitudes, and behaviors" (1989: 58).

The central belief here is that the cultures of immigrant peoples are the principal hindrance to their future prospects in North America, and that the American ideologies of individualism, self-sufficiency and hard work as a guarantor of success need to be inculcated in these future citizens of the United States before their arrival. . . . This discussion starts to raise questions not only about the connections between English in the world and social and economic power but also about the relationship between English and various cultural forms.

Ndebele (1987: 4) suggests that "the spread of English went parallel with the spread of the culture of international business and technological standardization". . . . Most important is the dominance of English in the domains of business, popular culture and international academic relations. As Flaitz (1988) has shown, it is through popular music that English is making a major incursion into French culture . . . .

In international academic relations, the predominance of English has profound consequences. A large proportion of textbooks in the world are published in English and designed either for the internal English-speaking market (United Kingdom, United States, Australia and so forth) or for an international market. In both cases, students around the world are not only obliged to reach a high level of competence in English to pursue their studies, but they are also dependent on forms of Western knowledge that are often of limited value and extreme inappropriacy to the local context. . . . Altbach (1981), for example, argues that much technological expertise in India has been inappropriate because "much of Indian science is oriented toward metropolitan models, because of the use of English, because of the prestige of Western science, and because of the foreign training of many key Indian researchers" (p. 613).

Other writers have claimed an even more fundamental role of English in the (re)production of global inequalities. Naysmith (1987), for example, suggests that English language teaching "has become part of the process whereby one part of the world has become politically, economically and culturally dominated by another" (p. 3). The core of this process, he argues, is the "central place the English language has taken as *the* language of international capitalism" (ibid.). Such a position, which suggests that English is an integral part of the global structures of dependency, has been explored at length by Robert Phillipson. He argues that *linguicism* – "the ideologies and structures which are used to legitimate, effectuate and reproduce an unequal division of power and resources (both material and non-material) between groups which are defined on the basis of their language (i.e., of their mother tongue)" (1988: 339) – is best seen within the broader context of *linguistic imperialism*, "an essential constituent of imperialism as a global phenomenon involving structural relations between rich and poor countries in a world characterised by inequality and injustice" (ibid.).

Most significantly, Phillipson's work demonstrates the limitations of arguments that suggest that the current position of English in the world is an accidental or natural result of world forces. Rather, through his analysis of the British Council and other organizations, Phillipson makes it clear that it has been deliberate government policy in English-speaking countries to promote the worldwide use of English for economic and political purposes. The British Council report for 1960–61, for example, draws a direct parallel between the advantages of encouraging the world to speak English (with the help of American power) and the history of US internal policies for its immigrant population: "Teaching the world English may appear not unlike an extension of the task which America faced in establishing English as a common national language among its own immigrant population" (cited in Phillipson 1988: 346). Ndebele (1987) also suggests that "The British Council . . . continues to be untiring in its efforts to keep the world speaking English. In this regard, teaching English as a second or foreign language is not only good business, in terms of the production of teaching materials of all kinds . . . . but also it is good politics" (p. 63). Given the connections outlined in this section between English and the export of certain forms of culture and knowledge, and between English and the maintenance of social, economic, and political elites, it is evident that the promotion of English around the world may bring very real economic and political advantages to the promoters of that spread. Indeed, Skutnabb-Kangas and Phillipson (1989) conclude that "it has been British and American government policy since the mid-1950s to establish English as a universal 'second language', so as to protect and promote capitalist interests" (p. 63).

Of primary importance to those of us working in English language teaching is the connection between our work and this global spread of English. Phillipson (1986) states that a primary purpose of his work is to gauge "the contribution of applied linguists and English Language Teaching Experts in helping to legitimate the contemporary capitalist world order" (p. 127). As I have suggested elsewhere (Pennycook 1990), it is incumbent on applied linguists to explore the interests served by our work. If we start to accept some of the critical perspectives outlined here, we must surely start to raise profound questions about our own practices. Certainly, these perspectives suggest that we must be highly suspicious of claims that the spread of English is natural, neutral, or beneficial.

[. . .]

Discourse, counter-discourse and the world in English

Of significance to the issues I wish to address in this chapter are, on the one hand, the continued acknowledgement of inequalities and dependencies between First and Third World countries and, on the other, an attempt to conceptualize these relationships in a way that avoids the reductionist and deterministic tendencies inherent in looking predominantly at socioeconomic relationships. Of fundamental importance is the elevation of notions of culture and discourse as principal factors in our understanding of the world. Although not belittling the importance of economic and material inequalities, I would argue that it is also crucial to understand how discourses construct and regulate our realities and operate through a diverse range of international institutions. Once we move beyond a view of the world as made up of competing states or as reducible to a set of socioeconomic relations, in favour of a view that also tries to account for diverse cultures and discourses constituting our subjectivities, then it also starts to become clear that language, and especially any international language, may play a far greater role in the world than had heretofore been considered. Importantly, too, this view suggests that people around the world are not merely passive consumers of culture and knowledge but active creators. In this section I shall explore the relationship between international discourses and English, and I shall discuss the importance of counter-discourses formed in English.

. . . First although I want to acknowledge the very great importance of work such as Phillipson's in its description of the structures of global language inequality, I also want to avoid what seems to be a foreclosure of discussion and possibilities by naming the spread of English as linguistic imperialism.

Phillipson describes a massive structure of linguistic imperialism and suggests ways of trying to counter this through language-planning policies. My position, however, is that we cannot reduce language spread to an imperialism parallel to economic or military imperialism. What I want to examine are the *effects* of the spread of English, how people take up English in their daily lives, what is done with "the world language which history has forced down our throats" (Achebe 1975: 220). By taking up the concept of discourse I am suggesting that the implications of the spread of English may be even greater than suggested in structuralist analyses because of the connection between English and international discourses, and that it may be almost impossible to solve these problems through language-planning policies since, as Luke *et al.* (1990) argue, "while language . . . can be 'planned', discourse cannot". And yet I also want to suggest that the concept of discourse allows for the construction of counter-discourses in English and may offer remarkable potential for change.

Language plays a central role in how we understand ourselves and the world, and thus all questions of language control and standardization have major implications for social relations and the distribution of power. . . . Once we start to deal with language as always political, never neutral, its relationship to other forms of power becomes easier to perceive.

Kachru (1986) quotes the Nigerian novelist Chinua Achebe (1975) in support of his arguments for the legitimation of the new Englishes. Achebe argues that it is neither necessary nor desirable for an African writer to be able to use English like a native speaker. Rather, he argues that English "will be able to carry the weight of my African experience. But it will have to be a new English, still in communion with its ancestral home but altered to suit its new African surroundings" (p. 223). But what do we mean when we talk about a new English? I want to argue that this is a far more complex question than simply a case of new words, new syntax or new phonology, that Achebe is concerned not so much with the structural diversity of English as with the cultural politics of new meanings, the struggle to claim and to create meanings in the political arenas of language and discourse. Significantly, Achebe's remark follows a quotation from the African American writer James Baldwin, who argues that:

> My quarrel with English has been that the language reflected none of my experience. But now I began to see the matter in quite another way. . . . Perhaps the language was not my own because I had never attempted to use it, had only learned to imitate it. If this were so, then it might be made to bear the burden of my experience if I could find the stamina to challenge it, and me, to such a test.
>
> (Cited in Achebe 1975: 223)

Achebe and Baldwin are referring to a political struggle over meaning, and it is in this domain that the notion of new Englishes becomes interesting. As Mazrui (1975) demonstrates, the relationship between English and politics is always complex. Although English has been one of the major languages of colonialism and neo-colonialism in Africa, a language linked to oppression, racism and cultural imperialism, it was also the language through which opposition to the colonizers was formed. "Among the functions of the English language in the Commonwealth must indeed be included a function which is unifying. What are often overlooked are some of the anti-Commonwealth tendencies which are also part of the English language" (1975: 191). On the eve of an election in Nairobi, Mazrui relates, the Kenyan political leader Tom Mboya stood in front of a vast crowd and recited the poem "If" by Rudyard Kipling. What are we to make of the use of a poem by one of the great apologists of imperialism in a political speech by a vehement opponent of imperialism and colonialism? According to Mazrui (1975: 209):

> The cultural penetration of the English language was manifesting its comprehensiveness. That was in part a form of colonization of the African mind. But when Rudyard Kipling is being called upon to serve the purposes of the Africans themselves, the phenomenon we are witnessing may also amount to a decolonizing of Rudyard Kipling.

What starts to emerge from these instances is a sense that language is a site of struggle, that meanings are always in flux and in contention. The process of using language against the grain, of the empire writing back to the centre (see Ashcroft *et al.* 1989), of using English to express the lived experiences of the colonized and to oppose the central meanings of the colonizers, is a crucial aspect of global language use . . . .

In looking at postcolonial literature, at forms of "writing back" in the language of the colonizers, I wish to avoid the same liberal pluralism of the writing on the new Englishes that we looked at earlier and that takes as its central concerns a notion of diversity and the legitimation of other standards. I am not here concerned with legitimating other forms of Commonwealth literature or "New literatures in English" so that they can be incorporated into the canon of English. Rather, I am interested in the ways in which these literatures in English are rich in struggles over meaning and opposition to the central definitions. As Ashcroft *et al.* (1989: 189) suggest, "A canon is not a body of texts *per se*, but rather a set of reading practices". Thus, the question is not so much one of replacing, validating or incorporating new forms of English language or literature, but rather of rethinking our understanding of language practices.

[. . .]

Discourses and languages can both facilitate and restrict the production of meanings. When we look at the history and present conjunction of English and many discourses of global power, it seems certain that those discourses have been facilitative of the spread of English and that the spread of English has facilitated the spread of those discourses. It is in this sense that the world is in English. The potential meanings that can be articulated in English are interlinked with the discourses of development, democracy, capitalism, modernization, and so on. And if we accept the argument that subjectivities are constructed in discourse (see e.g. Weedon 1987), then we can see how the spread of English is not only a structural *reproducer* of global inequalities, but also *produces* inequality by creating subject positions that contribute to their own subjectification. But it is also at this point that possibilities for resistance present themselves in alternative readings of Rudyard Kipling, postcolonial struggles in English, and the formation of counter-discourses.

[. . .]

I have been trying to suggest in this section, then, that if we elevate language, culture and discourse to a central role in the (re)production of global inequalities, the relationship between English and these inequalities becomes on the one hand stronger but on the other more open to resistance. If we see the relationship between power/knowledge in discourse and the power inscribed in words and produced in the struggle over meaning, we can start to understand not only the extent to which English is in the world and the extent to which it appears to run parallel to many forms of global oppression, but also the ways in which the world is in English, the ways in which the history of conjunctions between various discourses and English creates the conditions for people's complying with their own subjugation. . . . In the final section I shall try to suggest what implications such a view holds for teaching English around the world.

English teachers and the worldliness of English

I have suggested that the predominant paradigms of analysis of the spread of English around the world have by and large failed to problematize the causes and implications of this spread. They have dealt primarily with descriptions of varieties of English and have paused only to debate the questions of standardization and intelligibility. The spread of English is taken to be natural, neutral and beneficial. English language teachers, therefore, have been poorly served by a body of knowledge that fails to address the cultural and political implications of the spread of English. More critical analyses, however, show that English threatens other languages, acts as a gatekeeper to positions of wealth and prestige both within and between nations, and is the language through which much of the unequal distribution of wealth, resources and knowledge operates. Furthermore, its spread has not been the coincidental by-product of changing global relations but rather the deliberate policy of English-speaking countries protecting and promoting their economic and political interests. Thus, I have argued, English is in the world and plays an important role in the reproduction of global inequalities.

I have also suggested that when we consider the importance of language, culture and discourse in how we make sense of the world (and how the world makes sense of us), another aspect of the worldliness of English emerges: the extent to which the world is in English. By considering the relationship between language and discourse, it is possible to go beyond an understanding of the structural concordance of English and forms of global inequality to understand how people's subjectivities and identities are constituted and how people may comply with their own oppression. This, however, is by no means a deterministic thesis; it is not the structure of English that is important here but the politics of representation. And it is in this locus of struggle over meaning that counter-discourses can be formulated.

[. . .]

What, then, are the implications of all this for teachers and applied linguists? Rogers (1982) argues that, given the falsity of the hopes that English teaching provides, we should try to discourage the teaching of English. As the responses to Rogers' article rightly suggest, however, to deny people access to English is an even more problematic solution (Abbott 1984; Prodromou 1988). Although I think we should support language-planning policies aimed at maintaining languages other than English, there are also limits to the effectiveness of such policies. Phillipson's (1988: 353) "anti-linguicist strategies" may only be part of the picture. As long as English remains intimately linked to the discourses that ensure the continued domination of some parts of the globe by others, an oppositional programme other than one that seeks only to limit access to English will be necessary.

Elsewhere (Pennycook 1989b), I have argued that local forms of opposition can indeed be taken up. Following Foucault's (1980: 81) formulation, I suggested that by asking what forms of knowledge have been disqualified and subjugated by the dominant discourses, we could attempt to bring about the "insurrection of subjugated knowledges". More generally, I would suggest that counter-discourses can indeed be formed in English and that one of the principal roles of English teachers is to help this formulation. Thus, as applied linguists and English language teachers we should become political actors engaged in a critical pedagogical project to use English to oppose the dominant discourses of the West and to help the articulation of counter-discourses in English. At the very least, intimately involved as we are with the spread of English, we should be acutely aware of the implications of this spread for the reproduction and production of global inequalities.

References

Abbott, G. (1984) 'Should we start digging new holes?' *ELT Journal* 38 (2): 98–102.

Achebe, C. (1975) 'English and the African writer', in A. Mazrui, *The Political Sociology of the English Language* (Appendix B, pp. 216–23). The Hague/Paris: Mouton.

Altbach, P.G. (1981) 'The university as center and periphery', *Teachers College Record* 82 (4): 601–22.

Ashcroft, B., Griffiths, G. and Tiffin, H. (1989) *The Empire Writes Back: Theory and Practice in Post-colonial Literatures*. London and New York: Routledge.

Bamgbose, A. (1982) 'Standard Nigerian English: issues of identification', in B.J. Kachru (ed.) *The Other Tongue: English Across Cultures* (pp. 99–111). Urbana, IL: University of Illinois Press.

Cooke, D. (1988) 'Ties that constrict: English as a Trojan horse', in A. Cumming, A. Gagne and J. Dawson (eds) *Awarenesses: Proceedings of the 1987 TESL Ontario Conference* (pp. 56–62). Toronto: TESL Ontario.

Crystal, D. (1988) *The English Language*. Harmondsworth: Penguin.

Day, R. (1980) 'ESL: a factor in linguistic genocide?' in J.C. Fisher, M.A. Clarke and J. Schachter (eds) *On TESOL '80. Building Bridges: Research and Practice in Teaching English as a Second Language*. Washington, DC: TESOL.

Day, R. (1985) 'The ultimate inequality: linguistic genocide', in N. Wolfson and J. Manes (eds) *Language of Inequality* (pp. 163–81). Berlin: Mouton.

Fishman, J.A., Cooper, R.L. and Rosenbaum, Y. (1977) 'English around the world', in J.A. Fishman, R.W. Cooper and A.W. Conrad (eds) *The Spread of English* (pp. 77–107). Rowley, MA: Newbury House.

Flaitz, J. (1988) *The Ideology of English: French Perceptions of English as a World Language*. Berlin/New York/Amsterdam: Mouton de Gruyter.

Foucault, M. (1980) *Power/Knowledge: Selected Interviews and Other Writings, 1972–1977* (ed. Colin Gordon). New York: Pantheon.

Hindmarsh, R.X. (1978) 'English as an international language', *ELT Documents: English as an International Language* 102: 40–3.

Jespersen, O. ([1938] 1968) *Growth and Structure of the English Language*. Toronto: Collier-Macmillan.

Judd, E.L. (1983) 'TESOL as a political act: a moral question', in J. Handscombe, R.A. Orem and B.P. Taylor (eds) *On TESOL '83* (pp. 265–73). Washington, DC: TESOL.

Kachru, B. (1982a) 'Introduction: the other side of English', in B.J. Kachru (ed.) *The Other Tongue: English Across Cultures*. Urbana, IL: University of Illinois Press.

Kachru, B. (1982b) 'Models for non-native Englishes', in B.J. Kachru (ed.) *The Other Tongue: English Across Cultures* (pp. 31–57). Urbana, IL: University of Illinois Press.

Kachru, B. (1985) 'Standards, codification and sociolinguistic realism: the English language in the outer circle', in R. Quirk and H.G. Widdowson (eds) *English in the World*. Cambridge: Cambridge University Press.

Kachru, B. (1986) *The Alchemy of English: The Spread, Functions and Models of Non-native Englishes*. Oxford: Pergamon.

Luke, A., McHoul, A. and Mey, J.L. (1990) 'On the limits of language planning: class, state and power', in R.B. Baldauf, Jr. and A. Luke (eds) *Language Planning and Education in Australasia and the South Pacific* (pp. 25–44). Clevedon: Multilingual Matters.

Mazrui, A. (1975) *The Political Sociology of the English Language*. The Hague/Paris: Mouton.

Naysmith, J. (1987) 'English as imperialism?' *Language Issues* 1 (2): 3–5.

Ndebele, N.S. (1987) 'The English language and social change in South Africa', *The English Academy Review* 4: 1–16.

Nelson, C. (1982) 'Intelligibility and non-native varieties of English', in B.J. Kachru (ed.) *The Other Tongue: English Across Cultures* (pp. 58–73). Urbana, IL: University of Illinois Press.

Ngugi wa Thiong'o (1985) 'The language of African literature', *New Left Review* 150 (March/April): 109–27.

Pennycook, A. (1989a) 'The concept of method, interested knowledge, and the politics of language teaching', *TESOL Quarterly* 23 (4): 589–618.

Pennycook, A. (1989b) 'English as an international language and the insurrection of subjugated knowledges'. Paper presented at the Fifth International Conference of the Institute of Language in Education, Hong Kong, 13 December 1989: 'LULTAC '89'.

Pennycook, A. (1990) 'Towards a critical applied linguistics for the 1990s', *Issues in Applied Linguistics* 1 (1): 9–29.

Phillipson, R. (1986) 'English rules: a study of language pedagogy and imperialism', in R. Phillipson and T. Skutnabb-Kangas (eds) *Linguicism Rules in Education* (pp. 124–343). Denmark: Roskilde University Centre.

Phillipson, R. (1988) 'Linguicism: structures and ideologies in linguistic imperialism', in J. Cummins and T. Skutnabb-Kangas (eds) *Minority Education: From Shame to Struggle*. Avon: Multilingual Matters.

Platt, J., Weber, H. and Ho, M.L. (1984) *The New Englishes*. London: Routledge and Kegan Paul.

Prodromou, L. (1988) 'English as cultural action', *ELT Journal* 42 (2): 73–83.

Quirk, R. (1985) 'The English language in a global context', in R. Quirk and H.G. Widdowson (eds) *English in the World*. Cambridge: Cambridge University Press.

Richards, J.C. (1982) 'Singapore English: rhetorical and communicative styles', in B.J. Kachru (ed.) *The Other Tongue: English Across Cultures* (pp. 154–67). Urbana, IL: University of Illinois Press.

Rogers, J. (1982) 'The world for sick proper', *ELT Journal* 36 (3): 144–51.

Said, E. (1983) *The World, the Text and the Critic*. Cambridge, MA: Harvard University Press.

Skutnabb-Kangas, T. and Phillipson, R. (1989) 'Wanted! Linguistic human rights', *Rolig Papir* (Roskilde Universitetscenter) 44.

Tollefson, J.W. (1988) 'Covert policy in the United States refugee program in Southeast Asia'. *Language Problems and Language Planning* 12 (1): 30–42.

Tollefson, J.W. (1989) *Alien Winds: The Reeducation of America's Indochinese Refugees*. New York: Praeger.

Weedon, C. (1987) *Feminist Practice and Poststructuralist Theory*. Oxford: Blackwell.

Zuengler, J.E. (1982) 'Kenyan English', in B.J. Kachru (ed.) *The Other Tongue: English Across Cultures* (pp. 112–24). Urbana. IL: University of Illinois Press.

Zuengler, J.E. (1985) 'English, Swahili, or other languages? The relationship of educational development goals to language of instruction in Kenya and Tanzania', in N. Wolfson and J. Manes (eds) *Language of Inequality* (pp. 241–54). Berlin: Mouton.

Chapter 8

Branca F. Fabrício[1] and Denise Santos

(Re-) locating TEFL
The (re-) framing process as a collaborative locus for change

Introduction

Embedded in the debate around the (re-)location of TESOL is the fact that any relocation process involves, by definition, a movement from one locus to another. However, this new place does not lie somewhere as a territory already in existence, awaiting some kind of landing, but instead has to be crafted by those involved in any educational enterprise. In other words, this new place comes into existence as the outcome of participants' dynamic intersubjective activities. In this chapter, we will explore this creative movement in a Brazilian context and argue that the co-construction of particular interactive practices in the EFL classroom can orient teachers' and students' collective journeys towards the production of more critical understandings about the role of English in their social lives.

In order to support and clarify these claims, we start by discussing how English fits in the new global order and we then provide an account of how foreign language education in general, and TEFL in particular, fits in current educational policies in Brazil. We shall argue that, although these policies already point to important new directions concerning foreign language teaching and learning, their implementation in the classroom is far from straightforward. We then describe an innovation project in a Brazilian state school focusing on the cooperative processes of framing and interpretation through which awareness of central aspects of the EFL teaching-and-learning experience is mutually elaborated. We conclude by discussing the implications (and gains, in our view) of these new directions.

From: Fabrício, B. and Santos, D. '(Re-) locating TEFL: the (re-) framing process as a collaborative locus for change', in J. Edge (ed.), *(Re-) Locating TESOL in an Age of Empire*, Palgrave/Macmillan, pp. 65–83, 2006.

English within the new global order

Voices from varied fields of studies have been constructing a hegemonic discourse concerning our current experiencing of a period of complex social, cultural, political and economic changes whose pervasive and global impact has never been more far-reaching. Involving the breakdown and redrawing of boundaries of all sorts, at the macro- and micro-levels, these changes provide the context in which people must now make sense, interpret and (re-)construct all spheres of their existence – as learners in changing educational contexts; as professionals in changing workplaces; as citizens in changing public places; as meaning-makers in an emergent world of meaning-making possibilities (textual, visual, audio, spatial, electronic, virtual, and so on); as local community members in changing group rules and values; and as global community members in our increasingly globally interconnected lifeworlds (Cope and Kalantzis 2000). Globalized communications media (for example, mass media, electronic media and the world wide web) together with phenomena such as migration and diaspora force us to negotiate differences and diversity on a daily basis, intensifying this process of change.

It is true that new patterns of global economic and cultural exchanges are at the heart of a new contemporary order; indicative of this scenario is a new world order in which new practices come into being as a result of the extension of the market logic to different areas of social life, a process referred to as *marketization* of social life (Fairclough 1995, 2000). A myriad of expressions tries to capture the essence of this phenomenon: globalization, post-modernity, *PostFordism* (Kalantzis and Cope 2000), *Late Modernity* (Jameson 1991; Chouliaraki and Fairclough 1999), *Liquid Modernity* (Bauman 2000), or *Fast Capitalism* and *New World Order* (Gee et al. 1996), among others. In fact, what this multiple terminology indicates is the difficulty of naming new experiences and creating intelligibility about immediately lived moments. More recently Hardt and Negri (2000) have been referring to this global process as *Empire*, the contemporary form of sovereignty. Implying different relations from those of colonialism and imperialism, this new kind of supremacy has no fixed territory, static boundaries, or identifiable frontiers, being governed by transnational corporations joined by the hegemonic idea of global economy.

In this panorama, no single power centre can be identified as a world potency imposing, in a conspiratorial fashion, a global plan or monopoly upon other countries. It is true that the United States and the United Kingdom, for example, occupy central positions in the new order. However, in spite of their economic and political power, specific nations do not account on their own for the transformations in contemporary plural exchanges. Rather, deterritorialized rules and norms, reaching unprecedented breath and scope, are made legitimate by a supranational network of relationships which, favouring the economic dimension of social life, sustain what may appear to be a hegemonic reality. The contemporary Empire, unlike modern imperialism, has limitless and flexible frontiers whose borders are in constant dilation and flux. This constant expansion brings progress and wealth to developed countries at the same time that it blocks peripheral territories from access to global markets, free trade and opportunities in international commerce, promoting inequalities, societal hierarchy and exclusion to many.

The English language has increasingly had a central role in the globalization of this 'imperial' weft of connections, as a great part of the new economic, social, cultural, and political relations are being constructed in and mediated by English, the language of *Empire* and the language of techno-information society. The so-called 'Englishization' of the world is an important dimension of the new social order, and this process is inseparable from the historical and sociocultural contexts in which it operates. It is also inseparable from ongoing processes of globalization and localization (Graddol and Meinhof 1999). The phenomenon is therefore non-linear, complex and plural, producing hybrid identities and alterities as it engages social actors in important, different ways. English is used daily by people living in different parts of the globe and engaging themselves in multiple cultural-discursive practices. This scenario calls for a redefinition of the role of English, focusing on the complex workings of language amid power relations in a variety of social contexts.

It is within this post-colonial framework that the spread of the English language (and hence the spread of TESOL, and more specifically of teaching English as a *foreign* language, TEFL) is now to be conceived. These issues in the contemporary world cannot be approached separately from globalism as they are interwoven with political, economic, cultural and social aspects. It is for this reason that the idea of considering English as a lingua franca focusing only on its communicational role reflects a limited view of language and a limited view of social relations. Besides neglecting the fact that languages do not develop in a social vacuum, as they are intertwined with the values, attitudes and beliefs at play in different societies, this view does not conceive of language as discourse, i.e. as an active element in the construction of the social world. Approaching language as discourse means understanding its inseparability from the societies it is part of.

In the light of this scenario, how can the spread of English and the effects of the global–local dialogue be addressed in Brazil? How does it affect the TEFL context in the country? How can TEFL address all the complexities of this new social order in particular classrooms? In order to answer these questions it is important to understand the role played by the English language in Brazil. In what follows we therefore aim to provide an overview of socio-political aspects in the country associated with English in general, and TEFL in particular. We then contrast more mainstream positions in this respect with a few dissonant voices. After this discussion, we provide details of our study: an innovation programme which essentially seeks to develop alternative ways to (re-) locate the teaching of English in Brazil into a site crafted by multi-party manoeuvres interweaving debate, reflection, and awareness-raising of important socio-political issues attached to the spread of English today at both global and local levels.

English in Brazil: market-language hybridity

English and Portuguese do not simply 'sit happily together' in Brazil (Graddol *et al.* 1999: 18) as some may think. To subscribe to this belief is to conceive of language operating in the abstract, ignoring its performative force to alter states and produce meaningful effects as well as its constitutive role of social life and social relations. So, if language does have an impact on meaning-making processes in its community of users, a question is raised here: what kinds of meaning and social practices does the use of English create in Brazil?

On the one hand, because English is a central language in this globalized panorama (if not *the* central one), knowing English implies having access to information and multiple discourses – enlarging one's meaning repertoire (through reading, travelling, using the internet), opening doors to economic success (having access to better job opportunities, being promoted and so on) and participating in the world of fashion and entertainment. On the other hand, in a country such as Brazil, victimized by social imbalance and inequality, the benefits of the global language are limited to an economically privileged elite who can afford to pay the costs of exchange programmes abroad or enrolments in private language schools.[2] Therefore foreign language education creates one more great divide in a country where illiteracy, computer illiteracy, poverty, homelessness and unemployment separate most citizens from those few Brazilians who have access to global discourses.

However, English is everywhere in Brazil: in the labels of products at super-markets, on T-shirts and other fashion items, on billboards, in the names of shops and buildings (Thonus 1991), in marketing campaigns, in fast-food stores such as McDonald's and the like, in the American songs, sitcoms and movies that abound in the media, and in the flourishing of private English teaching institutions – a thriving market (Rajagopalan, 2003b). This situation leads to an interpretation that Brazil is undergoing some process of acculturation, as many Brazilians seem to be losing their cultural background and consuming non-critically the media's signals that English and everything about it is 'more cool' and better than Portuguese.

The indiscriminate and unrestricted use of English loans has led many academics to become alarmed with the so-called 'English invasion'. Pertinent discussions in the country involving linguists, applied linguists, educators, sociologists and even politicians have pointed to the fact that the Portuguese language is under constant assault, especially as Portuguese and English blend together in marketing practices, blurring the limits of their domains. The two advertisements below provide an eloquent picture of this phenomenon in Brazil, and the allure of the Anglo-Saxon culture that comes along with it:[3]

> Summer Comfort Collection: conforto combina com estilo. A prova está na linha de sandálias que seguem as *fashion trends*, na maior estabilidade, sem cansar a beleza.
> (Advertisement of a well-known shoe store in Brazil, 2002)

> Fuja do óbvio e ceda à tentação do NOVO *CLOSEUP RED FRUITS MINT max protection*. O único gel que combina o sabor selvagem das frutas vermelhas e a refrescância da menta.
> (Advertisement of a well-known Brazilian toothpaste brand, 2004)

The two advertisements are quite clear about the value the use of English tries to add to the products in focus: it adds style, originality and glamour to them (signalled by the constructions 'comfort goes with style', 'escape from the obvious' and 'giving in to the temptation'), standing as examples of the unsettling of boundaries of social life – between marketing practices in Portuguese and marketing practices in English, between economy and culture, between global and local, and so forth. This increasing flow across linguistic and cultural boundaries is due to the *globalization of discursive practices* (Chouliaraki and Fairclough 1999: 83) – a dimension of hybridity which is a significant facet of meaning-construction in contemporary social life.

In Brazil, the debate around this kind of hybridization involves different postures and reactions, sometimes assuming fierce contours. This is the case of some academics who advocate the protection of the national language from 'foreign invaders', an idea supported by some linguists and cultural fundamentalists.[4] Preaching the notion that the Portuguese language has to be defended from 'corruption and degeneration', this protectionist approach involves a monolithic and static understanding of language and culture, simplifying the complex processes involved in the relationship between language and culture – a dynamic relationship that no law can capture.

These polemical discussions, besides pointing to the complexity of the global–local dialogue, pose a problem to the TEFL scenario. If we approach the EFL classroom as a social scene in which a multitude of sociocultural texts are at play, we will see that it is a complex context and a privileged setting for cultural exchanges. However, how can teachers and students explore these multiple meaning-making processes when they come across meanings and identities produced by others? How do they help students who are coming into contact with different social and cultural organizations to avoid discriminatory attitudes and the restricting armour of ethnocentrism and monoculturalism? How do teachers prevent students from jumping to conclusions regarding the target culture, resorting to unhelpful cultural stereotyping?

TEFL in Brazil: canons and dissent

More critical readings of the social world tend to address contemporary discursive practices by investigating how language operates in a social sense, being necessarily invested with social, cultural, political and ideological connotations (Fairclough 1989; Pennycook 1999). Following this trend and problematizing the imbrication of language and power issues, many Brazilian applied linguists and educators approach TEFL in Brazil not only as an educational issue, but also a political issue. They have been defending a more political agenda concerning TEFL and have produced proposals focusing on ethics and critical thinking as central issues to deal with globalism, highlighting its importance in the construction of citizenship (e.g. Bohn 2003; Moita Lopes 2003; Rajagopalan 2003a). This is the approach that underlies the National Curricular Parameters for foreign language teaching in the country, recently issued by the Brazilian Ministry of Education and Culture (Secretaria de Educação Fundamental 1998). The excerpt below, extracted from the document, shows the political space the proposal intends to occupy in the Brazilian language education scenario:

> The teaching of foreign languages as part of the National Curriculum has a valuable constructive role as a constitutive part of students' formal education. It should involve a complex process of reflection of social, political and economic issues. These are important values in the process of empowerment, which leads to freedom. Putting it in different words, the teaching of foreign languages

in secondary schools (from age 10 to 14) is part of the construction of citizenship.

(Secretaria de Educação Fundamental 1998: 41, our translation)

Throughout the document, the political function of education in the formation of active citizens is highlighted, as the above fragment illustrates. It is clear that this proposal suggests an intervention in the social order through alternative directions for language education, other than the models currently in use, which highlight strictly grammatical, situational and/or communicative aspects of language. This new approach to English as a discipline moves away from more orthodox views, which advocate the sole use of the target language in the classroom, or which foreground knowledge about the structural components of the language as the primary goal in this educational process.

In spite of the ample debate around language education and its role in the contemporary scenario, conservative pedagogical practices are still at play, constituting an arena where conflicting paradigms coexist and a myriad of contradictory and paradoxical educational actions intersect. In Brazil, this new approach lives side by side with a frequently ill-defined communicative tradition, which tends to subscribe to notional-functional methodologies and to audiolingual structuralism. Often based on uncritical and apolitical understandings of language use, TEFL is usually operationalized as a decontextualized process focusing mainly on linguistic practice of the structural components of the target language at phonological, lexical, morphological and syntactic levels and promoting no connections with students' social world. Hardly ever are students encouraged to relate what they learn to their own experiences in the different social contexts they belong to, and this neglect may easily lead them to develop an idea that language is an abstract system disconnected from the social world.

This seems to be so because the transmission paradigm (Reddy 1979) is still strong, approaching communication as a process of sending/receiving messages and learning as a process involving information input and knowledge output. This modus operandi is based on the belief that cognition and cognitive life are individual and autonomous processes, existing independently from socio-cultural life – a reductionist understanding of the relationship between language, education and society, widely criticized by vygotskians and neo-vygotskians (Edwards and Mercer 1987; Mercer 1994, 1995; Wells and Chang-Wells 1992) among others.

Another problem is the fact that many teachers tend to base their work on the textbooks available on the market. By and large, these books deal with an isomorphic and homogenizing notion of culture, which naturalizes the cultural struggles and differences that are part and parcel of the cultures lived by those who use English in their everyday lives. According to studies analysing instructional materials being currently used in Brazil (Moita Lopes 2004; Santos 2002), we can say that a monocultural world inhabits EFL textbooks. Besides presenting the United Kingdom or the USA as unified nation-states standing for the Anglo-Saxon world, they do not problematize the cultural complexity and diversity of these two countries, which are becoming more and more multicultural.

Subscribing to recent theorization concerning foreign language education (Moita Lopes 2003, 2004; Pennycook, 2001; Rajagopalan, 2003a), it makes no sense, in the Brazilian TEFL scenario – a context that is hybrid per se – and in our increasingly multicultural world (one of the consequences of globalization), to depict the English-speaking world by ignoring the many countries in which English is spoken as an official language – such as South Africa, India and Singapore, to name but a few – based on the notion of imagined 'hegemonic' nation-states, in a world in which hybridity seems to be the keynote. However, in spite of all the debate around the inevitability of cross-breeding – and the contemporary understanding that all cultures are inherently *mestizas* (Canclini 1997) – the EFL area still adopts stereotypes, pasteurizations and generalizations as an explanatory bias of social behaviour, constructing a world inhabited by linguistic, cultural and social isomorphism. This approach does not allow for the critical fruition of cultural interchange.

Unfortunately, many teachers have been teaching English unaware of their educational and political role in the spread of the language and the values and power issues it represents, as if the sociocultural and the political domains were alien to them – drastically contrasting, as a corollary, with the orientation of the National Curricular Parameters mentioned above. This is so because there is still no professional cohesion in the area of elaboration and implementation of national educational policies. Furthermore, because these policies do not come along with massive investment in the area of teacher development, few institutions have adopted this new perspective. And more often than not, when this new stance inhabits schools, it is more as an empty discourse than as an actual social practice.

The study

Our data come from a Brazilian state school located in a major urban centre, with a population of about 1,500 students. Specifically, the class in which we carried out the study had a total of thirty-five students (of which about fifteen also attended private language schools) in their first year of secondary education and ranging from about ten to eleven years of age. The socio-economic profile of the class was mixed, including both middle-class and working-class students. The workload for English lessons was 1 hour and 40 minutes per week, and before we started our investigation students were used to engaging in extensive practice on structural components of the language, in dealing with decontextualized content, and in accepting a high level of control on the part of the teacher, Vera.[5] Vera, a woman in her late forties, routinely followed the approach presented in the English coursebook (adopted by her and the other staff members) whose methodology favoured the PPP ritual. Every lesson was organized predictably in terms of (1) *presentation* of new language; (2) *practice*, involving drilling, chorus repetition of correct sentences and mechanical grammar exercises; and (3) *production*, that is making sentences using the new structures and vocabulary. Consequently, the idea of approaching English as a topic for reflection rather than a code to be learnt was rather novel to her.

Nevertheless, Vera promptly accepted the idea of having her classes researched and observed by one of us, relating to this experience as a learning opportunity. Her only objection concerned the recording of her classes because she did not feel comfortable with either the cassette player or video camera – once she knew she was not doing a 'modern job'. According to her, the traditional methodology 'worked' with that group, but she invited the researcher to contribute with ideas, suggestions and comments on her practice. Due to personal problems, Vera had to go off on a leave for two weeks and asked if the researcher was willing to take over the classes for four consecutive sessions, and experiment with 'new methods', an invitation that was immediately accepted. This was the niche we were fortunate to have found to develop the work presented in this chapter.

Our study had as its primary goal the exploration of ways in which TEFL could be part of a more educationally relevant experience for these individuals, attempting to develop ways to guide young learners in a journey towards: (1) understanding the connection between language and society; (2) seeing themselves as agents in their meaning-making process; (3) challenging unquestioned practices and making them unstable; and (4) being able to read cultural manifestations critically. In so saying, we should acknowledge that our objectives did not follow mainstream implementations of TEFL in the Brazilian educational scenario and called for alternative support both at theoretical and more practical levels.

We have found Goffman's ([1974] 1986) theory of experience, especially his concept of *frame* (ibid.), particularly suitable to orient our work. According to Goffman (pp. 10–11) frames involve the 'principles of organization which govern events – at least social ones – and our subjective involvement in them'. Simply put, the framing of an event refers to how we answer the question: 'What is it that's going on here?' (p. 8), a perception which is not the activity of a single isolated individual consciousness, but rather a social phenomenon demanding interactional and interpretative procedures. Put in different words, making sense of what is going on around us and of interactions in progress is a collaborative process encompassing active operations by all interlocutors, which emerge from social and historically constituted discursive practices oriented by the tasks participants are engaged in and by the perceptual and interactive processes at play. That is to say that framings are co-constructed interpretation frameworks depending on contextual features as well as on interactants.

Following this line of thought, it could well be argued that in more conservative educational scenarios in Brazilian EFL classrooms, teachers and students would tend to frame these events as occasions in which they are expected to engage in mechanical practice of the language, of getting to know isolated words, of talking about grammar rules, and so on. This perception is not separate either from the kinds of activities teachers and students are used to carrying out in class or from the interactional routines within which they occur. However, as frames are dynamic and are constantly redefined (Tannen and Wallat [1987] 1993), we alternatively proposed that all participants collaboratively defined these events (or *framed* them) in novel ways. If frames are not fixed, situations that are apparently stable can be constructed outright. For this to happen, new practices, tasks and relationships, which are part of the framing process, have to be negotiated so that new perceptions, new meanings and new understandings are conjointly engendered.

A key issue in this re-framing process involved the redefinition of 'English'. Moving away from an emphasis on decontextualized language, characterized primarily in terms of its structural components, a redefinition was proposed in which English was to be approached by, above all, its sociocultural and political dimensions. In this respect, this study found support in research traditions emphasizing the central role played by talk in the meaning-making process (Heath 1982; Maybin and Moss 1993) and in education (e.g. Edwards and Westgate 1994: 15; Edwards and Mercer 1987; Mercer 1995; Wells and Chang-Wells 1992) and in the fact that classroom discourse is not a peripheral issue in the dynamics of classroom interaction but, rather, a nodal element which impinges upon the meanings constructed in interaction in decisive ways. Seen this way, students' L1 gained an important role in the English lesson: to become the medium through which interactants could negotiate these new meanings.

In more practical terms, this investigation involved other novel pedagogic practices – which helped to negotiate a new classroom frame – such as the adoption of a new furniture arrangement in the classroom: instead of the old pattern of sitting in rows, students started to sit in circles so that they acknowledged each other's presence in more democratic ways. Or, with regard to different participation structures, students moved from an excessive, if not total, dependence on the teacher and started to learn to acknowledge their peers as more-knowledgeable others as well. Also particularly important in this discussion was the incorporation of more unorthodox materials into the EFL classes, including cutouts from Brazilian texts in the media, or local containers and packages containing the English language (such as the ones commented on earlier), or Brazilian clothes displaying text in English, or locally produced textbooks aiming to foster critical awareness about the role played by English in Brazil. What all these texts have in common is that they represented English-in-the-new-global-order in ways particularly relevant to that local community of particular teachers and learners. Consequently, they were a relevant starting point for these individuals' reflection of the role of English in an age of Empire.

In the remainder of this chapter, we shall argue that this re-locating, or re-framing, process we advocate is not a straightforward one, nor an individual accomplishment on the part of particular students, or teacher. It is rather a necessarily lengthy, joint achievement of coparticipants who collaborate in interaction towards the creation of novel meanings.

The excerpt below is an English version of the initial steps in the development of critical and reflective positioning in this particular group of students. As explained earlier, this approach necessarily involved the use of students' L1 as the medium of communication towards the exploration of socio-political issues involving the target language. An appendix provides a transcription of the original interaction in Portuguese. This interaction takes place after the group has read a number of cutouts from local newspapers and magazines in which English coexists with Portuguese in taken-for-granted ways. Students have been asked to identify, and underline, the English words present in these texts and the following conversation,[6] led by one of us, then takes place:

Sequence 1

1	T	These words that you've underlined – do they all have equivalent
2		forms in Portuguese? //
3	Ss	Some do, some don't.
4	T	Some words // especially the ones related to fashion // *do* have

```
 5           corresponding words in Portuguese. The question then is // why
 6           do you think that happens? // Why is it that in our culture do
 7           T-shirts / newspaper articles // fashion articles / use English words
 8           when we have corresponding words in Portuguese? // Have you
 9           understood the question?
10    Ss     No!
11    T      I'll repeat // You have you noticed here / in these Brazilian
12           magazine and newspaper articles / an exaggerated use of English
13           words? // Why do we use 'hot dogs' when we have the word
14           'cachorro quente'? //
15    S1     Because sometimes it makes things more simple. For example,
16           'shopping center' and 'centro de compras' //
17    S2     I think that we use English because English is a universal
18           language //
19    S3     Because it's nicer//
```

Initially (lines 3 and 10), students frame the interaction resorting to rather conservative teaching-and-learning models: the teacher poses questions (initiation) and students respond (response), seeking to provide answers in chorus and in the shortest possible ways, signalling their understanding of what is appropriate regarding classroom behaviour. The many pauses verified throughout this sequence help to frame interaction as a didactic event in which one participant (the teacher) is expected to provide the stimulus the students are supposed to react to. Note here that, according to this interpretation, there is no place for individualities, for challenges, or for individualized stances.

The teacher's clarification of her provocative comments (lines 11–14) respresents a first attempt to negotiate a new frame. Then, very interestingly, what this excerpt suggests is that students start articulating attributes to the English language (namely, that it is economical, lines 15–16; universal, lines 17–18; and holder of an intrinsic aesthetic value, line 19) as if these attributes were givens, and non-problematical issues. These ideas, as discussed earlier, express some of the beliefs that circulate in Brazilian culture concerning English. Should the discussion have stopped there, the group would have probably reinforced a description of the local culture as 'less able', 'less important', or 'less attractive' than the anglo-culture – legitimizing in this way a characterization of the former as inferior to the latter.

Nevertheless, the teacher insists on engaging the group in a process of re-framing in which the naturalization of these notions can be collaboratively challenged. This is how the conversation unfolds:

Sequence 2

```
20    T      But I wonder if that's why we insist on using so many English words
21           when we have words in Portuguese //
22    S1     (looking at the teacher) We know some words better in English than
23           in Portuguese. Now we know some words in English that we don't
24           even know in Portuguese. Then it becomes easier to say them in
25           English /
```

26	S4	(looking at the teacher) It makes communication easier /
27	S5	(looking at the teacher) It calls people's attention if you use words in
28		English, like *new journalism* /
29	T	If you put the title '*Novo journalismo brasileiro*' on a magazine cover /
30		and you put 'New journalism' on the cover of another magazine //
31		It's the same magazine the same content / only the cover is different
32		// Which one will sell more? =
33	Ss	= The one in English.
34	T	Why?
35	S5	(looking at the teacher) The person will get engaged more easily /
36		She will think it's more interesting =
37	S6	= (looking at peers) People think that the quality of things that come
38		from abroad is better than what is ours /
39	S7	(looking at peers) I think people value what comes from abroad and
40		do not value our culture =
41	T	= That's it!
42	Ss	(claps)
43	S8	(enthusiastically, looking at peers) The United States has the
44		economic power. It's in fashion. Brazil follows the United States =
45	S7	= (looking at peers) When are we going to start valuing our culture?
46		We can invent things instead of copying them =
47	S1	= (looking at peers) We don't have to devalue our culture when we
48		learn the language from another culture. All cultures are interesting
49		and rich.

The invitation for further reflection (lines 20–21) leads students into further elaboration and it is interesting to see how Student 1 rehearses, in lines 22 to 25, a more sophisticated way of expressing her opinion than the one put forward previously (see lines 15–16). It is also important to note that this reformulation develops even further on into the interaction, culminating with the same student's articulation of a much more elaborated and engaged positioning in lines 47 to 49. Note here that this statement is the outcome of the collaborative interaction in progress.

In addition to the changes expressed by this particular student as this brief interaction develops, two further, important, re-directing processes can be perceived in the excerpt above. The first one is that students jointly construct themselves as active and critical learners who, in more quantitative terms, dominate the chorus of voices being heard in the discussion, given that the teacher, from a certain point on, shares interactional control with the students, who start negotiating the turn-taking system more freely. Also, in more qualitative terms, there are two issues to be highlighted here. The first one is that, from a certain point in the interaction onwards, students' utterances tend to build upon prior utterances and not to be merely disconnected voices produced here and there. Disconnection is evident in the sequence involving S1, S2 and S3 (lines 15 to 19), as students seem to ratify the teacher as their sole interlocutor, keeping eye-contact only with her. However, a more connected chain, involving mutual orientation, is found in the sequence involving S1, S4 and S5 (lines 22 to 28). It is clear that, from line 37 onwards, students attend to their interlocutors' viewpoints, and build upon them, showing that the meaning-making process is generated within interaction with peers.

A second important change in the development of this interaction seems to be triggered by the duet carried out by students S6 and S7 (lines 37 to 40), culminating with the teacher's emphatic feedback on line 41. The joint re-framing process is achieved by students' involvement in the discussion, signalled by their gaze, emphasis modulation and the dynamism generated by the amount of latching in their speech. Therefore, they move from a status of disengaged 'individuals' to interlocutors socially engaged in a process of mutual monitoring, constructing and displaying a new multi-party perception of the relationship between English and Portuguese.

What this interaction suggests is that new meanings can be constructed in the EFL classroom if the latter is collectively recontextualized to make room for and value the confrontation of all participants' voices. From this perspective, we reconceptualize TEFL as situated local practices through which teacher and students can redefine common-sense beliefs and craft fresh routes for global–local dialectics.

Language practices: a possible place for change

In this chapter we have argued that the EFL classroom can be the site of active and creative production of socially relevant meanings regarding the role of English within the new global order. We have suggested that, in order to achieve this goal, it is necessary to redefine a number of issues. Key to this reframing process is the redefinition of the goals, foci, resources, practices and procedures in the EFL class. By assuming a sociopolitical stance in TEFL, we are responding to global affairs which today, perhaps more than ever, cannot be ignored in the English teaching-and-learning process.

The implications of the stance we are suggesting here are various. First, by (re-) locating TESOL in this direction we are helping to develop language users who acknowledge the fact that languages are not devoid of sociocultural aspects, and that by using language individuals are necessarily acting in the social world. Secondly, this (re-)location positions students as active participants in their learning processes, given that their voices become central to the development of the new meanings constructed. Furthermore, this perspective fosters critical awareness of crucial aspects of current times once it engages teachers and students in the examination of local traditions within a broader scenario involving global issues.

In the context under investigation, this process of (re-)location was inaugurated through a set of procedures guiding our course of action: the task proper, involving text reading and debate; the selection of topic; the enhancement of critical thinking; the flexibilization of the turn-taking system; and the spatial arrangement, aspects which promoted a high degree of involvement among participants. The perceptions they co-constructed were situated in a web of discursive practices involving not only the rearrangement of the classroom setting but also the redefinition of rhetorical, didactic and interactional routines pertaining to TEFL events, which have made a 'frame' of difference. In fact, what these issues altogether show is the possibility of approaching the language of empire in critical and positive ways in times of a globalizing panorama.

Notes

1   I am grateful to CNPQ for the research grant (300715/02–1) which has made this work possible.
2   The teaching of a modern foreign language is obligatory in the curriculum of private and state schools in Brazil from the beginning of secondary education. However, the low-quality work often carried out in these contexts has created a common-sense assumption that it is impossible to learn a foreign language at school.
3   The translations of these advertisements are as follows: (1) Summer Comfort Collection: comfort goes with style. Proof can be found in the new sandals that follow the latest *fashion trends*, combining stability and beauty; (2) Escape from the obvious by giving in to the temptation of *CLOSEUP RED FRUITS MINT max protection*. The only gel that combines the wild flavour of red fruit and the freshness of mint.
4   For example, Aldo Rebelo, a well-known politician in Brazil, has launched a project for a polemic law to tackle the threat of the English invasion. For more details, see Rajagopalan 2003b.
5   This is a pseudonym, to preserve the anonymity of the participants in this study.
6   For transcription purposes we have used the following notation: (/) indicates a quick pause and (//) a longer pause; (parentheses) identify comments on non-verbal behaviour; (=) signals latching; underlined words stand for emphasis; and *italics* indicates words in Portuguese.

References

Bauman, K. (2000) *Liquid Modernity*. Oxford: Polity Press.
Bohn, H.I. (2003) 'The educational role and status of English in Brazil', *World Englishes* 22 (2): 159–72.
Canclini, N.G. (1997) *Culturas Híbridas*. Universidade de São Paulo: Edusp.
Chouliaraki, L. and Fairclough, N. (1999) *Discourse in Late Modernity: Rethinking Critical Discourse Analysis*. Edinburgh: Edinburgh University Press.
Cope, B. and Kalantzis, M. (2000) 'Designs for social futures', in B. Cope and M. Kalantzis (eds) *Multiliteracies: Literacy Learning and the Design of Social Futures* (pp. 203–34). London: Routledge.
Edwards, A.D. and Westgate, D.P.G. (1994) *Investigating Classroom Talk*, 2nd edn. London: The Falmer Press.
Edwards, D. and Mercer, N. (1987) *Common Knowledge: The Development of Understanding in the Classroom*. London: Methuen.
Fairclough, N. (1989) *Language and Power*. London: Longman.
Fairclough, N. (1995) 'Discourse across disciplines: discourse analysis in researching social change', *AILA Review*, n. 12: 3–17.
Fairclough, N. (2000) 'Multiliteracies and language: orders of discourse and intertextuality', in B. Cope and M. Kalantzis (eds) *Multiliteracies: Literacy Learning and the Design of Social Futures* (pp. 162–81). London: Routledge.
Gee, J., Hull, G. and Lankshear, C. (1996) *The New Work Order: Behind the Language of the New Capitalism*. Sydney: Allen & Unwin.
Goffman, E. (1974/1986) *Frame Analysis: An Essay on the Organization of Experience*. Harmondsworth: Penguin Books.
Graddol, D. and Meinhof, U.H. (eds) (1999) *AILA Review 13: English in a Changing World*. Oxford: Biddles Ltd.
Graddol, D., McArthur, T., Flack, D. and Amey, J. (1999) 'English around the world', in D. Graddol and U.H. Meinhof (eds) *AILA Review 13: English in a Changing World* (pp. 3–18). Oxford: Biddles Ltd.

Hardt, M. and Negri, A. (2000) *Empire*. Cambridge, MA: Harvard University Press.

Heath, S.B. (1982) 'What no bedtime story means: narrative skills at home and at school', *Language in Society* 11 (2): 49–76.

Jameson, F. (1991) *Pós-Modernismo: A Lógica Cultural do Capitalismo Tardio*. São Paulo: Ática.

Kalantzis, M. and Cope, B. (2000) 'Changing role of schools', in B. Cope and M. Kalantzis (eds) *Multiliteracies: Literacy Learning and the Design of Social Futures* (pp. 121–48). London: Routledge.

Maybin, J. and Moss, G. (1993) 'Talk about texts: reading as a social event', *Journal of Research in Reading* 16 (2): 138–7.

Mercer, N. (1994) 'Neo-Vygotskian theory and classroom education', in B. Stierer and J. Maybin (eds) *Language, Literacy and Learning in Educational Practice* (pp. 92–110). Clevedon: Multilingual Matters.

Mercer, N. (1995) *The Guided Construction of Knowledge: Talk amongst Teachers and Learners*. Clevedon: Multilingual Matters.

Moita Lopes, L.P. (2003) 'A nova ordem mundial, os parâmetros curriculares nacionais e o ensino de inglês no Brasil: a base intelectual para uma ação política', in L. Barbara and R. Ramos (eds) *Reflexão e ações no ensino-aprendizagem de línguas* (pp. 29–60). Campinas: Mercado de Letras.

Moita Lopes, L.P. (2004) *Ensino de inglês como espço de embates culturais e de políticas da diferença*. Programa Interdisciplinar de Lingüística Aplicada: Universidade Federal do Rio de Janeiro, mimeo.

Pennycook, A. (1999) 'Introduction: critical approaches to TESOL', *TESOL Quarterly* 33 (3): 329–48.

Pennycook, A. (2001) *Critical Applied Linguistics: A Critical Introduction*. Mahwah, NJ: Lawrence Earlbaum.

Rajagopalan, K. (2003a) *Por uma lingüística crítica: linguagem, identidade e a questão ética*. São Paulo: Parábola Editorial.

Rajagopalan, K. (2003b) 'The ambivalent role of English in Brazilian politics', *World Englishes* 22 (2): 91–101.

Reddy, M. (1979) 'The conduit metaphor', in A. Ortony (ed.) *Metaphor and Thought*. Cambridge: Cambridge University Press.

Santos, D. (2002) 'Learning English as a foreign language in Brazilian elementary schools: textbooks and their lessons about the world and about learning', *Paradigm* 2 (5): 25–38.

Secretaria de Educação Fundamental, (1998) *Língua estrangeira, Parâmetros Curriculares Nacionais [Foreign Language, National Curricular Parameters]*. Brasília, DF: Ministério da Educação.

Tannen, D. and Wallat, C. (1987/1993) 'Interactive frames and knowledge schemas in interaction: examples from a medical examination/interview', in D. Tannen (ed.) *Framing in Discourse* (pp. 57–76). New York: Oxford University Press.

Thonus, T. (1991) 'Englishization of business names in Brazil', *World Englishes* 10 (1): 65–74.

Wells, G. and Chang-Wells, G.L. (1992) *Constructing Knowledge Together: Classrooms as Centers of Inquiry and Literacy*. Portsmouth, NH: Heinemann.

Appendix

1	T	Todas essas palavras que vocês sublinharam têm correspondente em
2		português?//
3	Ss	Algumas sim outras não.
4	T	Muitas palavras // sobretudo as relacionadas à moda // têm
5		correspondente em português. A pergunta é // por que vocês
6		acham que isso acontece? // Por que na nossa cultura, camisetas /

7		artigos de jornal // artigos de moda / utilizam palavras em inglês
8		quando temos correspondentes em português? // Entenderam a
9		pergunta?
10	Ss	Não!
11	T	Vou repetir // Vocês verificaram / aqui em artigos de revistas e
12		jornais brasileiros / um uso exagerado de palavras em inglês // Por
13		que que a gente usa *hotdog* quando temos cachorro quente? //
14	S1	Às vezes, simplifica. Por exemplo, *shopping center* e centro de
15		compras//
16	S2	Eu acho que a gente usa inglês porque inglês é uma língua
17		universal //
18	S3	Porque é mais bonito //
19	T	Mas será que é por isso que a gente insiste em usar tantas palavras
20		em inglês quando a gente tem palavras em português //
21	S1	(olhando para a professora) Nós conhecemos muito mais
22		facilmente algumas palavras de um jeito em inglês que em
23		português. Hoje em dia a gente conhece algumas palavras em inglês
24		que a gente nem conhece em português. Aí fica mais fácil falar em
25		inglês /
26	S4	(olhando para a professora) Facilita a comunicação /
27	S5	(olhando para a professora) Chama mais atenção colocar uma
28		palavra em inglês, por exemplo, *new journalism* /
29	T	Se colocar na capa de uma revista o título 'Novo jornalismo
30		brasileiro' e na de outra 'New Journalism' // È a mesma revista,
31		com o mesmo conteúdo / só muda a capa // Qual vai vender mais?
32		=
33	Ss	= A em inglês.
34	T	Por quê?
35	S5	(olhando para a professora) A pessoa vai se interessar mais / Vai
36		achar mais interessante =
37	S6	= (olhando para os colegas) As pessoas acham que a qualidade do
38		que é de fora é melhor do que o nosso /
39	S7	(olhando para os colegas) Eu acho que as pessoas dão mais valor ao
40		que é de fora e desvalorizam a nossa cultura =
41	T	= Isso!
42	Ss	(aplausos)
43	S8	(de forma engajada, olhando para os colegas) Os Estados Unidos
44		têm o poder econômico. Está na moda. O Brasil segue os Estados
45		Unidos =
46	S7	= (olhando para os colegas) Quando a gente vai começar a
47		valorizar a nossa cultura? A gente pode inventar coisas em vez de
48		copiar =
49	S1	= (olhando para os colegas) A gente não precisa desvalorizar a nossa
50		cultura quando aprende a língua de outra cultura. Todas as culturas
51		são interessantes e ricas.

Chapter 9

Jennifer Jenkins

A sociolinguistically based, empirically researched pronunciation syllabus for English as an international language

Introduction: Changing Circumstances, Changing Pronunciation Goals

At the start of the twenty-first century, most applied linguists are familiar with the fact that English is now spoken by a considerably greater number of NNSs than NSs. Several scholars have already begun discussing the implications for English Language Teaching (see, e.g., Kachru 1992; Kachru and Nelson 1996; Kasper 1998; Pennycook 1999, 2000; Seidlhofer 1999; Widdowson 1994, 1997). And with the conceptual leap implicit in Cook's recommendation that 'language teaching would benefit by paying attention to the L2 user rather than concentrating primarily on the native speaker' and should 'apply an L2 user model' (1999: 185), second language acquisition researchers look set to enter the debate. Nevertheless, although this paradigm shift is finally gaining acceptance in theory, in practice it has so far had little impact on applied linguistic research design and even less on English language teaching or teaching materials: the NS remains a given, and the NS standard measure still reigns supreme.

[. . .]

Edited extracts from: Jenkins, J. 'A sociolinguistically based, empirically researched pronunciation syllabus for English as an international language', in *Applied Linguistics*, 23 (1): 83–103, Oxford University Press, 2002.

Received Pronunciation (RP), the prestige British accent, is thought to be spoken now in its pure form by fewer than 3 per cent of British Speakers of English (Crystal 1995: 365), while the majority of British people have either a regionally modified RP or a regional accent. The latter, unless overly broad (and with the exception of the still-stigmatized accents of Liverpool, Birmingham, and Glasgow), are fast gaining acceptance among the general public. There is, then, a growing awareness in Britain of a fact that sociolinguists have always recognized: that regional variation is the (acceptable) rule rather than the (unacceptable) exception. Turning to the case of EFL and other modern foreign languages, the purpose of learning is, by definition, to speak the target language as a 'foreigner' in order to facilitate communication with NSs of the language. Here, it seems reasonable to argue that the goal of pronunciation teaching should be the sufficiently close approximation of an NS accent such that it can be understood by NSs of that language. In this case, the choice of pedagogic model is (or should be) a matter of selecting the NS accent which will have widest currency among the learner's target (NS) community.

EIL is a different matter. Here, English is being learnt for international communication rather than for communication with its NSs. Speakers of EIL are not 'foreign' speakers of the language, but 'international' speakers. The EIL target community is no longer an NS British (or any other NS) one: it is an international community in which all participants have an equal claim to membership. An intrinsic part of this claim, it seems to me, is the right for speakers to express their (L1) regional group identity in English by means of their accent, as long as the accent does not jeopardize international intelligibility.

[. . .]

However, this is not to make a claim that as far as NNS English accents are concerned, anything is acceptable. The possibility of mutual unintelligibility is currently a cause of much concern. In Trudgill's words, there is 'a great fear . . . that English is now used so widely around the world, and is in particular used by so many non-native speakers, that if we are not careful, and very vigilant, the language will quite rapidly break up into a series of increasingly mutually unintelligible dialects, and eventually into different languages' (Trudgill 1998: 29). Trudgill himself considers this to be 'a perfectly sensible point of view' for a language that has more non-native than native speakers, and goes on to predict that while English lexis is likely to undergo a process of 'homogenisation' by means of 'Americanisation', English phonology will take the opposite route and undergo a process of disintegration.

In line with Trudgill's point, despite decades of teaching of RP and GA (General American), the NNS Englishes are thought to diverge from each other more in terms of pronunciation than of the other linguistic levels (see, for example, Ioup 1984). The links between accent and identity on the one hand and accent and articulatory motor skills on the other are, it seems, so ingrained that traditional English pronunciation teaching is destined to fail for all but a small minority of L2 learners. Hence pronunciation already has a greater potential to compromise mutual international unintelligibility than do the other linguistic levels. And the worst-case scenario is, as Trudgill implies, that the whole purpose of learning EIL – to engage in successful international communication – will be threatened by further phonological divergence. In order to prevent the disintegration of international phonological intelligibility there is, it follows, a strong case for pedagogic intervention of a new kind: intervention that is no longer based on idealized NS models or NS corpora, but that is both more relevant (in terms of EIL needs) and more realistic (in terms of teachability). Given its primary concern to promote international phonological intelligibility, as well as the broader purpose of developing a research-based pedagogy, a new pedagogy for EIL must be based on evidence drawn from EIL (NNS–NNS) interactions and, above all, from NNS listeners. It is to such evidence that we now turn.

Empirical research in EIL contexts

The purpose of this section is threefold: first, to demonstrate the extent to which intelligibility in NNS–NNS interaction can breakdown as a result of problems at the phonological level; secondly, to identify which specific phonological features are implicated in the breakdown; and thirdly, to consider two other factors which contribute to (un)successful EIL communication: the processing of contextual cues and the use of accommodation strategies.

The section is structured around the analysis of different types of data collected in EIL contexts.[1] The first set of data (five communication breakdowns drawn from the author's field data collected in a range of classroom and social situations) establishes the general fact of communication breakdown and provides evidence of specific phonological sources of mis- and non-communication. The second set (two recorded information exchange tasks) demonstrates that NNS interlocutors' attempts to accommodate (converge) at the phonological level (in other words, to adjust their pronunciation in order to bring it closer to one another's) in speech situations where intelligibility for their interlocutor is critical. The focus here is on which phonological features are selected for convergence and how the speaker resolves the problem. The purpose is to assess whether the features selected are those which have been identified as being likely to threaten EIL phonological intelligibility, and how satisfactorily the problem is resolved.

In both sets of data, the subjects are of upper-intermediate to low advanced level as recognized by the University of Cambridge Local Examinations Syndicate (UCLES) in that students hold the First Certificate of English (FCE) or the Certificate of Advanced English (CAE) qualification. In other words, these subjects have achieved a level of reasonable competence, but would not be considered fully bilingual in English. Because this is tantamount to saying that such speakers still have inter-languages, some authors refer to their spoken interactions with each other as 'interlanguage talk' (see, e.g., Duff 1986; Long and Porter 1985). My own use of the term interlanguage talk (ILT) relates specifically to this type of EIL interaction.

Examples of pronunciation-based miscommunication in interlanguage talk

We begin with five examples drawn from the author's field data. The majority of this data was collected over a period of three years in classroom and social settings, with the aim of establishing the extent to which miscommunication in ILT is caused primarily by problems at the phonological level. Over this period, I noted down every example of mis- and non-communication that occurred in my presence and, wherever feasible, discussed the cause(s) with the interlocutors involved. What emerged was a clear indication that although pronunciation was by no means the sole cause of ILT communication breakdown, it was by far the most frequent and the most difficult to resolve. The following five examples are typical of the errors which caused intelligibility problems for ILT interlocutors in the data, and exemplify the categories of phonological error which most often proved problematic: consonant sounds, tonic (or nuclear) stress, vowel length, and non-permissible (according to the rules of English syllable structure) simplification of consonant clusters.

[1] [aɪ ˈperɪd] = 'I failed'

In this example, an L1 Korean speaker of English had taken his driving test that morning. He entered the classroom after the lunch break, and announced that he had failed the test. His classmates (from a range of L1s), did not understand the significance of what he had said, and one followed the announcement with the enquiry 'Did you pass your test, Lee?' In this example, the typical Korean sound substitution of /p/ for /f/ had rendered the speaker's pronunciation unintelligible for his non-Korean receivers. There are several other examples in the field data of this speaker's /p/-/f/ sound substitution causing problems for receivers. For example, 'wife' pronounced 'wipe'; 'finish' pronounced 'pinish'; 'coffee' pronounced 'copy'; 'father' pronounced 'pader'.

[2] I smoke more than you DO = 'I smoke more than *you* do'.[2]

In this example, the speaker, an L1 Taiwanese speaker of English, and his Swiss-Italian interlocutor were discussing how many cigarettes a day they each smoked. The Swiss-Italian subject had just told the Taiwanese subject that she smoked around twenty a day. The latter replied that he smoked more than she did, but instead of putting tonic (nuclear) stress on the word 'you', where it would have indicated intonationally the contrast he was making lexically, he put it on the last item in the tone unit, that is 'do'. After three repetitions she still did not understand.

[3] Shakespeare's [bɑːspleɪs] = 'Shakespeare's birthplace'

In this case, a Japanese speaker was giving a short presentation to a mixed-L1 class. He announced the title of his talk as what sounded most like 'Shakespeare's bathplace' (although the /θ/ was pronounced /s/). During the presentation he described Stratford-upon-Avon, talked about Shakespeare's early years, his marriage to Anne Hathaway, his acting career, and his plays. When the student had finished speaking and offered his audience the opportunity to ask questions, the first was an enquiry about the connection between the content of the talk and a bath. Indeed, the majority of the group admitted to having thought the talk had concerned a bath, although they had not been able to identify a connection. The problem here was the substitution of /ɜː/ with /ɑː/, a substitution which frequently caused intelligibility problems in my data, and one which had previously been noted by others such as Schwartz (1980). On the other hand, the replacement of /θ/ with /s/ was not at all problematic – and this was a phenomenon which recurred regularly in the data.

[4] Have you got a blue VUN? = 'Have you got a *blue* one?'

Here we have an example of a combination of phonological errors which caused the most serious problems in my data: misplaced tonic (nuclear) stress along with a consonant substitution within the wrongly stressed word. An L1 Hungarian student of English was talking with three other students, respectively from Guatemala, (French-)Switzerland, and Brazil. They were using coloured pens to make posters for the classroom wall. At one point the Hungarian asked his fellow students if any of them had a blue pen. However, he not only placed tonic stress on the final item in the tone unit, but he also substituted the /w/ of 'one' with a /v/. The other students asked several times 'What is vun?' and only understood his meaning when the speaker located the pen he needed, and held it up, saying 'Blue vun like THIS'. It could be argued that the problem in this example was also lexical: the listeners may have assumed that 'vun' was a word unfamiliar to them. However, the same problem arises in my data when tonic stress is misplaced on words that are both familiar to listeners and contain no segmental errors. It seems, then, that any lexical difficulties of the kind encountered in example 4 are compounded by misplaced tonic stress.

[5] [dõ laɪzə fɪz ɒf 'skɔ] = 'Don't rise the fees of school.'

In this final example, another L1 Japanese speaker of English was giving a short presentation to her mixed-L1 class. She had been discussing education in the EC and, in particular, its high cost for international students such as herself and concluded her talk with the words 'don't rise the fees of school'. However, only the other Japanese students in the group understood her meaning, while the others remained completely baffled even after she had repeated the sentence four times. Eventually we 'translated' it word for word and the meaning was immediately clear despite the two lexicogrammatical errors ('rise' for 'raise'; 'fees of school' for 'school fees'). In this example, the several pronunciation errors all involve vowel length and consonant substitution. Both these error types are frequent causes of unintelligible pronunciation in my empirical data.

    [. . .]

The accommodation data: same-L1 and different-L1 interactions

To sum up so far, the ILT data indicate that certain pronunciation deviations, particularly in consonant sounds, vowel length and the placing of tonic stress, render an NNS's pronunciation unintelligible to an NNS interlocutor; and that when this happens, context and cotext do not provide much help in clarifying meaning. As far as sounds are concerned, this position is corroborated by a further set of data which investigate the extent of NNSs' attempts to accommodate towards the pronunciation of their interlocutors. Here, the sounds which speakers attempt to replace with something more targetlike (certain sounds that are liable to be affected by L1 transfer), tend to be the same sounds as those which appear in the field data to be crucial for intelligibility in ILT. In other words, it seems that, given the opportunity, NNSs engaged in ILT work out for themselves which features of their pronunciation are potentially unintelligible for their NNS interlocutors, and endeavour to replace them.

Traditionally the accommodation literature discusses the accommodative adjustments made by interlocutors in relation to an affective motivation (see, e.g., Giles 1973). That is, speakers make their speech more similar to that of their interlocutors because of their desire to be liked. But the early accommodation theorists also identified a motivation which they called 'communicative efficiency' and which they found to be particularly relevant to communication in a second language: the desire to be understood (Beebe and Giles 1984). What seems to happen in ILT, however, is that instead of converging on each other's pronunciation, when intelligibility is particularly important, speakers converge on what they construe as a more targetlike pronunciation.

The following extracts demonstrate this phenomenon. The two extracts compare the amount of L1 transfer when speakers are engaged in an exchange first with a partner from a different L1 and, secondly, with a partner from the same L1. In each case, the task is an information exchange. In the first, the Swiss-German speaker is describing a picture which his Japanese interlocutor has to identify from a choice of six. In the second, the Swiss-German speaker is describing a geometric pattern which his Swiss-German interlocutor is endeavouring to draw. In both transcripts, only those words containing non-targetlike sounds are transcribed phonetically.

Extract 1: SG1 (Swiss-German) in different-L1 pair

(J) indicates that the subject's Japanese interlocutor spoke briefly at this point.

1. Okay, it's a four storey house with two large balconies and one small balcon, this the
    wɪv   bælkɒnis ænt   dɪs
2. small balcon is on top – is the highest one (J) Balcon (J) I think it's the right word. And
    ænt
3. in front of the house are is a is a yes it's a road, and on this road is a a lorry. And and
    d̥ə   ɹəʊt   dɪs   ænt
4. in front of the house too there are is a parking a small parking space with let's say
    d̥ə   wɪv
5. one, two, three, four, five, six, seven, eight parked cars and most of the cars are
    kɑːɹs   də
6. covered with snow. And on the left side of the house there are there are four or five
    kəʊwəd   də   deəɹ
7. parked cars. Four are co-five are covered with snow and one is is, a red a red car is
    kəʊvət wɪv
8. not covered with snow. In the back of the hou-of the house you can see, on the right
    kəʊwəd wɪv   d̥ə
9. side of the back of the house is you can see a mountain with er covered with with
    wɪv   kɒvəd   wɪv
10. trees and snow of course. And there are a f-few houses behind this main house I
    ænt   bɪhaɪnt
11. described to you

Extract 2: SG1 in same-L1 pair

(SG2) indicates that the Swiss-German interlocutor spoke briefly at this point

1. All I can see is one square, it's (unintelligible) first with with two dia-dia-diagonals
              ɪs   wɪv wɪv   daɪægɒnæls

2. I guess, this is the word, and now in every every corner of your square is er, is
              wɜːɹt   ɒf   skveəɹ

3. another er, the square is yeah, a small square in every corners of your big square is a
    ænɒdəɹ

4. small one, and the length is about two, two-and-a-half, no three centimetres . . . (SG2).
              də leŋgs   sentɪmitəɹs

5. Yeah. So you have four small squares in the big square. Then you have the er a square
              hæf   skveəɹs   d̪ə   d̪en   d̪ə   skveəɹ

6. with the same size in the middle where the two diagonals diagonals crosses each
    wɪv də   saɪs   də   də   daɪægɒnæls

7. other, you have another square. (SG2) Same size as the other (unintelligible) (SG2)
            hæf   ɒd̪əɹ

8. Yes, you have then (SG2) parallel to the the length of the big square . . . Okay, then you
          hæf   də   leŋgs d̪ə

9. have, if you have drawn this er small one in the middle er the four corners of this
    hæf   dɹəun dɪs   zmɔːl   də   kɔːɹnəɹs dɪs

10. small square er hit the diagonals. (SG2) Then from there you draw a line to the middle
       skveəɹ   daɪægɒnæls   den   deəɹ dɹəu   də

11. of the white, the length of the big square, so it gives you er (SG2) Four (SG2) Yeah,
    ɒf   də leŋgs   də   skveəɹ   gɪfs

12. like arrows . . . They all have the same size . . . should have the same size.
    æɹəus   hæf   saɪs

(Jenkins 2000: 59–60)

In the above two exchanges, the amount of subject SG1's transfer differs both qualitatively and quantitatively. As regards the quantitative analysis, a chi square test was carried out on the types of items which were affected (or not) most frequently by transfer (for example, word-final consonant devoicing in the case of subject SG1). The two conditions (same-L1 and different-L1 pairs) were compared for the number of occurrences of transfer as a proportion of the total number of candidates for transfer. Significance was found at the level $p < 0.01$. In other words, the replacement of transfer with more targetlike sounds in the different-L1 pairs was not due to chance. Qualitatively, we can make a number of observations about the presence and absence of L1 transfer in these exchanges. For example, in Extract 1, the different-L1 dyad, transfer tends not to involve words which may be considered key to meaning (in the sense of being important content as opposed to structural words), and mainly occurs on the definite article, on the preposition 'with', and on 'and'. This is not at all the case in Extract 2, the same-L1 pair, where there are many occurrences of L1 transfer on key items such as 'diagonals', 'square', and 'arrows'.

In addition, many of the instances of transfer in Extract 1 involve only the dental fricatives /θ/ and /ð/, which my field data have consistently demonstrated not to affect intelligibility for NNS listeners. Where other transferred sounds are concerned, especially where these occur on key lexical items, the speaker appears to make a considerable effort to replace the transfers with a more targetlike sound. This is particularly noticeable in his endeavour to pronounce the word 'covered'. He has four attempts at this word, each time approximating target production more closely (see Extract 1, lines 6, 7, 8, and 9). However, he is aware of his problem and of his interlocutor's difficulty in interpreting this word. Because of this, he is careful to repeat the word 'snow' each time – even adding it in line 10 ('and snow of course') after he has attempted to convey its meaning by referring to the trees on the mountainside as well.

In contrast, the two Swiss-German interlocutors were appalled at the extent of their L1 phonological transfer when the recording of their exchange was played back to them. Nevertheless, they pointed out that they had found one another far easier to understand than their respective Japanese interlocutors. In responses to a questionnaire, it also emerged that in the different-L1 pairs, they had consciously been attempting to make adjustments in the direction of more targetlike pronunciation (in other words, to converge phonologically) for the sake of intelligibility for their interlocutors (the 'communicative efficiency' motivation), by replacing L1 transfer with closer approximations to target sounds where they judged this to be necessary. In these exchanges, the adjustments occurred chiefly on consonant sounds, so corroborating the evidence of my field data where consonant sounds proved to be the greatest barrier to phonological intelligibility in ILT.

[. . .]

For EIL, the most interesting implications of this accommodation data are that, given the opportunity to engage in ILT, learners become aware of the features of their own pronunciation systems which are liable to be unintelligible for interlocutors from other L1s, and endeavour to adjust these features. Clearly, they will be unable to do so unless the adjustments concerned are within their phonological and phonetic repertoires. Even then, they may often be able to make these modifications only with considerable difficulty, and be unlikely to do so reliably unless interlocutor intelligibility is crucial or interlocutor non-comprehension has been signalled.

Learners therefore need specific training to enable them to add to their phonological repertoires those features which are most important for intelligible pronunciation in EIL contexts. In addition, they need pedagogic help in order to develop their accommodation skills, so that they become more aware of the importance of making adjustments for specific interlocutors and more able to identify the occasions when this is necessary. In the following section we will consider what these two conclusions mean for classroom pronunciation teaching.

A PROPOSAL FOR EIL PRONUNCIATION TEACHING

The Lingua Franca Core

The empirical evidence above provided the basis for a phonological syllabus for EIL learners: the Lingua Franca Core (LFC). This consists of those phonological and phonetic features which, from an analysis of all the miscommunication and accommodation data (of which the above are a small selection), seem to be crucial as safeguards of mutual intelligibility in ILT. Concentrating on these items is likely to be more effective than attending to every detail in which an NNS's pronunciation differs from that of the (standard) pronunciation of an NS. Additionally, it is also more relevant, since the syllabus no longer attempts to address the comprehension needs of an NS listener when, as we have already noted, in EIL the listener is more likely to be an NNS.

The following is a summary of the main core items:

1. *The consonant inventory with the following provisos:*
- some substitutions of /θ/ and /ð/ are acceptable (because they are intelligible in EIL);
- rhotic 'r' rather than non-rhotic varieties of 'r';
- British English /t/ between vowels in words such as 'latter', 'water' rather than American English flapped [r];
- allophonic variation within phonemes permissible as long as the pronunciation does not overlap onto another phoneme, for example Spanish pronunciation of /v/ as [β] leads in word-initial positions to its being heard as /b/ (so 'vowels' is heard as 'bowels' etc.).

2. *Additional phonetic requirements:*
- aspiration following word-initial voiceless stops /p/ /t/ and /k/ e.g. in [pʰɪn] ('pin') as compared with /spɪn/ ('spin'), otherwise these stops sound like their voiced counterparts /b/ /d/ and /g/;
- shortening of vowel sounds before fortis (voiceless) consonants and maintenance of length before lenis (voiced) consonants, for example the shorter /æ/ in 'sat' as contrasted with the longer /æ/ in 'sad', or the /iː/ in 'seat' as contrasted with that in 'seed'.

3. *Consonant clusters:*
- no omission of sounds in word-initial clusters, e.g. in promise, string;
- omission in middle and final clusters only permissible according to L1 English rules of syllable structure, e.g. 'factsheet' can be pronounced 'facsheet' but not 'fatsheet' or 'facteet';
- /nt/ between vowels as in British English 'winter' pronounced /wɪntər/ rather than American English where, by deletion of /t/, it becomes /wɪnər/;
- addition is acceptable, for example 'product' pronounced [pərˈɒdʌkʊtɔ] was intelligible to NNS interlocutors, whereas omission was not, for example 'product' pronounced /ˈpɒdʌk/.

4. *Vowel sounds:*
- maintenance of contrast between long and short vowels, for example between 'live' and 'leave';
- L2 regional qualities acceptable if they are consistent, except substitutions for the sound /ɜː/ as in 'bird', which regularly cause problems.

5. *Production and placement of tonic (nuclear) stress:*
*   appropriate use of contrastive stress to signal meaning. For example, the difference in meaning in the utterances 'I came by TAXi' and 'I CAME by taxi' in which nuclear stress is shown in upper case. The former is a neutral statement of fact, whereas the latter includes an additional meaning such as 'but I'm going home by bus'.

Non-core features

In effect, what I am claiming is that the items which are excluded from the LFC are not crucial to intelligibility in EIL contexts, and that they can therefore be considered as areas in which L1 transfer indicates not 'error' but (NNS) regional accent. In other words, what we have here is a redefinition of phonological and phonetic error for EIL: one which incorporates the sociolinguistic facts of regional variation instead of regarding any deviation from NS pronunciation as a potentially harmful error (the EFL perspective). It should be acknowledged, nevertheless, that NNS comprehension has not been widely researched in terms of responding to NS and NNS talk, and more research would be crucial for this proposal to gain empirical validity.

In the following seven cases, the eschewing of an NS way of pronouncing in favour of an NNS way (usually influenced by L1 transfer) was not found in my data to cause intelligibility problems for an NNS interlocutor. In addition, as many pronunciation teachers are only too well aware, some of these features seem to be unteachable. That is, however much classroom time is spent on them, learners do not acquire them. It may be that the rules are not sufficiently generalizable (as in the case of pitch movements) or are too complex (as with word stress), or that the item is heavily marked, infrequent in the world's languages and unnatural (as with /θ/ and /ð/). It may even be that (false) NS intuitions have misleadingly led us to believe in the existence of certain aspects of NS pronunciation such as timing and the link between pitch movement and grammar (see above).

Where the problem is one of overcomplexity or lack of generalizability, it may be that the best teachers can do is to draw learners' attention *receptively* to these items to prime learners for future acquisition outside the classroom, should the possibility of extended exposure present itself. A further benefit of presenting these items receptively is that it might be helpful for learners to be aware of these features in terms of both their own comprehension of NSs and their understanding of the differences between their own pronunciation and that of NSs. Having said that, however, it is worth repeating that a lack of these items did not emerge from my data as threatening intelligibility in EIL interaction. So one could argue that in these cases, it is perhaps NSs who need to make receptive adjustments rather than expecting NNSs to alter their production in EIL contexts. The non-core areas are as follows:

1. The consonant sounds /θ/, /ð/, and the allophone [ɫ].
2. Vowel quality, for example the difference between /bʌs/ and /bʊs/ as long as quality is used consistently.
3. Weak forms, that is the use of schwa instead of the full vowel sound in words such as 'to', 'from', 'of', 'was', 'do'; in EIL the full vowel sounds tend to help rather than hinder intelligibility.

4. Other features of connected speech, especially assimilation, for example the assimilation of the sound /d/ at the end of one word to the sound at the beginning of the next, so that /red peɪnt/ ('red paint') becomes /reb peɪnt/.
5. The direction of pitch movements whether to signal attitude or grammatical meaning.
6. The placement of word stress which, in any case, varies considerably across different L1 varieties of English, so that there is a need for receptive flexibility.
7. Stress-timed rhythm.

The development of accommodation skills

Finally, in addition to training in the core items, learners need EIL practice to enable them to develop their accommodation skills in relation to a wide range of different-L1 interlocutor groups, and to be able to respond quickly to phonological-based interlocutor incomprehension by adjusting their pronunciation. Since the majority of NNSs who engage in EIL communication are not of bilingual proficiency (that is, they engage in ILT), we cannot presume that they will produce the core items with 100 per cent accuracy all the time. This is less important, however, than having an item within their repertoire and being able to respond to a specific interlocutor's needs as and when they arise. ILT pair and group work should prove highly beneficial in this regard.

A basic problem for the development of EIL accommodation skills is the fact that the vast majority of English teaching takes place in same-L1 classrooms in the learners' own countries. As Bygate (1988: 76–7) has pointed out, same-L1 group work 'at least allows and at worst encourages fossilization and the use of deviant L2 forms' (though it should be noted that the main thrust of Bygate's article is that, in other respects, same-L1 group work is not necessarily disadvantageous). On the other hand, interlanguage talk practice leads to precisely the opposite scenario, since attempts to converge are more likely to result in replacement of transfer if intelligibility for an interlocutor is potentially threatened; that is, it will result in replacement of transfer in the core phonological and phonetic areas.

In addition, whereas interlanguage talk practice is also helpful at the *receptive* level by providing learners with exposure to a range of EIL accents other than their own, same-L1 practice simply reinforces learners' familiarity with their own accent. However, as things stand for the majority of learners, the only accent they are likely to hear in the classroom other than their own is that of RP- or GA-accented speakers on recorded materials.

The best way forward may therefore be for course materials producers to give some thought to the development of video and audio tapes designed specifically to provide exposure to a range of NNS accents, and for English language teaching institutions to set up video conferencing activities with institutions in other L1 areas. This would seem to be a more realistic approach than to hope for an increase in the availability of mixed-L1 classes around the world. It would also solve a basic contradiction, which is that while mixed-L1 student groups are optimum for the development of accommodation skills, the optimum teacher, as Seidlhofer (1999) argues, is often a bilingual English speaker who shares her students' L1. This teacher will have acquired the core pronunciation features but will also have clear traces of her regional accent.

She thus provides a more pedagogically realistic and sociolinguistically reasonable model for her students.

Despite making sense, these proposals are, none the less, likely to prove controversial. One issue which they will need to address is that of what learners want to learn. While some learners are likely to respond positively to the concept of L2 regional accents, others will no doubt share the view of Andreasson, who argues that 'it would . . . be far from a compliment to tell a Spanish person that his or her variety is Spanish English. It would imply that his or her acquisition of the language left something to be desired' (Andreasson 1994: 402). Similarly, research by Dalton-Puffer *et al.* (e.g. 1997) into Austrian learners' attitudes to pedagogic models has found that RP and GA are preferred to Austrian-English accents. The problem is compounded by the fact that at present there is no academic course entitled 'English as an International Language'. The result is that the common-sense philosophy underpinning the EIL pronunciation proposals, with their addition of an intelligibility dimension to communicative competence (by specifying core and non-core pronunciation features) and their promotion of accommodation skills, remains largely unrepresented and, therefore, uncomprehended. Efforts will need to be made to argue the EIL case more widely and even then, it will be important not to patronize those learners who, having heard the arguments, still wish to work towards the goal of a native speaker accent, by telling them they have no need to do so.

It is nevertheless to be hoped that in the not too distant future English pronunciation research and teaching will come to terms with the changed socio-linguistic environment in which they take place, and will generate more empirical research of the kind described above, instead of relying on intuition, laboratory experiments and corpora of NS speech.

Notes

1   The total database consists of approximately 30 hours of recorded interactions from both classroom groupwork and paired conversations and information exchanges set up outside the classroom; and of field notes of communication breakdowns made over a four-year period in classroom and social settings.
2   Upper case is used to indicate that the word was pronounced with tonic stress.

References

Andreasson, A.-M. (1994) 'Norm as a pedagogical paradigm', *World Englishes* 13 (3): 395–409.
Beebe, L. and Giles, H. (1984) 'Speech-accommodation theories: a discussion in terms of second language acquisition', in H. Giles (ed.) *International Journal of the Sociology of Language. The Dynamics of Speech Accommodation*. Amsterdam: Mouton.
Bygate, M. (1988) 'Units of oral expression and language learning in small group interaction', *Applied Linguistics* 9 (1): 59–82.
Cook, V. (1999) 'Going beyond the native speaker in language teaching', *TESOL Quarterly* 33 (2): 185–209.
Crystal, D. (1995) *The Cambridge Encyclopedia of the English Language*. Cambridge: Cambridge University Press.

Crystal, D. (1997) *English as a Global Language*. Cambridge: Cambridge University Press.

Dalton-Puffer, C., Kaltenboeck, G. and Smit, U. (1997) 'Learner attitudes and L2 pronunciation in Austria', *World Englishes* 16 (1): 115–28.

Duff, P. (1986) 'Another look at interlanguage talk: taking task to task', in R. Day (ed.) *Talking to Learn: Conversation in Second Language Acquisition*. Rowley, MA: Newbury House.

Giles, H. (1973) 'Accent mobility: a model and some data', *Anthropological Linguistics* 15: 87–105.

Graddol, D. (1997) *The Future of English?* The British Council.

Ioup, G. (1984) 'Is there a structural foreign accent? A comparison of syntactic and phonological errors in second language acquisition', *Language Learning* 34 (2): 1–17.

Jenkins, J. (2000) *The Phonology of English as an International Language*. Oxford: Oxford University Press.

Kachru, B.B. (1992) 'Models for non-native Englishes', in B.B. Kachru (ed.) *The Other Tongue: English Across Cultures*. Urbana, IL: University of Illinois Press.

Kachru, B.B. and Nelson, C.L. (1996) 'World Englishes', in S.L. McKay and N.H. Hornberger (eds) *Sociolinguistics and Language Teaching*. Cambridge: Cambridge University Press.

Kasper, G. (1998) 'A bilingual perspective on interlanguage pragmatics', in J.H. O'Mealy and L.E. Lyon (eds) *Language, Linguistics and Leadership. Essays in Honor of Carol M.K. Eastman*. Honolulu, Hawai'i: University of Hawai'i.

Long, M.H. and Porter, P. (1985) 'Group work, interlanguage talk, and second language acquisition', *TESOL Quarterly* 19 (2): 207–28.

McArthur, T. (1998) *The English Languages*. Cambridge: Cambridge University Press.

Pennycook, A. (1999) 'Pedagogical implications of different frameworks for understanding the global spread of English', in C. Gnutzmann (ed.) *Teaching and Learning English as a Global Language*. Tubingen: Stauffenburg Verlag.

Pennycook, A. (2000) 'The social politics and the cultural politics of language classrooms', in J.K. Hall and W.G. Eggington (eds) *The Sociopolitics of English Language Teaching*. Clevedon: Multilingual Matters.

Schwartz, J. (1980) 'The negotiation for meaning: repair in conversations between second language learners of English', in D. Larsen-Freeman (ed.) *Discourse Analysis in Second Language Research*. Rowley, MA: Newbury House.

Seidlhofer, B. (1999) 'Double standards: teacher education in the Expanding Circle', *World Englishes* 18 (2): 233–45.

Seidlhofer, B. (2001) 'Closing a conceptual gap: the case for a description of English as a lingua franca', *International Journal of Applied Linguistics* 11 (2): 133–58.

Trudgill, P. (1998) 'World Englishes: convergence or divergence?' in H. Lindquist, S. Klintberg, M. Levin and M. Estling (eds) *The Major Varieties of English. Papers from MAVEN 97*. Vaxjo: Acta Wexionensia.

Widdowson, H.G. (1994) 'The ownership of English', *TESOL Quarterly* 28 (2): 377–89.

Widdowson, H.G. (1997) 'EIL, ESL, EFL: global issues and local interests', *World Englishes* 16 (1): 135–46.

PART THREE

Applied linguistics in action

Guy Cook and Sarah North

Introduction to Part Three

Part 3 presents ten chapters, each of which engages with a real-world problem that applied linguistics can contribute to understanding and ameliorating. We begin with two case studies which both involve legal aspects, one relating to cross-cultural issues, the other to workplace communication. Jieun Lee investigates the way that evidence from Korean-speaking witnesses is interpreted during courtroom examination. She shows that pragmatic failure may occur when language which is inexplicit in Korean creates ambiguity in English, forcing interpreters to provide their own clarification. Pointing out how this may distort the evidence, Lee argues that interpreters should be able to inform the court of such difficulties. The role of applied linguistics in this case is to draw attention to the problems inherent in a process which the court might otherwise regard as purely mechanical.

Alison Wray and John Staczek also deal with the legal aspects of a failure in communication, this time between speakers of different varieties rather than different languages. At issue was whether the use of the phrase 'coon ass' in a Louisiana workplace constituted racial discrimination. Although the defence provided evidence of a dialect use unrelated to the racially offensive term 'coon', the court upheld the view that lack of intention was no defence. In this extract, the writers show how psycholinguistic factors can make language users blind to possible interpretations of their words, highlighting the need for sensitivity to language varieties in the workplace.

The next two chapters involve not only different areas of application, but also a different research approach that draws on quantitative data. To analyse the discourse of dementia patients, Katinka Dijkstra *et al.* identify particular features relating to conciseness, coherence and cohesion, and compare their frequency for patients with early-, middle-, late-stage dementia. While this part of the research enables a better understanding of the problem, they also go on to suggest how nursing home aides might ameliorate it by increasing use of facilitative techniques in conversation with late-stage dementia patients.

Jane Hurry *et al.* also directly address an area of practice, in this case the teaching of spelling. Their research involved a 'quasi-experiment' in which they provided teachers with a course of morphology and comprehension, and then compared their pupils' spelling scores with those of a control group. The hypothesis was that teaching children about morphemes would improve their spelling, and the results provide support for this claim. As the writers recognise, however, transforming research evidence into teacher practice is not straightforward, and is affected by factors such as policy documentation, teacher motivation, and classroom time.

Continuing the focus on education, the next chapter takes a critical look at needs analysis – a procedure that has been widely used to inform decisions on syllabus design in ESP (English for Specific Purposes). Rebeca Jasso-Aguilar questions the tendency to analyse needs in terms of institutional requirements, rather than what would best serve the interests of the individuals concerned. Her own analysis of the needs of hotel maids in Waikiki involved participant observation (while working as a hotel maid herself), and uncovered discrepancies between institutional and individual needs. Jasso-Aguilar raises questions about 'whose needs?' that reflect an issue for applied linguistics generally – 'whose problems?'.

Applied linguistics has most often focused on the problems associated with English as a foreign language, and the following three chapters explore this area in the light of evidence from corpus studies. The chapter by Scott Thornbury and Diana Slade (from their book *Conversation: From Description to Pedagogy*) illustrates a number of features that occur in naturally occurring conversational data, and suggests a 'core-grammar' as a basis for the developing learners' conversational competence. This 'core-grammar' contains a large amount of formulaic language, and the argument is that such language may provide a better way in to English conversation than a traditional grammar syllabus.

The chapter by Anne O'Keeffe, Michael McCarthy and Ronald Carter (from their book *From Corpus to Classroom: Language Use and Language Teaching*) also reflects the 'lexical turn' in language pedagogy, with greater attention to developing learners' ability to understand and use lexical phrases. This extract focuses in particular on the teaching of idioms, questioning whether materials designed purely on the basis of intuition can provide an accurate reflection of real use. Using corpus evidence to identify the most frequent idioms, the writers suggest that these might provide more appropriate targets for learners of English, and consider the role of language awareness activities to heighten understanding of their use in context.

O'Keeffe *et al.* refer to Prodromou's work on idioms, which provides the next chapter in this Part. This highlights a problem from the perspective of the learner rather than the teacher, arguing that 'as far as idiomaticity is concerned, L1-users are "playing at home", with rules they can bend according to need. L2-users are "playing away", and, if they break the rules, they are penalized'. Together with a plea for greater tolerance of learner creativity, Prodromou also questions native speaker norms as a valid model for English as a lingua franca (paralleling the arguments put forward by Jennifer Jenkins in Part 2 concerning phonological norms).

While creativity has been touched on in earlier chapters, it comes to the fore in the next chapter, where Philip Seargeant examines a literary text using the techniques of stylistics. Stylistics analyses the choices people make in their use of language, and how such choices produce a distinctive manner of expression. As Carter and Simpson put it, 'The general impulse [of stylistics is] ... to draw eclectically on linguistic insights and to use them in the service of what is generally claimed to be a fuller interpretation of language effects than is possible without the benefit of linguistics' (1989: 6). The problem that Seargeant considers is different from those considered so far, as it concerns the choices made by a writer in representing the perception of time in narrative. If literature and literary criticism are regarded as 'real-world' activity, then this sort of analysis may also claim to be concerned with real-world problems, and thus to fall under the heading of applied linguistics.

In the final chapter, Greg Myers addresses the problem of ensuring that public forums open out effective debate as part of democratic procedures. Myers questions the reliability of opinion surveys that assume that language simply needs to transmit opinions clearly, rather than recognising that the interaction may itself help to shape the opinions. However, he regards the role of applied linguists in helping to resolve the problem as mitigated by a number of factors, including the role of other experts, disciplinary biases, different conceptualisations both of the problem and of the nature of language, and the different timescales in academic as opposed to 'real-world' problem solving.

Myers' reflections on the role of applied linguistics provides a suitable conclusion to this volume, drawing together some of the strands that have emerged in the preceding readers, and reminding us to question 'our discipline, our framing of problems, our assumptions about language, the scope and scale of research, our own disciplinary biases, and our relation to wider audiences'.

References

Brazil, D. (1995) *A Grammar of Speech.* Oxford: Oxford University Press.
Carter, R. and Simpson, P. (1989) *Language, Discourse and Literature: An Introductory Reader in Discourse Stylistics.* London: Unwin Hyman.

Chapter 10

Jieun Lee

Interpreting inexplicit language during courtroom examination

Introduction

Court interpreting may be provided at various stages of court proceedings from empanelling the jury to sentencing, but in this chapter the term *court interpreting* is limited to interpreting provided during witness examination in the courtroom of English speaking countries. It is important that the court hears in the target language the oral evidence given in the language other than English rendered as closely as possible, in terms of content as well as register and style, to that provided in the original utterances. It has been argued that in an adversarial court system the speech style of the witness affects the power of testimony, namely its credibility and convincingness (O'Barr 1982). As such, the court interpreter's alterations of the style of original speech in interpreted renditions may have implications for the court proceedings, in particular by influencing the credibility of the witness and the power balance in adversarial courts (Berk-Seligson 2002; Hale 1997a, 2004; Fraser and Freedgood 1999). Nevertheless, discrepancies between the semantic and pragmatic equivalence of original speech by witnesses from culturally and linguistically diverse backgrounds (henceforth, CALD witnesses) and the interpreted rendition is not at all uncommon (see Berk-Seligson 2002; Jacobsen 2003; Hale 1997a, 1997b, 2002, 2004).

An additional complexity arises where CALD witnesses with low socio-economic and educational backgrounds produce non-standard and dialectically variant linguistic features, or include – as any witness can – ambiguous and confused speech in their

Edited from: Jieun Lee 'Interpreting inexplicit language during courtroom examination', in *Applied Linguistics*, 30 (1), Oxford University Press, 2009.

testimony. Such incoherent and ambiguous speech is perceived by court interpreters as the greatest challenge in court interpreting (Hale 2004, 2007), yet this topic has not been the subject of close analysis in the interpreting literature. In particular, there has been no research into how such speech by some CALD witnesses may be perceived as difficult to interpret, and how such difficulties can be dealt with by court interpreters. Focusing on the ambiguity contained in some CALD witnesses' evidence, this chapter will examine firstly why such speech may be challenging for court interpreters, and secondly, what strategies interpreters use to cope with these situations, which may have implications for court proceedings.

Context in court interpreting

Context plays a key role in determining the meaning of utterances (Linell 1997). With limitations of space, it is impossible to discuss the concept of context in detail. Based on Ochs's definition of context (1979: 2–6), suffice it to say here, however, that the key concept of context includes the talk, and the physical setting in which a talk is situated, and the extra-situational context that extends beyond the local talk. The line between text and context may sometimes be blurry. "Interpretation of each utterance depends on information provided by earlier utterances in the sequence and it constitutes information necessary for interpreting later utterances" (Janney 2002: 458). Courtroom examination is illustrative of what conversational analysts label as "the doubly contextual" nature of utterances (Heritage 1984: 242; Drew and Heritage 1992: 18) in that previous utterances influence the following utterances in a series of questions and answers (Ehrlich 2001: 31). This chapter underscores the view that talk-in-interaction during courtroom examination is both context-shaping and context-renewing (e.g. Heritage 1984; Drew and Heritage 1992; Goodwin and Duranti 1992).

As participants in communication events may not share a similar level of knowledge and information, the court interpreter does not have full and equal access to a body of knowledge shared by other participants in the court proceedings. The witness has firsthand experience with the incident or the people involved, and thus may have more information about or access to the particular context. Trial judges and lawyers possess sufficient knowledge about the case through the legal procedures preceding the witness examination. By comparison, the court interpreter's access to the context is limited to the local context unfolding at each turn in court examination.

Furthermore, the prevalent mode of interpreting during the examination of CALD witnesses, referred to as liaison interpreting, adds to the difficulty of accurate interpretation. This mode of interpreting, which can be considered as short consecutive interpreting, is characterised by constant interactions between communicative parties, namely those of the witness and the examining lawyer. Relatively short chunks of information are proffered at every turn, for example, a word, a clause or a few clauses, or a few sentences at most. Provision of piecemeal information at every turn may cause the interpreter to draw on context heavily. However, contextual clues available to the interpreter may be incomplete, that is restricted to local cohesion (Hatim and Mason 1997: 50). Therefore, each utterance tends to be treated as a self-contained, *decontextualised* unit of meaning, and the interpreter relies on the linguistic features of each utterance (e.g. Linell 1997; Hatim and Mason 1997; Wadensjö 1998). This may have the effect of the court interpreter having to draw premature conclusions about the message with limited contextual knowledge. Pure inductive and deductive skills may partially compensate for the lack of contextual knowledge, but the accuracy of the interpreted evidence may nonetheless still be at risk.

Pragmatic ambiguities abound in natural language use (Green 1996: 11), but communication is possible because both the speaker and the hearer are assumed to follow certain communication conventions or maxims, such as Grice's Cooperative Principle (Grice 1975). The speaker produces utterances assuming that the hearer can understand by the same practical reasoning and contextualising operations that they apply to social conduct in general (Schiffrin 1994: 234). The speaker should also make their intended meaning comprehensible to the hearer in order to communicate. Expectation of relevance may guide the hearer to the meaning of the speaker's utterances (Grice 1975; Sperber and Wilson 1986), but the ambiguity of the meaning should be negotiated through communicative interactions (e.g. Brown and Yule 1983; Schiffrin 1994; Gumperz 1999).

Negotiation of meaning through communicative interactions is also true of interpreter-mediated communications (Wadensjö 1998; Mason 2006). Just as spoken discourse requires constant confirmation between the participants to ensure they understand the same thing in the same way due to the inherent ambiguity of spoken language (Scollon and Scollon 2001: 78), clarification or checking may be needed in interpreting other people's utterances in courtroom interactions. However, the constraints on the role and behaviour of the court interpreter imposed by the institution may not encourage such checking or clarification. The restrictive role ascribed to the court interpreter limits the interpreter's freedom to ask the witness for clarification when it is needed. In the solemn atmosphere of the courtroom, frequent requests for clarification might be perceived as indicating the interpreter's incompetence, and as an unnecessary disturbance of the smooth flow of the proceedings, and consequently may act as a threat to the face of the interpreter who wants to maintain professional dignity. The intrusive actions of the interpreter may influence jurors' evaluation of witnesses and lawyers, however, the impact caused by the interpreter's interruption is far less than the one caused by the interpreter's alterations to the pragmatic meaning of witnesses' utterances (Berk-Seligson 2002: 195).

Inexplicit source language

Courtroom discourse is a highly institutionalised discourse, constrained by evidentiary rules (Hunter and Cronin 1995; Maley 2000). Legal discourse, which is often characterised by explicitness and precision, does not tolerate ambiguity or multiple interpretations (Luchjenbroers 1991). Witnesses are required to be explicit in giving evidence (Lakoff 1990: 100, 130). However, lay witnesses, particularly those from CALD backgrounds, may lack understanding of the discourse style expected in court proceedings, and may also lack the skills necessary to communicate adequately in such contexts. Not being aware of the level of explicitness required in the courtroom, where the alleged event and actions are reproduced in words, witnesses may inadvertently produce ambiguous and incoherent speech by not providing enough information.

Perceiving a witness's speech as coherent depends on the provision of adequate contextual information. Coherence is also dependent on the speaker's and the hearer's willingness to negotiate coherence in the same manner as they negotiate meaning in interactions (Bublitz and Lenk 1999: 154). To return to interpreter-mediated courtroom examination, it may be argued that a witness's inexplicit utterances may sound incoherent or ambiguous to the interpreter whose contextual information is limited to the physical setting of the courtroom and the linguistic context created and renewed during examinations.

Inexplicit language generally refers to utterances which require the hearer to rely on context to understand meaning (Cheng and Warren 1999; Warren 2006). In other words, if there is limited access to the context, the use of inexplicit language may result in pragmatic failure (Dines 1980; Cheng and Warren 2003). This chapter focuses on instances of pragmatic failure where the speaker misjudges the extent of the shared knowledge of the hearer, namely the interpreter and make inexplicit utterances. Thus, inexplicitness in the witness's utterance may inevitably require clarification for accurate interpretation. I argue that, although inexplicitness in CALD witnesses' evidence is largely due to their use of an informal discourse style, it may also be due to the linguistic differences of the language used by CALD witnesses in relation to the language of the court. The linguistic features of some languages such as Korean may create extra burdens for interpreters in maintaining appropriate levels of accuracy in interpreting. Given that research in interpreting studies has yet to examine various cross-linguistic issues in spoken language in a variety of language combinations, a study of the discourse of courtroom examination of Korean speaking witnesses will contribute to the literature by shedding light on linguistic issues in inter-lingual communication involving one of the under-researched languages in courtroom settings.

Some features of Korean morphology and syntax may be problematic when interpreting into English. I will briefly discuss three grammatical features of Korean that may be relevant to court interpreting.

Firstly, there is no strict marking of singularity and plurality in Korean. The plural marker attachment is not as obligatory as in English. See example (1) below:

(1) *Pay-ka*   *pakwuni-ey*   *iss-ta.*
     Pear-NOM   basket-LOC   there_is-DECL
     Pear   basket-in   is/exists
     There is a pear in the basket/There are pears in the basket.
     (Note: Nominative case markers – NOM; Locative case markers – LOC; Declarative verb ending – DECL.)

The noun *pay* (pear) can be used without any qualifier. Quality is specified only when it is important information. When quantifiers or numerals appear in sentences, the plural marker is often not used.

Secondly, Korean does not have a single form that indicates definiteness, which is indicated by demonstratives in some cases (Kim 1985: 895; Sohn 1993: 278).

This means that a decontextualised utterance such as (1) does not give the interpreter all the information necessary to meet the grammatical conventions of English, such as indicating the plurality or singularity of the pear and definiteness of the basket.

Thirdly, Korean predicates do not agree in number, person or gender with their subjects, but sentence-ending forms mark varying degrees of deference and politeness (Kim 1985: 895). This means that the verb form in Korean is not an indicator of plurality/singularity, person or gender. Accordingly, in order to ensure an accurate rendition, the interpreter is required to make an appropriate decision based on the context, or to ask for clarification.

Fourthly, Korean makes frequent use of ellipsis. The means of conveying inexplicitness may vary in each language, but ellipsis, substitution, deixis and reference are the main forms whereby inexplicitness is conveyed in both English and Korean. The discussion in this chapter is limited to ellipsis, a feature which is used for the sake of brevity, economy, and informality in communication across all languages (e.g. Carter and McCarthy 1995; Swan 1995; Yang 1996; Nariyama 2004). None-theless its prevalence is more common in Korean, even in written language (e.g. Kim 1989; Yang 1996; Lim 1996; Kim 1998).

Korean is a discourse/situation-oriented language in that contextually understood elements, whether they are subject, object or any other major sentential element, are often left unexpressed (Sohn 1993: 7–8). Person pronouns may be omitted from all syntactic positions (e.g. subject, direct object, indirect object, etc.) whenever they are contextually recoverable (Sohn 1993: 282). Explicit subjects mark emphasis or contrast (Sohn 1993: 282; Yang 1996; Kim and Jung 2006: 97–100). While the subject in subordinate clauses cannot be ellipted in English, both subjects as well as indirect object can be ellipted in Korean (see (2) below).

(2) *Kkok*   *kayahamyen*   *yaykihay- cwul- key.*
     surely/really   go-have to-if   tell/speak-for_one's_benefit-I_will
     surely/really   if Ø have to go   (I)'ll tell Ø
     If (she/he/you/they) have to go, I'll tell (her/him/you/them).

If the hearer does not know who the speaker is going to tell, the inexplicit utterance is ambiguous to the hearer. Without contextual information, inexplicit utterances may sound ambiguous, even incoherent. Given that the case is presented through, and is dependent on, oral evidence in court proceedings, misinterpretation of inexplicit language could have serious consequences.

The study

The aim of this study was to examine the circumstances in which inexplicit language used by CALD witnesses creates a problem of ambiguity of meaning, and how court interpreters handle this issue in court interpreting. The study involved Korean–English interpreting discourse, which has so far not been investigated in the body of court interpreting studies, and, it is hoped, this study may shed a new light on aspects of inexplicitness of witnesses' speech.

The data

Approximately eighty hours of audio recordings of criminal proceedings, provided by the court, form the data for this study. These hearings took place in New South Wales (NSW) local and district courts between 2003 and 2007. The basic information on the data is presented in the table below (see Table 10.1). Case 4 and Case 6 were the only trials where observation in the courtroom was at least partly possible. Five Korean interpreters and fourteen Korean-speaking witnesses were engaged in the proceedings analysed in this study. Some interpreters were engaged in more than one trial. Four of the interpreters involved were interviewed by the author some time after the court proceedings to obtain their feedback about court interpreting in general.

A simplified version of the Jeffersonian transcription system (see Hutchby and Wooffitt 1998: 73–92) has been used for transcribing the court recordings (see transcription conventions in Appendix). For the benefit of non-Korean readers, Korean Romanization according to the Yale system has been used, and an English translation has been provided in italics next to the Korean utterances in a separate column. Adaptation was needed for the presentation of Korean language utterances, however. Because of syntactical differences, such as word order, the exact positioning of pauses and overlaps was not possible in English translations. Accordingly, only the transcripts of original utterances contain such information as pauses and overlaps.[1]

Findings

The inexplicit language of the Korean-speaking witnesses created more problems at the beginning of the proceedings and during the examination-in-chief than in cross-examinations. This is not surprising considering that context is yet to be created through extended questioning and answers. Considering also the cooperative nature of examination-in-chief, inexplicitness in Korean witnesses' utterances may not be regarded as the product of intentional evasiveness. Of the different types of ellipsis, ellipted subjects created the highest level of ambiguity of meaning and consequently posed a challenge for the interpreter who did not have sufficient contextual information to interpret accurately.

Table 10.1 Profile of the data

Case No.	Jurisdiction	Matter	No. of the Korean-speaking witnesses in each case	Interpreter No.
1	Local court	Assault	Two: complainant and defendant	1 & 2
2	Local court	Assault	Three: complainant, witness, and defendant	1 & 2
3	District court	Aggravated robbery	One: victim	1
4	District court	Aggravated robbery	Two: victim and witness	3 & 4
5	District court	Aggravated sexual assault	Four: complainant, accused, two other witnesses	2,4 & 5
6	District court	Influencing the witness	Three: defendants	2 & 3

Four extracts were taken from the court proceedings to highlight the issue of interpreting inexplicit language during witness examination. In the following extracts, the following abbreviations are used: C = Crown Prosecutor; DC = Defence Counsel; J = Judge; I = Interpreter; W = Witness; Ø = Ellipsis. Extract 1 is taken from the Crown witness's evidence-in-chief in Case 4. This witness's husband had been kidnapped, assaulted, and robbed by Kim, the ex-husband of his cousin, as well as by other defendants. This excerpt took place several minutes after the examination started on Day 5 of the trial. The interpreter (Interpreter 4) had not taken part in this trial before. Consequently, this fresh interpreter lacked contextual knowledge of the specific matter before the court. In the discourse preceding this extract, it had been stated that Kim called the witness's husband and suggested a meeting with him. Because of these previous utterances, which provided the context, three pronouns contained in the prosecutor's question (in turn 1) were specific.

Extract 1, Case 4, examination-in-chief

Original utterances	Author's translation of Korean utterances
1 C: (2.4) did he say why he was going to meet him?	
2 I: (0.4) way kulul mannalyeko hantako malul hayssupnikka kuka?	did Ø say why Ø was going to meet him, he?
3 W: (0.4) e ihonhan ttaluy ttaluy osul cenhaycwuntako hayssssupnita.	Ø said Ø pass divorced daughter's, daughter's clothing.
4 I: (.) it was said that (0.9) uh because in order to pass, (0.2) in order to pass the:: clothings of the daughter, (1) from the divorced (.) WIFE,	
5 W: (1.8) uh=	
6 I: =in order to pass clothings (1.5) of the daughter, (1.9) who is from the divorced wife.	
7 C: (0.5) ok. (1) now, did did you know anything about (0.6) the: (1) daughter's clothing? that's the (1.4) before that phone call?	
8 I: (0.7) tangsinun ku cenhwaka oki ceney ku ttaluy, i: ossey kwanhayse, i: alko issnun key issessesssupnikka?	before the phone, did you uh know anything about the daughter's uh clothing?
9 W: (.) tulun ceki ebssupnita.	Ø never heard.
10 I: [never ne-]	
11 W: [Central] Coast-ey salmyense imi ihonul han sangthayeyse, (1) amwukesto cwucil anhasssupnita.	while Ø living on the Central Coast already divorced, Ø did not give anything.
12 I: (0.5) I'd never heard anything. (1) were, they were living in Central Coast, (0.2) were living in Central Coast, (0.7) and (0.8) after the situation of divorce took place, (1) u::h nothing given. (1) excuse me, prosecutor, (1.3) uh the witness has spoke with very few words meagre words. (1) in interpreting, (0.3) this is a the most difficult task how much should I ADD to make the meaning understood by the English speaker, the meaning=	

The prosecutor asked if the witness's husband told her why he was going to meet Kim. The witness's responses contain inexplicitness (in turn 3 and turn 11). In turn 3, the witness was inexplicit in relating to the court the reason her husband gave for meeting Kim. With limited contextual information available to the interpreter at this stage, the ambiguity of meaning resulted from the ellipted subjects for the verb *cenhaycwunta* (pass/give). There was uncertainty about who was saying the statement and also who was giving or receiving the clothes because the witness did not specify the subjects. Multiple interpretations may be possible for this response:

(a) "Kim said he wanted to meet my husband to receive the clothing of a divorced daughter from him".
(b) "Kim said he wanted to meet my husband to give him the clothing of a divorced daughter".
(c) "My husband said he wanted to meet him to receive the clothing of a divorced daughter from him".
(d) "My husband said he wanted to meet him to give him the clothing of a divorced daughter".

Prior to this extract, the witness had given evidence that Kim and his wife had divorced while Kim was in prison. This contextual information may have offered a key to interpret the utterances in question. However, the witness's utterance *ihonhan ttal* (divorced daughter) posed another problem in interpreting the utterance correctly. Since Kim was in the physical setting of the courtroom, the interpreter could tell his age and could see that he was too young to have a divorced daughter, and consequently interpreted "divorced daughter" as referring to Kim's divorced wife's daughter (see turns 4 and 6). This reveals a part of a complex cognitive process of interpreting whereby the interpreter draws on context surrounding the communication settings to determine the meaning. Whether it was an ethically correct decision to convey the intended meaning of misspoken words or unidiomatic expressions is beyond the scope of this chapter. Brief hesitations in the interpreted renditions when the interpreter interpreted inexplicit utterances may be an indication of the interpreter's decision-making process (see pauses marked by numbers in parentheses in turn 6 for example).

The grammatical features of interpreted renditions reveal this interpreter's strategy to cope with inexplicit language. Interpreter 4 chose not to make the ellipted subjects explicit by using a passive voice such as "it was said that" (in turn 4), and did not indicate who was giving or receiving by using the "in order to" clause, which would have sounded like an incomplete and ungrammatical sentence to the English-speaking audience.

A couple of turns later, the prosecutor asked if the witness knew anything about the clothing Kim said he would give to her husband (in turn 7). The witness's response, briefly interrupted by the interpreter, continued in turn 11, but it was inexplicit again with the subjects for three verbs, namely "live", "divorce" and "not give", ellipted. The subject ellipses suggest that each verb would share the same subject. Otherwise, it would be very ambiguous and confusing. Plausibly, the witness may have assumed that the interpreter would have enough knowledge to follow her evidence. However, inexplicit subjects, when access to context beyond the local context was required, made it difficult for the interpreter to render her answer accurately. The interpreter first used a dummy subject "they" as in "they were living" and then omitted the subject when rephrasing it, as in "were living in Central Coast" (in turn 12). The subject "they" which was initially used by the interpreter has a reference that is not known. If Kim had been divorced from his wife, "they" could not have referred to Mr and Mrs Kim, and it was not known where the former Mrs Kim lived at that time. The interpreter also avoided making ellipted subjects explicit by using the passive voice in "nothing given" (in turn 12).

It is noteworthy that the interpreter immediately informed the prosecutor of the interpreting issue after completing the interpretation (in the sixth line of turn 12). The interpreter may have been concerned about the comprehensibility of the interpreted renditions containing ungrammatical utterances. In the discourse that follows Extract 1, which is not presented here, as the interpreter tried to explain the intended meaning of the inexplicit language, the judge interrupted, encouraging the interpreter to "just translate" what was said. The judge also assured the interpreter by saying that the court followed the evidence because they had been listening to other witnesses' evidence for the past few days. According to the judge, the courtroom audience, who had more knowledge about the extra-situational context surrounding the alleged offence, had little trouble in understanding the interpreted evidence despite the grammatical inadequacy of some translations.

Most of the interpreters interviewed were reluctant to interrupt the proceedings for clarification, and their coping strategies varied. Interpreter 4 was the only interpreter who disclosed difficulties with interpreting during courtroom examination. Interviews with interpreters revealed that they were aware that inexplicit language, particularly ellipted subjects, was problematic in court interpreting, and that they often used the passive voice to avoid specifying subjects ellipted in the original utterances of witnesses. Given that grammatical choices represent a particular perspective on events (Duranti 1994), the interpreters' dependence on the use of passive voice may unnecessarily give an impression that the witness seeks to obscure the agent or diminish their responsibility.

Extract 2 is also taken from the examination-in-chief of a Crown witness, but this time from Case 3. Interpreter 1 had interpreted for this witness for the second consecutive day in this trial. The witness was a victim of the crime committed by Ben Kim and others. The prosecutor asked how his relationship with Ben Kim's father had been strained. According to the witness's evidence leading up to this point, Ben's father and the witness were acquainted with each other and had introduced Ben and Mary to each other. Mary was going out with Ben, and also worked for Ben's father. She was living at this witness's home at the time, but she did not come home until very late on the night being discussed in the extract. She called him very late saying that she was at a karaoke bar. Ben Kim's father was also at the bar with Mary, and he asked the witness to come and join them in the early hours of the morning.

Extract 2, Case 3, examination-in-chief

	Original utterances	Author's translation of Korean utterances
1	W: kulayse (0.4) cenun e ppalli thayksi thaywese ponyatala kuleko cenhwalul kkunhesssupnita.	*and Ø asked Ø to send Ø home by taxi, and Ø hung up phone.*
2	I: (0.3) so I asked him, put Mary in a cab quickly, and make he–(1) uh make her come ho:me, (0.5) and I just hung up.	
3	W: (3) kulikon tto cenhwaka wasssupnita,	*and there was phone call again*
4	I: (0.2) but I had a call again,	
5	W: tto naolako haysssupni°ta°.	*Ø said again come out*
6	I: (0.6) uh (2) requesting me to come out and meet him=	
7	W: =cenun mosnakantako hako,=r	*I said Ø couldn't go out,*
8	J: =can you just repeat that?	
9	I: uh I had a call from HIM again,	
10	J: yeah=	
11	I: =req-requesting me, to come and meet, (0.3) with him.	
12	DC (2.7) can I ask him who he is your honour.	
13	I: kuka nwuka nwukwunyakuyo=	*who-who is he?*
14	W: =Be-Ben Kim °apeci°	*Be-Ben Kim's father*
15	I: Ben Kim's father.	
16	W: (2) kulayse e mosnakanta kulehko,	*so Ø said Ø can't go out*
17	I: so I told him I can't.	
18	W: elma hwuey iltan icey thayksi thako cipulo ONtako, (0.4) cenhwaka tasi wasssupnita.	*a while later there was phone call again saying that Ø coming home by taxi*
19	I: (0.2) I had a call uh little bit later that, (0.6) she was coming home. (0.8) so, nwuka ontakoyo?	*who's coming?*
20	W: (0.8) Ben Kimbako Maryhako	*Ben Kim and Mary*
21	I: it was Ben Kim's father and Mary were coming home.	
22	L: (1.5) and to your place	*to your home*
23	I: (1) ponin cipuloyo?	*yes*
24	W: yey	

This witness's utterances at every turn contained ellipted subjects. Nevertheless, when the preceding utterances provided the context for the interpreter to understand the ellipted subjects and objects, it did not hinder interpreting the witness's utterances in turns 1, 3, 5, 16. The interpreted renditions indicate that the interpreter made all the ellipted subjects explicit to produce grammatically adequate renditions in English (see turns 2, 4, 6, 17).

This extract shows that judges as well as lawyers, both examining lawyers and other lawyers, do clarify the meaning during examination. When the witness resumed giving evidence, the judge asked for repetition of the previous interpreted evidence (in turn 8). Immediately after the interpreter finished rendering the witness's utterances, one of the defence lawyers asked for clarification of the "him" which was contained in the interpreted rendition (in turns 11 and 12). The lawyers representing each defendant were interested in finding out exactly who did what and how it was done because such information was crucial for determining the evidence and consequently for the outcome of the case.

It is noteworthy that a few turns later, in turn 18, the witness's inexplicit language caused a problem in interpreting since there was more than one interpretation as to who was coming home. There was a possibility that Ben Kim's father, who was allegedly drunk and had insisted that the witness come out at that hour, might have invited himself to the witness's home. Since there is no subject-verb agreement in Korean, it was impossible to determine whether Mary was coming by herself or whether she had company. The interpreter asked the witness directly who was coming home (in turn 19) without asking for the court's permission to clarify this. The witness responded that it was Ben Kim and Mary that were coming home at the time. It is not known whether it was the witness's slip of the tongue and whether the interpreter intentionally altered the interpreted rendition. The interpreted rendition (in turn 21) shows that the interpreter translated "Ben Kim" into "Ben Kim's father". In fact, Ben Kim had not been mentioned earlier in his testimony or later.

Whenever clarification was needed due to ellipted subjects creating a difficulty in interpreting, Interpreter 1 did not ask for the court's permission to seek clarification, and did not disclose to the court what the minor conversation was about or why such a clarification was needed. As a consequence, the court had no knowledge of the difficulty faced by the interpreter; and the court might have formed a suspicion that something underhand had transpired (Popovic 1991: 46).

Extract 3 is from another case (Case 4) in which Interpreter 3 had to interpret inexplicit utterances. The Crown witness in this case gave evidence at two separate trials on the same matter involving different co-defendants, and is thus the same witness as the one appearing in Extract 2. Up to this point in the examination, the court had heard from the Crown witness that he was assaulted, robbed and detained in a residential unit. However, it was not revealed at this stage of the examination that the victim had travelled with his kidnappers until the police found him. Therefore, it can be said that a new context was being created when new information was sought by the prosecutor, who asked whether the defendants mentioned where he was going (in turn 1).

The witness simply responded that Ben Kim talked about going to the Central Coast (in turn 3) without specifying *who* was going to the Central Coast. Although the prosecutor's question implied that the witness was going somewhere, the ellipted subject in the witness's utterance may have been perceived as ambiguous by the interpreter. It may be due to the interpreter's tendency to treat each utterance as a decontextualised utterance. The interpreter used a dummy subject, "someone", in the interpreted rendition (in turn 4) in place of the ellipted subject. A brief pause before the interpreter uttered "someone" may be an indication of extended processing or momentary hesitation by the interpreter. Hesitations were common when

Extract 3, Case 4, examination-in-chief

		Original utterances	Author's translations of Korean utterances
1	C:	and did anybody say where you were going?	
2	I:	(0.7) nwukwulato mwe tangsinul (0.2) etilo teyliko kantatenci mwe eti kantanunci yaykihaysseyo?	*did anybody say where to take you or going anywhere?*
3	W:	(0.7) kulen yaykinun ah (1.3) °uh° (1.9) Ben Kimi Central Coastlul ku kaya toentako kulen yaykilhaysseyo.	*such talk uh Ben Kim said Ø had to go to Central Coast.*
4	I:	(0.5) Ben Kim said (1.9) someone is going to Central Coast.	
5	C:	(1.2) to the Central Coast?	
6	I:	(0.2) Central Coastlo nwuka kantayyo?	*who's going to Central Coast?*
7	W:	icey ku Central Coast ccokulo (1) icey kal kelako incey kulehkey yaykilul,	*Ø said Ø (be) going toward Central Coast Ø said so*
8	I:	(0.3) Ben Kim said (1) they were going towards Central Coast.	
9	C:	(1.2) did he say why=	
10	I:	=way=	*why*
11	C:	=you be going to the Central Coast?	

interpreting inexplicit language of Korean witnesses which were ambiguous or polysemous.

The prosecutor did not seek to clarify who was referred to as "someone" in the interpreted rendition (see turn 5). To the prosecutor, this information was already known and contained in her question. The prosecutor simply checked whether it was the Central Coast. However, the interpreted rendition of the prosecutor's checking question points to the interpreter's curiosity. While the prosecutor asked "to the Central Coast" to confirm the place of destination, the interpreter asked who was going to the Central Coast, which was an attempt to clarify the inexplicit subject (see turns 5 and 6). Despite such an attempt, the witness, perhaps not aware of the interpreter's problem, merely responded that Ben Kim talked about going to the Central Coast, thus not answering the interpreter's question. As a consequence, the interpreter used another dummy subject, "they", in the interpreted rendition in place of the ellipted subject (in turn 8). However, the prosecutor ignored these inexplicit references and asked only about the reason behind the trip to the Central Coast (in turns 9 and 11). It may be because the prosecutor thought the subject was already explicit in her questions (see turns 1 and 11). Other participants, such as the defence lawyer and the judge, did not seek clarification either, perhaps because this information was obvious to them or insignificant.

Interpreter 3 covertly sought clarification from the witness without informing the court of the recurring interpreting problem deriving from inexplicit utterances. Extract 3 shows that Interpreter 3 produced grammatically adequate renditions adding subjects arbitrarily. Such restraint from disclosing the perceived difficulty in interpreting resulted in somewhat inconsistent evidence (e.g. the use of "someone" and "they" in turns 4 and 8). [. . .] In an interview, Interpreter 3 stated that subjectless sentences were one of the challenges of court interpreting, but she said that she tended to draw out the intended meaning from the context if possible, and refrain from interrupting the proceedings unless it was a matter of significance.

The results of this study indicate that ambiguity deriving from inexplicit language, particularly ellipted subjects, poses a challenge for the accurate interpretation of evidence when ellipted subjects are not recoverable from the context, particularly when there is a possibility that more than one person is involved. In addition, when references are related to the extra-situational context about which the interpreter lacks knowledge, there is an increased risk of misinterpretation. The findings reveal that court interpreters generally do not reproduce the ambiguity of the meaning deriving from inexplicit utterances. They omit or modify the witnesses' utterances to make them comprehensible and grammatically adequate, based on their judgement of the intended meaning, which may not only be unethical but may also result in misinterpretation of the original meaning. Such modifications corroborate other studies into Spanish–English court interpreting which indicate that interpreters tend to raise the register by rendering more coherent and comprehensible interpretations than the original (e.g. Berk-Seligson 2002: 142–5; Hale 1997a: 204–5; 1997b: 52; 2004: 156–7).

Interpreters' nondisclosure in addition to unwillingness to self-correct or admit errors may be considered as unprofessional conduct and may even be thought to be a matter of contaminating the evidence. When the interpreter misjudges the gravity of misinterpretation of inexplicit language, it may have significant legal implications. This study indicates that the court cannot be aware of the challenges faced by court interpreters in inter-lingual communication unless interpreters inform the court of inexplicit utterances and their need for clarification. If this clarification does not occur, the court will not be alerted to any potential inaccuracy in the interpreted renditions caused by the inexplicit utterances of CALD witnesses.

Notwithstanding this, interpreters' attempts to draw the attention of the court to the ambiguity of the precise meaning of witnesses' utterances and to request clarification have not always been welcome in the court (Morris 1995). Considering that there has been little discussion to date on when court interpreters' intervention or mediation is justified and when it is not – because it is often perceived as something other than interpreting – it is understandable why most of the court interpreters tended to provide comprehensible renditions rather than interrupting the proceedings and reproducing inexplicitness in interpreted renditions. As long as the court assumes that interpreting is a mechanical process, interpreters may have to make hard decisions as to how to deal with inexplicit utterances. This may result in their overstepping the boundaries of their prescribed role of faithfully rendering original utterances into the language of the court.

Conclusion

Drawing data from the discourse of Korean–English interpreting in Australian court examinations, this chapter has examined ambiguities contained in the inexplicit language used by Korean speaking witnesses and the ways interpreters deal with this issue in the court. This chapter has demonstrated that cross-linguistic differences tied with grammatical conventions as well as context-specific discursive practice conventions add to the challenge of interpreting Korean witnesses' utterances into English.

Ambiguity of witnesses' inexplicit utterances was more evident in examination-in-chief than in cross-examination in this study. Given that key information related to the offence is presented before the court during examination-in-chief and evidence given in examination-in-chief through the interpreter remains in the official court records, misinterpreted evidence, which may seem trivial, may take on greater significance in adversarial court proceedings.

The data analysed in this chapter were limited to criminal court proceedings, but the findings may equally apply to civil proceedings. These findings, based on Korean interpreting in Australian courts, may not be generalised to all CALD witnesses and all community languages used in the courtroom. However, given that Asian languages such as Chinese and Japanese display similar grammatical features of subject ellipsis to Korean (e.g. Oh 2006, 2007; Lee and Yonezawa 2008), the cross-linguistic issues examined in this chapter may also cause a problem related to the accuracy of interpreted evidence in court cases involving such languages that may not require explicit subjects in as strict manner as English. This theme needs further research, but clearly has potentially significant implications for the courts, whose duty it is to seek to obtain evidence as accurately as possible.

This chapter infers from the study that court interpreters should not be held responsible for making sense of ambiguous utterances. Instead, it is recommended that they disclose any interpreting issues which derive from cross-linguistic differences, namely the use of inexplicit language, to the court or, if this proves to be too difficult or inappropriate, they should reproduce the inexplicitness in interpreted renditions so that the court may direct the witness to be more explicit. Interpreters should make every effort to avoid altering oral evidence.

Considering the significance of potential implications of alterations and modification of original utterances in adversarial courtrooms, legal professionals as well as court interpreters need to appreciate that clarification may be necessary for the sake of achieving interpreting accuracy. The court should be informed that seeking or providing clarification is not necessarily a matter of displaying some deficiency in the interpreter's language ability or interpreting skills. The objective should be to create an environment where the interpreters feel encouraged to alert the court to interpreting issues without the fear of putting their competence in doubt. Only when interpreters feel free to disclose such issues related to the integrity of evidence, unafraid of losing face, will the court be able to hear the evidence accurately, as it wishes and as it is required.

Appendix

Transcription conventions

[]   overlapping talk
=   latching utterances
:   elongated vowel sounds. The more, the slower the enunciation is (e.g. :::).
CAPITALS emphasis
,   continuing intonation
.   a stopping fall in tone. It does not necessarily indicate the end of a sentence.
?   rising intonation
( )   The number in brackets indicates a time gap in seconds.
( )   Empty parenthesis indicates the presence of an unclear fragment.
(( )) Non-verbal activity
° °   soft voice

Notes

1   All the names that might be indicative of identities have been changed to protect the
       privacy of the people involved. I tried to provide a literal translation, even if it looks
       ungrammatical, to indicate the absence of grammatical equivalents. Alternative
       translation is also provided when there is ambiguity of meaning.

References

Berk-Seligson, S. (2002) *The Bilingual Courtroom: Court Interpreters in the Judicial Process*
       (2nd edn). Chicago, IL: University of Chicago Press.
Brown, P. and Yule, G. (1983) *Discourse Analysis*. Cambridge: Cambridge University Press.
Bublitz, W. and Lenk, U. (1999) 'Disturbed coherence: "Fill me in"', in W. Bublitz,
       U. Lenk and E. Ventola (eds) *Coherence in Spoken and Written Discourse*. Amsterdam/
       Philadelphia, PA: John Benjamins.
Carter, R. and McCarthy, M. (1995) 'Grammar and the spoken language', *Applied Linguistics*
       16 (2): 141–58.
Cheng, W. and Warren, M. (1999) 'Inexplicitness: what is it and should we be teaching
       it?' *Applied Linguistics* 20 (3): 293–315.
Cheng, W. and Warren, M. (2003) 'Indirectness, inexplicitness and vagueness made clearer',
       Pragmatics 13 (3): 381–400.
Dines, R.R. (1980) 'Variation in discourse – "and stuff like that"', *Language in Society*
       9: 13–31.
Drew, P. and Heritage, J. (1992) 'Analysing talk at work: an introduction', in P. Drew
       and J. Heritage (eds) *Talk at Work: Interaction in Institutional Settings*. Cambridge/New
       York: Cambridge University Press.
Duranti, A. (1994) *From Grammar to Politics: Linguistic Anthropology in a Western Samoan Village*.
       Berkeley, CA: University of California Press.
Ehrlich, S. (2001) *Representing Rape: Language and Sexual Consent*. London and New York:
       Routledge.
Fraser, B. and Freedgood, L. (1999) 'Interpreter alterations to pragmatic features in trial
       testimony'. Paper presented at the annual Meeting of American Association for Applied
       Linguistics (6–9 March 1999).

Goodwin, C. and Duranti, A. (1992) 'Rethinking context: an introduction', in A. Duranti and C. Goodwin (eds) *Rethinking Context: Language as an Interactive Phenomenon*. Cambridge: Cambridge University Press.

Green, G.M. (1996) *Pragmatics and Natural Language Understanding* (2nd edn). Mahwah, NJ: Lawrence Erlbaum Associates.

Grice, H.P. (1975) 'Logic and conversation', in P. Cole and J. Morgan (eds) *Syntax and Semantics, Vol. 3: Speech Acts*. New York: Academic Press.

Gumperz, J.J. (1999) 'On interactional sociolinguistic method', in S. Sarangi and C. Roberts (eds) *Talk, Work and Institutional Order: Discourse in Medical, Mediation and Management Settings*. Berlin: De Gruyter.

Hale, S. (1997a) 'Clash of world perspectives: the discursive practices of the law, the witness and the interpreter', *Forensic Linguistics* 4 (2): 197–209.

Hale, S. (1997b) 'The treatment of register variation in court interpreting', *The Translator* 3 (1): 39–54.

Hale, S. (2002) 'How faithfully do court interpreters render the style of non-English speaking witnesses' testimonies? A data-based study of Spanish-English bilingual proceedings', *Discourse Studies* 4 (1): 25–47.

Hale, S. (2004) *The Discourse of Court Interpreting*. Amsterdam/Philadelphia, PA: John Benjamins.

Hale, S.B. (2007) *Community Interpreting*. Basingstoke: Palgrave Macmillan.

Hatim, B. and Mason, I. (1997) *The Translator as Communicator*. London/New York: Routledge, 36–60.

Heritage, J. (1984) *Garfinkel and Ethomethodology*. Oxford: Basil Blackwell.

Hunter, J. and Cronin, K. (1995) *Evidence, Advocacy and Ethical Practice: A Criminal Trial Commentary*. Sydney/Adelaide/Brisbane/Canberra/Melbourne/Perth: Butterworths.

Hutchby, I. and Wooffitt, R. (1998) *Conversation Analysis*. Cambridge: Polity, 73–92.

Jacobsen, B. (2003) 'Pragmatics in court interpreting: additions', in L. Brunette, G. Bastin, I. Hemlin and H. Clarke (eds) *Critical Link 3: Interpreters in the community*. New York/Amsterdam: John Benjamins.

Janney, R.W. (2002) 'Context as context: vague answers in court', *Language & Communication* 22: 457–75.

Kim, E.I. and Jung, Y.C. (2006) 'Subject ellipsis and ambiguity condition', *Eoneokwahakyeonku* 37: 93–112.

Kim, J.N. (1998) 'A retrospection on the phenomena of ellipsis in Korean: ellipted subjects in embedded clauses', *Kukeohak* 32: 201–15.

Kim, N.I. (1985) 'Korean', in B. Comrie (ed.) *The World's Major Languages*. London/Sydney: Croom Helm.

Kim, S.R. (1989) 'The phenomena of ellipsis in Korean and its types', *Keonkuk University Nonmunjib* 29 (2): 53–70.

Lakoff, R.T. (1990) *Talking Power: The Politics of Language in our Lives*. New York: Basic Books.

Lee, D. and Yonezawa, Y. (2008) 'The role of the overt expression of first and second person subject in Japanese', *Journal of Pragmatics* 40: 733–67.

Lim, G.H. (1996) 'A study of Korean ellipsis phenomenon', *Eomunhak* 57: 281–319.

Linell, P. (1997) 'Interpreting as miscommunication', in Y. Gambier, D. Gile and C. Taylor (eds) *Conference Interpreting: Current Trends in Research*. Amsterdam/Philadelphia, PA: John Benjamins.

Luchjenbroers, J. (1991) 'Discourse dynamics in the courtroom', La Trobe Papers in Linguistics 4. Retrieved from www.latrobe.edu.au/linguistics/LaTrobePapersin Linguistics/Vol%2004/O6Luchjenbroers.pdf on 15 November 2007.

Maley, Y. (2000) 'The case of the long-nosed potoroo: the framing and construction of expert witness testimony', in S. Sarangi and M. Coulthard (eds) *Discourse and Social Life*. Harlow/New York: Longman.

Mason, I. (2006) 'On mutual accessibility of contextual assumptions in dialogue interpreting', *Journal of Pragmatics* 38 (3): 359–73.

Morris, R. (1995) 'The moral dilemmas of court interpreting', *The Translator* 1 (1): 25–46.

Nariyama, S. (2004) 'Subject ellipsis in English', *Journal of Pragmatics* 36 (2): 237–64.

O'Barr, W.M. (1982) *Linguistic Evidence: Language, Power, and Strategy in the Courtroom*. New York: Academic Press.

Ochs, E. (1979) 'Introduction: what child language can contribute to pragmatics', in E. Ochs and B. Bambi (eds) *Developmental Pragmatics*. New York: Academic Press.

Oh, S.Y. (2006) 'English zero anaphora as an interactional resource', *Research on Language and Social Interaction* 38 (3): 267–302.

Oh, S.Y. (2007) 'Overt reference to speaker and recipient in Korean', *Discourse Studies* 9 (4): 462–92.

Popovic, J. (1991) 'The magistrates' court', in G. Bird (ed.) *Law in a Multicultural Australia*. Melbourne: National Centre for Cross-Cultural Studies in Law.

Schiffrin, D. (1994) *Approaches to Discourse*. Singapore: Blackwell.

Scollon, R. and Scollon, S.W. (2001) *Intercultural Communication* (2nd edn). Oxford: Blackwell.

Sohn, M.H. (1993) *Korean*. London/New York: Longman.

Sperber, D. and Wilson, D. (1986) *Relevance: Communication and Cognition*. Oxford: Basil Blackwell.

Swan, M. (1995) *Practical English Usage* (2nd edn). Oxford: Oxford University Press.

Wadensjö, C. (1998) *Interpreting as Interaction*. London/New York: Longman.

Warren, M. (2006) *Features of Naturalness in Conversation*. Amsterdam/Philadelphia, PA: John Benjamins.

Yang, M.H. (1996) 'Ellipsis in Korean', *Kukeokukmunhak* 117: 125–57.

Chapter 11

Alison Wray and John J. Staczek

One word or two?

Psycholinguistic and sociolinguistic interpretations of meaning in a civil court case[1]

What weighting should be given, in a court case, to psycholinguistic explanations of an alleged offence? We review the case of an African American plaintiff who claimed that her receipt at work of a framed document with the title 'Temporary *Coon Ass* Certificate' from a white male supervisory-level employee in the same agency constituted racial discrimination in the workplace. Dialect research conducted by JJS, as expert witness for the prosecution, demonstrated that the dialectal use of *coon ass* to refer to Cajuns (white settlers of French descent) was restricted to the states of Louisiana and south-eastern Texas. It was argued by the prosecution to be unreasonable to expect someone from another part of the USA to know the meaning of the word. The jury found in favour of the plaintiff. The prosecution case rested upon the premise that when a word is unknown, it will be interpreted by breaking it down into smaller units, in this case *coon* and *ass*, both derogatory terms, the former strongly racist. We explore the psycholinguistic rationale for this assumption, and its converse, that when a word is well known to an individual, (s)he may fail to see how it is constructed.

Psycholinguistic considerations

Wray (2002) begins her book *Formulaic Language and the Lexicon* with the following anecdote:

Extracts from: Wray, A. and Staczek, J.J. 'One word or two? Psycholinguistic and sociolinguistic interpretations of meaning in a civil court case', in *Speech, Language and the Law*, 12 (1): 1–18, Equinox, 2005.

In a series of advertisements on British TV early in 1993 by the breakfast cereal manufacturer Kellogg, people were asked what they thought Rice Krispies were made of, and expressed surprise at discovering the answer was rice. Somehow they had internalized this household brand name without ever analyzing it into its component parts.

(p. 3)

Why should this happen? She proposes that: 'overlooking the internal composition of names is a far more common phenomenon than we might at first think . . . [and] it is actually very useful that we can choose the level at which we stop breaking down a chunk of language into its constituent parts' (pp. 3–4). In the course of her book, Wray draws on an extensive critical examination of the research literature to demonstrate that the internal composition of phrases and polymorphemic words is, indeed, often overlooked, and also develops a psychological model of how we learn and store lexical material, that accounts for why it comes about (see later).

In the trial, the expert witness for the defence was asked whether he viewed *coon ass* (or the more usual *coonass*) as a single word or two words. In reply, he compared it to the word *firefly*: '*firefly* is not *fire* or *fly*; it's a *firefly*. It's an expression used together' (trial transcript: direct examination of the expert witness for the defence, 22 August 1997, p. 14). In the case of *firefly* there is, of course, a clear hint as to why it gained its name; that it relates to its component parts. However, internally complex words and multi-word strings often have an apparent etymology that is misleading, with subcomponents that do not represent what they seem to. Thus, the *ladybird* or *ladybug* is so-called not because it is female or resembles a lady, but because it was traditionally a creature of 'Our Lady', the Virgin Mary (compare the German *Marienkäfer*, 'Mary's beetle'). A *penknife* is not a knife that is the size or shape of a writing implement, but a knife originally designed for sharpening quills (*pen* = 'feather').

What of *coonass*, then? If we set aside the single proposal, discussed earlier, that the term takes the form it does because it first referred to black Cajuns, and if we follow instead the more reliable etymology from French, then *coonass* is no more made up, historically, of *coon* and *ass* than *carpet* is made up of *car* and *pet* or *browsing* is made up of *brow* and *sing*. Any association with African Americans is after the event, and imposed by outsiders.

But does that make the externally imposed, albeit historically false, interpretation any less real to those who make it? More appositely here, does the 'innocent' etymology of a word or phrase excuse insensitivity on the part of its contemporary users? In order to assess this issue, we need to return to Wray's proposal that words and phrases are not always broken down into their smallest components. She identifies several interrelating reasons why that might occur. One is well exemplified above: in many cases an apparently polymorphemic word does not, in fact, break down in components that help one work out the meaning. The same applies to phrases, from the clearly irregular *by and large* through to many multi-word expressions whose internal oddity we could easily overlook (e.g. *perfect stranger*; *broad daylight*; *in order to*). In these instances, there will be no benefit in examining the word or phrase too closely. However, that cannot be the root of the issue, for how would the user *know* that the word or phrase was partly or entirely non-compositional, unless by attempting to do that analysis?

Wray's explanation is that when we encounter new words and phrases, we only break them down to the point where we can attribute a reliable and useful meaning, and then we stop. She terms this strategy *needs-only analysis* (Wray 2002: 130–2). Needs-only analysis suggests that people who have been raised in Louisiana or south-east Texas will, having encountered the term *coon ass* and having accepted without question that it refers to a Cajun, have had no reason to engage in further analysis of it. This could go some way to explaining how the sender of the *coon ass* certificate apparently failed to anticipate the possibility of a misunderstanding. Furthermore, it could account for why the expert witness for the defence felt that he did not need to look the phrase up 'because I know what it means'; why he described the racial interpretations as 'not standard meanings' (trial transcript, cross-examination of the expert witness for the defence, 22 August 1997, p. 44); and why, in response to the prosecution's question, 'You realize, don't you, that the term *coon ass* used in the District of Columbia addressed to Blacks would be an explosive term, fighting words, right?', he could say, 'I don't know. I don't know. I mean, I honestly don't know' (ibid., p. 60).

In contrast, someone who is not familiar with the word has an additional 'need', and will therefore engage with more analysis by breaking down the incomprehensible whole into comprehensible parts, naturally using the word-break as the morphological boundary. The result is two words with independent meanings, *coon* and *ass*, the relationship between which then has to be established. English requires a pragmatic approach to the interpretation of juxtaposed nouns (and some other pairs). A range of grammatical or semantic relationships is possible, and largely unpredictable: a *hand stand* is a means of bodily inversion, not an object designed for resting the hand; a *pastry case* is a pie base made out of pastry, not a carrying receptacle for pastry; and a *foot pump* is a pump activated by the foot, not a device for inflating it.

Apparent paradigms are not always helpful. A *smartass* might be 'an ass [< donkey] that is smart' or 'a person with an ass [< arse] that is smart'. But a *coonass* fits neither interpretation easily, since *coon* is not easy to construe as an adjective. *Shitface*, apparently similar to *coonass* in representing a derogatory qualification to a body part, offers a similarly limited parallel: it makes little sense to speak of an *ass* that is covered in, or reminiscent of, *coon*.

In fact, it may be pointless to seek to assign exact meanings to these defamatory terms. Perhaps all they need to do is raise in the mind of the beholder the sense that there is some sort of semantic juxtaposition between the components, without specifying what it is. If so, then the decoding that is required by a person encountering *coon ass* for the first time is minimal: no more than the recognition that there are two components, both derogatory. It may be quite unnecessary to develop any sense of whether, in combination, they mean 'an ass who is also a coon', 'a coon who is also an ass', 'an ass with the colour or status of a coon', 'a coon with the status of an ass', 'a person with a coon's ass', or whatever. English permits all these possibilities, but appears ambivalent about which is the best match.

In this light, it may be significant to note the plaintiff's account of her first sight of the certificate:

Q: Now, let me direct your particular attention to June 14, 1995. Do you recall that day?
A: . . . When the meeting began, I pulled out my center desk drawer to get a pad upon which to write, and there was a large frame that was on top blocking the pad that I usually keep in my center desk drawer. When I pulled it out, the first thing I saw was 'coon.' I didn't see 'temporary.' I didn't see 'ass.' All I could see was 'coon.' . . . I was shocked. I was outraged. The frame took me back to when the schools in West Virginia were integrated.

   . . .

Q: What did the term 'coon ass' mean to you?
A: To me, it's a pejorative term. Coon is a pejorative term that's used to refer to Negroes, blacks, African Americans, what have you . . .

(trial transcript: direct examination of the plaintiff
by plaintiff's attorney, 20 August 1997, pp. 36, 38)

In her account of this first sight of the certificate, the plaintiff does not refer to *ass* at all. Her interpretation of *coon ass* was, it seems, entirely driven by her sighting of the word *coon*.

What of the sender? Although he may never have needed to break down *coon ass* into its components to derive meaning, nevertheless, he would presumably only need to have once caught sight of the word *coon* on its own on the certificate to have noticed, and quite differently computed, its meaning as a separate item. Yet he appeared never to have made the connection between *coon* and *coon ass*:

Q: You're familiar with the term 'coon,' aren't you?
A: Yes, sir, I am.
Q: You understand that that has a racially-derogatory meaning?
A: Yes, sir, I do.
Q: And you have known that for some time, haven't you?
A: Yes, sir, I have.
Q: And you knew that the term 'coon' has a racially-derogative meaning to African Americans at the time that you prepared the certificate that's been marked as Plaintiff's Exhibit Number 1, isn't that true?
A: That's correct.

(trial transcript: cross-examination of defence witness
by plaintiff's attorney, 21 August 1997, p. 40)

His claim is particularly striking in view of the fact that an African American colleague (PW) of the plaintiff did attend the site visit:

Q: And you met her and showed her around the site?
A: Yes, I did.
Q: And you gave [PW] a 'Coon Ass Certificate' that looks just like this except it has [PW]'s name.
A: That's correct, sir.

Q: And you later found out that Miss [PW] had objected to that certificate as well, isn't that correct?

A: That's correct, sir. And as soon as she objected to that, just like [the plaintiff] objected to her certificate, an immediate apology was sent to both of them.

Q: Did the thought occur to you in May of 1995, when you handed Ms. [PW] a 'Coon Ass Certificate' with her name on it, issuing the certificate to her, that she might consider it racially offensive?

A: No, sir, I did not.

> (trial transcript: cross-examination of defence witness
> by plaintiff's attorney, 21 August 1997, p. 42)

In short, the sender claimed that even having seen that PW was African American, it still did not occur to him to associate the term *coon ass* with the term *coon*. This makes most sense from the perspective of *needs-only analysis*, and would be a case of 'constituent blindness' brought about by the strong and consistent association of a specific meaning with *coon ass* as a holistic item. More accurately, it would be 'pseudo-constituent blindness', since *coon* and *ass* are not, historically or actually for the dialect speakers, constituents of the whole. For such individuals to see *coon* and *ass* in *coon ass* is – the word break notwithstanding – comparable to a standard English speaker noticing *sea* and *son* in *season*.

Conclusion

So, what does a word mean? Clearly, no man is an island where language is concerned, and we would be unwise to follow Humpty Dumpty in claiming that 'when I use a word it means just what I choose it to mean – neither more nor less' (Carroll 1871/1970: 269). We operate within, and across, speech communities, and whatever we may intend by a word, we must be constantly aware of how it is, or could be, received by others. Nevertheless, we may, for good psycholinguistic reasons, be blind to the internal construction of a word or phrase in our own variety, while that same internal construction is all too plain to those unfamiliar with the item. If such blindness is the default, and awareness of other possible interpretations is essentially serendipitous, or else a product of imagination or a fascination for etymology (false or real), is it reasonable to expect that a word with strong local cultural associations will always, and necessarily, be viewed as potentially ambiguous even though, within its own realm of application, it is not?

The judge and jury are put into a difficult situation in such cases, assuming that they take both parties to have made an innocent interpretation of the disputed term. The judge, in his summing up, stated:

> [T]o determine . . . whether the Temporary Coon Ass Certificate was racially offensive, you should consider [the sender's] intent to discriminate or not to discriminate against blacks, the subjective effect of the forwarding of the certificate on [the plaintiff], and the impact it would have had on any reasonable person in [the plaintiff's] position.
>
> (trial transcript: summary of the judge, 25 August 1997, p. 19)

The judge allows for the possibility that while the sender's intent was non-discriminatory, the impact on the plaintiff was nevertheless one of deliberate discrimination. Achieving a ruling therefore entailed deciding which of the two was more justified in their blindness to the other's perception. For linguistic awareness cuts both ways: the sender might have been expected to have an awareness of non-dialect users' interpretations of *coon ass*, but, similarly, the recipient might have been expected to spot, from the various indicators, that she was reading an unfamiliar dialect term.

This linguistic awareness, we have argued, may rest on more than the words themselves. The plaintiff's initial sight of the certificate, when the word *coon* was all she saw, may have blinded her to the possibility that *coon ass* meant something other than *coon* + *ass*. Meanwhile, the sender did not deny familiarity with the word *coon* and its racist meaning, only any awareness that *coon ass* might be construed by a person who did not know the term, as containing the word *coon*. We propose that her constituent awareness, and his constituent blindness, are entirely natural consequences of our approach to linguistic processing.

Just how a court should handle such psycholinguistic considerations is another matter. They could clearly have some bearing on the issue of intent, but it could still be argued that however explicable the oversight might be in psycholinguistic terms, it is part of the educational level required of a manager or supervisor that he or she will be language-aware in relation to differences between linguistic varieties used, and encountered, in the workplace. At the very least, the outcome of this case, as also, by implication, the *nignog* incidents in the UK, suggests that individuals in a socially responsible position are expected to appreciate the singularity of their own dialect or slang forms to a sufficient extent that they will refrain from using them with people likely to be unfamiliar with – or to misconstrue – their meaning.

Note

1   This chapter is taken from the second half of the article, which focuses on psycho-linguistic factors.

References

Carroll, L. (1871/1970) 'Through the looking glass', in M. Gardner (ed.) *The Annotated Alice* (rev edn). Harmondsworth: Penguin.

Wray, A. (2002) *Formulaic Language and the Lexicon*. Cambridge: Cambridge University Press.

Chapter 12

Katinka Dijkstra, Michelle Bourgeois, Geoffrey Petrie, Lou Burgio and Rebecca Allen-Burge

My recaller is on vacation

Discourse analysis of nursing-home residents with dementia

Memory problems that are caused by dementia can be reflected in conversations in different ways. A woman with dementia, for instance, can comment about her memory loss, speak in an incoherent manner, or do both. A clear example of this is the following statement made by a dementia patient when talking to her caretaker: "My recaller is on vacation. Maybe you can help me find it." The choice of the metaphor suggests an awareness of a temporary loss of memory and reflects the inability of the patient to convey the message in a coherent and concise manner.

In this example, the speaker was aware of her memory loss. It is doubtful, however, that she was aware of deficits in the coherence of her discourse and if this awareness lasts through advanced stages of impairment. An analysis of discourse characteristics in conversations of dementia patients could lead to a better understanding of how cognitive impairment affects discourse in different stages of impairment even if the patients are unaware of their discourse deficits and memory loss.

The study we discuss here examines discourse characteristics of people in the early, middle, and late stages of dementia at different levels, either throughout the discourse (discourse level) or at the level of different units or segments of discourse (utterance level). Our focus is on three basic discourse components—conciseness, coherence, and cohesion—and how they occur in discourse of people in different stages of dementia.

Edited extracts from: Dijkstra, K., Bourgeois, M., Petrie, G., Burgio, L. and Allen-Burge, R. 'My recaller is on vacation: discourse analysis of nursing-home residents with dementia', in *Discourse Processes*, 33 (1), Taylor and Francis, 2002.

Cohesion in discourse is the result of linguistic elements forming structural or semantic relations between discourse components (Ripich and Terrell 1988). In linguistic and discourse studies, *cohesion* refers to the surface indicators of relations within and between sentences (De Santi *et al.* 1994; Halliday and Hasan 1976; Liles and Coelho 1998). These indicators can be pronominal references (*referential cohesion*), verb tense (*temporal cohesion*), or other linguistic elements such as conjunctions (*causal cohesion*; Liles and Coelho, 1998). Cohesion is disrupted when references, verb tense, and conjunctions are used incorrectly by the speaker. This may result in discourse errors at the sentence level and may negatively affect the logical flow of the sentences.

Coherence in discourse is the result of appropriate topic maintenance in discourse (Albrecht and O'Brien 1995; Hakala and O'Brien 1995; Laine *et al.* 1998; McNamara and Kintsch 1996; Ulatowska and Chapman 1991). Coherence reflects a mechanism in discourse that cannot be reduced to linguistic code but involves discourse components at a cognitive level as well. *Coherence* can be defined locally as an indication of how closely an utterance (sentence) is related in topic and content to the immediately preceding utterance, or globally as an indication of how closely an utterance is related to the general topic initiated by the conversation partner (Laine *et al.* 1998). Global and local coherence presumably are represented differently in a person's discourse, with local coherence incorporating new information with immediately preceding information at the utterance level and global coherence representing thematically higher order structures of discourse (Hakala and O'Brien 1995; McNamara and Kintsch 1996).

Conciseness is a third building block for discourse. Without information to add to the topic of conversation, a conversation partner will be reluctant to continue the conversation. Moreover, verbosity may reflect cognitive disorganization of the speaker and tire the conversation partner (Ripich and Terrell 1988). *Conciseness* is therefore both an indicator of the informativeness and relevance of discourse (Hier *et al.* 1985; Tomoeda and Bayles 1993).

To illustrate how the basic components for discourse—cohesion, local and global coherence, and conciseness—may appear in discourse of people with dementia, an excerpt from a middle-stage dementia patient is listed and explained in Table 12.1.

The excerpt illustrates correct local (utterance-to-utterance) coherence throughout the segment, and (thematic) global coherence towards the end. The excerpt is concise, with all but one utterance contributing new information (information units) to the conversation. Temporal cohesion, referential cohesion, and causal cohesion are present for all but two utterances (Utterance 3 and 7) in which the referent lacks an antecedent. With the basic components of discourse intact, this part of the conversation shows few deficits, except for the incorrect referential cohesion and the revision in Utterance 2.

Coherence, cohesion, conciseness, and other discourse characteristics of people with dementia have been studied extensively. These studies mostly compared discourse of people with dementia to discourse of healthy older adults (De Santi *et al.* 1994; Laine *et al.* 1998; Tomoeda *et al.* 1996; Ulatowska and Chapman 1991). Findings showed that throughout the discourse, patients with Alzheimer's disease (AD) changed topics more abruptly in conversations and had more difficulty relating new topics to old topics compared to healthy controls (Garcia and Joanette 1997).

Table 12.1 Example of discourse components in conversation of a middle-stage dementia patient

Conversation Sample	Discourse Components
1. The place was called *Sacre Coeur de Marie*	IU, L, T
2. In Ru, in Fra . . ., in Belgium	IU, L, Rev
3. And so they put me there to stay	IU, L, C, Ra, T
4. Where in the meantime I was a little wild, you know.	IU, L, C, T
5. I got into fights.	IU, L, T
6. Yeah.	L
7. But everyone still more or less liked me because I had a sense of humor.	IU, L, C, Ra, T
8. So there I stayed till I was almost 17 years old.	IU, G, C, T

Note. IU = information unit; L = local coherence; T = temporal cohesion; Rev = revision; C = causal cohesion; Ra = referent without antecedent cohesion; G = global coherence.
Coherence (local = L, global = G)
Cohesion (temporal = T, referential = R, causal = C, referent without antecedent = Ra)

They had difficulty elaborating on topic information appropriately because of their failures to maintain the topic of conversation (Mentis *et al.* 1995).

Additionally, AD patients manifested problems in keeping processed information activated from utterance to utterance. This was reflected in less-cohesive discourse of AD patients compared to that of healthy controls (Ripich and Terrell 1988) and a higher frequency of empty and indefinite words (i.e. words that have no meaning or nonspecific words; e.g. *stuff* and *thing*) and aborted phrases compared to healthy controls in a picture description task (Hier *et al.* 1985).

What was relevant for our study was that specific discourse characteristics seem to occur in specific stages of dementia, whereas other discourse characteristics are mostly present in AD discourse but not related to different stages of impairment. Aborted phrases, for instance, occurred predominantly in AD discourse but were as prevalent in early- as in late-stage dementia (Hier *et al.* 1985; Tomoeda *et al.* 1996). Indefinite terms occurred mostly in the discourse of middle-stage dementia patients (Bayles 1985), whereas revisions and empty speech were found to occur most in discourse of late-stage dementia patients (Tomoeda *et al.* 1996). Other studies related increases in discourse deficits to increased dementia severity, such as decreases in conciseness and cohesion with advanced impairment (Hier *et al.* 1985; Kempler 1991; Tomoeda *et al.* 1996; Ulatowska *et al.* 1988).

The benefit of discourse analyses that relate the occurrence of discourse characteristics to stages of impairment is a better understanding of when cognitive abilities in a dementia population start to decline to the extent that they become apparent in discourse. This will then provide deeper insight in the impact specific memory processes such as working memory capacity have on discourse components.

[. . .]

There are several cognitive mechanisms that might explain why cognitive impairments are reflected in discourse. More limited cognitive resources appear to hinder continued activation of processed information from utterance to utterance and throughout a conversation. This presumably has a negative impact on the coherence, cohesion, and conciseness of a conversation, preventing the dementia patient from keeping track of a conversation topic, continuing to add information, or keeping track of antecedents of referents during the conversation. Deficits in semantic memory might hinder the production of informative and cohesive discourse on an utterance level when specific words can not be retrieved or words can not be put together in meaningful sentences, resulting in indefinite words and empty speech.

It can be hypothesized that the deficits discussed previously will become more apparent with the progression of dementia, resulting in predominantly empty, indefinite, noncohesive, nonconcise, and incoherent discourse at the late stages of impairment. The severity of these deficits could be related to the demands placed on working memory resources and semantic memory that may or may not exceed the available resources available to the patient in a certain stage of dementia. We can assume that discourse level characteristics, such as global coherence, conciseness, and elaborations on the topic of conversation, require more cognitive resources than utterance level discourse characteristics, such as local coherence and cohesion. Discourse level characteristics require activation of conversation topics throughout the conversation, whereas utterance level characteristics require activation of information that is relevant from utterance to utterance. Therefore, discourse level characteristics such as global coherence are expected to be more affected in earlier stages of impairment than characteristics at the utterance level, such as cohesion, which are expected to be affected in late-stage dementia but relatively preserved in earlier stages.

Apart from available cognitive resources and access to semantic information, communication strategies of an unimpaired conversation partner could affect discourse of dementia patients. This conversation partner may be able to compensate for some of the memory deficits of dementia patients by providing cues or repeating information that help the patients to remember relevant information, or keep information activated long enough to formulate a coherent response.

Several studies have supported the assumption that communication partners can help people with dementia to communicate more effectively (Bayles *et al.* 1987; Lamar *et al.* 1994). For instance, an adequate communication strategy such as turn taking was supported among AD patients by their conversation partner who increased response time, repeated information, and alerted AD patients when it was time to answer (Lamar *et al.* 1994). Another study showed that young adults adopted a modified form of "elderspeak" when addressing older listeners who pretended to have cognitive impairments. Their speech was shorter, more informative, and repetitious when talking to impaired listeners than when talking to unimpaired listeners. In particular, repetitions and grammatical simplifications were found to benefit comprehension of adults with AD (Kemper *et al.* 1998). When unimpaired communication partners talked to patients with AD, these partners assumed a greater burden to repair breakdowns in the conversation (Watson *et al.* 1999).

It is likely that conversation partners in nursing homes, such as nursing aides, take on a similar role to repair breakdowns in their conversation with nursing-home residents with dementia. They may facilitate the conversation with a cognitively impaired person either by initiating a topic of conversation, encouraging the person to speak, or repeating previous information to keep the person on track and providing

Table 12.2 Conversation sample illustrating facilitative strategies

Conversation Sample	Facilitative Strategies
A: Where did you go today?	
R: We haven't left the place.	
A: You haven't left the place today?	Repetition
R: I don't think so.	
A: You didn't go to the Capitol today?	Cue
That big, old building, that big old white building	Cue, Cue
You didn't go there?	Repetition
R: I don't think so.	
A: You don't think so?	Repetition
Did you get on a bus today?	Cue
R: Huh?	
A: Did you get on a bus today?	Repetition
R: Yes.	
A: You got on a bus?	Repetition
R: And that's where we went.	
A: Yes, to the Capitol.	Cue
R: Umm hmm.	
This is my problem. My recaller is on vacation. (. .)	
Maybe you can help me find it.	

Note. A = nursing aide; R = resident.

cues. For instance, if a resident has trouble keeping track of the immediately preceding utterance, the nursing aide may repeat that utterance or paraphrase the utterance to keep the resident focused. The nursing aide may also encourage the resident to continue talking by making positive and encouraging statements, such as "that's good" or "go on." Similarly, if the resident does not remember a particular event, a nursing aide may provide specific information that can help the resident remember that event.

To illustrate how memory problems occur during conversations and how an attentive conversation partner can help to solve these problems, a segment of a transcript is presented in Table 12.2. In the conversation, a middle-stage dementia resident had trouble remembering that she had gone to the capitol building by bus that morning. Only when the nursing aide cues her about the specifics of the trip did the resident remember that she actually went there.

We can expect conversational partners to be more facilitative in conversations with people in later stages of dementia than in conversations with people in earlier stages because the latter generally do not manifest memory difficulties that often. Conversational partners can accomplish facilitative communication through repetitions, encouragements, and cues, as well as extra turns in the conversations to keep the patient with dementia focused on the conversation.

It is beyond the scope of this study to assess specific contributions of working memory and semantic memory deficits on discourse. Therefore, we test general research questions rather than specific hypotheses regarding discourse characteristics in conversations between people with dementia and their conversation partners:

1. Do people in different stages of dementia display differences in discourse and utterance level characteristics in conversations?
2. Are deficits in discourse level characteristics more apparent in earlier stages of the disease compared to discourse characteristics at the utterance level?
3. Are deficits in utterance level characteristics more apparent in late-stage dementia compared to earlier stages of the disease?
4. Are nursing aides, as conversation partners of dementia patients, more facilitative—through cues, encouragements, turns, and repetitions—in conversations with middle- and late-stage dementia residents than with early-stage patients?

Method

Participants

Residents. Sixty patients with dementia residing at seven nursing homes in the Tallahassee, Florida area participated. Residents who had a primary or secondary diagnosis of dementia (mostly probable AD) from their primary care physician, the staff physician of the nursing home, or the neurologist of the local hospital were asked for written consent. Residents had to be at least fifty-five years of age and have retained some expressive and receptive language abilities (Bourgeois 1993). All residents were screened for vision and hearing impairments.

    Nursing aides. Thirty-three nursing aides who were assigned to the selected residents participated as a conversation partner; thirty nursing aides were African American, two were White, and one was Asian. Twenty-nine nursing aides were women. Their average age was thirty-six years (*SD* = 7.2); their average educational attainment was fourteen years (*SD* = 0.89), with a range between eleven and fifteen years of education. Nursing aides had conversations with one to five assigned residents.

Procedure

Conversational samples. Videotaped conversations between the sixty nursing-home residents with dementia and their nursing aides were transcribed verbatim for discourse analysis purposes. An equal number of conversations with early-, middle-, and late-stage dementia residents (twenty each) were selected for analysis.

    The conversations were five-minute, interview-style conversations (timed with a countdown timer) between a resident and his or her nursing aide, during which the aide was instructed to prompt the resident to talk about his or her family, life, and day. The nursing aide was instructed not to ask other questions than those three and only to provide prompts, such as "tell me more," if the resident stopped talking. These instructions were given verbally while the nursing aide was walking with a member of the research team to the location of the interview and repeated just before the beginning of the interview. Additionally, the three questions were listed on a piece of paper that the nursing aide kept with him or her during the interview. This ensured that the initiating component of nursing aides' discourse (three questions and prompts to urge residents to keep talking) was constant across the sample.

Facilitating strategies, however, were not prompted by the research team and reflect spontaneous facilitation by the nursing aide.

Despite differences between nursing aides and residents in their sociodemographic background (ethnic background, educational background), no apparent communication problems arose between the two communication partners during the conversations. All of the nursing aides knew the residents prior to the interview, which should have reduced potential communication problems by the time of the conversation. Most of the nursing aides were aware of the residents' condition of dementia, although they did not exactly know what stage of dementia they were in at the moment of conversation.

Transcripts were segmented following conventional sentence boundaries and information contour. Sentence fragments, such as incomplete sentences, revisions of a previous utterance, and additions to the previous utterance following a pause were considered as separate utterances. Lexical fillers such as *well* and *let's see* were transcribed as separate utterances if they occurred at the beginning or end of another utterance. If they occurred within an utterance, they were transcribed as being part of that utterance.

The transcripts were analyzed according to discourse level (Table 12.3) and utterance level (Table 12.4) analysis schema for residents and a discourse analysis schema for nursing aides (Table 12.5).

Table 12.3 Discourse level analysis schema for resident discourse

Categories and References	Examples	Frequency
1. Number of words (Kemper *et al.* 1998; Shadden 1998; Tomoeda *et al.* 1996)	Well I was born	
2. Number of unique words (Hier *et al.* 1985)	Well I was born	
3. Number of information units relevant, truthful, nonredundant utterances (Bayles *et al.* 1987; Shadden 1998)	I went to school in uh New Jersey.	1
4. Conciseness: Information units-words (Hier *et al.* 1985; Tomoeda and Bayles 1993; Tomoeda *et al.* 1996)	I was born in 1916.	1/5
5. Elaborations, number of elaborations on the topic of conversation (Shadden 1998)	No, I went to grade school first of course And then high school	1
6. Disruptive topic shift, abrupt shift of topic (Garcia and Joanette 1997; Mentis *et al.* 1995)	And they're both with the Lord. You are a good-looking woman.	1
7. Topic maintenance: Number of elaborations on the topics divided by the number of disruptive topic shifts (Coelho 1994)	It is a very nice place. Have you met this lady?	1/1
8. Global coherence: Number of utterances that represent the topic of conversation (Korolija 2000; Laine *et al.* 1998)	Well I was born and raised in Ohio.	1

Table 12.4 Utterance level discourse analysis schema for resident discourse

Categories and References	Examples	Frequency
1. Incorrect pronominal referencing (Shadden 1998; Ulatowska and Chapman 1991)	And I was not always it, any idea?	1
2. Aborted phrases, incomplete phrases not revised within two succeeding sentences (Tomoeda *et al.* 1996)	Well I am supposed to have.	1
3. Empty phrases: Utterances with little or no content (Ulatowska *et al.* 1988)	First and then and that and that was all	1
4. Repetitions: Near and complete repetitions (Bayles *et al.* 1987; Hier *et al.* 1985; Shadden 1998)	Just, just, just books.	2
5. Indefinite terms: Nonspecific words (Ulatowska *et al.* 1988)		
6. Revisions: Incomplete phrases that were restated in a complete form within two succeeding sentences (Shadden 1998; Tomoeda *et al.* 1996)	And uh, so I come out to lunch at, oh approximately eleven, no not eleven, but uh, ten.	1
7. Local coherence: Number of utterances that are semantically connected to the preceding sentence (Laine *et al.* 1998)	Yeah, can you tell me about your day? Well, uh, I start getting ready to get up around seven or something	1
8. Cohesion: Number of utterances that include:		
a. Temporal: Correct verb tense	No, I don't think so.	1
b. Referential: Correct pronominal reference	My mother was a baroness when she married my father.	1
c. Simple causal: Simple conjunctions	Well, I just hung along with some village children.	1
d. Complex causal cohesion: Complex conjunctions (De Santi *et al.* 1994; Ulatowska and Chapman 1991)	So there I stayed till I was almost 17 years old.	1

Table 12.5 Discourse analysis schema for nursing aide discourse

Categories and References	Examples
1. No. of utterances (Kemper *et al.* 1998; Ripich *at al.* 1991)	"Tell me more."
2. Total no. of questions	"Anything else you can tell me about?"
3. Total no. of prompts	"Tell me about your day."
4. Facilitators:	
Repetitions: Repeating utterance	R: She works all the time. A: She works all the time.
Encouragements: Keep conversation going	R: I had a [unintelligible] on my shoulder. A: Ok, That's good.
Cues: Provide missing information	R: And uh, and uh, and with a . . . A: Keyboard. R: Yeah.

Note. R = resident; A = nursing aide.

'Discourse level categories included characteristics that could be assessed throughout the discourse, such as words and unique words, or reflect coherence or information building elements throughout the discourse, such as global coherence, topic maintenance, and conciseness. Utterance level categories included characteristics that could be assessed at an utterance level, such as empty phrases and indefinite terms, or reflect cohesion or coherence building elements from an utterance-to-utterance level, such as referential or causal cohesion, or local coherence.

Additionally, discourse of the nursing aide was analyzed for its facilitating, questioning, or prompting nature. To our knowledge, no such schema exists yet. Facilitators were divided into repetitions, encouragements, or cues based on their potential to enhance the dementia patient's ability to talk and be more coherent, cohesive, and concise in their conversation.

To illustrate the application of the discourse schema, three excerpts of conversations are listed in the Appendix to this chapter with the coding categories.

Results and discussion

Resident discourse

Table 12.6 displays the data for the discourse level variables. As shown in Table 12.6, early-stage dementia residents had higher occurrences of discourse level characteristics than late-stage dementia residents, except for the category disruptive topic shifts that occurred significantly more in the conversations of late-stage dementia patients. This supports our assumption that early-stage dementia residents are better able to keep information from the conversation activated throughout the conversation and to integrate this information with topic information than late-stage dementia residents.

Table 12.6 Means and standard deviations and F values of discourse level categories for residents

Discourse Categories	Early Stage		Middle Stage		Late Stage		Group	F
	M	SD	M	SD	M	SD		
1. Words	641.2	155.7	542.6	164.0	456.0	160.8	E > L	6.68**
2. Unique words	243.9	57.6	196.2	43.4	187.7	63.9	E > M, L	5.94**
3. Information units	43.6	14.0	41.3	16.1	20.1	13.6	E, M > L	15.74***
4. Conciseness	82.9	12.2	74.1	16.8	56.3	24.4	E, M > L	10.64***
5. Elaborations	12.0	7.2	7.5	5.5	7.1	4.5	E > M, L	4.31*
6. Disruptive shifts	5.1	2.5	5.7	2.4	13.5	8.4	L > E, M	15.94***
7. Topic maintenance	2.5	1.5	1.6	1.4	0.8	0.8	E > L	8.60**
8. Global coherence	21.0	23.1	5.6	4.4	6.3	5.5	E > M, L	7.80**

Note. E = early stage; M = middle stage; L = late stage.
* *p* < .05. ***p* < .01. ****p* < .001.

Specifically, in their conversations, compared to late-stage dementia residents, early-stage residents used (a) more words; (b) more unique words; (c) more information units; (d) had more concise discourse; (e) used more elaborations per topic; (f) had higher topic maintenance; and (g) had higher global coherence. Early-stage dementia residents also used more unique words, elaborations on topic, and had higher global coherence than middle-stage dementia residents. Middle-stage dementia residents used more information units, were more concise, and had fewer disruptive shifts in their conversations than late-stage dementia residents.

The results indicate that, apart from the profound differences between early- and late-stage residents in discourse, there are differences between early- and middle-stage dementia discourse and middle- and late-stage dementia discourse as well. Global coherence, elaborations on topic, and unique words apparently put such high demands on cognitive resources that people in the middle stages of dementia are not as able to use these discourse components in a conversation compared to early-stage dementia residents. Being informative and concise, however, are relatively preserved abilities for middle-stage dementia residents, whereas they are compromised at the late stage of dementia.

Table 12.7 shows the data for utterance level discourse categories. Occurrence for utterance level categories was higher in conversations of early-stage dementia residents than late-stage dementia residents, except for empty speech and indefinite words that were more prevalent among late-stage dementia residents. The assumption that early-stage dementia residents are better able to keep information activated during the conversation, on an utterance-by-utterance basis, than late-stage dementia residents seems to be supported.

Table 12.7 Means and standard deviations of utterance level discourse categories for residents

Discourse Categories	Early Stage		Middle Stage		Late Stage		Groups	F
	M	SD	M	SD	M	SD		
1. Incorrect referents	4.7	2.0	3.8	2.2	8.3	5.9	L > E, M	7.79**
2. Aborted phrases	4.9	2.3	1.8	2.6	1.5	1.5	–	2.48
3. Empty phrases	2.6	1.1	2.1	3.1	5.4	10.2	L > E, M	3.56*
4. Repetitions	3.4	2.8	5.9	6.6	16.5	27.4	L > E	3.41*
5. Indefinite words	4.6	3.6	7.2	5.5	14.8	10.0	L > E, M	11.54***
6. Revisions	5.3	3.3	2.0	3.8	0.6	1.8	–	0.30
7. Local coherence	66.2	28.9	68.0	16.9	45.6	18.0	E, M > L	6.42**
8. Cohesion								
a. Temporal	71.6	17.7	61.4	18.2	50.6	20.0	E > L	6.34**
b. Referential	23.8	12.5	25.9	21.3	13.5	8.5	M > L	3.93*
c. Simple causal	27.9	11.1	21.2	11.0	17.8	13.7	E > L	3.68*
d. Complex causal	14.3	10.2	9.8	8.8	4.8	6.1	E > L	6.33**

Note. E = early stage; M = middle stage; L = late stage.
*$p<.05$. **$p<.01$. ***$p<.001$.

Specifically, higher occurrences of discourse characteristics in conversations of late-stage dementia residents were found for (a) incorrect referents; (b) empty phrases; (c) repetitions; and (d) indefinite words. No significant differences in occurrence across the stages of dementia were found for aborted phrases and revisions. Early-stage dementia residents showed (a) higher local coherence; (b) higher temporal cohesion; (c) higher causal cohesion, than late-stage dementia residents in their conversations. Middle-stage dementia residents showed fewer incorrect referents, empty phrases, indefinite words, higher local coherence, and higher referential cohesion in their conversations than late-stage dementia patients. This supports the assumption that abilities needed to establish local coherence and cohesion are relatively preserved among middle-stage dementia residents.

The aforementioned results indicate distinct differences in discourse between residents across stages of dementia. Table 12.8 presents a summary of the results with a profile of discourse characteristics per stage. Only discourse characteristics that showed a statistically higher or lower occurrence are included. The table illustrates that for discourse level characteristics—in particular, the ones that put high demands on cognitive resources such as global coherence and topic elaborations—middle-stage dementia residents are more similar to late-stage dementia residents and different from early-stage dementia residents. The occurrence of utterance level characteristics in conversations, however, shows more similarities between early- and middle-stage dementia residents than late-stage dementia

Table 12.8 Discourse profiles for residents in early-, middle-, and late-stage dementia

Level	Early	Middle	Late
Discourse			
1. Words	■		□
2. Unique words	■	□	□
3. Information units	■	■	□
4. Conciseness	■	■	□
5. Elaborations	■	□	□
6. Disruptive topic shifts	□	□	■
7. Topic maintenance	■		□
8. Global coherence	■	□	□
Utterance			
1. Incorrect pronominal referents	□	□	■
3. Empty phrases	□	□	■
4. Repetitions	□		■
6. Indefinite words	□	□	■
7. Local coherence	■	■	□
8. Cohesion			□
a. Temporal	■		□
b. Referential		■	□
c. Simple causal	■		□
d. Complex causal	■		□

Note. ■ = significantly higher occurrence; □ = significantly lower occurrence.

residents, especially characteristics that concern local coherence and cohesion. Apparently, coherence, cohesion, and conciseness are discourse components that closely relate to the cognitive abilities and access to semantic memory of the speaker.

To summarize, the answer to the first research question, "Do people in different stages of dementia display differences in discourse at utterance level characteristics in conversations?" is "Yes." Specific discourse patterns in different stages of dementia can be distinguished. At the discourse level, conversation of middle- and late-stage dementia residents is less unique, elaborate, and globally coherent than that of early-stage residents. Moreover late-stage dementia residents are less informative, concise, and topic oriented and more disruptive in their conversations than other residents. At the utterance level, conversations of late-stage dementia residents are more repetitive, empty, indefinite, and less cohesive and locally coherent than conversations of early-stage dementia residents.

The second research question can be answered as well: "Are deficits in discourse level characteristics more apparent in earlier stages of the disease compared to discourse characteristics at the utterance level?" Some discourse level conversation characteristics, such as global coherence, elaborations on topic, and unique words only occurred more in early-stage dementia discourse. Other characteristics, however, such as information units and conciseness were equally present in early- and middle-stage dementia discourse. These last two characteristics may be relatively preserved in early to middle stages of cognitive decline.

The question whether deficits in utterance level characteristics are more apparent in late-stage dementia discourse compared to early-stage dementia discourse can be confirmed too. Most utterance level discourse deficits, such as incorrect referents, empty speech characteristics, and indefinite words, as well as lower occurrences for local coherence and cohesion were found mostly in conversations of late-stage dementia residents. Local coherence and cohesion seem to be relatively preserved in early and middle stages of impairment.

We focus on nursing aide discourse characteristics in their conversation with dementia patients to answer the fourth research question: "Are nursing aides more facilitative through cues, encouragements, turn taking, and repetitions in conversations with middle- and late-stage dementia residents than with early-stage residents?"

Nursing aide discourse

As shown in Table 12.9, nursing aides were not more facilitative when talking to middle- and late-stage dementia residents, as expected, but instead used more facilitative techniques when talking to early-stage dementia residents. Specifically, aides used fewer questions; more facilitators; and more encouragements, in conversations with early-stage dementia residents than with late-stage dementia residents. There were no differences in nursing aide discourse with regard to the use of prompts, repetitions, and cues in conversations with early-, middle-, and late-stage dementia residents.

The high incidence of questions nursing aides asked late-stage dementia patients could be the result of a conversation strategy to keep the conversation going when talking to less talkative residents. In other words, nursing aides possibly consider question asking to be a facilitative strategy for late-stage dementia residents who appear

Table 12.9 Means and standard deviations for discourse categories of nursing aides

Discourse Categories	Early Stage		Middle Stage		Late Stage		Groups	F
	M	SD	M	SD	M	SD		
1. Utterances/turn	132.5	104.5	121.0	85.4	76.9	33.1	–	2.67
2. Questions	33.4	17.0	46.6	14.8	49.8	15.7	L > E	5.98**
3. Prompts	16.1	12.4	13.9	9.9	19.5	16.2	–	0.98
4. Facilitators	50.6	16.8	42.7	17.8	34.7	16.5	E > L	4.31*
a. Repetitions	20.0	15.2	18.8	10.2	21.2	8.7	–	1.28
b. Encouragements	29.0	17.1	20.9	15.9	12.4	8.7	E > L	6.64**
c. Cues	8.4	4.7	7.9	4.9	6.7	3.5	–	0.87

Note. E = early stage; M = middle stage; L = late stage.
*$p < .05$, **$p < .01$.

to be less talkative. Results of a nursing-home study (Bourgeois *et al.* 2001) showed that nursing aides ask more questions of less talkative residents than talkative ones.

The research question of whether nursing aides use facilitative communication techniques more when talking to middle- and late-stage dementia residents than early-stage residents has to be answered with a "No." Results indicate the opposite instead: an increased use of facilitative techniques in conversations with early-stage residents. The high occurrence of questions when talking with late-stage dementia patients suggests that nursing aides try to repair communication breakdowns in conversation with severely impaired residents by using questions instead of facilitators or encouragements.

Conclusion

This study has provided deeper insight in discourse deficits among dementia patients throughout conversations and on an utterance-by-utterance basis. Specifically, it helped to answer four research questions. First, significant differences between early-, middle-, and late-stage dementia residents were found for a large number of discourse characteristics. Second, discourse level characteristics occurred differently in discourse of early-stage dementia residents on one hand and middle- and late-stage discourse on the other hand. Third, utterance level characteristics appeared differently in early- and middle-stage dementia discourse on one hand and late-stage dementia discourse on the other hand. Global coherence, as an example of a discourse level category, was affected in an earlier phase of the disease process than, for instance, local coherence and cohesion as examples of utterance level categories. Fourth, nursing aides used more facilitative conversation techniques when talking to early-stage dementia residents than when talking to late-stage dementia residents. It seems that aides do not provide cues, repetitions, and encouragements where they are needed most—with the late-stage dementia residents—but instead opt for the strategy of asking questions when talking to them. Possibly, using facilitative communication techniques with early-stage dementia residents has contributed to the coherence, cohesion, and conciseness of their discourse.

These findings are unique in the sense that the discourse characteristics described here have not been linked systematically to stages of dementia and levels of discourse. They suggest certain patterns of discourse following stages of cognitive decline. Discourse components that put high demands on cognitive resources, such as global coherence, are affected earlier in dementia than discourse components that require continued activation of information on an utterance-by-utterance basis, such as cohesion and local coherence. Further research could study these patterns in greater detail, for instance by relating the occurrence of discourse components to measures of working memory.

A next step for this study could be an expansion of the discourse analysis to include others, such as fellow residents without dementia. This would make possible a comparison of coherence, cohesion, and conciseness in discourse of early-stage dementia residents and residents without dementia. It would be interesting to assess the extent to which these discourse components are preserved in early-stage dementia residents compared to their cognitively unimpaired counterparts.

Another possibility would be to include people other than nursing aides as conversation partners, such as family members and fellow residents, and to see if and to what extent they use facilitative communication techniques with residents in different stages of dementia. Family members, for instance, may be better able to provide cues in cases where they are needed, for they know the resident better. Fellow residents, especially friends, might feel more inclined to be encouraging, for their conversations are an important means of passing time during the daily nursing-home routine. Fellow residents without social ties to the dementia patients, however, may avoid having conversations with them, for lucid residents in nursing homes tend to avoid residents with cognitive impairments as if dementia were contagious (Carstensen *et al.* 1995; Kaakinen 1992).

The discourse analysis schema could further be expanded to assess effects of communication-enhancing intervention programs (cf. Allen-Burge *et al.* 2001; Bourgeois *et al.* 2001; Ripich *et al.* 1998). If nursing aides are trained to communicate more effectively with cognitively impaired nursing-home residents, we could expect benefits for the coherence, cohesion, and conciseness of their conversations. Facilitators such as cues and repetitions may prove to be beneficial for local coherence or cohesion, whereas encouragements could urge the residents to talk more within the time frame of a five-minute conversation.

If nursing aides want to help find the "recaller" of a resident with memory problems when this recaller is on vacation, they can have a substantial and positive impact on improving the communicative abilities of this person.

References

Albrecht, J.E. and O'Brien, E.J. (1995) 'Goal processing and the maintenance of global coherence', in R.F. Lorch, E.J. O'Brien and J. Edward (eds) *Sources of Coherence in Reading* (pp. 263–78). Hillsdale, NJ: Lawrence Erlbaum Associates.

Allen-Burge, R., Burgio, L.D., Bourgeois, M.S., Sims, R. and Nunnikhoven, J. (2001) 'Increasing communication among nursing home residents', *Journal of Clinical Geropsychology* 7: 213–30.

Almkvist, O. (1996) 'Neuropsychological features of early Alzheimer's disease: preclinical and clinical stages', *Acta Neurological Scandiavica Supplementum* 93: 63–71.

Baddeley, A. (1986) *Working Memory*. Oxford: Oxford University Press.

Bayles, K.A. (1985) 'Communication in dementia', in H. Ulatowska (ed.) *The Aging Brain: Communication in the Elderly* (pp. 110–34). Boston, MA: College-Hill.

Bayles, K.A., Kaszniak, A.W. and Tomoeda, C.K. (1987) *Communication and Cognition in Normal Aging and Dementia*. London: Taylor and Francis.

Bourgeois, M.S. (1993) 'Effects of memory aids on the dyadic conversations of individuals with dementia', *Journal of Applied Behavior Analysis* 26: 77–87.

Bourgeois, M.S., Dijkstra, K., Burgio, L. and Allen-Burge, R. (2001) 'Memory aids as an AAC strategy for nursing home residents with dementia', *Journal of Augmentative and Alternative Communication*.

Carstensen, L.L., Fisher, J.E. and Malloy, P.M. (1995) 'Cognitive and affective characteristics of socially withdrawn nursing home residents', *Journal of Clinical Geropsychology* 1: 207–18.

Coelho, C.A. (1994) 'Cognitive framework: a description of discourse abilities in traumatically brain injured adults', in C.A. Coelho, B. Liles and R.J. Duffy (eds) *Discourse Analysis and Applications: Studies in Adult Clinical Populations* (pp. 95–110). Hillsdale, NJ: Lawrence Erlbaum Associates, Inc.

De Santi, S., Koenig, L., Obler, L.K. and Goldberger, J. (1994) 'Cohesive devices and conversational discourse in Alzheimer's disease', in R.L. Bloom, L.K. Obler, S. De Santi and J. Ehrlich (eds) *Discourse Analysis and Applications: Studies in Adult Clinical Populations* (pp. 201–14). Hillsdale, NJ: Lawrence Erlbaum Associates, Inc.

Diesfeldt, H.F.A. (1992) 'Impaired and preserved semantic memory functions in dementia', in L. Bäckman (ed.) *Memory Functioning in Dementia* (pp. 227–60). Amsterdam: North-Holland.

Ehrlich, J.S., Obler, L.K. and Clark, L. (1997) 'Ideational and semantic contributions to narrative production in adults with dementia of the Alzheimer's type', *Journal of Communication Disorders* 30: 79–99.

Folstein, M.F., Folstein, S.E. and McHugh, P.R. (1975) 'Mini-mental state: a practical method for grading the cognitive state of patients for the clinician', *Journal of Psychiatric Research* 12: 189–98.

Garcia, L.J. and Joanette, Y. (1997) 'Analysis of conversational topic shifts: a multiple case study' *Brain and Language*, 58: 92–114.

Hakala, C.M. and O'Brien, E.J. (1995) 'Strategies for resolving coherence breaks in reading', *Discourse Processes* 20: 167–85.

Halliday, M.A.K. and Hasan, R. (1976) *Cohesion in English*. London: Longman.

Haut, M.W., Roberts, V.J., Goldstein, F.C., Martin, R.C., Keefover, R.W. and Rankin, E.D. (1998) 'Working memory demands and semantic sensitivity for prose in mild Alzheimer's disease', *Aging, Neuropsychology, and Cognition* 5: 63–72.

Hier, D.B., Hagenlocker, D. and Schindler, A.G. (1985) 'Language disintegration in dementia: effects of etiology and severity', *Brain and Language* 25: 117–33.

Kaakinen, J.R. (1992) 'Living with silence', *The Gerontologist* 32: 258–64.

Kemper, S., Ferrell, P., Harden, P., Finter-Urczyk, A. and Billington, C. (1998) 'Use of elderspeak by young and older adults to impaired and unimpaired listeners', *Aging, Neuropsychology, and Cognition* 5: 43–55.

Kempler, D. (1991) 'Language changes in dementia of the Alzheimer type', in R. Lubinski, J.B. Orange, D. Henderson and N. Stecker (eds) *Dementia and Communication* (pp. 98–114). Philadelphia, PA: Decker.

Kemper, S., Rash, S.R., Kynette, D. and Norman, S. (1990) 'Telling stories: the structure of adults' narratives', *European Journal of Cognitive Psychology* 2: 205–28.

Korolija, N. (2000) 'Coherence-inducing strategies in conversations amongst the aged', *Journal of Pragmatics* 32: 425–62.

Laine, M., Laakso, M., Vuorinen, E. and Rinne, J. (1998) 'Coherence and informativeness of discourse in two dementia types', *Journal of Neurolinguistics* 11: 79–87.

Liles, B.Z. and Coelho, C.A. (1998) 'Cohesion analysis', in L.R. Cherney, B.B. Shadden and C.A. Coelho (eds) *Analyzing Discourse in Communicatively Impaired Adults* (pp. 65–84). Gaithersburg, MD: Aspen.

McNamara, D.S. and Kintsch, W. (1996) 'Learning from texts: effects of prior knowledge and text coherence', *Discourse Processes* 22: 247–88.

Mentis, M., Briggs-Whitaker, J. and Gramigna, G.D. (1995) 'Discourse topic management in senile dementia of the Alzheimer's type', *Journal of Speech and Hearing Research* 38: 1054–66.

Orange, J.B. and Purves, B. (1996) 'Conversational discourse and cognitive impairment: implications for Alzheimer's disease', *Journal of Speech-Language and Audiology* 20: 139–53.

Ripich, D.N. and Terrell, B.Y. (1988) 'Patterns of discourse cohesion and coherence in Alzheimer's disease', *Journal of Speech & Hearing Disorders* 53: 8–15.

Ripich, D.N., Vertes, D., Whitehouse, P. and Fulton, S. (1991) 'Turn-taking and speech act patterns in the discourse of senile dementia of the Alzheimer's type patients', *Brain and Language* 40, 330–43.

Ripich, D.N., Ziol, E. and Lee, M.M. (1998) 'Longitudinal effects of communication training on care-givers of persons with Alzheimer's disease', *Clinical Gerontologist* 19, 37–55.

Salmon, D.P., Heindel, W.C. and Butters, N. (1991) 'Patterns of cognitive impairment in Alzheimer's disease and other dementing disorders', in L. Bäckman (ed.) *Memory Functioning in Dementia* (pp. 37–44). Amsterdam: North Holland.

Shadden, B.B. (1998) 'Sentential/surface-level analysis', in L.R. Cherney, B.B. Shadden and C.A. Coelho (eds) *Analyzing Discourse in Communicatively Impaired Adults* (pp. 35–64). Gaithersburg, MD: Aspen.

Tomoeda, C.K. and Bayles, K.A. (1993) 'Longitudinal effects of Alzheimer's disease on discourse production', *Alzheimer Disease and Associated Disorders* 4: 223–36.

Tomoeda, C.K., Bayles, K.A., Trosset, M.W., Azuma, T. and McGeagh, A. (1996) 'Cross-sectional analyses of Alzheimer disease effects on oral discourse in a picture description task', *Alzheimer Disease and Associated Disorders* 10: 204–15.

Tulving, E. (1985) 'Ebbinghaus's memory: what did he learn and remember?' *Journal of Experimental Psychology: Learning, Memory and Cognition* 11: 485–90.

Ulatowska, H.K. and Chapman, S.B. (1991) 'Discourse studies', in R. Lubinski, J.B. Orange, D. Henderson and N. Stecker (eds) *Dementia and Communication* (pp. 115–32). Philadelphia, PA: Decker.

Ulatowska, H.K., Allard, L. and Donnell, A. (1988) 'Discourse performance in subjects with dementia of the Alzheimer type', in H. Whitaker (ed.) *Neuropsychological Studies of Nonfocal Brain Damage* (pp. 108–31). New York: Springer-Verlag.

Watson, C.M., Chenery, H.J. and Carter, M.S. (1999) 'An analysis of trouble and repair in the natural conversations of people with dementia of the Alzheimer type', *Aphasiology* 13: 195–218.

Appendix A

Excerpts From Three Transcripts with Coding: Early-, Middle-, and Late-Stage Dementia

Stage	Codes
Early	
A: Yeah, so tell me about your day today.	Prompt
How's your day going so far?	Facilitator: Repetition
R: Oh. Ok	Information unit, local coherence, 1 word, 1 unique word
A: Umm, so how'd you start off this morning?	Question
R: Alright.	Information unit, local coherence, 1 word, 1 unique word
I went over and helped,	Information unit, correct verb tense, local coherence, 5 words, 5 unique words, elaboration
one of the ladies has a problem trying to get about.	Information unit, correct referent, correct verb tense, local coherence, 11 words, 11 unique words, elaboration
A: Oh, Rose,	Facilitator: Cue
R: I'm trying to think what her name is.	Information unit, correct verb tense, correct referent, 9 words, 6 unique words
A: Yeah the lady sitting in the wheel chair that you just said you'd be back to.	Facilitator: Cue
Middle	
A: How many children do you have?	Question
R: Two	Information unit, 1 word, local coherence, 1 unique word
A: Two?	Facilitator: Repetition
Two daughters?	Facilitator: Cue
R: Umm humm.	Information unit, local coherence
A: What are their names?	Question
R: C. and L.	Information unit, simple conjunction, local coherence, 3 words, 3 unique words
A: Oh, C. and L.	Facilitator: Repetition
Late	
A: Tell me about your day.	Prompt
Tell me about your day.	Facilitator: repetition
R: Well it was a nice day.	Information unit, correct verb tense, correct referent, simple conjunction, local coherence, 6 words, 6 unique words
And it was always nice children‑and God love them.	Empty phrase, simple conjunction, incorrect referent, correct referent, 10 words, 5 unique words
You don't have to [unintelligible].	Correct verb tense, 4 words, 4 unique words

Note. A = nursing aide; R = resident. Initials are used instead of full names

Chapter 13

Jane Hurry, Terezinha Nunes, Peter Bryant, Ursula Pretzlik, Mary Parker, Tamsin Curno and Lucinda Midgley

Transforming research on morphology into teacher practice

It is difficult to transform research evidence into teacher practice; indeed it has been argued that educational research is not very useful to teachers. In this chapter, we explore teacher knowledge about a relatively new area of research concerning the role morphemes play in spelling, and seek to transform their practice. We find that although reference to morphology is beginning to be made in English policy documents, teachers make limited use of morphology in their practice. After attending a course on the role of morphemes in spelling, teachers' own awareness of morphology increased and this was reflected in their practice. This in turn caused their pupils to make significant gains in spelling, compared to a control group. This reinforces the proposition that explicit instruction about morphemes is helpful to children's learning. It demonstrates the fact that research can be transformed into teacher practice, but it also illustrates the difficulties. Policy documentation alone is insufficient. Professional development can effect change but this may be hard to sustain. Children's gains are contingent on teachers continuing to dedicate class time to focused intervention.

Extracts from: Hurry, J., Nunes, T., Bryant, P., Pretzlik, U., Parker, M., Curno, T. and Midgley, L. 'Transforming research on morphology into teacher practice', *Research Papers in Education* 20 (2): 197–206, Taylor and Francis, 2005.

Background

The role of morphemes in children's reading and spelling

Our starting point is a desire to improve children's literacy skills. We have taken a particular theoretical position: that enabling children to understand underlying principles will be a powerful way of improving their performance in practical tasks. Foregrounding the power of conceptual understanding has a long tradition (e.g. Piaget 1978; Karmiloff-Smith 1992). In the context of literacy, the importance of understanding the alphabetic principle is a well-known example of the significance of conceptual understanding (e.g. Frith 1985). A less well-researched concept, which is our focus here, is that of morphology.

A morpheme is the smallest part of a word that carries meaning, so that can be a whole word, like 'cat' or just part of a word like the 's' in 'cats' or the suffix 'less' in 'careless'. Our language is a morphological jigsaw which we manipulate all the time to increase our word power: e.g. verbs created from nouns – paint balling, texting, etc. But despite the fact that morphemes are one of the key building blocks of words in any language, many of us are unconscious of our morphological expertise. This is frequently the case with skills that are learnt early in our development. We argue that if children's attention is explicitly drawn to the morphemic structure of English it will provide a conceptual base which will support their learning to read and spell.

Treiman and Cassar (1997) summarise the principle developmental theories of spelling development (Gentry 1982; Henderson 1985; Ehri 1986). They differ in some details but they all recognise that early spelling development is characterised by an increasing use of phonic strategies. As spellers mature, they build a greater repertoire of sight spelling and begin to understand the meaning relations among words which they use to help them spell. For example, Ehri (1986) identifies three broad stages of spelling development:

1. Semi-phonetic: Spellers represent sounds or syllables with letters that match their letter names: R (are), U (you), LEFT (elephant).
2. Phonetic: The child can symbolise the entire sound structure of words in their spellings but the letters are assigned strictly on the basis of sound (Treiman and Cassar 1997).
3. Morphemic: The child becomes more aware of conventional spelling, employing visual and morphological information in spelling. For example, children learn to represent the 't' sound at the end of past tense regular verbs with 'ed' (Nunes et al. 1997).

There is a debate about when children start to use their knowledge of morphemes in their spelling. Treiman et al. (1994) find some evidence of five year olds using simple morphological relations to guide their spelling. Nunes et al. (1997) suggest that seven- and eight-year-old children are entering the morphemic stage in spelling. Henderson (1985), who writes about derivational spelling (e.g. 'heal' and 'health'; 'confide', 'confident' and 'confidential'), suggests that children do not start applying these principles until around 10 or 11 years old. In fact, the ramifications of the function of morphemes in English are considerable and it seems probable that children's understandings of morphemes and word derivations develop over a number of years, possibly well into adulthood (e.g. Nunes *et al.* 1997). Nonetheless, there is some consensus that from the age of seven years onwards children can certainly benefit from explicit instruction in morphology (Treiman & Cassar 1997). Our research with children confirms that teaching them about morphemes produces significant gains in spelling (Nunes *et al.* 2003).

Teacher practice

School policies and structures determine what happens in the classroom, a fact which led Adey (2004) to remark on the 'futility of trying to change teaching practice by working with just one or two teachers from a school'. However, the teacher's own plans, practices, knowledge and beliefs also have an impact on children's learning in many domains, including literacy (e.g. Clark and Peterson 1986; Shulman 1987; Grossman 1990; Zancanella 1991; Fisher *et al.* 1996).

We have a particular interest in teachers' knowledge. In the context of the primary school curriculum, adults tend to have implicit rather than explicit knowledge of fundamental concepts. Within our framework, we argue that the explicit knowledge of these concepts is not only a powerful aid to learning, but also to teaching. Lack of consciousness of the underlying principles one applies to read, spell and do arithmetic becomes an issue when one has to teach these skills. Thus, the first step in transforming our research with children into teachers' practice is to ensure that teachers have explicit knowledge of the role of morphemes in reading and spelling. This has been referred to as content knowledge (Shulman 1987) and can be seen as 'the "stuff" of a discipline: factual information, organizational principles, [or] central concepts' (Grossman *et al.* 1989: 27).

Increasing teachers' explicit content knowledge is unlikely to be sufficient to change their practice. They need to be convinced that it is valuable to teach their pupils about morphology; they need to know how to do it, they need to have the resources to do it and they need to know that it is sanctioned by the educational frameworks within which they operate.

To persuade teachers of the value of teaching morphology explicitly, they need to be informed about the research base, but ideally also to see how it works in their own classroom. The importance of teacher motivation in the process of educational change is well recognised (e.g. Leithwood *et al.* 1992; O'Day 1996).

To know how to teach about morphemes, teachers need to transform their conceptual understanding into forms that make sense to their students, what Shulman (1987) refers to as 'pedagogical content knowledge'. Joyce and Weil (1986) argue that the knowledge which underpins skilled practice develops through repeated cycles of (i) developing a conceptual knowledge structure, (ii) teaching a lesson guided by this knowledge structure, (iii) obtaining feedback about the adequacy of the teaching strategies, and (iv) refining the knowledge structure. They estimate that teachers need thirty hours of practice to perfect a new teaching technique.

The provision of resources to teach about morphemes will make it easier for teachers to enter this cycle, both practically, in the sense that some of the work is done for them, but also conceptually, as the materials can provide more detail about the role of morphemes in children's learning. It is the nature of conceptual understanding that it involves making multiple connections between existing aspects of knowledge. Concepts cannot simply be transmitted, they need to be assimilated and accommodated (to use Piaget's terminology).

Fortunately, teaching morphology is sanctioned by the educational framework within which English teachers operate. However, this needs to be made clear to teachers.

Aims of the study

In the study reported here, we first wished to explore the extent of teachers' explicit knowledge of morphology and their reference to morphology in their practice. We then wanted to see if we could increase both their knowledge and their reference to morphemes in their teaching of spelling. In our evaluation of this professional development we document both teachers' reactions to the course and its impact on their pupils' spelling.

Method

Research design

The research was carried out in two phases. In the first phase, a survey was conducted to document teachers' awareness of morphology. The second phase involved a quasi-experiment. Teachers were invited to attend a ten-session course focusing on morphology and comprehension and compared with similar teachers not attending the course. [. . .]

Intervention. Teachers attended a ten-session literacy course covering comprehension and morphology. The course was delivered over one school term. There were three main aspects to the morphology part of the course: an introduction to theories and research about morphology and literacy; involvement of teachers in the intervention and research process; the provisions of a practical set of materials, including lively PowerPoint slides and teachers' notes, to enable teachers to 'do' explicit morphology in their classrooms. The underlying principle of the morphology materials was to help children see how words could be divided into roots and stems, each contributing to the meaning (and the spelling) of the word. Throughout the scripted sessions, children were encouraged not just to answer questions but to give reasons for their answers, often discussing and working in pairs. As morphemes often have a grammatical function (plurals, past tense of verbs, changing a verb to a noun, etc.) the children did some exercises to familiarise them with verbs, nouns and adjectives. For example, children were asked to decide if a word fitted in a sentence: e.g. 'We saw a *sing* in the town centre'. They were then introduced to a range of derivational morphemes, starting with prefixes and suffixes such as 'un' and 'less', that changed the meaning of a word in an obvious way. Next, they worked with inflectional morphemes that changed the type of word, e.g. teach to teach*er*, verb to noun. They were asked to try out stems with different beginnings and endings, always thinking about how this changed the meaning, and how adding morphemes changed the way a word was spelt. Does *hop* become *hoping* or *hopping*? Why does *say* have a 'y' but *said* have an 'i'? And does that have anything to do with *baby* and *babies*? They were asked to try to find spelling rules, for example, for when to use 'ion' and when to use 'ian'.

Prior to running the ten-session course we had run three short in-service courses as a pilot. Feedback from these courses was that: advanced warning was needed to make a space for the use of intervention materials in the termly plan; teachers valued discussion with other teachers; provision of the theoretical and evidence base for the course content was important. This feedback was used to refine the final course. For example, teachers were advised well before the course to make space in their plans for spelling sessions. At the beginning of the course, the theoretical and evidence base was introduced following teachers' discussion of their own techniques of teaching spelling and connections made. Teachers were also provided with selected readings. The research design was discussed and teachers identified suitable control classes within their schools. They were given a seven-session spelling intervention and asked to try it out in their classroom over the term. They were asked to record their experience of the sessions, and the way their pupils responded in a diary. When teachers attended the course at the university, they discussed how their children did in the tests, how the sessions were going, how they would approach the next sessions. We examined samples of children's writing; we discussed how this tied in with the theoretical side and the readings; they heard from other teachers who had tried the same system; they discussed approaches to teaching spelling between themselves; and we wrestled with the practicalities of handing out information, teaching materials, etc. Through this process we attempted to integrate theory and practice.

Results

[. . .]

Phase two – intervention effects

How teachers changed

On the first session of the course, the most frequently mentioned methods of teaching spelling were:

- Look, cover, write, check (13 out of 20 – two thirds of teachers mentioned this)
- Letter strings/letter patterns (12 out of 20)
- Spelling rules (magic 'e', plurals of words like 'baby'), particularly using mnemonic strategies, e.g. 'ought': O u great hairy teacher (12 out of 20)
- Phonic strategies (11 out of 20)
- Learning whole words (high frequency words, technical words, words identified as difficulties for individual children) (9 out of 20)
- Proof reading of various kinds (9 out of 20)
- Spelling investigations (7 out of 20)
- Spelling banks and dictionaries (6 out of 20)
- Kinetic learning of various kinds (5 out of 20).

The use of prefixes, suffixes or roots was only spontaneously mentioned four times and there was only one reference to morphemes.

We also asked the teachers to write down their definition of a morpheme. Of the twenty teachers who completed this pre-course questionnaire, a quarter knew that it was a small chunk of a word which had meaning. Other responses varied, e.g. 'God knows', 'something to do with spelling', the most common definition was 'a unit of sound'. This confirmed the findings of our earlier survey, that primary teachers have quite limited explicit knowledge of morphemes. One teacher reflected that much of her own knowledge of grammar was picked up rather than taught:

> I learnt the majority of my English grammar indirectly. I don't consciously remember being taught present, past and future tenses in the same way as they were taught in my French classes. [French] was taught through a structure specific approach and informed my understanding of the English language.
>
> (Teacher 55)

At the end of the course we asked the teachers to give us their definition of a morpheme again. Of the seventeen teachers for whom we had data at the beginning and the end of the course, three had defined a morpheme fairly accurately at the beginning and sixteen out of seventeen at the end. Teachers tended to consider phonological awareness as 'an essential foundation in the learning of reading and spelling', but saw that teaching children about morphology also had important benefits for seven to eleven year olds. All but one of the teachers reported that the course had changed their approaches to teaching spelling. As expected, most mentioned that they would teach more explicit morphology, making connections between spelling, grammar and meaning. However, they changed in a number of other ways too. Several teachers mentioned that they would take spelling more seriously, for example focusing one (one hour) literacy session per week on spelling and/or taking a more structured approach to teaching spelling. They also saw spelling as having more creative possibilities such as class discussions and investigations. A number of teachers thought that using computer generated materials had been good fun and effective and had encouraged them to try this again in the future. Seven out of the seventeen teachers spontaneously mentioned that they would like to introduce the use of spelling journals. This was not something that we had suggested but something that the teachers had discussed between themselves during the course. We had hoped that the course would be an interaction between us and the teachers, but worried that in the end, the tremendous pressure of dealing with all the practicalities would squeeze this luxury out. It seems that some dialogue did go on between teachers despite everything.

We have no comprehensive information about whether or not the change in practice was sustained, but fear that in many cases it was not. Seven of the teachers wanted to work with us in the next school year, having twice-termly meetings to share practice and assessing the progress of their children. In reality, teachers found it hard to attend sessions outside school once the course was completed and only three of the seven teachers systematically used the materials.

The impact on their pupils' spelling

Before the course, the children in the control classes were fairly evenly matched with the children receiving the morphology intervention, except for Year 3 where the control group was substantially better on both spelling (t = 2.0, df = 203, p < 0.05, Table 13.1) and pseudo-word spelling (t = 2.4, df = 177, p < 0.02, Table 13.2). Around seven weeks later, all the children had improved, but the morphology group had made larger gains than the control group (overall, three times as much). Statistical significance was assessed by fixed order regression where pre-test was entered in the first block and experimental group in the second. Overall, the morphology group had made significantly more progress than the control group on both spelling and pseudo-word spelling. The intervention showed a moderate effect size (0.50, B = 3.3, p < 0.001) on the spelling test and 0.48 (B = 3.5, p < 0.01) on the pseudo-word test, which is impressive for a class level intervention.

In one very large Year 5 class (with forty-five children), children had been randomly assigned to do the morphology tasks, some comprehension tasks or the standard classroom programme. This is a particularly strong design because the

Table 13.1 Children's scores on spelling test: by teaching condition and year group

	Pre-test				Post-test			
	Control group		Morphology group		Control group		Morphology group	
Year group	mean	(sd)	mean	(sd)	mean	(sd)	mean	(sd)
Year 3	64	(24)	57	(23)	64	(22)	62	(23)
Year 4	65	(25)	65	(27)	68	(25)	70	(26)
Year 5	74	(22)	72	(21)	76	(19)	76	(20)
Year 6	75	(26)	76	(22)	77	(24)	86	(16)
Total	69	(24)	65	(25)	71	(23)	71	(23)

Table 13.2 Children's scores on pseudo-word spelling test: by teaching condition and year group

	Pre-test				Post-test			
	Control group		Morphology group		Control group		Morphology group	
Year group	mean	(sd)	mean	(sd)	mean	(sd)	mean	(sd)
Year 3	52	(23)	43	(26)	52	(25)	57	(23)
Year 4	54	(27)	53	(30)	61	(25)	57	(28)
Year 5	58	(25)	53	(25)	61	(24)	60	(24)
Year 6	65	(26)	64	(25)	69	(25)	73	(25)
Total	57	(25)	51	(27)	59	(25)	59	(26)

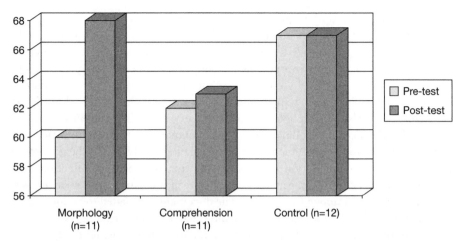

Figure 13.1 Year 5 class, randomly assigned to condition (pre- and post-test spelling)

children were randomly assigned and were getting no different treatment in class except for the interventions. In this class, the children who received the morphology tasks did significantly better than the other two groups on spelling (Figure 13.1: difference between groups assessed by Analysis of Variance, $F = 3.6$, $p < 0.01$, where pre-test was entered as a co-variant) and the children who received the comprehension tasks made more progress on comprehension. The impact of the intervention does not seem to be the result of having something new but with the morphology training itself.

[. . .]

Discussion

There are two driving forces underpinning this research. The first is the power of an idea, a conceptual understanding. The second is how that idea is transformed into practice. The concept explored is the role of morphology in spelling, interesting because it has a fundamental role in the way our language is constructed, but our understanding of this concept is largely implicit.

Transforming research into teacher practice is a complicated business. In the research that is the focus of this study, the process of transformation had already begun. English policy documents identify the role of morphology in teaching spelling. However, when we looked at teachers' practice, reference to morphemes was limited and patchy. No teacher spontaneously mentioned the word morpheme, and when asked, most teachers were unaware of its meaning. This suggests the absence of an explicit knowledge of the concept of the way morphology governs the spelling construction of English. Although teachers talked about aspects of morphology, most commonly in the context of verb endings and prefixes and suffixes, they normally focused on the visual patterns, failing to make a link between this and the meaning function. Observation in the classroom confirmed that children were rarely taught about the morphological dimension of our language.

Apparently, policy on morphology has not translated consistently into practice. Smith and Smith (1992) discuss the complex relationship between policy and research. The policy documents themselves are not a transparent reflection of existing research knowledge. In our case of morphology, layers of documentation give different messages, no doubt written by different authors with different understandings of what is important in teaching spelling and different levels of explicit knowledge of morphology. Also, 'morphology' covers a very wide and complex range of morphemic influences on spelling. To a limited extent, the teachers' practice that we observed reflected the documentation on morphology fairly well. Where practical activities in the documentation emphasised the link between an inflection or a derivational morpheme and meaning, a link between morpheme and meaning was more likely to be mentioned by teachers. The documentation failed to communicate the pervasive role of morphology in spelling and teachers' existing knowledge influenced the extent to which they implemented those elements that were unambiguously described.

Our own attempts at transforming teachers' practice could focus on the concept of morphology and offer materials for use in the classroom which made the role of morphology in spelling more explicit. There was little difficulty in increasing teachers' understanding of morphology. Changing their classroom practice, even in the short term, was more difficult. It is difficult to make changes to practices which are already governed by previous behaviour and a range of hierarchical structures. As Joyce and Weil (1986) have documented, the teachers themselves have to be part of the transformation. It is easy to underestimate how much effort it takes teachers to make this transformation. No materials can be taken into the classroom and used without adaptation. The teachers who worked with us had to differentiate the materials in the classroom. Access to technology varied and this influenced a number of aspects of the teaching process, medium of instruction, timing and location. Some teachers had access to computers and classroom projectors, others had not. Some could operate within the classroom; others had to use the assembly hall or a computer suite, etc. Teachers vary in their pedagogy. Some teachers encouraged children to investigate and discuss the ideas; others preferred a more formal style of pedagogy.

Despite the difficulties, the teachers did change their practice, to varying degrees, and this had a positive impact on their pupils' spelling. The pupils of teachers attending the course made significant gains in spelling compared to children in similar classrooms receiving standard instruction. The effect size of 0.50 was impressive for a whole class intervention delivered by teachers just learning a technique for the first time. The intervention is quite a focused and practical one, despite its conceptual base, and this probably contributed to its impact. Exactly what aspect of the intervention caused the change is less clear. We would like to say that it was due to teachers' conceptual awareness of morphology. However, there are a number of other contenders. The classic alternative explanation is that the children did better just because they were being exposed to something new. There are a couple of reasons why this seems unlikely. The teachers of half of the control children were attending a maths course which was also exposing the pupils to novel practices. In one of the intervention classrooms, some children received the morphology materials and others comprehension materials also covered on the course. The morphology children made significant gains on spelling, the comprehension children on comprehension. Another alternative explanation for children's spelling gains is that teachers spent more classroom time teaching spelling. This was certainly an effect of the intervention. We had seen from the survey phase of our research that there is not a great deal of teaching time dedicated to spelling in the standard classroom and the teachers on our course commented that they were spending more time teaching spelling than they would normally. In the year following the course, one school clarified what aspect of our intervention was improving children's spelling. Just improving teachers' explicit knowledge of morphology was not enough. In the Autumn term, the teacher who had been on the course did not have an opportunity to use the morphology materials. During this term, her new group of pupils made no greater gains in spelling than the other children in the school, despite the fact that this teacher did have explicit understanding of the role of morphology. Increasing the amount of time on spelling did not explain the gains entirely either. When her class was compared with a parallel class (the NLS condition) receiving the same amount of additional spelling instruction, her morphology group made significantly more progress than the children having additional NLS spelling activities. However, additional curriculum time was helpful. Both these classes made significant spelling gains compared to a control class and to their own progress in the previous term. The ingredients for change in pupils' performance appear to be teacher knowledge and dedicated teacher time.

We conclude that it is possible to transform research into teacher practice, but we must add a cautionary note. In the year following our course, despite teachers' commitment to the techniques introduced, a proportion, probably the majority, did not use them systematically. Consistent application of the techniques will require another layer of transformation back up through the policy cycle to make a more prominent place for morphology in the classroom.

References

Adey, P. (2004) *The Professional Development of Teachers: Practice and Theory*. London, Kluwer.

Clark, C.M. and Peterson, P.L. (1986) 'Teachers' thought processes', in M.C. Wittrock (ed.) *Handbook on Research in Teaching* (3rd edn) (pp. 255–96). New York: Macmillan.

Ehri, L. (1986) 'Sources and difficulty in learning to spell and read', in M.L. Wolraich and D. Routh (eds) *Advances in Developmental and Behavioural Paediatrics* (Vol. 7) (pp. 121–95). Greenwich, CT: JAI.

Fisher, C.J., Fox, D.L. and Paille, E. (1996) 'Teacher education research in the English language arts and reading', in J. Sikula, T. Buttery and E. Guyton (eds) *Handbook of Research on Teacher Education* (2nd edn) (pp. 410–41). New York: Macmillan.

Frith, U. (1985) 'Beneath the surface of developmental dyslexia', in K. Patterson, M. Coltheart and J. Marshall (eds) *Surface Dyslexia*. London: Lawrence Erlbaum Associates Ltd.

Gentry, J.R. (1982) 'An analysis of developmental spelling in GYNS AT WRK', *The Reading Teacher* 36: 192–200.

Grossman, P.L. (1990) *The Making of a Teacher: Teacher Knowledge and Teacher Education*. New York: Teachers College Press.

Grossman, P.L., Wilson, S. and Shulman, L.S. (1989) 'Teachers of substance: subject matter knowledge for teaching', in M. Reynolds (ed.) *Knowledge Base for the Beginning Teacher* (pp. 23–36). Elmsford, NY: Pergamon.

Henderson, E. (1985) *Teaching Spelling*. Boston, MA: Houghton Mifflin.

Joyce, B. and Weil, M. (1986) *Models of Teaching* (3rd edn). Englewood Cliffs, NJ: Prentice Hall.

Karmiloff-Smith, A. (1992) *Beyond Modularity: A Developmental Perspective on Cognitive Science*. Cambridge, MA: Bradford.

Leithwood, K., Begley, P. and Cousins, J. (1992) *Developing Expert Leadership for Quality Schools*. London: Falmer Press.

Nunes, T., Bryant, P. and Bindman, M. (1997) 'Spelling acquisition in English', in C. Perfetti, L. Rieben and M. Fayol (eds) *Learning to Spell* (pp. 151–70). London: Laurence Erlbaum.

Nunes, T., Bryant, P. and Olsson, J. (2003) 'Learning morphological and phonological spelling rules: an intervention study', *Scientific Studies of Reading* 7: 289–307.

O'Day, J. (1996) 'Incentives and student performance', in S. Fuhrman and J. O'Day (eds) *Rewards and Reform: Creating Educational Incentives that Work*. San Francisco, CA: Jossey-Bass.

Piaget, J. (1978) *The Development of Thought: Equilibration of Cognitive Structures*. Oxford: Blackwell.

Shulman, L.S. (1987) 'Knowledge and teaching: foundations of the new reform', *Harvard Educational Review* 57 (1): 1–22.

Smith, G. and Smith, T. (1992) 'From social research to education policy: 10/65 to the Education Reform Act 1988', in A. Halsey and C. Grouch (eds) *Social Research and Social Reform; Essays in Honour of A.H. Halsey* (pp. 245–71). Oxford: OUP.

Treiman, R. and Cassar, M. (1997) 'Spelling acquisition in English', in C. Perfetti, L. Rieben and M. Fayol (eds) *Learning to Spell* (pp. 61–80). London: Laurence Erlbaum.

Treiman, R., Cassar, M. and Zukowski, A (1994) 'On the status of final consonant clusters in English syllables', *Journal of Verbal Learning and Verbal Behavior* 23: 343–56.

Zancanella, D. (1991) 'Teachers reading/readers teaching: five teachers' personal approaches to literature and their teaching of literature', *Research in the Teaching of English* 25 (1): 5–32.

Chapter 14

Rebeca Jasso-Aguilar

Sources, methods and triangulation in needs analysis

A critical perspective in a case study of Waikiki hotel maids[1]

NA and social engineering

Recently, a great deal of emphasis has been placed on needs analysis (NA) for occupation-specific VESL (Vocational English as a Second Language) and other ESP (English for Specific Purposes) courses, often motivated by pressing time constraints, limited financial resources, and institutional and learner expectations (Chambers 1980; Cumaranatunge 1988; L. West 1984). Institutional VESL and ESP curricula, however, face strong criticism from critical educators. Auerbach (1995) questions NA for the workplace as the basis for curriculum development for ESL students altogether, arguing that the process is often performed by outsiders whose information comes from institutions with clearly defined expectations of what they want the workers/students to do. Such information, she argues, can only be transformed into a curriculum whose goals are to serve the interests of institutions which have traditionally marginalized ESL speakers, socializing them into passive acceptance of subservient roles. Likewise, Tollefson (1989, 1991) denounces a covert policy in which language training for specific purposes channels immigrants into marginal occupations that offer no opportunity to gain additional language or job skills, ensuring that they will have enough English to perform adequately in minimum-wage jobs while avoiding any welfare dependency, yet not enough to move beyond those levels of employment. While these concerns regarding the occasional misuse of NA are valid, in this chapter I explore a different methodology – different from traditional approaches to NA – and the possibility to use findings critically, so as to overcome the potential pitfalls.

Edited extracts from: Jasso-Aguilar, R. 'Sources, methods and triangulation in needs analysis: a critical perspective in a case study of Waikiki hotel maids', in M. Long (ed.) *Second Language Needs Analysis*, pp. 127–58, Cambridge University Press, 2005.

The position taken in this chapter follows Long, who acknowledges that institutional curricula could clearly lead to a potentially serious problem of "social engineering of the worst sort", but suggests that the possible exploitation of workers undertaking these courses:

> . . . would be better seen as the result of Machiavellian government policy, pernicious business practices and gross dereliction of duty by educational administrators, not as the result of NA or specific purpose course design per se. It would involve an abuse of NA, but is neither its inevitable corollary nor reason to forego its positive effects.
>
> (Long, to appear: 10)

Although Auerbach opposes institutional NA and predetermined curricula, it is clear that the collaborative investigation of what is important to students, which she advocates, implies NA beyond the workplace (without excluding it), and that this NA is an ongoing process. Long advocates use of multiple sources and methods, insiders (with expertise) as better informants than outsiders, and triangulation of sources and methods. Triangulation, a commonly used procedure in anthropology, involves (with many variants) systematic comparison of interim findings from two or more sources, methods or combinations thereof, and an attempt to validate the researcher's (in this case the needs analyst's) interim findings by presenting them to the informants, and/or by seeking confirmation or disconfirmation of the current analysis. By using multiple sources and methods, and triangulation, Long believes that the main problem for which Auerbach opposes NA, that is, the learners' needs being identified only from the point of view of institutions and manipulated to their own advantages, can be overcome. Under the type of NA advocated by Long, Auerbach's approach falls short, since it considers the students and their lives and experiences the only source that should inform the curriculum. Long questions the reliability of many students as sources on their own needs, especially if they are new to the job or activity they are to perform, and Drobnic *et al.* (1978: 320) reminds us that "linguistically naive students should not be expected to make sound language decisions concerning their training" (cited in Chambers 1980: 26).

With these considerations in mind, this study set out to identify the tasks performed by the maids (or 'housekeepers') in a Waikiki hotel in order to complete their daily routine at the hotel, and the language involved in those tasks. One concern was to find out whether language was needed to perform the tasks, whether or not the maids perceived this need, and to what extent the lack of language abilities might have affected their performance. Another concern was to identify the needs and wants of both the maids and institutional representatives and to interpret any discrepancies.

Orientations in NA for the workplace: sources and methods

Some attempts have been made to identify efficient methods and sources of information for NA for the workplace. L. West (1984) suggests use of various sources, such as job description manuals, job site observations, tape-recording of conversations in the workplace, surveys, and specific questions that "can elicit key information about the language requirements of a job". For L. West, syllabus design derives from a logical analysis of the job. What that means, however, and who defines it, remain unclear.

Prince (1984) recommends *goal analysis*, which is what a company feels is the need for a course and its expected results, *job analysis*, which is the description of the job, and *language analysis*, which is the work-oriented language, which will include procedures, policies, etc., and which will emphasize the names of tools, supplies and other job terminology. In Prince's approach, workers are interviewed for information related to the job only, such as time spent on different tasks and to determine the degree of involvement. Prince also suggests that the analyst should consider the "company climate", tactfully asking workers questions about, for example, what they think the company values are. One presumes that these questions will be asked in the learners' native language, although this is not suggested and neither is any methodology for investigating "company climate".

R. West (1994) provides an overview of what has been done, said and written about NA. What is striking about his account, just like L. West's, is how little attention has been paid to learners as a source of information, especially compared to other sources. Little attention, either, has been paid to the sociopolitical environment of the workplace or to the sociopolitical environment of the workers outside the work-site. (Prince does seem to take the sociopolitical environment of the workplace into consideration, although it is not clear to what extent and how it is incorporated.) West enumerates ten different methods of data collection, suggesting that these methods ensure coverage of most of the (one presumes, crucial) areas. Of nine areas listed, only three (general personal background; language background; and attitudinal and motivational factors) seem to be related to issues outside the workplace. These areas, particularly attitudinal and motivational factors, suggest that a view of the workers' world outside the job is taken into account for NA purposes.

R. West's state of the art NA in language teaching and Long's (to appear) chapters dedicated to NA have some points in common. They both agree on the advantage of utilizing multiple sources, and on the importance of selecting adequate information-gathering instruments. They regard the language intuitions of expert analysts and applied linguists as not necessarily reliable sources representative of language use in a field. They also agree that there is often a difference between learners' needs and learners' wants, although the degree to which they differ will vary among learners. Two crucial issues neglected by West (and indeed by the people he cites), but which Long treats in detail, are: (i) the need to establish a unit of analysis in terms of which needs will be identified, and (ii) the need for triangulation of sources.

Long (1985, and elsewhere) proposes *task* as the (non-linguistic) unit of analysis. For Long, task is a more viable unit of analysis than such options as situations or communicative events, among other reasons, because more relevant information for course designers is available in task-based occupational analyses by domain experts and other sources. Task-based occupational analyses reveal more about the dynamic qualities of target discourse than do text-based analyses; they also circumvent the domain expert's usual lack of linguistic knowledge and the applied linguist's usual lack of content knowledge. As such, they minimize the pervasive problem of finding informants who are competent in the academic, occupational or vocational area of interest and also knowledgeable about language use in that area. Once target tasks for a particular group of learners have been identified, domain experts (not necessarily the learners, unless they have expertise) can easily and reliably supply information which will later be analyzed by applied linguists, materials writers, teachers and learners. Another, and by no means less important, advantage of tasks is their role in preparing students as agents of social change:

> Steps are taken, both in pedagogic task design and in the area of methodology, to make learners aware of their potential as social actors, not merely passive observers, in determining task outcomes, and when necessary, in *redefining* tasks.
> (Long, to appear: 29)

Where sources are concerned, Long suggests appropriate combinations of language teachers with prior experience with learners in the program, people now undergoing or who have completed the education program, those already employed in the occupation for which the perspective learners are preparing, current or future subject area teachers or employers, documents, such as job descriptions and course reading lists, and published NA literature. Long emphasizes the need for triangulation, a process that involves the use of multiple-data-collection methods and may also involve the incorporation of multiple data sources, investigators, and theoretical perspectives. Triangulation contributes to the trustworthiness of the data and increases confidence in research findings (Glesne and Peshkin 1992: 24). Prolonged engagement in the field, persistent observation and triangulation are procedures used by researchers working within the qualitative research or naturalistic research traditions to help them validate their data and to increase the credibility of their interpretations (Davis 1992). 'Qualitative research' is an umbrella term for many kinds of research approaches and techniques, including 'ethnography', a term that has recently become fashionable in NA and ESL studies; 'naturalistic research' is a descriptive term that implies that the researcher conducts observations in the natural environment, that is, where people live and work (Watson-Gegeo 1988).

[. . .]

When the need arises for NA beyond the workplace

Goldstein (1992) provides an account of female factory workers learning English as a second language. Although hers is not an NA but a study of language choice, the use of ethnography allowed her to see the discrepancies between students' situations for language use and the content of their ESL class. While lessons were composed of communicative tasks related to their work, such as polite ways to ask for tools, the particular sociocultural environment of the workplace made it unnecessary for the women to be polite with one another, and it even made the use of English unnecessary. The majority of the women were Portuguese, their language choice was Portuguese, and they did not associate the use of English with getting ahead in the workplace. Their supervisor was a bilingual speaker of English and Portuguese, eliminating the need for English in supervisor–worker communication. On the assembly line, the use of Portuguese brought workers together, enabling them to meet efficiency and time standards, while the use of English generated conflicts, especially among the least proficient ones. Goldstein concluded that while English-language training is not always necessary for functioning well at work or for economic survival and/or mobility, there are still good reasons for women working and living in languages other than English to participate in ESL classes. She suggested looking at the larger picture of these (and other) women's lives and finding needs that can be addressed by providing language training to expand their options for functioning not just as a cheap labor force but as functional members of English-speaking societies. What she was arguing for, in fact, was NA beyond the workplace.

The study

The present study was mainly carried out at one of the many large hotels in Waikiki, one belonging to a well-known chain. In addition, two observations were performed at a smaller site belonging to the same company. The great majority of maids in these hotels are Filipino, Chinese, Korean, and Vietnamese women. As previously mentioned, the study set out to identify the tasks and language needed to perform a housekeeper's job. Two concerns guided the study: (i) to find out whether language was needed to perform the tasks, whether or not the maids perceived this need, and to what extent the lack of language abilities might have affected their performance; and, (ii) to identify the needs and wants of both the maids and the institutional representatives, and to interpret any discrepancies.

At the time I contacted the human resources person, Sandra, she was in the process of starting an English course for the hotel maids because, out of approximately 1,000 housekeepers employed at the chain, "five hundred could benefit from learning English" (personal communication). She had begun to do her own NA of the language needs of the maids, and had already selected a consulting company to develop the curriculum. For this purpose, a task force had been assembled, composed of people with expertise in different areas who, in one way or another, had contact with the hotel maids: maintenance, security, housekeeping, front desk, and human resources. Sources for the study reported here included the human resources person, the executive housekeeper, various housekeepers and supervisors, task force meetings, morning/afternoon briefings, documents, such as job and routine descriptions, and the ESL curriculum designed by the task force. Sources will be discussed at more length in the following sections.

Methodology

Methods and sources used in this study were as follows.

Methods:
1   Participant observations (with tape-recording and note-taking)
2   Unstructured interviews
3   Written questionnaires (given to housekeepers and to co-workers).

Sources:

1   Three housekeepers (day and evening shifts)
2   Human resources person
3   Executive housekeeper: the person at the top of the housekeeping hierarchy
4   Various supervisors and housekeeper assistants: personnel between the executive housekeeper and the hotel maids in the housekeeping hierarchy
5   Task force weekly/biweekly meetings
6   Morning briefings
7   Housekeeping room
8   Documents (job descriptions, safety procedures, etc., all in English).

I conducted five participant observations, three observations corresponding to the day shift (8:00 am – 4:00 pm) and two to the evening shift (3:00 pm – 11:00 pm) between March and July, 1996. Unstructured interviews with the housekeepers were conducted as part of conversations during our work together; interviews with the human resources person and the executive housekeeper were more formal, in that time was set aside for the purpose, and some discussion of my ongoing research and findings took place during these sessions, as well. Written questionnaires for the housekeepers (Appendix A) consisted of twenty-nine items aiming at identifying tasks and language use both at work and outside the job. Co-workers' questionnaires (Appendix B) contained twelve items aimed at identifying situations in which housekeepers needed English to interact with them, as well as the co-workers' perceptions of communication difficulties and language needs of the housekeepers. Both questionnaires were written in English.

The task force was composed of personnel with expertise in the areas of maintenance, security, housekeeping, front desk, and human resources. The NA process followed by the task force consisted of one-hour brainstorming sessions (most of which I attended), reflections and discussions of the previous session, more brainstorming, and so on, i.e., predominantly the use of intuitions. The results of these meetings were several lists of situations which, according to the task force, the maids were most likely to encounter on a regular basis, the tasks they were more likely to perform, the language they were more likely to hear, and language they should be able to speak, read or write in such situations. Aside from Chris, the housekeeper executive, most people participating in the task force could be considered outsiders to the housekeepers' group, in the sense that they were not housekeepers and had never worked as such. To one degree or another, all thought they knew the situations and the language that the housekeepers encountered on a daily basis. Participant observation would later disconfirm these intuitions.

Supervisors and housekeeper assistants, besides having experience and seniority as housekeepers, are fairly proficient English speakers. They may be responsible for answering the phone and performing duties in the housekeeping room, and may help in the training or supervision of new housekeepers. Supervisors also conduct the morning briefings at the smaller branches of the hotel chain, where there may not be an executive housekeeper. The morning briefings are conducted daily from 8:00–8:30 am. The executive housekeeper briefs the hotel maids on routine housekeeping issues, as well as special events in the hotel. The housekeeping room is the place where guests call with housekeeping requests; paged messages from and to the housekeepers are also received and sent here. Uniforms, pagers, keys and room assignments are kept and distributed here, which makes the place buzz with activity at the beginning and end of the work day.

Participant observation ranges along a continuum from observation to active participation (Glesne and Peshkin 1992). I chose the latter because I was interested not only in identifying but in experiencing the tasks and situations that housekeepers face during a day's work, the language they hear, and the language they use. Because I also wanted to identify the language needed for training new personnel, I requested to be trained in the same fashion as a new housekeeper. This training essentially consists of pairing up the new housekeeper with an experienced one, after the apprentice has undergone a session on procedures and safety measures for the workplace with the executive housekeeper. If the apprentice's English proficiency is very low, this session will be conducted with the help of an interpreter, usually one of the housekeepers who speak the same language as the apprentice. The training occurs on the spot, the experienced housekeeper demonstrating how to do the job rather than explaining how to do it. Due to the context-embedded nature of the talk, names of objects are often substituted by "this" and "that", "go like this", "put like this". As found by Svendsen and Krebs (1984), nothing is expressed that cannot be seen. After the new housekeepers have mastered the routine tasks the job involves, descriptions and explanations are even less useful; housekeepers can go about their work with almost no need to speak, with the only item to read being their room-assignment sheet, and the only items to write being the times at which they start and finish a room, whether the safe box was opened, etc., on the same assignment sheet.

A day in the life of day-shift hotel maids at this hotel in Waikiki goes as follows. They arrive at the hotel, check their time cards at the clock located in the hall and change into their uniform in the locker room, where they place their belongings in a locker. They pick up their keys and room assignments (a sheet with the occupancy on their floor, names and number of guests, checkouts, etc.) at the housekeeping room, and join the rest of the maids in the dining-room, where they have some free coffee and chat until briefing time. Speakers of the same language tend to group together and converse in their native language. (This was a fact that seemed to bother some people, as indicated at a meeting by one member of the task force: "They don't want to learn English. If there's one who speaks a little English they'll rely on her for everything. They all hang out in their little groups. We're trying to break that up."). The executive housekeeper, Chris, comes into the dining room at 8:00 am and the morning briefing takes place. The briefing is in English, and Chris makes sure that there is at least one supervisor or assistant housekeeper (fairly proficient speakers of English) at each table, so they can translate and/or explain to the maids in case they find themselves unable to understand what Chris is saying.

After the briefing, the maids go to the housekeeping room to get their pagers (everybody carries one) and their keys and room assignments if they have not yet done so. Since they will have left everything ready for the next day (towels, sheets, supplies, etc.) at the end of their previous shift, they are ready to go straight to their floors. A particular floor is assigned to a housekeeper, and her daily workload is the cleaning of sixteen rooms on that floor. The amount of work required for each room is variable, depending on the type of room (single, double, extra beds added, children staying, etc.) and whether it is a checkout room or not. At one end of each floor there is a small room, a closet, where the housekeeper's cart is kept; there are also shelves of linens, towels, and other items, as well as cleaning supplies. Housekeepers are responsible for replenishing these items every day after they finish their rooms and before they go home, so as to avoid wasting time the next day trying to collect all the needed supplies before work. The room-assignment sheet allows them to know the number and size of sheets, towels, and supplies (shampoo, hand lotion, shower caps, etc.) they will need to place on their carts.

Once they have packed their carts with everything they need, they go to the rooms, knock on the door and say "Housekeeping", wait a few seconds, and repeat the procedure before opening the door with their own key. They open the door slowly while saying "Hello", and, once they are convinced that the room is empty, they open the door wide, get the vacuum cleaner into the room, and station the cart in front of the door as if blocking it, a safety procedure specified in the housekeepers' manual. A complete, step-by-step set of the tasks involved in the process of cleaning rooms is included in this manual, which is given to the housekeepers during the initial session on procedures and safety measures. Cleaning routines as well as bed-making procedures are taught during the training period and their mastery encouraged, since they are designed to reduce time, effort and fatigue. Participant observation allowed me to witness that the housekeepers do in fact follow this routine in every room they clean.

At lunch time, which consists of 30 minutes between 11:00 am and 1:00 pm, the housekeepers usually sit together with speakers of the same language, share food and chat. After lunch they continue working until they finish cleaning their sixteen rooms, which usually occurs around 4:00 pm. Before heading down to the house-keeping room, they make sure that they leave everything ready for the next working day. They return their keys, pagers and assignment sheets to the supervisors at the housekeeping room, check their time cards, and head back home. These last activities are not performed silently, as the housekeepers turn the end of a day's work into an opportunity to socialize in their own languages.

Participant observation showed that the job of day-shift housekeepers occurs in solitude, with very few situations in which the need for English language arises. By the time they go up to clean their rooms, most of the guests have left, and even encounters with the few guests still around do not require more language than short greetings ("Hi", "Hello", "Good morning/afternoon").

While doing the participant observation, my informants (the hotel maids I had been paired up with) and I engaged in conversation. They were usually interested in my personal life, and willing to talk about their own. This is an important aspect pointed out by Goldstein (1992), related to how newcomers are incorporated in the workplace network, and how friendships are formed and become the basis for support in the workplace. Unstructured interviews were conducted between conversations about families and lives outside the workplace, including questions about the need for English in their work and the problems related to their lack of English proficiency, as well as what they thought it would be useful to learn in an English class. Conversations between my informants and myself, interactions that the housekeepers go through, and paged messages they receive in a day's work, were all tape-recorded. Morning briefings were tape-recorded, as well, and the desk clerk answering the phone in the housekeeping room was recorded during a one-hour session, too. These phone calls were mostly from guests who had some requests for the housekeeping department, or from housekeepers who were requesting something or reporting room discrepancies.

Triangulation and comparisons of sources and methods

Participant observation proved to be the most useful method, allowing me to experience first-hand the tasks involved in being a hotel maid, as well as the language and situations involved. Because it gave me access to various sources in similar situations, participant observation allowed me to triangulate sources and interpret discrepancies among sources' different perceptions of the same situation or issue. It also made it possible to confirm or disconfirm outsiders' predictions, as well as to explain some of those predictions. Sandra, for example, who had once dressed and worked as a housekeeper for a day to learn about their situations and language needs, had stated she was "amazed at how much interaction goes on with the guests" (personal communication). I, conversely, was amazed at how little interaction was going on between my informants and the guests, and between myself and the guests (see Appendix C).

In qualitative field work one must look for recurring patterns not only of what happens during observations but also of what does not happen, and try to understand why people do what they do (Wolcott 1995). This led me to notice that the interactions between the guests and myself usually occurred after I made eye contact with them and smiled while keeping eye contact, a deliberate effort on my part to encourage interaction. Even this effort, however, did not result in anything more than a simple greeting, thus casting doubt on Sandra's generalization. An interpretation of this difference is that quite possibly Sandra was the one initiating the interactions, not to mention the fact that her physical appearance must have been an unusual sight in this environment. Sandra is an obviously Caucasian woman while the great majority of the housekeepers, as mentioned before, are Filipino, Chinese, Korean, and Vietnamese. I am not suggesting racist attitudes here, but rather an assumption on the part of guests that the housekeepers cannot speak English, and that, therefore, they choose not to interact unless they have a need. Because it must have seemed so obvious that Sandra could speak English, they probably felt more inclined to interact with her. (At this point, it should be mentioned that I am not, and do not look, Caucasian, a fact that could have led guests to believe that I was in fact a housekeeper, unable to speak much English.) Neither am I implying that the housekeepers are unfriendly, or that they do not smile at the guests. My informants in fact smiled a lot, but one could hardly expect them to go out of their way to create opportunities for conversation, when they had sixteen rooms waiting to be cleaned.

Several task force predictions were cast in doubt by the results of participant observation. One situation, the one correct prediction, occurred twice: guests with no key asking to be let into their rooms. The prediction for the language most likely to be used by the guest (and heard by the housekeeper) was "But this is my room", spoken by an adult in an argumentative tone, to which the appropriate responses could be "Can you please run your key through the door?", "I need to see/check /be sure/verify that this is your room.", "I'm sorry, it's for your safety." and a suggestion that, if the guest continued arguing, the housekeeper should leave and call security. In the two cases in which this situation arose the guests were actually children who behaved more politely than the task force had predicted. The first situation arose during the day shift, when an approximately ten-year-old girl came back to her room and found nobody in. Josy (the day-shift housekeeper I was shadowing) and I were in the room across the hall, and the girl asked Josy, "Could you please open the door? (pointing to her door). My grandfather is not here." Josy, a fairly proficient speaker of English, just looked at her assignment sheet, verified that the guests in the particular room included a child, and opened the door for her. Notice that the prediction made by the task force was incorrect not only in the type of interlocutor and the tone of the request, but also in that they did not even consider that the guest might give an explanation for making such a request – in this case the girl explaining why she was asking to be let into the room.

The second instance occurred during the evening shift. A group of soccer players (three 13- and 14-year-old boys) came back to their rooms before the person in charge (and holding the key) did. The following is an excerpt from a rather lengthy conversation:

Boy 1:   Can you guys open it? (talking to Kris, the evening-shift housekeeper, and me, pointing at his door).
Kris: No. Sorry.
Boy 1:   But it's our room.
Kris: Can you call front desk? . . . They open it for you.
Boy 2:   What?
Kris: There's a phone over there (pointing at the phone at the end of the hall).
Boy 3:   What do we say, can you show us how to do it?
Kris: Just . . .
Boy 1:   How long will it take?
Kris: . . . the room number (she tries to tell them what to say when calling the front desk, as they fight over who should make the phone call; they go to the phone and return to the cart).
Boy 1:   Today somebody just opened it for me.
Boy 3:   Can we show you like . . . our names are there . . . or . . . look, I got something here (he shows Kris some kind of ID).
Boy 2:   Oh yeah! Oh let me tell you what's inside.
Boy 3:   Look . . . look . . . right here . . . I'm in the room (showing an ID with his name) . . . I don't know if you have like . . . a list with names of people staying in the room.

The conversation continues for a while. The point is that, although the one prediction for this situation made by the task force was correct, it fell very short of providing an account of the type and amount of interaction and negotiation that occurred.

As a source, the task force relied heavily on intuitions about hypothetical situations related to the task force members' own domains, and theorized about the language used in such situations. Their predictions concerning situations for small talk/greetings and closing a conversation with guests did not materialize during my participant observations. In cases of emergencies, however, people in specific departments do expect housekeepers who report to them to use some formulaic language, especially in the area of safety. Whether this formulaic language is used or not remains unknown; these are situations which almost never arise.

Participant observation also led to the identification of sources which had not been considered initially, like the morning briefings and the housekeeping room. It was while working with my informants that the usefulness of the paged messages as a source of language needs became obvious, and I realized that while working with one informant would provide access to the messages she received, tape-recording the messages in the housekeeping room would provide access to the messages sent to all housekeepers in the hotel. This confirms the emergent nature of qualitative research, where the "selection strategy evolves as the researcher collects data" (Glesne and Peshkin 1992: 25). In naturalistic inquiry, rarely does the researcher have a prespecified study design or a set of prespecified questions; responses to initial questions lead to new questions, and, coupled with observations, they allow discovery of alternative and complementary sources and methods which initially would have not been considered or even thought of (Glesne and Peshkin 1992; Wolcott 1995).

The following are examples of language used in paid messages to maids (1) and the language used to deal with guests' phone requests (2, 3) in the housekeeping room (for more examples see Appendix D). (XXX indicates unclear speech or difficult-to-transcribe words; the speaker is an evening supervisor, Celina.):

(1)   (Name), 719 would like service now. Room 719 service now. Thank you. Room XXX needs clean sheets.

(2)   Good evening, housekeeping, Celina. Yes yes yes . . . they want roll-away bed? OK, bye bye (she hangs up and pages the runner). The bedroom 602 need roll-away bed, 602 roll-away bed. Thank you.

(3)   Good evening, housekeeping, Celina . . . mhm . . . two coffee mugs, OK . . . Pardon? . . . No it's not free, we just let you borrow . . . OK thanks (hangs up and pages the runner). XXX also bring two coffee mugs in room 2706 . . . two coffee mugs in room 2706. Thank you.

Although these requests usually go to the runner[2] first, what makes them very important as a source is that they are the type of request with which the guests approach the maids if they see them, before calling housekeeping.

Morning briefings were undoubtedly the most important source of English for the housekeepers. The issues dealt with at these meetings ranged from those strictly related to their daily work (like supplies and guests) to institutional information (such as surveys and new policies) and institutional 'bonding' (like reciting the company's values and practicing Christmas carols). Problems related to personal feelings and touchy situations on the job also have an important place in these meetings, making them potentially very rich situations for language learning and language socialization (see the excerpt from Sakamaki's briefing below). The following are excerpts of some of the briefings, conducted at the main branch by the executive housekeeper (Chris) and an assistant housekeeper (Maria), and by supervisors (Janet and Sakamaki) at a smaller branch of the hotel chain.

Chris:
OK I talk to XXX manager. Remember you folks brought up yesterday about the XXX combination, yeah? . . . We have been ordering extra linen because is almost like four people per room, yeah? Four- four teenagers per room, OK? . . . And it's a lot . . . just . . . take the stuff off the beds and put them back . . . as far as vacuuming . . . if you cannot you cannot . . . OK? . . . because . . . we cannot expect you to pick up and move their XXX bags and move all their shoes because that's four people yeah? . . . If only one or two guests, no problem, but four, yeah?

Maria:
OK . . . you can call in sick, yeah? . . . Please try to call one day before in order that we . . . will call for replacement, yeah? Right away . . . cause it's very hard if you call us and let us know "I will call it back later" . . . then try to re-do the schedule, yeah? Especially late at night when nobody, Chris, Lina or XXX are no here, yeah?

Janet:
Very good. OK let's make the briefing short. We got a couple of things more for you. Regarding supplies . . . please, when you service your room, double check: toilet paper, kleenex, soap, shampoo. We're still getting calls from the guests early in the morning no more . . . OK? . . . always should have . . . back up . . . tissue paper, toilet paper, yeah? So please, take good care of your guests, OK?

Sakamaki:
. . . If you really need XXX or comments, please comment . . . please comment with a supervisor, no . . . no talking to other people . . . OK? . . . If you think is not right, is not fair, so . . . XXX schedule and you now you talking to everybody . . . please comment . . . for example, Marasita, for example, "Ah is not fair how come I get too much check out and she only gets two." I talk to Marasita and Marasita not gonna help . . . right? . . . So you gotta go see who can help you out the problem . . . OK? . . . Understand, yeah?

Unstructured interviews provided more and better quality information than questionnaires. As mentioned before, questions to the housekeepers were asked informally, more as part of casual conversations during our work together, thus allowing me to begin the process of building rapport with my informants and developing trust, both crucial aspects of qualitative research (Glesne and Peshkin 1992). The following responses provide some insight into various sources' perceptions of the need for English at work.

Josy (day-shift housekeeper):
Researcher: Do you think that to do your work, you need to speak English very well?
Josy: No (without hesitation). You mean the housekeepers?
Researcher: Yes, for example, for your job. How much do you use English?
Josy: Ah . . . (she keeps working while she seems to be thinking).
Researcher: That you have to use English.

Josy: You have to (repeating my words) . . . Ah! (seems to suddenly remember) because talk the guest, yeah? But they don't understand too English, yeah? They say, "Yes, yes, yes." You know, the Chinese, like that.

Researcher: And does that sometimes create problems?

Josy: Yeah problem, because they don't understand the . . .

Lao (evening housekeeper in charge of the public area):

Because some guests, yeah, they asking me, you know uh uh plenty questions but I cannot answer. Some guests, they listen, yeah? They say, "Oh, you no talk nice." But I tell, you know, if you go English class, yeah, you can talk nice and you . . . and when they listen, they feel comfortable. If no, you English class, yeah? You English no good, yeah? Some thinking like that, you know. I like help people, you know, but sometimes you don't understand. It's hard.

Celina (an evening supervisor):

. . . usually we just show it (the job) to them and they just follow, how to clean . . . not too much problem . . . they (the maids) get evaluated . . . cleaning, bodysavers (procedures to increase safety, efficiency, and to reduce fatigue). Good in cleaning is what is important.

Sandra (the human resources person):

The reason we have an English program starting is the hotel's focusing on more guests' services and trying to be friendly and be a host to everybody, to have each employee be a host to each guest rather than "Oh it's the front desk job to greet people and if I'm a housekeeper, I can just say hello and that's it." The way the company puts it, "to show our *aloha*[3]." Sometimes we get, ah, negative comments cards (regarding the housekeepers). They say things like "I asked for this and I didn't get it." But mostly is like "And can't you even get staff that speak English?" More like whiny, irritated.

Chris (the executive housekeeper):

To be able to explain to the guest that either because of their English or their under-standing they're not able to help them, but maybe they can refer them or put them on the phone with the managers, you know, at least tell them that. If they can just put the guests at ease and let them know that although I cannot help you, I can have someone help. Yeah, that would be it. I'm sure the guests wouldn't be upset about that. As for emergencies, they know what to do. They know what to say. I think the more we practice with them, the more they will feel comfortable. Like towards the afternoon, when the guests will be coming back, even. You know. If you tell them just "Hi," they'll say something else, you know. "Hi, how are you today? I'm fine." And it goes on. You know (laughs). They [the housekeepers] might shy away from that. I don't want them to be worried about what the guests might say.

Josy's, Lao's, Celina's, Sandra's and Chris' responses are a clear example of the differences in perceptions that different sources can have of the same phenomenon (Cumaranatunge 1988), and of how those perceptions can vary according to whether they are insiders or outsiders. It is clear that Josy, a fairly proficient English speaker, does not perceive English as necessary for the housekeeping job, nor regards chit-chatting with guests as part of her work. Celina seems to agree with Josy when she asserts that "Good in cleaning is what is important." Josy also hints that this pressure to talk to guests can generate problems since there are some guests who are not English speakers and engage in conversation when they in fact do not understand what the maid is asking or saying. Lao's perceptions of interactions with the guests as necessary for her job make sense for two reasons: the evening shift operates a schedule when the majority of the guests come back from the beach and get ready for dinner, and the public area includes places where there is constant traffic of guests, like the lobby, the front desk, the conference rooms, the halls, and the bathrooms. This causes Lao to have substantially more contact with guests than any of the day-shift housekeepers. Sandra, an outsider representing institutional interests who has no experience working as a housekeeper, seemed to regard the need for the maids to chit-chat as the most relevant need, while Chris, also an institutional representative, offered a different, more on-target perspective of the maids' English needs in their work. This should not be a surprise, however, for Chris is hardly an outsider. The executive housekeeper is at the top of the housekeeping hierarchy, with housekeeper assistants and supervisors between her position and the hotel maids. Her work involves a great deal of knowledge and performance of those occupations, besides interviewing and hiring new personnel and acting as a liaison between housekeeping and the rest of the departments. In part because of the nature of the job, and perhaps also because of Chris' personality (very involved with, and supportive of, the housekeepers), she is well aware of what goes on in a housekeeper's job on a daily basis, which makes her able to understand and share the insiders' perceptions. Also, it is not unusual for housekeepers to come to her with language questions related to dealing with doctors and other situations outside the workplace (personal communication). In addition, she is the person in charge of dealing with guests' complaints, which gives her an insight into their needs in terms of services provided by the housekeepers. It is this combination of knowledge that makes her responses more elaborated and focused on concrete facts, as compared to the responses from some other sources. Chris fits several criteria for Selinker's good informant:

> a NS, well trained and competent in the field of interest, used to dealing with NNSs attempting to function in that domain, caring about their success in doing so, able to explain what experts in the domain do, and willing to revise initial answers after follow-up questions if wrong the first time . . . should have a feel for the technical language in the domain, an openness to language teaching and LSP.
>
> (Selinker 1979)

Chris was aware of how little interaction goes on between guests and maids, and also of the background knowledge and pragmatics involved in chit-chatting, which makes casual conversation more complex than it seems – a fact that can discourage the housekeepers in their language efforts. For both reasons, she did not regard it as a major need the way Sandra did. During the interviews, she often expressed a desire to help the housekeepers succeed at the job, although this desire was expressed rather in institutional than personal terms: "We want them to succeed."

The following responses address the question of what it was thought would be useful to learn in an English class. This question was oriented towards investigating the various sources' perceptions of the housekeepers' language needs.

Chris:

Work terminology, only because XXX they have a lot of communication with the clerk, and most of the XXX, the guest requests or discrepancies uh one example would be the parts of the XXX, the knob, the light bulb, the switch, whatever, outlet. We use the terminology that the guest would most likely use from the mainland. For example, we call uh the lanai (a Hawaiian word) "lanai", whereas the guests call it "balcony", so they (the housekeepers) should know both. I'm not saying that they should use the other term, but they should know both.

Kris (the evening-shift housekeeper in charge of rooms and non-public areas such as offices):

. . . to learn about the hotel, name of things. Some people don't know how to say it, like toilet paper. To practice the things in the hotel.

Lao:

Simple English like "go see doctor", yeah? Then uh, "Meet a friend". You know. I just want learn the simple English. You know. When we go travel, we need English. Oh, you know, where I stay now, you know, I need to go somewhere, you know, "Can you tell me, you know, this hotel?" You know.

Lao also mentioned the questions that guests usually ask her: "Where's the market?", "Where's ABC store?" (a popular souvenir store chain), "How can I get to Ala Moana?" (a very large shopping center), "What bus I take?", "Where can I eat the Chinese food . . . the good . . . the good one?", questions about safety of Honolulu, oh "Here at night 11 o'clock, can you go outside? Is dangerous?" You know, like that.

Again, discrepancies between Lao's and Chris' perceptions can be explained by the nature of their jobs. Chris' job takes place mainly in empty rooms and offices, which makes knowing names of items more necessary than knowing how to answer guests' questions. In addition, Lao's English proficiency is higher than Chris', a fact that could make her ready, and willing, to learn language beyond what is needed for the job. Kris agrees with Chris and once again offers a more on-target perspective when she suggests the need for housekeepers to learn the names of things and the terminology used by the guests. Appendix D shows that many of the interactions in the housekeeping room involve requests of specific items.

Questionnaires provided little information related to either language or tasks, confirming Long's assertion that domain experts (in this case, the housekeepers) who have reliable introspections about language are exceptions, not the rule (although, admittedly, these domain experts were ESL speakers, and the questionnaires were in English). The questionnaires were administered during three morning briefings, with Chris going over each question and having a supervisor or assistant housekeeper help at each table. Not surprisingly, there were several questionnaires which had similar answers, probably what the housekeepers had explained or suggested to them by the supervisor at their table.

Responses to the questionnaires followed certain patterns according to nationality. All the Filipino housekeepers, for example, answered "yes" to question 4 (Did you study English in your home country?) and questions 8 and 9 (Do you speak English now? Do you speak English at work?), and reported not having any problems communicating with co-workers or guests (questions 11a, b, c). Most of the non-Filipino housekeepers, on the contrary, answered "no" to question 4 and left question 8 unanswered, or answered "a little", yet more than two thirds did not report having difficulties communicating (in English) with co-workers or guests (questions 9 and 11a, b, c). The English proficiency of the Filipino housekeepers varied, but it was higher than that of the rest of the housekeepers. Thus a similar answer among speakers of markedly different language proficiency is a discrepancy to be accounted for. A plausible explanation would depend on the language they use: if they communicate with co-workers using either a shared native language or Hawaii Creole English (HCE or "Pidgin"), which most of the housekeepers (including the Filipinas) seem to speak better than so-called "standard" English, then there seems to be no reason for having communication problems. Where communication with guests is concerned, if most of their communication is reduced to simple greetings, then it is understandable that they do not perceive any difficulty. This suggests more evidence of the unreliability of (many) learners' perceptions regarding their language needs.

Most housekeepers indicated their daily room assignment sheets and the surveys that the hotel conducts among workers as both reading and writing needs for the job (questions 12–15). Some indicated Saturday briefings and newspapers as reading needs as well. A variety of items were specifically indicated in answers to question 18 (What would you like to learn in an English class?): "writing", "spelling", "vocabulary", "correct grammar", "improve speaking", "learn everything at work". How many of these are objective needs and how many subjective needs or 'wants' (Long 2005; R. West 1994) cannot be determined, since it is difficult to know exactly what is meant by such responses as "improve speaking" and "correct grammar". They could refer to "standard" English, which Lao hints at in a statement of hers about the need to learn to "talk nice", and which Chris clearly refers to in some of her comments on what the maids should learn.

Most of the housekeepers' co-workers' answers to their questionnaires did not report any difficulty in communicating with the housekeepers (questions 6 and 8). However, all of them expressed a need for the maids to take English classes (question 12) "so they can understand", "so we can communicate", "improve English language", etc. These answers show a discrepancy which can only be partially accounted for with the same explanation given above for the housekeepers' answers (the use of HCE or "Pidgin" facilitates communication between co-workers and housekeepers). It is possible that when co-workers answered "yes" to question 6 (Do you ever speak English to the housekeepers?), and "no" to question 8 (Is it difficult communicating with them in English?), they may have meant HCE (which is, after all, a variety of English) and "standard" English when they answered question 12. This may explain why co-workers implied difficulty in understanding and communicating with the housekeepers (question 12) after denying such difficulty in questions 8 and 9, and it may imply a perception on their part of the housekeepers' need to learn "standard" English. This explanation would agree with Lao's and Chris' perceptions mentioned above. These interpretations, however, remain speculative.

One particular questionnaire was quite informative in regards to the view of an outsider (the assistant general manager) as to the maids' language needs. This individual perceived the maids as able to "get by" with their English skills, a fact that probably reflects the general feeling, and explains why most co-workers and maids did not perceive communication difficulties. This person also took into account the need for a "better command of the language" not only in the workplace but outside, as well, and seemed quite aware of the frustration that Lao expressed when she reported being unable to understand what guests wanted or liked.

A point of concern regarding the questionnaires was the number of questions that were not answered. Most housekeepers left questions 19–29, which refer to language use and needs outside the workplace, unanswered. A plausible explanation may be language difficulty, which highlights the importance of using the native language for written introspections. Lack of time may have played a role as well: the questionnaires were answered during morning briefings, which usually had a packed agenda. The lack of response to so many questions also highlights the importance of piloting questionnaires.

Conclusion

This study has shown the value of using multiple sources and methods for identifying learners' needs, the general reliability of insiders, and the frequent unreliability of outsiders. Participant observation proved to be crucial not only for familiarizing the researcher with the tasks and language involved in the maids' work, but also for identifying more sources, and triangulation allowed identification of the most reliable ones. This is bad news for applied linguists who make a living out of materials design and curriculum development based on their and other outsiders' intuitions: they are likely not providing their students with a realistic picture of the types of tasks, interlocutors, interaction patterns, and background knowledge involved.

The use of multiple sources also showed that different actors in a social setting have different perceptions of similar tasks and situations, which leads them to different objective and felt needs. Conflicts are bound to arise because their views often differ, and because the actors involved do not hold the same power in social settings. In this study, for example, it was found that the language necessary for the tasks that the hotel maids have to perform in their job is very limited, and a lack of English-language skills does not affect their performance. Conversely, institutional representatives perceive a need for the housekeepers to develop better language skills that will allow them to engage in "chit-chatting" with guests to show the company's "aloha", a strategy geared towards increasing business. This should lead us as researchers and curriculum designers to reflect on "the very obvious question of whose needs are we concerned with and how they are determined" (Chambers 1980: 26).

That an institutional need – clearly not perceived as such by the housekeepers – can be the motivation behind establishing a task force, a curriculum, and a language course, is a clear example of how power can be exercised in decision-making. Needs analyses are usually the result of institutional mandates, and are usually paid for with institutional money, but there is also the issue of who pays for language training. In this study, the company believed that the cost should be shared by itself and the housekeepers, on the basis that it would provide benefits to both (human resources person, personal communication). However, language training that does not meet the needs of students is a recipe for failure from the standpoint of motivational factors, and plain unfair when one considers that the housekeepers would be paying with both money and time.

There is no implication here that English-language training is unnecessary or undesirable, and I would like to remind the reader of Goldstein's (1992) suggestion of looking at the larger picture to find needs that must be addressed in order to expand students' options in English-speaking societies. In conducting an NA, it is necessary to examine the social context in which actors live their lives critically, as well as the power differentials involved. As researchers and curriculum designers, we must strive for a critical perspective based on dialogue with, rather than observation and manipulation of, people (Comstock 1982).

The use of qualitative research methods, and, more specifically, of ethnography, can help achieve this goal, by taking into account the social context of people's lives, and by allowing them to express their own voice and needs, as opposed to the researcher's, or the institution's. Although the study reported here was not an ethnography, the use of several qualitative research methods, multiple sources, and triangulation allowed for inclusion of learners' voices. These voices clearly disagreed with institutional needs and interpretations, and expressed their own. Further ethnographic research is suggested in order to identify language and literacy needs the housekeepers have outside the workplace, to create a curriculum that will truly engage them in language learning, so as to allow them to become active and functional members of an English-speaking society (Goldstein 1992), not merely cheap labor capable of reporting cleaning discrepancies in their rooms and greeting guests in "standard" English.

Notes

1   This is a revised and expanded version of the paper with the same title that first appeared in *English for Specific Purposes* 18, 1, 1999, 27–46.
2   The runner is an employee who is dispatched to the rooms to deliver items requested by the guests.
3   *Aloha* is a Hawaiian word with several meanings. In this context, it would indicate the company's friendliness and desire/effort to make the guests feel at home and have a pleasant stay.

References

Auerbach, E.R. (1995) 'The politics of the ESL classroom: issues of power in pedagogical choices', in R. Tollefson (ed.) *Power and Inequality in Language Education*. Cambridge: Cambridge University Press.

Chambers, F. (1980) 'A re-evaluation of needs analysis in ESP', *The ESP Journal* 1 (1): 25–33.

Comstock, D.E. (1982) 'A method for critical research', in E. Breedo and W. Seinberg (eds) *Knowledge and Values in Social and Educational Research*. Philadelphia, PA: Temple University Press.

Cumaranatunge, L. (1988) 'An EOP case study: domestic aids in West Asia', in D. Chamberlain and R.J. Baumgardner (eds) *ESP in the Classroom: Practice and Evaluation* (pp. 127–33). ELT Document 128. London and Oxford: The British Council in Association with Modern English Publications (Macmillan).

Davis, K.A. (1992) 'Validity and reliability in qualitative studies. Another researcher comments', Research Issues. *TESOL Quarterly* 26 (3): 605–8.

Drobnic, K., Trimble, L. and Trimble, M.T. (eds) (1978) 'Mistakes and modifications in course design: an EST case history', in *English for Specific Purposes: Science and Technology*, (pp. 313–21). English Language Insitute, Oregon State University, Corvallis: Ore.

Glesne, C. and Peshkin, A. (1992) *Becoming Qualitative Researchers: An Introduction*. White Plains, NY: Longman.

Goldstein, T. (1992) 'Language choice and women learners of English as a second language', in K. Hall, M. Bucholtz and B. Moonwoman (eds) *Locating Power: Proceedings of the Second Berkeley Women and Language Conference*, Berkeley, CA: Berkeley Women and Language Group.

Long, M. (ed.) (2005) *Second Language Needs Analysis*, Cambridge University Press, pp. 127–58.

Long, M.H. (1985) 'A role for instruction in second language acquisition: task-based language teaching', in K. Hyltenstam and M. Pienemann (eds) *Modeling and Assessing Second Language Development* (pp. 77–99). Clevedon, Avon: Multilingual Matters.

Long, M.H. (to appear) *Task-based Language Teaching*. Oxford: Blackwell.

Prince, D. (1984) 'Workplace English: approach and analysis', *The ESP Journal* 3 (2): 109–15.

Selinker, L. (1979) 'The use of specialist informants in discourse analysis', *International Review of Applied Linguistics* 17 (2): 189–215.

Svendsen, C. and Krebs, K. (1984) 'Identifying English for the job: examples from the health care occupations', *The ESP Journal* 3: 153–64.

Tollefson, J.W. (1989) *Alien Winds: The Reeducation of America's Indo-Chinese Refugees*. New York: Praeger.

Tollefson, J.W. (1991) *Planning Language, Planning Inequality*. New York: Longman.

Watson-Gegeo, K. (1988) 'Ethnography in ESL: defining the essentials', *TESOL Quarterly* 22 (4): 575–92.

West, L. (1984) 'Needs assessment in occupation-specific VESL or how to decide how to teach', *The ESP Journal* 3: 143–52.

West, R. (1994) 'Needs analysis in language teaching', *Language Teaching* 27 (1): 1–19.

Wolcott, H. (1995) *The Art of Fieldwork*. Newbury Park, MA: Sage.

Appendix A: Housekeepers' questionnaire

Name _____

1. Where are you from?
2. What language do you speak?
3. How many years did you go to school in your home country?
4. Did you study English in you home country?   Yes____ No____
5. How long have you been in the United States?
6. How long have you been working as a housekeeper?
7. What things do you do every day at work?
8. Do you speak English now?
9. Do you speak English at work?   Yes____ No____
10. If you answered No, why not?
11. If you answered Yes,
     a) Who do you speak English with?
     b) When do you speak English with them?
     c) Is it difficult communicating with them?
12. Do you sometimes need to read English at work?   Yes____ No____
13. If you answered Yes, what do you need to read?
14. Do you sometimes need to write in English at work?   Yes____ No____
15. If you answered Yes, what do you need to write?
16. Have you ever studied English in the United States?   Yes____ No____
17. Would you like to study English?   Yes____ No____
18. If you answered Yes, what things would you like to learn in your English class?
19. Do you speak English outside the job?   Yes____ No____
20. If you answered Yes, when do you speak English?
21. Does somebody help you with English when you go shopping, or when you go to the doctor, etc.?   Yes____ No____
22. If you answered Yes, who helps you?
23. What language do you speak at home with your family and friends?
24. Do you have children?   Yes____ No____
     How many?
     What languages do they speak?
25. Are your children in school?   Yes____ No____
26. Do you sometimes go to meetings at your children's school?
27. Can you understand what teachers and parents say at those meetings?   Yes____ No____
28. Does somebody help you with English at those meetings?   Yes____ No____
29. Did somebody help you answer this questionnaire? Who?

Appendix B: Co-workers' questionnaire

Occupation _____

1. Do you speak English?
2. What things do you do every day at work?
3. For reasons of work, do you need to speak with the
   housekeepers?   Yes___ No___
4. If you answered Yes, please describe the work situations in
   which you need to speak to them.
5. In what language do you speak to them? Please write as
   many languages as you use.
6. Do you ever speak English to the housekeepers?   Yes___ No___
7. If you answered Yes, in what situations?
8. Is it difficult communicating with them in English?   Yes___ No___
9. If you answered Yes, can you explain the difficulties?
10. Do the housekeepers sometimes need to read messages
    from you, or write messages to you in English?   Yes___ No___
11. If you answered Yes, can you explain in what situations?
12. Based on your experience working at the hotel and with the housekeepers,
    what do you think it would be good for them to learn in an English class?
    What do you think are the languages that they need to learn most? Please give
    as many examples as you can think of. Thank you.

Appendix C: Examples of interactions with guests

Examples of interactions with guests that occurred during the five sessions of
participant observation (interactions already included in the chapter, such as those
with guests asking to be let into their rooms, are not repeated here).

Interactions with guests during day-shifts. None of these interactions occurred
because the guests stopped to chat; they interacted while passing by. FG = female
guest; MG = male guest.

(1) MG: Hello.
    Researcher: Hello, how are you.
    FG: Hello, good morning.
(2) MG and FG: Good morning.
    Researcher: Good morning, how are you today.
    MG: Fine, yourself?
    Researcher: Fine thank you. Have a good day.
(3) MG: Finished for the day? (making a gesture)
    Researcher: I wish.
    MG: You wish! (laughs)

Interaction that took place when a guest wanted the maid (Shu) to wait a few more minutes before servicing the room:

(4) Shu: (Knocks on the door). Housekeeping.
     FG (Japanese):   (Opens the door) Yes?
     Shu: Housekeeping.
     FG: How about 15 minutes . . . we'll go out?
     Shu: OK.

Shu moves to another room, and a few minutes later the guest calls back:

     FG: OK lady.
     Shu: OK. Thank you.

Interaction that took place when two guests (Korean females) returned and their room was still being serviced.

(5) FG: For you (pointing at two dollar bills on the night table).
     Researcher: Oh, thank you.

Interaction that occurred during the evening shift. There was usually a housekeeper and a supervisor working together in the rooms during the evening shift. Chris is the housekeeper, Celina is the supervisor.

(6) Child: Excuse me, do you have a swimming pool?
     Chris: Yes, ten(th) floor.

Interactions that occurred between the housekeeper in charge of the public area (Lao), during the evening shift. There was only one maid working in the public area, and she would be "pulled out" from her duties there during busy times when extra help was needed in the rooms.

While emptying ashtrays in the lobby:

(7) FG: Hello, how are you.
     Lao: Hi.

In the hall outside the meeting room, with guests coming out of a meeting:

(8) FG: Good evening.
     Lao: Hi, good evening.
     MG: Hello . . . you got to clean up (smiling).
     Lao: Yes (she smiles and nods)
     Guest: I know what it is like. I have to do it sometimes.

Interactions while cleaning the women's bathroom in the basement, where there was a new Chinese–Japanese restaurant.

(9) FG 1:   Hello.
     Lao: Hi.

FG 2:	Hi . . . (she hesitates to come in since we are cleaning the floor) am I interrupting something?
Lao:	Hi.
Researcher:	No, just go ahead.

Interaction with the front desk clerk (FDC) when cleaning the front desk area:

(10) FDC:	Hi Lao, how are you
Lao:	Hi XXX.
FDC:	How's your son?
Lao:	Very big! . . . XXX pounds.
FDC:	Wow! He's soon going to outweight you.
Lao:	Yes! (laughing).
FDC:	(To me) Are you shadowing tonight?
Researcher:	Yeah.

Appendix D: Examples of phone calls and paged messages

Examples of phone calls and paged messages received and sent in the housekeeping room during an evening shift observation.

Examples of paged messages:

(1) (Name), 719 would like services now. Room 719 service now. Thank you.
(2) Room____needs clean sheets.
(3) Room____needs service. Room____. Thank you.
(4) Call housekeeping, housekeeping, call housekeeping. Thank you.

Examples of the evening supervisor (Celina) attending phone requests from guests in the housekeeping room. Messages would then be paged to the runner or to the housekeepers:

(5) Good evening, housekeeping, Celina. Yes, yes, yes . . . they want roll-away bed? OK, bye bye. (She then hangs up and pages the runner):
(6) The bedroom 602 need roll-away bed, 602 roll-away bed. Thank you.
(7) Good evening, housekeeping, Celina. Pardon me? What . . . ah . . . what do you want to . . . oh we have only toothbrush, toothpaste . . . that's all we have complimentary . . . no we have only XXX mhm OK . . . that's all we have I think. And besides that we have the lobby, we have the store in the lobby where you can buy those things . . . we have toothpaste . . . and we have toothbrush . . . how about toothpaste . . . OK . . . bye bye.

She hangs up and turns to me "He's asking for deodorant", she says. She pages the runner:

(8) Call housekeeping please call housekeeping. Thank you.

The phone rings, it is the runner who had just been paged:

(9)   Good evening, housekeeping, Celina . . . XXX OK room 2706 . . . ah they like toothbrush and toothpaste and comb.

(10)   Good evening, housekeeping, Celina mhm two coffee mugs, OK . . . pardon? No it's not free, we just let you borrow . . . OK thanks.

Celina pages the runner:

(11)   XXX also bring two coffee mugs in room 2706 . . . two coffee mugs in room 2706. Thank you.

(12)   Good evening, housekeeping, Celina mhm oh OK yeah we have do . . . we have vacuum too OK . . . you need the . . . to vacuum the carpet? OK we have some ah some things to XXX up. OK. I'll page my runner and sen(d) to XXX room XXX right? So you need a vacuum only . . . OK Thanks. (Celina pages the runner):

(13)   XXX please bring one vacuum in room 2215, the guest would like to borrow it. Room 2215 like to borrow vacuum.

(14)   Good evening, housekeeping, Celina. Yes Kris . . . OK is it occupied room? OK thanks, bye.

This was a call from Kris, the evening maid, reporting a problem she had encountered in one room. Celina pages maintenance:

(15)   Room 2914 the bathtub stopper is not working . . . Room 2914 the bathtub stopper is not working. Thank you.

Example of Celina calling housekeeping to report discrepancies in a room while working with Kris:

(16)   Celina: 805 you said maid service, yeah? . . . it's ah vacant room . . . is it XXX? Double check. (She hangs up and a few minutes later her pager beeps with the following message):

(17)   805 continental room need to be cleaned before 9 o'clock. 805 continental room need to be cleaned before 9 o'clock.

After hearing the message she turns to Kris:

(18)   So they want the room clean, Kris.

Example of Celina responding to the paged message "Call housekeeping, please call housekeeping."

(19)   Renato, you paged me. Yeah . . . 29? Right now? OK. OK. Goodbye. (A TV repairer is going up to fix the TV in room 29 and Celina must let him in and stay with him until he finishes his job.)

Example of Kris paging housekeeping to make a request:

(20)   I need one shower curtain, 805.

Chapter 15

Scott Thornbury and Diana Slade

The grammar of conversation

Introduction

There are at least two common misconceptions about the grammar of spoken language: it is assumed either that spoken grammar is simply written grammar realized as speech, or that spoken grammar is a less complex, even degenerate, form of its written counterpart. The first assumption seems to underlie the conventional pedagogic wisdom that the written grammar of the language is sufficient for the learning of both writing *and* speaking, as if the written grammar was the 'default' grammar, from which all language choices flowed. The following dialogue (from a textbook published in 1947), while extreme, exemplifies the way written language is often presented as if it were speech:

> The other day, on getting into the train, I found a Frenchman in my carriage, and the following conversation took place:

> Englishman: Good morning, sir. Isn't it lovely weather? Are you travelling far?
>
> Frenchman: No, sir, I get out at the first stop, the next station before Leeds.
>
> Englishman: Oh? Then I travel farther than you. I have to go as far as Glasgow. I get there early tomorrow morning. Do you know this line well? It is one of our best main lines.
>
> Frenchman: Oh no, not at all. It is the first time I have ever travelled on it; I have not been long in England . . . etc.
>
> (Hübscher and Frampton 1947: 63–4)

Edited extracts from: Thornbury, S., Slade, D. 'The grammar of conversation', in *Conversation: from description to pedagogy*, pp. 73–86, 90–6 and 100–3, Cambridge University Press, 2006.

The recognition that spoken language is characterized by, among other features, repetitions and simplifications – such as contractions, ellipsis and a lack of clausal complexity – began to emerge in teaching materials in the 1960s and 1970s. It may be no coincidence that, around the same time, dramatists and novelists were also attempting to capture the flavour of spoken language through the use of similar stylistic devices.

Despite this acceptance of the distinctiveness of both written and spoken language, any differences were generally treated as being stylistic (i.e. a question of formality), or as resulting from the demands of performance factors, or simply as symptoms of laziness and lack of care. The distinction between what Saussure termed *langue* (that is to say, the underlying linguistic system) and *parole* (the actual utterances the speaker produces), was commonly invoked to describe – if not explain – the differences between written language and speech. Similarly, Chomsky distinguished between what he called *competence* and *performance*, and noted that 'a record of natural speech will show numerous false starts, deviations from rules, changes of plan in mid-course, and so on', but insisted that such performance phenomena 'cannot constitute the actual subject matter of linguistics' (1965: 4).

Thus spoken grammar continued to occupy an inferior position and seldom merited a footnote, let alone a full-blown description, in either descriptive or pedagogic grammars. Even the shift to a greater naturalism in coursebook dialogues only went so far. The following criticism by Crystal and Davy is just as applicable thirty years later:

> People in textbooks, it seems, are not allowed to tell long and unfunny jokes, to get irritable or to lose their temper, to gossip (especially about other people), to speak with their mouths full, to talk nonsense, or swear (even mildly). They do not get all mixed up while they are speaking, forget what they wanted to say, hesitate, make grammatical mistakes, argue erratically or illogically, use words vaguely, get interrupted, talk at the same time, switch speech styles, manipulate the rules of the language to suit themselves, or fail to understand. In a word, they are not *real*.
>
> (1975: 3)

More recently, the case for 'real English', including a recognition of the distinctive and systematic nature of spoken grammar, has been argued vigorously, particularly by researchers working with corpora of spoken language (such as the CANCODE corpus). Carter and McCarthy contend that 'written-based grammars exclude features that occur widely in the conversation of native speakers of English . . . and with a frequency and distribution that simply cannot be dismissed as aberration' (1995: 142). Biber *et al.* go further, and argue for the primacy of spoken grammar: 'Conversation is the most commonplace, everyday variety of language, from which, if anything, the written variety, acquired through painstaking and largely institutional processes of education, is to be regarded as a departure' (1999: 1038). Of course, this does not mean that the two grammars are so different as to deserve separate treatment. On the basis of their corpus data, Biber *et al.* conclude that so many language features are shared that 'the same "grammar of English" can be applied to both the spoken and the written language'. Nevertheless, as McCarthy points out, 'we should never *assume* that if a grammar has been constructed for written texts, it is equally valid for spoken texts. Some forms seem to occur much more frequently in one mode or the other, and some forms are used with different shades of meaning in the two modes' (1998: 76). In the rest of this chapter we shall be looking at those grammatical forms that occur more frequently, or are used differently, in casual conversation as compared to other registers.

Complexity

One issue that has attracted a good deal of attention is the apparent syntactic simplicity of casual conversation. This simplicity has been attributed both to its informal nature and to the constraints of real-time production. Halliday, however, takes issue with this view, arguing that 'the sentence structure [of speech] is highly complex, reaching degrees of complexity that are rarely attained in writing' (1985: xxiv). This is because, while the complexity of writing resides in the way lexical content is densely packed into fairly simple grammatical frames, 'the complexity of spoken language is more like that of a dance; it is not static and dense but mobile and intricate' (ibid.). This mobility and intricacy is in turn due to the fact that the context of spoken language is 'in a constant state of flux, and the language has to be equally mobile and alert'. He gives, as an example of the fluidity and intricacy of spoken language, the following:

> but you can't get the whole set done all at once because if you do you won't have any left to use at home, unless you just took the lids in and kept the boxes, in which case you wouldn't have to have had everything unpacked first; but then you couldn't be sure the designs would match so . . .
>
> (Halliday 1985: xxiv)

Some evidence for this intricacy can be found in corpus data. Biber *et al.*, for example, note that 'speakers in conversation use a number of relatively complex and sophisticated grammatical constructions, contradicting the widely held belief that conversation is grammatically simple' (1999: 7). One example of this complexity that they identify is the use of complex relative clause constructions of the type *There's so many things that I want to learn*. . . . Nevertheless, they also note that the real-time production demands of conversation result, on the whole, in shorter and simpler clauses, less variation, and a reliance on certain more-or-less fixed sentence frames that are less grammatical than lexical in the way they are retrieved and deployed (1999: 964). McCarthy makes a similar observation:

> Anyone who looks at large amounts of informal spoken data . . . cannot fail to be struck by the absence of well-formed "sentences" with main and subordinate clauses. Instead, we often find turns that are just phrases, incomplete clauses, clauses that look like subordinate clauses but which seem not to be attached to any main clause, etc.
>
> (1998: 79–80)

In fact, the very terms *sentences*, *main clauses*, *subordinate clauses* etc. sit uncomfortably with spoken data. They belong to a 'text-on-the-page' view of language, where the constituents of sentences can be unpacked and analysed after the event, so to speak, producing what Brazil calls 'a hierarchical constituent-within-constituent account of how language is organised' (1997: 4). Such a product-derived account fails to capture the *processes* by which the grammar of speech is realized. Moreover, many features of spoken language – such as *heads* and *tails* (see below) – simply cannot be accounted for by 'sentence grammar'. Brazil, therefore, proposes a view of spoken grammar that is essentially dynamic, one in which we regard discourse as 'something that is now-happening, bit by bit, in time, with the language being assembled as the speaker goes along' (1997: 37). Such a view helps explain the seemingly fragmented, even inchoate, nature of transcribed talk. It may also put to rest the question of the relative complexity of written and spoken language: they are both complex, but in quite different ways.

To return to Halliday's example (quoted above), clearly the planning in advance of this utterance in its entirety, including the embedding within it of a number of subordinate clauses, would simply be beyond the capacity of most speakers' working memories, given that working memory has a span of only about seven items (whether single words or multi-word units). Moreover, the pause that would have been required in order to formulate such an utterance would have been unacceptably long for most conversational situations.

It is much more likely that the utterance was assembled in stages, each successive stage building on its predecessor, and each planned locally, so that the effect is something like the following (although in the absence of prosodic information – e.g. pausing and intonation – we can only guess):

but you can't get the whole set done all at once
+ because if you do
+ you won't have any left to use at home
+ unless you just took the lids in
+ and kept the boxes
+ in which case you wouldn't have to have had everything unpacked first
+ but then you couldn't be sure the designs would match
+ so . . .

The complexity is achieved not by embedding constituents within a pre-determined sentence frame, but through the successive (and potentially limitless) accumulation of individual clause-like units. The logical connections between such units are indicated using discourse markers (*but*, *because*, *unless*, *in which case*, *so* . . .) to signal the incremental twists and turns of the speaker's train of thought. While the cumulative effect of these 'add-ons' appears syntactically complex, each segment is relatively simple – for example, every clause in the above text begins with *you*.

Nor is spoken language always conveniently packaged into clauses. In the following text, the segments in italics are non-clausal, that is they resist analysis in terms of combinations of subject and verb, or subject + verb + object, etc:

Chris: It's a nice area.
Doris: *Bardwell Park.*

Mark: Is it?

Gary: It's pretty dead. It's only a small shopping centre.

Chris: *Oh yeah, well* you don't really go to that shopping centre. Where I live it's the worst shopping centre in Sydney. They opened a new dress shop and I could see the pink carpet going in and all and I thought *gee a nice trendy dress shop. Thank goodness.* 'Cause there's nothing there. You know what it is? *A middle-class boutique for the middle-age set.*

Gary: *Yuck.* And everybody wears brown boots.

Doris: *Yeah?*

Chris: *Nothing worse. You know too, too dressy.*

(Authors' data)

Non-clausal material partly consists of a large class of items called *inserts* (Biber *et al.* 1999), which include response words (*Oh yeah*), discourse markers (*well*), back-channel devices (*yeah?*), and interjections (*gee, thank goodness, yuck*). Inserts are stand-alone items – they do not enter into syntactic relations with other structures. A second class of non-clausal material consists of isolated phrases or clausal fragments which *are* capable of forming elements of clause-and-sentence structures. Hence they are called *syntactic non-clausal units* (Biber *et al.* 1999). Examples include answers to questions (*A middle-class boutique for the middle-age set*), repetitions or elaborations of previous content (*Bardwell Park*), and evaluative comments (*nothing worse*).

Biber *et al.* (1999) use the term *C-units* as an umbrella term for both clausal and non-clausal units, and consider such units to be the building blocks of spoken grammar – what sentences are to written grammar.

Heads and tails

The complexity of spoken language, then, is achieved incrementally. One effect of this incremental construction – and one that the grammar of written language does not generally share – is that the body of the message is preceded and followed by optional slots into which matter (typically non-clausal) may be inserted, as in these italicized instances from the preceding extract:

oh *a friend of ours in Paddington*, they had to move out of the flat

she was sitting in her living room and a hailstone fell through the skylight, *this old Italian woman*

I think I don't know many people who have been affected except you and I. *That much.*

These optional slots either before or after the body of the message are known, respectively, as *heads* and *tails*. The head slot typically consists of a noun phrase which serves to identify key information such as the topic and to establish a common frame of reference for what follows – whether a statement or a question:

Junket, I mean you have junket and stewed rhubarb

Filing. I'd love a whole day, one weekend, when there's nobody around to do it.

You know how kids they always say if they can't get their own way they're going to kill themselves?

Good ground out there is it? (cf: Is it a good ground out there?)

Where a narrative follows, the head slot can accommodate the *abstract* component of a story structure, according to Labov's (1972) model. The abstract is a short statement of what the story is going to be about:

Kedgeree, I remember saying to my mum I've got to take a pound of fish next week we're making kedgeree

Note that noun phrase heads often result in such 'non-grammatical' constructions (by written grammar standards) as sentences with two subjects:

[Where I live] [it]'s the worst shopping centre in Sydney.

oh [a friend of ours in Paddington], [they] had to move out of the flat

[The bloke behind], [he] can't see

[His mate with him], [he] hit a tree.

Heads thus fulfil a discourse function, because one of their roles is to fore-ground the topical focus of what follows. Another discourse function of head-slot items is to flag the direction of the talk and its connection to preceding talk, and so it is common to find discourse markers and other interactional signals in this position, as in the italicized examples in this short extract:

Di: You cannot drink on the job
Jessie: *Right yes* and if they did set him up what would they do? *I mean* how could you get him sacked?
Judy: *Well* they just would-
Di: *Really in a way* they don't really have to get anybody *I mean to say* if you are not doing the right thing and you feel there's this pressure on and they watch you like a hawk . . . in the end you're really going to crack
                                                                          (Authors' data)

While the head slot fulfils a largely prospective function, the tail slot is more retrospective in its use, serving to extend, reinforce, mitigate, clarify or otherwise comment on, what the speaker is saying or has just said. Typical tail-slot items are:

- *question tags*: Croatia's Yugoslav, *isn't it*? That Parramatta's good side, *aren't they*?;
- *interrogatives*: There's a nice big pub there, *no*? They started already *or*?;
- *reinforcement tags*: you're in trouble, *you are*;
- *noun phrase identifiers*: Yeah she's nice *Robyn*; They hate the Yugoslavs *the Croats*; Jeff's the other guy from Wollongong *that photo you saw*;
- *evaluative adjectives*: He drops them anywhere, *terrible*;

- *vague category identifiers*: you know high mass *and all the rest*; you trying to make me talk *or something?*;
- *comment clauses*: The things he does, *I don't know*; I was down there Sunday *I think*; That's a bit unfair *I reckon*.

Discourse markers and interactional signals can also occupy the tail slot, as in:

> Before we know it they've got Swiss bank accounts *you know*
> And, and as I said the language *you know I mean really*
> It's nice like that *though*
> Oh I shouldn't really do this *but*

Vocatives – such as *How are you, Jessie?*; *Good morning, brother* – are other common tail-slot items, and are more usually found in the tail slot than the head slot. If placed in the head slot, they tend to function as attention solicits, whereas tail-slot vocatives have the function 'of adjusting or reinforcing the social relationship between the speaker and the addressee' (Biber *et al.* 1999: 1112). McCarthy and O'Keeffe (2003) use spoken corpus data to show that, in casual conversations, there is a fairly equal distribution of vocatives among speakers, and that this can be interpreted as a display of solidarity. This is consistent with Carter and McCarthy's contention that tails are 'an important part of what may be called *interpersonal grammar*, that is to say speaker choices which signal the relationships between participants and position the speaker in terms of his/her stance or attitude' (1995: 151).

Grammatical incompletion

Because of the pressure of online planning, and the jointly constructed nature of conversation, spoken language is often ungrammatical, even by its own relatively 'relaxed' standards. For example, utterances are either left incomplete or non-standard usages arise through syntactic 'blending' – that is, where there is a grammatical mismatch between the start of an utterance and its completion. Here are some instances of typical incompletions and blends:

- *abandonment* (where the speaker abandons or re-starts an utterance):
  Odile: I'm so glad the kids were not there because you know that hole is just above Debbie's head . . .
- *interruption* (incompletion caused by the interruption of another speaker):
  Grace: I was speaking to erm . . .
  Odile: Oh my god I hadn't thought about that . . .
- *completion by other speakers*:
  Rob: . . . they had to move out of the flat because the whole . . .
  Grace: . . . roof collapsed
- *blending*:
  I think there's there's the colour I like is a sort of a buttery yellow.

The fact that such non-standard forms not only exist but are tolerated by native-speaker interlocutors suggests that to demand 100 per cent accuracy in speaking activities in the classroom may not only be unrealistic but unwarranted.

Ellipsis

Unlike grammatical incompletion, ellipsis is the deliberate omission of items, such as subject pronouns and verb complements, that are redundant because they are recoverable from the immediate context, either the linguistic context or the situational one. We have already seen how a lot of non-clausal conversational material is elliptical, as in question-and-answer exchanges such as the following:

Chris: Is your wife working? She going back to work?
Gary: When she gets motivated I suppose
Chris: Good on her, stands her ground.
Chris: You going to stay in your mum's house?
Gary: Nah – moving . . . probably. Might move into a, Bardwell Park.

Here, the omitted elements have been re-instated between brackets:

Chris: Is your wife working? [Is] she going back to work?
Gary: [She's going back to work] when she gets motivated I suppose
Chris: Good on her, [she] stands her ground.
Chris: [Are] you going to stay in your mum's house?
Gary: Nah [I'm] moving . . . probably. [I] might move into a, Bardwell Park.

Note that omitted items can consist of single words and phrases (*is*, *she*) or whole clauses (*she's going back to work*). Commonly omitted items include sentence subjects (*[she] stands her ground, [I] might move . . .*), subjects and operators (*[I'm] moving*) and auxiliary verbs (*[Is] she going . . ., [are] you going*). Ellipses most frequently occur at the beginning of utterances rather than in their middle or at their end. This is because it is at the beginning of utterances that *given* (as opposed to *new*) information is usually incorporated – information that is more readily recoverable from the context, and hence redundant. Final ellipsis is common in replies to questions, or in comment questions (see below), where repetition is avoided by omitting any words following the operator (*do* in each of the following instances; omitted items in brackets):

Di S: Do you think women sw-swear as much here at each other?
Judy: Oh they do [swear at each other] here.
Judy: I think they're awful.
Jess: Do you [think they're awful]?

'Ellipsis is pervasive in spoken discourse' (Carter and McCarthy, 1997: 14). This is particularly the case in language-in-action talk – that is, talk that accompanies the performance of some activity, where situational factors, plus the need for brevity and concision, render relatively elaborated language superfluous.

Deixis

Because conversation takes place in a shared temporal and spatial context (unless, of course, it is over the telephone), speakers frequently make direct reference to features of the immediate situation. They do this using *deictic* expressions. Deixis derives from the Greek term for 'finger' and is used to mean 'pointing with language'. In other words, using language devices such as personal pronouns, demonstratives (*this* and *that*), and adverbials (such as *here, there, now, then*), speakers can make reference to such features of the immediate context as themselves and the other people present (what is called *personal deixis*), the immediate space (*spatial deixis*), and the time (*temporal deixis*). Even on the telephone, speakers can 'point' to contextual features, using deictic expressions, as in **This** *is Dan. Is Louise* **there**? and *What's the weather like* **there now**? Deixis is mainly realized through lexical choices, but we have included it as part of the grammatical description of conversation since the bulk of the words that comprise deictic expressions are function words rather than content ones.

In the following extract deictic references are italicized:

Father: Look *I* fixed *this*.
Girl 1: *You* did?
Father: Okay.
Girl 1: Thank *you*, Dad.
Father: No worries.
Girl 1: Dad. Can *you* do *this* for *me*?
Father: *You*'ll have to press *this* extremely hard.
Girl 1: Ah hm.
Girl 2: And *you* don't have to use *that*.

(OZTALK)

The relatively high proportion of deictic expressions in casual conversation in comparison with other spoken genres, and the even higher proportion of deictic expressions in spoken language as compared to most written language, is one of the reasons why the reading of transcripts of conversation is so difficult. This is particularly so in the case of language-in-action talk (see above).

[. . .]

Tense and aspect

The way tense and aspect are used in conversation generally parallels their uses in other registers. That is, tense is used as a grammatical marker of time, while aspect serves to distinguish between verbal situations that are seen as in progress (or not) or complete (or not). However, there are important differences in the frequency and distribution of these verb forms – differences that reflect both the 'here-and-now' nature of conversation, as well as its largely interpersonal function.

The present tense is by far the most common tense in casual conversation, outnumbering past tense forms by roughly four to one (Biber *et al.*), a fact that 'reflects speakers' general focus on the immediate context' (1999: 457). It is used primarily to refer to current states or to current habitual behaviour, as in this extract in which a group of women are looking at holiday photos (present tense forms – including present perfect, but excluding modal verbs – are italicized):

Beaches

Judy: What *are* their beaches like? *Are* they pebbles?

Di: You *get* sand, you *get* pebbles, you *get* yuck. This was a sandy beach, but as you can see it's not really golden.

Judy: You're not riding on sand *are* = = you?

Di: = = No . . .

Judy: You *know* what you *look* like? You should be here?
         You should be in an Omo ad, you *know*, really you *got** the smile and then the bright lights.

Di: There's there's sand.

Deidre: And there's rock.

Di: Yeah well, further up the coast *is* all this rock.
         Imagine lying on that in your bikinis!

All: [laugh]

Di: They *go* down there with their little deck chairs . . .

Deidre: And their shelves = =

Judy: = = You can always tell English people at the beach

Deidre: You can . . .

Judy: They always *wear* their short socks and their sandals.
         Have you ever seen them?

All: [laugh]

* in this instance *got* is considered an elliptical form of *have got*

(Authors' data)

Present tenses with past reference (also called the *historic present*) are sometimes used in narratives in order to create immediacy, either in setting the scene, or in order to signal the *complicating event* (Labov 1972), as in this example:

Russell Stouffer mints

Irene: I'm on a diet and my mother *buys* . . .

Zelda: You're not!

Irene: My mother *buys* these mints . . .

Zelda: Oh yeh.

Irene: The Russel Stouffer mints. I said. 'I don't want any Mum'. 'Well, I don't wanna eat the whole thing.' She *gives* me a little tiny piece, I *eat* it. Then she *gives* me another = =

Henry: = = Was

Irene: = = so I threw it out the window.

(after Schiffrin 1987: 80–1)

Jokes in particular lend themselves to the use of the historic present (*There're these two goldfish in a tank. One of them says to the other. 'How do you drive this thing?'*). On the whole, however, tellers of narratives and personal anecdotes favour past tense forms over present tense ones, with only occasional shifts into the present. The majority of past forms in casual conversation occur in narratives. In the following short extract, the speaker constructs her narrative by weaving together past simple, past continuous, past perfect and present simple forms with all the skill of a filmmaker varying between wide-angle shots, flashbacks and close-ups (past tense forms underlined; present tense forms in italics):

> I <u>came</u> out I <u>was filing</u> the sheets and I'<u>d done</u> up to the 50s and I <u>was coming</u> out for a cigarette and I *sit* down, and the minute I <u>sat</u> down, <u>lit</u> up a cigarette, she <u>looked</u> out of the window and she *can* see me so I just sort of <u>slid</u> behind the boxes where all our papers *are*

(Authors' data)

Progressive aspect is found in past narrative (as in the above extract: *was filing, was coming*) to provide the narrative 'frame' for the key events in a narrative, as well as being frequently used for reporting verbs (see below). But on the whole progressive verb forms are relatively uncommon in conversation, being outnumbered by simple forms by roughly twenty to one (Biber *et al.* 1999). Of these progressive forms the majority (70 per cent) are in the present (ibid.). Curiously, progressive aspect is more common in American conversational data than in British data (ibid.).

Perfect aspect is also far less frequent than simple forms in conversation, even taking into account *have got*, the single most common present perfect in British English. The present perfect is often used to comment on changes, such as when reporting news, or commenting on situations whose effects are evident at the time of speaking, as in these two extracts:

Extract (1)
Keith: *He's changed.*
Jim: *I have changed.*
Steve: *He's shaved* his mo' off.
Gary: You ought to see it. It's unbelievable.

Extract (2)
Pauline: What'*ve they done* to the seats?
Bron: They're all re-covered, yeah.
Pauline: With what?
Gary: Yeah, all the floors *have been redone.*
Bron: It was, it was velvet where I was.
Pauline: Mmm.
Bron: Which was up in the circle.
Pauline: Mmm.
Bron: Don't know what it was downstairs, but all the *paintings have been restored.*
Pauline: Oh good.
Bron: And all the gilt'*s been done* and the chandeliers *have been* . . .

In contrast to the progressive, perfect aspect is less frequent in American English than in British English (Biber *et al.* 1999). Combinations of perfect and progressive aspect, as in the present perfect progressive, are even rarer, across all dialects. (This fact suggests that the amount of time devoted to these verb forms in conventional teaching materials may be somewhat disproportionate, a point that will be taken up at the end of this chapter.)

Perfect aspect is most commonly found in its present form (*have been, have done* etc*). The relatively rare past perfect (*had been, had done* etc.) has a 'backgrounding' function – typically referring back to a time prior to the main focus of a narrative:

Jessie: And what was it like when you first saw him? Were you really = = nervous?
Di: = = Well I was hanging out of a window watching him in his car, and I thought 'oh God what about this!'
Jessie: [laughter]
Di: And *he'd combed* his hair and shaved his eyebrows = = and
Jessie: *Had you seen* a photo of him?
Di: Oh yeah, I had photos of him, photos . . . and *I'd spoken* to him on the phone.
Jessie: Did you get on well straight away?

(Authors' data)

McCarthy points out that the past perfect is often used in indirect speech reports (. . . *And then when I finally went they said I*'d chipped *this bone*; 1998: 74) and to provide background information of an explanatory or justificatory type:

. . . Cooksie drove cos *he'd been driving all night* and he drove the minibus down

(McCarthy 1998: 74)

The use of the past perfect to background information in this way suggests to McCarthy that the verb form has a discoursal macrofunction at a level beyond the sentence, allowing speakers to organize their message in terms of the relative importance of its propositions. The same may be said for the use of continuous aspect in narratives, which, as we have seen, is commonly used to frame events:

I remember *we were sitting* for our analytical chemistry exam and *I was sitting* there, and I thought 'Geez I can feel something on my foot'. And *I am trying* to think, but there's something on my foot . . .

(Authors' data)

Such pragmatic uses of different combinations of tense and aspect are not always easily captured by traditional pedagogical rules, suggesting to McCarthy that '[spoken] grammar is often most adequately explained by referring to contextual features and, above all, by taking into account interpersonal aspects of face-to-face interaction' (1998: 86). A case in point is the use of the passive voice, also very rare in talk. According to Biber *et al.*, only 2 per cent of finite verbs in conversational data are in the passive form, which they attribute to the fact that 'conversation, having a human-centred concern with people's actions, thoughts and stances, usually does not demote the subject, who is often the speaker' (1999: 477). However, to maintain topic consistency – and where the agent is either not known or can be taken for granted – the passive is sometimes employed, as in this extract (passive clauses are italicized):

Richard

Jessie: Mmm, what's happened about Richard?

Judy: Ah about Richard. Ah nothing [laughs]. *He's been spoken to*. It'll be a sort of
a watch and wait = = something.

Jessie: = = Yeah, what do you reckon is going to happen?

Judy: Not a thing.

Jessie: What could they do to him?

Di: Richard's not a very nice person anyway. He just doesn't fit into the system
in general. It's not nice what's happening to him, but the thing is he is em
creating the situation just as much as what they . . . because *he's been caught
drinking on the job* [whispers] which is no good you know and he hasn't been
really doing his job properly anyway . . .

(Authors' data)

Modality

Modality is another area of grammar that is best understood by taking into account
the interpersonal features of its contexts of use. Modality, very broadly, has to do
with the way speakers indicate their attitudes or judgements with regard to the message
in hand, as in utterances like *X probably happens* or *X should happen* or *I think X might've
happened*, in contrast to bald assertions of fact of the type *X happens* or *X does not
happen* or *X didn't happen*. Modality is signalled principally by the use of modal verbs
(*must*, *may*, *will*, *could* etc.), along with the marginal modals (*need to* and *ought to*),
and the so-called semi-modals such as *have to*, *be supposed to*, *be going to*, *had better*.
However, as McCarthy points out 'large numbers of "lexical" words (nouns,
adjectives, verbs and adverbs carry the same or similar meanings to the modal verbs'
(1991: 84–5).

Analysis of corpus data (e.g. Biber *et al.* 1999) suggests that the use of fully
modal, marginal modal, and, especially, semi-modal verbs is more common in
conversation than in other registers (such as news reports, fiction or academic prose).
This is hardly surprising, given conversation's largely interpersonal function and the
fact that modality is strongly associated with the expression of interpersonal meaning.
Eggins, for example, notes that 'the systems of Mood and Modality are the keys to
understanding the interpersonal relationships between interactants' (1994: 196).
This is particularly salient where an imbalance in terms of power – whether due
to social distance, gender, or other contextual factors – requires some speakers to
defer to others. Such deference is frequently realized by means of modality. In fact,
wherever any threat to face is felt to be imminent, modal systems are employed to
defuse such a threat. In this short exchange between clerical staff, the participants
are discussing work schedules, a potential source of friction. Expressions of modality
are italicized (King George is the name of a hospital):

Work schedules

Bron: We are *going to* have a lot of admissions to do this afternoon.

Pauline: Is Jenny there, by the way? And what's she doing?

Bron: Well, Jenny and I'*ll* finish the admissions now, but Sue's going at half past
three and she's half done King George.

Pauline: Oh is she? Why is she going early?

Bron: She *needs to* go to the post office, so *apparently* she asked if she *could* go early and make up the time.

Pauline: Oh well. Jenny *better* stay and help me with those then.

Bron: Yeah. 'Cause we haven't started on them yet.

Pauline: Mmm.

Bron: And of course she's pulled all the EASY King George.

Pauline: Oh well, I don't suppose she's any idea of what *could* happen. And I said on Monday she *can* do PA because it's different to King George.

(Authors' data)

In the above extract a number of common modal meanings are realized, and can be divided into those that express a speaker's judgement as to the likelihood of an event (whether past, present or future) – what is called *extrinsic modality* – and those that express the speaker's judgement of the desirability, necessity or permissability of an event occurring – that is, *intrinsic modality*. Likelihood (whose shades of meaning include predictability, certainty and theoretical possibility) is represented by these examples:

> We are *going to* have a lot of admissions to do this afternoon. [prediction]
> I don't suppose she's any idea of what *could* happen. [possibility]

Intrinsic modal meanings in the extract include:

> Jenny and I'*ll* finish the admissions now. [volition]
> She *needs to* go to the post office. [obligation]
> Jenny *better* stay and help me. [desirability]
> And I said on Monday she *can* do PA. [permission]

Note that *I don't suppose* (as in *I don't suppose she has any idea of what could happen*) can also be classed as a form of modality, in that it indicates the speaker's assessment of the situation as being uncertain.

[. . .]

What do learners need to know?

What is it, then, that learners need to know about grammar in order to achieve conversational competence? First of all, what they probably *don't* need to know is a lot of the formal grammar that is typically presented in EFL materials. Pedagogical grammar is essentially *written* grammar – that is, it is a grammar derived from an analysis of the written language. It is the grammar which, by virtue of being more thoroughly researched as well as more prestigious, is customarily taught to EFL learners. As was pointed out earlier, it is this grammar which determines the content of much of the coursebook 'conversations' students are exposed to in the course of their studies. Yet many of the grammar items that are ingeniously incorporated into such conversations – and whose presentation and practice can take up a good deal of classroom time – only rarely feature in authentic conversational data.

The second point that needs to be made is that conversation places fewer demands on learners in terms of grammar – in its conventional sense – than do other registers such as academic prose or more formal spoken genres. Indeed, spoken grammar shares a number of the features of interlanguage grammar. Ochs (1979), for example, in comparing planned and (relatively) unplanned discourse, notes that in the latter there is greater use of grammatical features that are associated with the early stages of language acquisition. These features include less frequent use of definite articles and a preference, instead, for demonstratives (as in '*this* place where I go'); greater use of active rather than passive constructions; and more frequent use of the present as opposed to past or future verb forms. According to Givón (1979), these features are typical of what is called a *pragmatic* language mode, as opposed to a *syntactic* one. Other features of a pragmatic mode include short verbal clauses with a low proportion of noun phrases per verb, and reduction and simplification of grammatical morphology.

There is a danger, however, that, as more and more features of spoken grammar are identified and described, they become a focus of instruction in their own right. Thus, valuable time may be wasted teaching learners about syntactic noun-clausal units or ellipsis or heads and tails when their natural tendency, in the interests of simplification, is to use these features anyway. An extreme statement of the scepticism is Prodromou's: 'The status of spoken English may be a subject of debate in Applied Linguistics but I do not think it is for language teachers' (1997: 20). Prodromou argues, instead, for a methodology that 'takes the students' interlanguage as a starting point and seeks to build on that rather than on language imposed from the outside'.

It is this thinking that underlies the so-called *lexical approach* to course design, including the design of materials that foreground the lexical needs of learners, e.g. Willis (1990) and Lewis (1993). It is also the view that informed the research undertaken by Gairns and Redman in the preparation of an intermediate-level general English course (2002a). They were interested in comparing the output of intermediate level learners with that of more advanced learners (rather than with native speakers, on the grounds that a 'native speaker model represented a target that was unattainable for intermediate learners of English' (2002a: 2)). They therefore recorded and transcribed learners at these two different levels performing a variety of speaking tasks. Among their findings, they noted that:

- *Modal verbs* appeared frequently in the higher-level output, but were notably scarce in the intermediate data, especially *will*, *would*, *might*, *could*, *should*.
- *Tenses* were still generally problematic at intermediate level, but backshift in reported speech seemed largely superfluous.
- Learners at the intermediate level seemed to shy away from adverbs. *Very* appeared everywhere, but not some of the high-frequency adverbs found in the more advanced-level data, such as *extremely*, *slightly*, *occasionally*, *fortunately* etc.

What they found most significant was the fact that 'learners lacked a wide range of frequently occurring lexical items, many of them lexical chunks, which are an important part of sounding natural, either in your own or another language' (Gairns and Redman 2002b: 6). Again, this is a finding consistent with the view that spoken language consists, to a large extent, of prefabricated lexical 'chunks', as argued by Pawley and Syder (1983) and Nattinger and DeCarrico (1992), among others.

Nevertheless, based on the findings reviewed in this chapter, there seem to be good grounds for arguing for the acquisition of a 'core grammar' as a basis for developing conversational competence, and that this grammar would include the following features:

- some basic conjunctions (*and*, *so*, *but*) in order to string together sequences of clausal and non-clausal units;
- the use of deictic devices (*here/there*, *now/then*, *this/that*, etc.) to anchor utterances in the immediate context, and to refer to other contexts;
- a command of simple verb tense forms, both present and past, and the ability to use the latter to sequence narratives;
- familiarity with the use of aspect both to frame and to background information in narratives, as in *it was snowing . . . I'd been working . . .*
- a knowledge of the most frequently occurring modal and semi-modal verbs (i.e. *can*, *will*, *would*, *have to*, *going to*, *used to*) and the ability to use these to express both intrinsic and extrinsic meanings;
- the ability to formulate questions, especially *yes/no*- but also *wh*- questions (but not perhaps question tags and comment questions which – although frequent – are syntactically complex, and can readily be replaced by lexical items such as *no?* and *really?*):
- a repertoire of head- and tail-slot fillers – principally discourse markers – items which perhaps belong to the lexicon rather than the grammar; and
- one or two all-purpose quotatives, of the *he said . . . and then I said . . .* type.

Clearly this is a very short list, and bears little relation to the fairly elaborate grammar syllabuses of standard ELT materials. This is not to say that such syllabuses are ineffective nor that this core grammar guarantees conversational competence. For a start, it assumes that learners have sufficient communicative strategies to compensate for any deficiencies in their linguistic competence. It is also difficult to avoid the conclusion that a significant proportion of what we have identified as core grammar is reducible to formulaic language of a lexical, rather than strictly grammatical, nature. In other words, a repertoire of sentence starters, discourse markers, back-channel devices and so on, may provide the learner with a more effective bridge-head into conversation than any number of traditional syllabus items such as *tenses* or *conditionals* and so on.

References

Biber, D., Johansson, S., Leech, G., Conrad, S. and Finegan, E. (1999) *Longman Grammar of Spoken and Written English*. Harlow: Longman.

Brazil, D. (1997) *The Communicative Value of Intonation in English*. Cambridge: Cambridge University Press.

Carter R. and McCarthy, M. (1995) 'Grammar and the spoken language', *Applied Linguistics* 16 (2): 141–58.

Carter, R. and McCarthy, M. (1997) *Exploring Spoken English*. Cambridge: Cambridge University Press.

Chomsky, N. (1965) *Aspects of the Theory of Syntax*. Cambridge, MA: MIT Press.

Crystal, D. and Davy, D. (1975) *Advanced Conversational English*. London: Longman.

Eggins, S. (1994) *An Introduction to Systemic Functional Linguistics*. London: Pinter.

Gairns, R. and Redman, S. (2002a) *Natural English Intermediate Teacher's Book*. Oxford: Oxford University Press.

Gairns, R. and Redman, S. (2002b) 'A spoken syllabus', *English Teaching Professional* 25: 5–7.

Givón, T. (1979) *On Understanding Grammar*. New York: Academic Press.

Halliday, M. (1985) *Spoken and Written Language*. Geelong: Deakin University Press.

Hübscher, J. and Frampton, H. (1947) *A Modern English Grammar*. Lausanne: Librairie Payot.

Labov, W. (1972) *Language in the Inner City*. Philadelphia, PA: University of Pennsylvania Press.

Lewis, M. (1993) *The Lexical Approach: The State of ELT and the Way Forward*. Boston: MA: Heinle.

McCarthy, M. (1991) *Discourse Analysis for Language Teachers*. Cambridge, Cambridge University Press.

McCarthy, M. (1998) *Spoken Language and Applied Linguistics*. Cambridge: Cambridge University Press.

McCarthy, M. and O'Keeffe A. (2003) ' "What's in a name?": vocatives in casual conversations and radio phone-in calls', in P. Leistyna and C. Meyer (eds) *Corpus Analysis: Language Structure and Language Use*. Amsterdam: Rodopi.

Nattinger, J. and DeCarrico, J. (1992) *Lexical Phrases and Language Teaching*. New York: Oxford University Press.

Ochs, E. (1979) 'Planned and unplanned discourse', in T. Givón (ed.) *Syntax and Semantics: Vol. 12. Discourse and Syntax*. New York: Academic Press.

Pawley, A. and Syder, F.H. (1983) 'Two puzzles for linguistic theory: nativelike selection and nativelike fluency', in J.C. Richards and R.W. Schmidt (eds) *Language and Communication*. New York: Longman.

Prodromou, L. (1997) 'From corpus to octopus', *IATEFL Newsletter* 137: 18–21.

Schiffrin, D. (1987) *Discourse Markers*. Cambridge: Cambridge University Press.

Willis, D. (1990) *The Lexical Syllabus*. London: Collins.

Chapter 16

Anne O'Keeffe, Michael McCarthy and Ronald Carter

Idioms in everyday use and in language teaching

Introduction

Everyone loves idioms – teachers and learners alike. They offer a colourful relief to what can otherwise be a rather dull landscape of grappling with difficult grammar rules, learning new word lists, doing tests, and so on. Publishers are aware of this and offer materials specially devoted to idiom-learning, and there are good learners' dictionaries of idioms available for English, including corpus-based ones. A search through the back issues over decades of important language teaching journals such as *ELT Journal* and *TESOL Quarterly* will reveal continual mention of idioms, usually as part of vocabulary teaching or the teaching of language and culture, and mostly not seen as anything special or peculiar in the language teaching repertoire, albeit a challenge. However, in a book by one of the authors of this chapter (McCarthy 1998), it was noted that there was a shortage of information on how idioms are actually used in everyday communication, and it was argued that better information on actual use might benefit pedagogy. McCarthy offered spoken corpus examples in an attempt to remedy that lack of perspective; here we take the question further and offer more corpus evidence, and, in addition, look at teaching applications.

We also consider the question of whether idioms, because of their cultural resonance and their status as 'badge of membership' of the speech communities from which they spring, have any place in a world where English is often used as a

Edited extracts from: O'Keeffe, A., McCarthy, M., Carter, R. 'Idioms in everyday use and in language teaching', in *From Corpus to Classroom: Language Use and Language Teaching*, pp. 80–94, Cambridge University Press, 2007.

lingua franca and/or by learners and expert users (or SUEs) who may have no desire to claim membership of the native-speaker culture.

In our earlier research, we used the word 'idiom' to mean strings of more than one word whose syntactic, lexical and phonological form is to a greater or lesser degree fixed and whose semantics and pragmatic functions are opaque and specialised, also to a greater or lesser degree. This overlaps, of course, with the characteristics of a number of everyday chunks, many of which, although they form part of our most ordinary everyday language, are, nonetheless, 'idiomatic' in the sense that their forms are unpredictable and the relationship between their form and meaning is not always one-to-one (e.g. *on the other hand, this that and the other, all the rest of it, thank you very much*). In this chapter, however, we shall confine our attention to the other end of the spectrum: items which have, traditionally, been included in intuition-based language teaching materials probably just because they are low-frequency but very colourful and, consequently, psychologically more salient and accessible to expert users than the frequent, everyday chunks. These are the opaque 'idioms' beloved of language teaching, such as *kick the bucket* (= die), *hit the sack* (= go to bed), and so on. These are fixed and relatively inflexible in form and word-by-word analysis fails to yield their unitary meaning. The questions we want to raise in this chapter are: Are the intuition-based materials a good reflection of language use in terms of what actually occurs in a corpus and what are the functions of such items? And how far can the automated processes of corpus analysis assist us with items which are, of necessity, low frequency and unpredictable?

McCarthy (1998) proposed that idiomatic expressions were not merely colourful alternatives to their literal counterparts, but that they encoded important cultural information and often performed discourse roles that could best be observed in real data. Idiom selection seemed not to be random and unmotivated. Written corpus research, showing idioms functioning as evaluative devices, often found in authorial comment segments in texts, seemed to underline this view of idioms as non-random (Moon 1992). McCarthy (ibid.) focused on spoken data, and here we take that research on these colourful, low-frequency idioms in spoken language further.

Finding and classifying idioms

Since computers do not know what an idiom is, automatic retrieval of idioms using conventional software is only partially possible, despite recent advances in the recognition of syntactic patterns involving idiom-prone words (see Volk 1998 for a discussion of the difficulties and some solutions), and the exploitation of latent semantic analysis (put simply, the likely absence of semantically related words within and surrounding the idiomatic expression; see Degand and Bestgen 2003). One can generate lists of recurring chunks, but such lists are massive and still have to be sifted manually to decide which items can be classified as idioms and which not, and the lists do not provide contextual information – one still has to call up the contexts to fully research the idioms. One can also simply load a pre-compiled dictionary of idioms and ask the computer to search for their occurrences in the corpus. However, this necessarily presupposes that the dictionary has already recorded all the idioms in common circulation, which may not be so, and, again, one still has to bring up the contexts to research the items properly.

Certain everyday words do seem to be 'idiom-prone', probably because they are the foundations of basic cognitive metaphors. These would include parts of the body (*eye, shoulder, hand, nose* and *head* all generate a number of idioms), money (the metaphor that living is akin to spending money can be seen in idioms such as *money talks, put your money where your mouth is, the smart money,* and so on), light and colour (*be in the dark, shed light on, give the green light, have green fingers,* etc.) and other basic notions. A corpus can be searched productively simply by starting with such basic words. The word-form *face* has 520 occurrences in CANCODE, and a reading of the 520 concordance lines yields no less than fifteen idiomatic expressions, of which the following occur three times or more:

let's face it	20
on the face of it	10
face to face	6
keep a straight face	4
face up to	4
till you're blue in the face	3
fall flat on one's face	3
shut your face	3

So, although the process of analysis is not entirely automatic, much can be gained by doing searches on basic, everyday words.

However, a corpus does contain extended examples of the usage of its speakers and writers, and we should not forget that we can also read its entire texts, however time-consuming and, at times, tedious this may be. We therefore chose files at random from the CANCODE spoken corpus and a same-sized sample of conversations from the North American segment of the CIC, and read through the conversations as continuous texts, noting each idiomatic expression as we encountered it. This, and our subsequent procedure, was similar to that followed by Simpson and Mendis (2003). After finding 100 idioms in each of the British and American datasets, we then attempted to classify them according to their syntactic and pragmatic functions in context. This is only a partial solution to the problem but does give us a useful window into idioms in their actual contexts of use.

The opaque idioms fell into the following categories (with examples of their realisations):

1 Clausal expressions evaluating people's actions and personal states (*look down one's nose at sb* (BrE), *give sb a hard time* (AmE))
2 Clausal expressions evaluating things and events (*make sense, it's a small world* – in both datasets)
3 Names for people (*man/woman of the world* (BrE), *sugar daddy* (AmE))
4 Names for things and events (*pub crawl* (BrE), *small talk* (AmE))
5 Discourse routines and interjections (*there you go* (BrE), *here's the thing* (AmE))
6 Miscellaneous adjectival, adverbial and prepositional expressions (*by and large* (BrE), *top notch* (AmE))

The strongly evaluative nature of idioms comes out in the list of 100 items. Even the miscellaneous syntactic types show this (e.g. *by and large*, *as deaf as a post*, *till you're blue in the face*). A number of the expressions can be seen to support discourse functions such as marking staging-points in conversations (*here's the thing*, *let's face it*, *there you go*).

Here is an example of *here's the thing*, signalling an important point in the discussion:

S1:   What about the French Canadians? Do they celebrate Independence Day?
S2:   Well I mean **here's the thing**. I mean there is certainly a city of Montreal parade.

(CIC North American)

Relatively few analysts have attempted to describe idiom use in naturally-occurring spoken data, but those that have (Strässler 1982; Norrick 1988; Drew and Holt 1988 and 1995; Powell 1992) have all underlined the evaluative role of idioms and their discourse functions, which we return to below in section 4.5.

Frequency

The next procedure was to investigate the total frequency in the whole of the CANCODE corpus and the whole of the CIC sample for each item in the 100-item lists. It turns out that frequency varies greatly, with expressions such as *there you go*, *figure sth out*, *(not) make sense*, *once in a while*, *how come* and *fair enough* enjoying hundreds of occurrences, while about 20 per cent of all the items occur only once. The two lists are comparable. Figure 16.1 shows the distribution of items in the different functional classes for the two datasets.

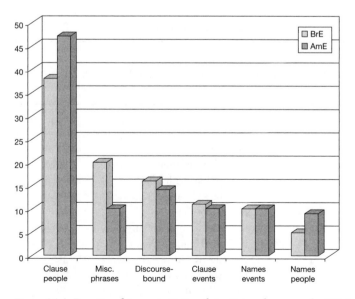

Figure 16.1 Functional types in BrE and AmE (random sample 100 items each)

To get a handle on what these frequencies might mean for pedagogy, it is worth noting that any item occurring ten times or more would find its place in the top 7,000 items if dovetailed into the lemmatised list of single-word items in CANCODE. Any item occurring twenty times or more would find a place in the top 5,000 items in the CANCODE single-item list. A range of 5,000 to 7,000 words is often seen as realistic for the receptive vocabulary size of high intermediate to advanced level EFL students (Hever 1997; Waring 1997). It would therefore seem reasonable to suggest items in our lists occurring ten or more times, and any other idioms which can be shown to occur with such frequency, as possible targets for study if teachers and learners decide they want to explore a set of native-speaker idioms at the upper intermediate or advanced level. The top twenty items from the CANCODE 100 list are shown in Table 16.1; those from the American sample in Table 16.2.

Table 16.1 Twenty idioms occurring ten or more times (from the CANCODE 100 idiom list)

	Idiom	Occurrences		Idiom	Occurrences
1	fair enough	240	10	good god	44
2	at the end of the day	221	11	be/have a/some good laugh(s)	41
3	there you go	209	12	the only thing is/was	41
4	make sense	157	13	good grief	38
5	turn round and say	139	14	keep an/one's eye on	37
6	all over the place	75	15	half the time	34
7	be a (complete/right/ bit of a/absolute/real) pain (in the neck/arse/ bum)	73	16	up to date	30
			17	take the mickey	25
			18	get on sb's nerves	24
8	can't/couldn't help but/ -ing	69	19	how's it going	21
9	over the top	53	20	along those lines/the lines of	20

Table 16.2 Twenty idioms occurring ten or more times (from the 100 North American idiom list)

	Idiom	Occurrences		Idiom	Occurrences
1	figure sth out	348	11	piss sb off	53
2	once in a while	278	12	ahead of time	50
3	(not) make (any) sense	276	13	put up with sth	44
4	(no) big deal	179	14	be sick of sth	43
5	screw up	151	15	make fun of sb	40
6	oh my gosh!	149	16	stay away from sth	40
7	how come . . .?	111	17	it all comes/came down to	40
8	oh boy!	71	18	throw up	35
9	freak out	56	19	what's up with . . .?	30
10	get over sb/sth	54	20	I'll be darned!	30

The lists (in Tables 16.1 and 16.2) certainly offer a variety of types over and above the traditionally favoured clausal ('verb + complement') types and includes prepositional expressions, discourse routines, interjections, nominal compounds and a trinomial expression (*left, right and centre*), offering a rich menu of different types for study. We should bear in mind, though, that this is a random list and not necessarily an accurate cross-sectional picture of idioms in spoken British/Irish and American English, but it does seem to capture something of the richness and variety of idioms in everyday native-speaker conversations, and is preferable, we would argue, to lists drawn up entirely on the basis of intuition, where the colourfulness and consequent psychological salience of some expressions may blind us to their low frequency and limited usefulness, and where only an impoverished range of formal types may be represented.

Meaning

We began by saying that idioms are characterised by degrees of opacity of meaning, with prototypical examples being quite opaque (e.g. *take the Mickey, be hung over*). There are certainly many idioms of this kind, where, in the absence of contextual clues, there is no way of decoding the unknown expression by examining its constituent parts. However, there are two considerations which appear in the literature that suggest that apparently opaque meaning may offer an opening to good pedagogy. The first is the often partial literalness of expressions and the ability of the mind to 'image' literal meanings and to go from them to possible figurative interpretations. These include those which Yorio (1980) refers to as 'recoverable' images, giving as examples expressions such as *bumper to bumper* and *shake hands* (see also Lazar 1996; Boers and Demecheleer 2001). Where there are similarities in the basic concepts across languages, the interpretation of figurative expressions can be expected to be easier (Charteris-Black 2002). Horn (2003) further relates degrees of transparency of interpretation to potential for syntactic flexibility, offering a useful link between form and meaning'.

A second consideration, the literature on cognitive metaphors suggests that basic metaphors, often universally comprehensible, underlie many idiomatic expressions; for example, the idioms *let the cat out of the bag* and *spill the beans* share the underlying metaphorical construct of the human mind as a 'container', from which thoughts/information can be released suddenly and involuntarily. There is also evidence to suggest that such metaphors may be activated by key words in the idioms (Tabossi and Zardon 1993). McGlone *et al.* (1994) suggest that speakers do not ignore the non-idiomatic meanings of individual words in idiomatic expressions, and that even in opaque idioms literal meanings of component words are in some sense activated, or at least are potentially available. Underlying metaphors, Gibbs (1994) and Gibbs and O'Brien (1990) argue, partly enable language users to make sense of idiomatic expressions (see also Kövecses and Szabo 1996).

But meaning, as always, is best apprehended in context, and in actual contexts of use one can observe relevant aspects of semantic and pragmatic meaning. A case in point is the expression *be a (complete/right/bit of a/absolute/real) pain (in the neck, etc.)*: of its seventy-three occurrences in the CANCODE corpus, fifty-two refer to things and events and situations, while 21 refer to people. The expression *(let sth.) wash over sb.*, on the other hand, is only used with non-human subjects referring to events and situations. Knowing whether an idiom typically refers to people and things or only to one or the other is clearly an important aspect of knowledge of the expression and is best observed in context. Good dictionaries of idioms encode such information for the user, based on large-scale observations of corpora. But corpora also enable us to immerse ourselves in longer contexts and thus to observe functional aspects of idioms, such as who uses them and when. This is typically done by expanding concordances to include long segments of texts or whole texts.

Functions of idioms

McCarthy (1998) gave examples of idioms functioning in various generic patterns, such as the characteristic 'observation–comment' pattern, where speakers make an observation about some phenomenon in the world and then evaluate it, with idioms typically occurring in the evaluative segment:

S1:   Well I thought you were gonna go on holiday.

S2:   +yeah. The thing – well I don't think I'm gonna do that now cos none of us can get together at the right time when we want to do it. Which **is a pain in the arse**.

(CANCODE)

[An informal discussion about a book the speakers have read]

S1:   Yet it made a lot of political statements as you were saying, a lot of comments [S2: Mm. Yeah. Yeah.] on even the way the world is today.

S2:   Today. Yeah. I thought that.

S3:   + But I I just felt the whole book was written **tongue in cheek**. I think that was, that was initially his whole point he was just laughing at us. He's **taking the Mickey**.

(CANCODE)

S1:   There's no fast food.

S2:   There's just nothing really nice.

S3:   There's not that many [name of popular restaurant chain] around either.

S2:   No there's only one on um Route twenty-two across from=

S3:   Yeah.

S1:   It's terrible.

S2:   Yeah. And then I was thinking, go and get a sandwich.

S1:   Yeah.

S2:   And then by the time I go to and find a parking spot.

S1:   **You're starving to death**. Yeah.

(CIC North American)

In the examples above we have three cases of factual observations or claims, followed by evaluative comments, with idioms performing their characteristic function of evaluation. It is worth noting that in two of the three cases, the comment/evaluation is performed by a speaker other than the one who makes the initial observation. This illustrates the important interactive functions idioms can perform, creating and reinforcing interpersonal relations, projecting informality, camaraderie and social bonding. It also underscores the fundamental characteristic of conversation as jointly created.

McCarthy (1998) distinguished between the 'event line' and the 'evaluation line' in narratives, with idioms signalling the evaluation line, as can be seen in the following example. (For further examples see McCarthy and Carter 1994: 111.)

[Speaker 1 is recounting a story about her car windscreen wipers breaking down]

S1:   Colin erm fixed it sort of you know disconnected the windscreen wipers and that was like in the first week. [S2: Mm mm.] So now it's started raining a bit more I thought I'm gonna have to get it sorted you know. Cos I ended up walking when it's not raining you know and and, no, sorry, I've ended up walking when it's raining rather than the other way round.

S2:   Yes. Yeah. Yeah. Yeah. Which **doesn't really make sense** does it.

S1:   No. So I thought I'm gonna get this sorted.

(CANCODE)

McCarthy (1998) noted that narrative codas are a particular example of the more general phenomenon of summing up gist at points along the way in a discourse, offering 'formulations' or paraphrases of where participants feel they have got to and judgements of the general significance of what has been said so far (Heritage and Watson 1979). The following example illustrates this summarising function of idioms:

S1:   I actually went last weekend with, my father was in town and we went and looked at used cars around town. Uh, and I, you know, I found like a nineteen eighty-four Regency Ninety-eight with only forty-six thousand miles on it and that was pretty good condition, uh.

S2:   Yeah.

S1:   But I also found a nineteen eighty Volvo, uh, station wagon +

S2:   Right.

S1:   +that was in just super condition. I mean there's not a dent on the outside body, the inside is clean it's had the same owner for years.

S2:   Right.

S1:   It, it has about eighty thousand miles on it but that's all right, you know, the engine's in excellent shape and I think it would last me probably another fifty or sixty thousand miles.

S2:   Yeah.

S1:   So, I guess **I'm kind of in limbo** waiting to see what the insurance is, you know, company is going to do, to see whether or not I can get one of these cars.

(CIC North American)

Other general conversational contexts where idioms are found were also noted by McCarthy (1998) and by Powell (1985, 1992), including more creative aspects of idiom usage, the 'unpacking' of idioms and word play (see also Fernando 1996; Carter and McCarthy 2004).

Idioms in specialised contexts

Here we consider the occurrence of idioms in more specialised contexts, and focus on two areas, spoken business English and academic English. Neither context is immediately associated with the occurrence of idiomatic expressions in most people's minds, perhaps owing to the early days of ESP/LSP in the 1970s and 1980s, where the focus was often on the more informational/transactional functions of language at the expense of the interpersonal. However, there is no shortage of idioms in business and academic data. Using the one-million-word CANBEC spoken English corpus, McCarthy and Handford (2004) observed how the discussion of problems among business colleagues was often given an informal flavour in an atmosphere of camaraderie by the use of idioms. The business data in CANBEC is predominantly about problem-solving and consensus making (e.g. striking deals, deciding on courses of action), and the occurrence of idioms often supports these core goals. An example from the data illustrates this, where evaluations of people's roles in creating and solving problematic issues is foregrounded:

[Recorded at an internal meeting between the technical manager and a technician in a British internet service provider company.]

S1:   Okay. So we know full well the account manager's not gonna tell them cos the account manager **doesn't give two hoots**. All right. So the next person it comes from is DLM who send the customer a fax and I know DLM haven't been doing that because they they realize that they're gonna **get it in the neck** from the customer. Cos the customer will see a thing which says 'Right let's do a concrete example'. So let's say a customer says be on site by nine.

S2:   Yeah.

[1 min]

S1:   For this and of course the overtime will just be deducted from = Well either the overtime'll be deducted from the account manager or somehow Componet'll just pay this which I can't believe will happen.

S2:   Yeah.

S1:   Yeah? So it'll get deducted from the account managers which means the account managers'll **be up in arms** but then tough. Cos **the buck's gotta stop somewhere** and I don't see why it should stop with well I don't see why it necessarily should stop with BJE.

S2:   Yeah.

S1:   Well it's been on the agenda. And I mailed you about it. I mailed the whole team about it. Cos in your= Well either way it's got to be resolved.

S2:   Yeah.

S1:   Cos it's a **it's a pain in the arse for everybody** at the minute.

S2:   I know I know. I know.

S1:   All right?

S2:   Yeah.

(CANBEC)

Such data raises similar issues for the LSP context to those which native-speaker casual conversation data do for the teaching of general spoken English, that is to say a high degree of intimacy and in-group membership is projected by such idiomatic usage. Many students of business English may never find themselves in such chummy native-speaker environments or indeed ever doing business with native speakers at all, yet nonetheless conducting their affairs in English. As always, the use or rejection of such material in any individual pedagogical context should be left to teachers and learners to decide, especially in the business domain, where students are likely to be mature individuals perfectly capable of making their own decisions as to what they wish to study. The point is that the specialised corpus offers the opportunity to explore business cultures and to see how idiomatic language is exploited in characteristic ways, albeit in a context where such study may not have as its goal the acquisition and use of such language.

A similar case can be made for academic English, though here perhaps the need to confront the actual language used is usually more pressing, since so many students travel to study and live in countries where English is a native language. Simpson and Mendis (2003), using the 1.7 million-word MICASE corpus of spoken academic English, found that idioms were distributed across all types of academic disciplines and situations, with no particular concentrations in any one context, and that idioms constituted a 'not-insignificant feature of the lexical landscape of academic speech' (p. 427). Idioms occur in the MICASE data with a variety of functions, including the observation-comment function already mentioned in this chapter, as well as description, paraphrase and other functions. Simpson and Mendis (ibid.) offer a list of useful idioms for the spoken academic contexts and in their list one can see how many of the idioms serve the description and evaluation of knowledge and its transmission, with items such as *bottom line, the big picture, come into play, get a grasp of, get to the bottom of things, go off on a tangent*, etc.

Following up on Simpson and Mendis' study, Murphy and O'Boyle (2005) performed a similar analysis on twenty hours of data from the one million-word LIBEL Corpus of Academic Spoken English. Murphy and O'Boyle found overlaps with MICASE in both forms and functions (e.g. both corpora had *bottom line, down the line, come into play, hand in hand, thumbs up, get a handle on, take one's word for it*), and found thirty-seven idioms in their twenty hours of data, distributed fairly evenly across monologic and dialogic data, as were the idioms in MICASE. Murphy and O'Boyle additionally found idioms such as *on the same track, lose track of (the meaning), both sides of the same coin, the other side of the coin, part and parcel, the nitty gritty, take on board*, again showing the relationship between the construction and transmission of disciplinary knowledge and the informality and interpersonal and cultural bonding projected in the use of these idioms. If it is true that idioms do project a high degree of interpersonal closeness, then it is further worthy of note that the monologic academic data seem to be as interpersonally charged, at least in this respect, as dialogic contexts, in both studies.

Examples from the spoken academic data segment of CIC showing the use of some of the idioms mentioned are given here. Both examples strike friendly, informal notes in what are otherwise formal contexts. The first is a law lecture, perhaps typically conceived of as a rather dry, impersonal affair, and the second is a seminar on politics where the seminar leader obviously feels a necessity to bring the students to the nub of the issue in a non-threatening way:

[From a lecture on contract law]

> To what extent are terms and contracts between business controlled by the Act? Now w= how would you answer that? [long pause] Well, er you need, you know you have to **get a handle on** er saying to what extent are terms and contracts between business. Well erm what sections of the Act I mean is the Act designed and is its application dependent on whether contracts are between businesses or whether they're between businesses and consumers or not?
>
> (CIC)

[From a politics seminar]

> No. It's You've actually all around the point. You're scattered around the point. The critical point is they devalued because. You're telling me what happened when they devalued like structural adjustments all that. Let's just **get down to the nitty gritty**. They devalued because of huge IMF pressure on France to cut the currency link. The IMF have been saying These countries are in the mire. they can't repay debt. They're never going to get anywhere.
>
> (CIC)

The two studies of spoken academic data and the study of spoken business data seem to suggest that using specialised corpora focusing on particular discourse communities can produce insights into how idioms are used to create and reinforce particular cultures and types of relationships within the members of those communities. In support of this, we may note that Wenger (1998) points to the importance of jokes, stories, lore, idioms and metaphors, which become the routine ways of confronting problems in institutions and which help to construct and solidify communities of practice. Idioms have been shown to be created among small groups or those with shared interests (for example, see Gibbon 1981), right down to partnered couples, where intimacy is often accompanied by private lexicons of expressions (see Hopper *et al.* 1981).

Idioms in teaching and learning

In a pioneering investigation of a substantial non-native-user spoken English corpus, Prodromou (2005) raises fundamental questions about what he calls the 'paradox' of idiomaticity: the very thing which, for native speakers, promotes ease of processing and fluent production (Fillmore 1979) seems to present non-native users with an insurmountable obstacle. Try as they may, many advanced SUEs (Prodromou 2003a and b) still have problems with idioms, even when they have mastered most other aspects of the language system. And Prodromou is not alone in adducing evidence of these high-level difficulties; many studies have shown under-use of idioms among learners and other non-native users in comparison with native-speaker data, or avoidance of idioms in favour of single-word or other more literal alternatives, or errors in form and function (Bahns *et al.* 1986; Kellerman 1986; Hulstijn and Marchena 1989; Yorio 1989; Arnaud and Savignon 1997; De Cock 1998, 2000; Altenberg and Granger 2001; Meierkord 2005).

Several problems seem to lie at the root of the apparent 'deficit' (a term used guardedly here) in idiom-learning and use as opposed to the impressive levels of grammatical and non-idiomatic lexical proficiency in English which many SUEs achieve. Firstly, because of their varying degrees of syntactic and lexical flexibility, and because of their often specialised pragmatic attributes, idioms are, simply difficult to get right. Secondly, as Irujo (1986) pointed out, idioms, even when correctly produced, can sound strange on the lips of non-native users. One often hesitates to use idioms in a foreign language even if one knows them; it is as if one is claiming a cultural membership and identity one has no right to or does not wish to lay claim to. In this situation, there can be no question of a 'deficit' of any kind. Thirdly, as Prodromou convincingly shows, idioms do not just 'pop up' in native-speaker speech; rather they occur as part of:

> . . . a more extended and diffuse phenomenon that generates subtle webs of semantic, pragmatic and discourse prosodies. It is through these situated webs of signification that L1-users achieve fluency and the promotion of self rather than in the manipulation of isolated idiomatic units *in vacuo*.
>
> (Prodromou 2005: 2)

Prodromou also refers to 'networks of semantic, discourse and pragmatic prosodies' (ibid.: 295). The CANBEC business data in the example on p. 220 well illustrates this notion of a 'situated web' or network of meanings in the way idioms weave in and out of the talk alongside other pragmatic markers and serve to structure the problem-solving episode while creating a particular type of relationship and collegiate bond for the participants. Such appropriate, contextualised use, embedded in the native user's lifetime experience of sociocultural practices, cannot simply be 'picked up' in a language course, however intensive and however authentic the data learners are exposed to. Native speakers may well be taught spelling, pronunciation and grammar and aspects of formality during their years of schooling, but they are generally not *taught* the appropriate use of idioms; it is a longterm 'priming' (Hoey 2005) of the items which build in the native user over many years. There are several possible pedagogical conclusions which can be drawn from these three militating factors.

The first conclusion might be not to bother with idioms at all, since (a) they are simply too much of a formal obstacle and it may be better to focus on learning and using the many thousands of single words which can largely do the same job, at least from the view-point of propositional meaning and (b) for many, interpersonal and sociocultural meaning will be a (useless or unnecessary) luxury. Provided the learning community of teachers and students are content with this, then such a choice should be respected. We might, at this point, however, still make a useful distinction between the needs of learners and the desirability of increased language knowledge and awareness among teachers during teacher education (see Liu 1998).

A second option is to question the input–output metaphor that informs a lot of thinking about language learning. Partly due to the dominance of utilitarian approaches to language learning from the 1970s onwards, the more traditional, belletristic approaches to language learning (which typically included literary and cultural studies) have slipped into the twilight in many areas of the world. But there is still undoubtedly a place in many educational contexts for learning about the colourful, cultural aspects of language and for observing cultures as they live through their words and actions, without any presupposition that the goal is short-term or even long-term lexical acquisition or production. There is indeed room for 'play' in language, the sheer enjoyment of handling words and expressions, uttering them and sharing them. Such a non-utilitarian view of language learning also opens the door to allowing the non-native learner to appropriate idiomatic expressions and make them their own. As Kramsch and Sullivan (1996) argue, learners may be encouraged to 'acquire correct and idiomatic forms of English, but then use these forms with the poetic licence of the non-native speaker' and 'create their own context of use according to the values cherished in their national, professional-academic, or institutional culture' (p. 210). In situations which are not threatened by the sanctions of tests and consequent risk of failure, such explorations can be motivating, enjoyable and creative. And where non-native speakers use idioms, with whatever degree of departure from the native-speaker norm, as long as comprehensibility for the target listeners is not impaired, there should be no necessary censure or labelling of 'error'. A recent example, on the junior version of the annual *Eurovision Song Contest*, broadcast primarily to a non-native-speaking European audience in English and French, was seen in the programme anchor's reference to 'being back on tracks', after the restoration of a break in the show's continuity. British native-speaker usage only permits singular *track* here, but in situations such as this, what Weinert (1995: 195) refers to as 'faulty grammatical rules' that seep into conventionalised language usage need not be seen as problematic at all (Prodromou 2005 gives further examples of non-native variations on native-speaker norms).

A third recourse is to engage in the teaching of idioms based on sets of relatively more frequent ones, ones which non-native users are at least likely to hear and see when confronted with native-speaker data, whether it be printed or electronic media, or films, TV and popular music, especially in an age of increasing global availability of such material. If this be the choice, then we would argue that basing one's evidence on a spoken corpus would be most likely to offer the best preparation for what the learner is likely to hear. In this respect, we would support the kinds of language awareness activities and exposure to corpus data (albeit edited and in longer extracts than just single concordance lines) which Simpson and Mendis (2003) have shown to be both usable and popular with their students. Simpson and Mendis (ibid.) and Murphy and O'Boyle (2005) show that it is possible to extract useful lists of the most frequent idioms from their specialised corpora. In these specialised cases the dividends in terms of increased comprehension and motivation are likely to be tangible, but the same will probably also be the case with more general spoken data.

Language awareness means discussing, perhaps through one's own language and looking at data, why idioms are being used and by whom (for example in advertising texts, where idioms are often used to project a friendly, informal relationship between the advertiser and the potential customer, a situation more likely to be conducive to successful sales). The role of the first language in terms of either positive transfer or idiom-avoidance is a complex one, but there is some evidence that, in the mental processing of collocations, formulaic sequences and idioms in a second language, the first (or third or fourth) language plays a role (Nesselhauf 2003; Spöttl and McCarthy 2004). Some materials on teaching idioms draw on transfer, or lack of it, between languages, for example McLay (1987), which offers speakers of some European languages cues in their L1 to assist them in choosing the appropriate English idiom (see Figure 16.2).

The more contexts observed, the more likely it is that greater insights will be available as to what idioms are and what they are for. The discussion may indeed range from whether such items are worth studying, or whether they may be worth learning for receptive purposes, or whether they may be worthy of serious attention in the same way that other vocabulary is. Unless teachers and learners find themselves in the unenviable position of being forced by the curriculum to study idioms, language awareness sessions open the way to making informed choices.

The importance of looking at idioms in context has benefits for the awareness of recurrent formal features too, as Coulmas (1981) has argued. In this chapter, we have suggested that a wide variety of idiom types are in everyday circulation in native-speaker English; seeing these in actual contexts of use will give a better feel for their distribution than simply studying a list of idioms. Lattey (1986) suggests organising the contexts in which idioms occur on the basis of recurrent pragmatic functions (for example, interaction of speaker and listener, speaker and outside world, positive evaluations and negative evaluations of people and phenomena, etc.), rather as our data sampling and categorisation suggested. McCarthy and O'Dell (2002), using a database of idioms extracted from the Cambridge International Corpus, in their self-study materials for idioms, organise contexts around typical conversational areas (e.g. *dealing with problems, reacting to what others say*), as well as more notional, metaphorical and topic-oriented areas (e.g. *necessity and desirability, colour, weapons and war*). Figure 16.3, an extract from their book, attempts to build practical

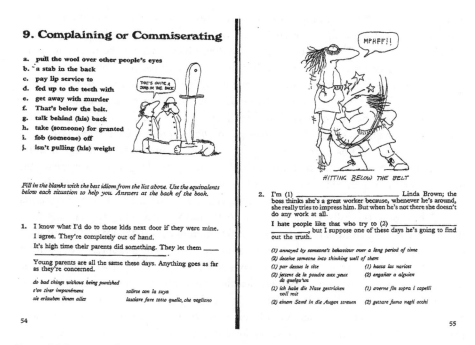

Figure 16.2 Extract from *Idioms at Work* (McLay 1987: 54–5)

Reacting to what others say
Complete phrases

Possible stimulus	Response	Meaning of response
I understood everything he said to me in French. I was just pretending not to	Really? **You could've fooled me!**	You do not believe what someone says about something that you saw or experienced yourself
Josh adores cowboy films!	**There's no accounting for taste(s)!**	You can't understand why someone likes or doesn't like something
Are you prepared to hand in your notice to stop them going ahead with their plans?	Yes, **if all else fails!**	If all other plans do not work
What do think of the Labour candidate in the election?	**The lesser of two evils,** I suppose.	It is the less unpleasant of two bad options
How did we get into this terrible position?	**One thing just led to another.**	A series of events happened, each caused by the previous one
It was such a stupid thing to say to her	I know, **I'll never live it down!**	You think that you have done something bad or embarrassing that people will never forget
My boss just congratulated me on my report. Should I ask him for a pay rise now?	Yes, go on. **Strike while the iron is hot.**	Do something immediately while you have a good chance of success
How are you going to live on such a small salary?	I don't know – **one way or another.**	You are not sure exactly how yet, but it will happen

Figure 16.3 Extract from *English Idioms in Use* (McCarthy and O'Dell 2002: 38)

pedagogy around the observation-comment function discussed in this chapter, where a second speaker typically uses an idiom to comment on something in the first speaker's utterance. The follow-up exercise then gives students the opportunity to produce similar comment-utterances using idioms, in response to stimulus utterances.

Wright (1999) includes sections on metaphors in the organisation of the contents of his teaching material for idioms. These include animal metaphors (see also Nesi 1995), metaphors based on parts of the body, and various other categories, including conceptual metaphors such as *Life is a journey* and *Business is war*. Given the discussions on the role of metaphor in the mental processing of idioms, this would seem to be a laudable approach with great potential for increasing language awareness and improving comprehension (see Boers 2000, who also suggests classroom activities).

Replicating in the classroom and in materials, however artificially, the contexts in which idioms typically occur is likely to be more motivating to learners than decontextualised attempts to understand and remember these tricky items, not least because in actual contexts idioms often contain their own paraphrases or at least many clues as to their meaning. We have seen, for example, that idioms occur naturally in narratives, and so helping learners incorporate idioms into their own personal narratives and histories may assist in acquiring at least receptive competence. Encouraging learners to connect idioms with their own personal experiences (Bergstrom 1979), or any kind of personalisation, is widely considered to be a good aid to learning. One can begin with skeletal narratives and then work on them to add, where appropriate, idiomatic expressions. McCarthy *et al.* (2006: 100) build idioms into a narrative and suggest grouping the idioms according to different stages of the story as an aid to learning. All this can be done in a context where it is understood that the object of the exercise is not necessarily productive use outside of the class, but rather the building of receptive knowledge, the fostering of memorability and the development of language awareness.

Earlier we mentioned that idioms, with all the sociocultural baggage they bring with them, might have no place in a world where English is used as lingua franca (ELF). However, some things need clarifying. It has yet to be demonstrated that ELF exists as a *variety* of English rather than as a *function* of the use of English, which responds to every context differently (rather in the way that people adapt their language for use with small children or animals). The assumption that ELF is a variety brings with it several common inferences: that the variety is in some way a 'reduced' form of the native variety, that the reduced repertoire can inform a consequently reduced syllabus, and that idioms are likely to be one of the features that can be dispensed with. If it could be shown that ELF is a variety (or, more likely, a series of varieties manifesting differently in different parts of the world) and that the variety or varieties was characterised by an idiom-free, efficient lexicon, then there may be good arguments for de-emphasising idioms. Here, once again, there would be no question of talking about a 'deficit'. But if we are in fact talking about a function of English, then there would seem to be no a priori reason to 'reduce' anything; users would make their own choices from their available repertoire of forms, just as any normal person does when adapting to any context. Much research still remains to be done in this area, and until satisfactory evidence can be brought to bear on the nature of ELF, the jury must remain out, though recent research by Roberts (2005) suggests that there is no obvious lack of orientation to interpersonal meaning in ELF situations. We need more information on how ELF users achieve interpersonal harmony and construct human relations, and what part, if any, idiomatic expressions play in such interactions. In the meantime, what seems to persist, despite the healthy and vigorous debates, is teachers' and learners' natural curiosity towards and interest in idioms, and it is in the service of that positive interest that corpus-based studies can best make their contribution by providing evidence of the forms and functions of idioms in use. This chapter has shown that there are no easy answers as to how we get from corpus to classroom in the case of idioms, but the corpus evidence does suggest, both formally and functionally, ways in which idioms might be incorporated into teaching in a manner which better reflects their actual use and which can engage students with this area of language without necessarily pressuring them into using a type of vocabulary which displays such a strong claim to native-speaker ownership.

References

Altenberg, B. and Granger, S. (2001) 'Grammatical and lexical patterning of *make* in student writing', *Applied Linguistics* 22 (2): 173–94.

Arnaud, P. and Savignon, S. (1997) 'Rare words, complex lexical units and the advanced learner', in J. Coady and T. Huckin (eds) *Second Language Vocabulary Acquisition* (pp. 157–200). Cambridge: Cambridge University Press.

Bahns, J., Burmeister, H. and Vogel, T. (1986) 'The pragmatics of formulas in L2 learner speech', *Journal of Pragmatics* 10: 693–723.

Bergstrom, K. (1979) 'Idioms exercises and speech activities to develop fluency', *Collected Reviews* Summer: 21–2.

Boers, F. (2000) 'Metaphor awareness and vocabulary retention', *Applied Linguistics* 21 (4): 553–71.

Boers, F. and Demecheleer, M. (2001) 'Measuring the impact of cross-cultural differences on learners' comprehension of imageable idioms', *ELT Journal* 55 (3): 255–62.

Carter, R.A. and McCarthy, M.J. (2004) 'Talking, creating: interactional language, creativity and context', *Applied Linguistics* 25 (1): 62–88.

Charteris-Black, J. (2002) 'Second language figurative proficiency: a comparative study of Malay and English', *Applied Linguistics* 23 (1): 104–33.

Coulmas, F. (1981) 'Idiomaticity as a problem of pragmatics', in H. Parret, M. Sbisà and J. Verschueren (eds) *Possibilities and Limitations of Pragmatics* (pp. 139–51). Amsterdam: John Benjamins.

De Cock, S. (1998) 'A recurrent word combination approach to the study of formulae in the speech of native and non-native speakers of English', *International Journal of Corpus Linguistics* 3: 59–80.

De Cock, S. (2000) 'Repetitive phrasal chunkiness and advanced EFL speech and writing', in C. Mair and M. Hundt (eds) *Corpus Linguistics and Linguistic Theory. Papers from ICAME 20 1999* (pp. 51–68). Amsterdam: Rodopi.

Degand, L. and Bestgen, Y. (2003) 'Towards automatic retrieval of idioms in French newspaper corpora', *Literary and Linguistic Computing* 18 (3): 249–59.

Drew, P. and Holt, E. (1988) 'Complainable matters: the use of idiomatic expressions in making complaints', *Social Problems* 35 (4): 398–417.

Drew, P. and Holt, E. (1995) 'Idiomatic expressions and their role in the organisation of topic transition in conversation', in M. Everaert, E-J. van der Linden, A. Schenk and R. Schreuder (eds) *Idioms: Structural and Psychological Perspectives* (pp. 117–32). Hillsdale, NJ: Lawrence Erlbaum Associates.

Fernando, C. (1996) *Idioms and Idiomaticity*. Oxford: Oxford University Press.

Fillmore, C.J. (1979) 'On fluency', in C.J. Fillmore, D. Kempler and W.S.Y. Wang (eds) *Individual Differences in Language Ability and Language Behavior* (pp. 85–102). New York: Academic Press.

Gibbon, D. (1981) 'Idiomaticity and functional variation: a case study of international amateur radio talk', *Language in Society* 10 (1): 21–42.

Gibbs, R.W. (1994) *The Poetics of Mind: Figurative Thought, Language, and Understanding*. New York: Cambridge University Press.

Gibbs, R.W. and O'Brien, J.E. (1990) 'Idioms and mental imagery: the metaphorical motivation for idiomatic meaning', *Cognition* 36: 35–68.

Heritage, J. and Watson, D. (1979) 'Formulations as conversational objects', in G. Psathas (ed.) *Everyday Language* (pp. 123–62). New York: Irvington Press.

Hever, B. (1997) 'Tests for estimating vocabulary size'. Göteborgs Univärsitet. Available at: www.wordsandtools.com/flat_structure.htm.

Hoey, M.P. (2005) *Lexical Priming: A New Theory of Words and Language*. London: Routledge.

Hopper, R., Knapp, M.L. and Scott, L. (1981) 'Couples' personal idioms: exploring intimate talk', *Journal of Communication* 31 (1): 23–33.

Horn, G.M. (2003) 'Idioms, metaphors and syntactic mobility', *Journal of Linguistics* 39: 245–73.

Hulstijn, J. and Marchena, E. (1989) 'Avoidance: grammatical or semantic causes?' *Studies in Second Language Acquisition* 11: 241–55.

Irujo, S. (1986) 'A piece of cake: learning and teaching idioms', *ELT Journal* 40 (3): 236–42.

Kellerman. E. (1986) 'An eye for an eye: crosslinguistic constraints on the development of the L2 lexicon', in E. Kellerman and M. Sharwood Smith (eds) *Crosslinguistic Influence in Second Language Acquisition* (pp. 35–48). Oxford: Pergamon Press.

Kövecses, Z. and Szabo, P. (1996) 'Idioms: a view from cognitive semantics', *Applied Linguistics* 17 (3): 326–55.

Kramsch, C. and Sullivan, P. (1996) 'Appropriate pedagogy', *ELT Journal* 50 (3): 199–212.

Lattey, E. (1986) 'Pragmatic classification of idioms as an aid for the language learner', *International Review of Applied Linguistics* XXIV (3): 217–33.

Lazar, G. (1996) 'Using figurative language to expand students' vocabulary', *ELT Journal* 50 (1): 43–51.

Liu, D. (1998) 'Ethnocentrism in TESOL: teacher education and the neglected needs of international TESOL students', *ELT Journal* 52 (1): 3–10.

McCarthy, M.J. (1998) *Spoken Language and Applied Linguistics*. Cambridge: Cambridge University Press.

McCarthy, M.J. and Carter, R.A. (1994) *Language as Discourse: Perspectives for Language Teaching*. London: Longman.

McCarthy, M.J. and Handford, M. (2004) '"Invisible to us": a preliminary corpus-based study of spoken business English' in U. Connor and T. Upton (eds) *Discourse in the Professions. Perspectives from Corpus Linguistics* (pp. 167–201). Amsterdam: John Benjamins.

McCarthy, M.J. and O'Dell, F. (2002) *English Idioms in Use*. Cambridge: Cambridge University Press.

McCarthy, M.J., McCarten, J. and Sandiford, H. (2006) *Touchstone. Student's Book 4*. Cambridge: Cambridge University Press.

McGlone, M.S., Cacciari, C. and Glucksberg, S. (1994) 'Semantic productivity and idiom comprehension', *Discourse Processes* 17: 167–90.

McLay, V. (1987) *Idioms at Work*. Hove: Language Teaching Publications.

Meierkord, C. (2005) 'Interaction across Englishes and their lexicon', in C. Gnutzmann and F. Intemann (eds) *The Globalisation of English and the English Language Classroom* (pp. 89–104). Tübingen: Gunter Narr Verlag.

Moon, R. (1992) 'Textual aspects of fixed expressions in learners' dictionaries', in P.J. Arnaud and H. Béjoint (eds) *Vocabulary and Applied Linguistics* (pp. 13–27). Basingstoke: Macmillan.

Murphy, B. and O'Boyle, A. (2005) 'LIBEL CASE: a spoken corpus of academic discourse'. Paper read at *The American Association for Applied Corpus Linguistics* at the University of Michigan, Ann Arbor 12–16 May 2005.

Nesi, H. (1995) 'A modern bestiary: a contrastive study of the figurative meanings of animal terms', *ELT Journal* 49(3): 272–8.

Nesselhauf, N. (2003) 'The use of collocations by advanced learners of English and some implications for teaching', *Applied Linguistics* 24 (2): 223–42.

Norrick, N. (1988) 'Binomial meaning in texts', *Journal of English Linguistics* 21 (1): 72–87.

Powell, M. (1985) 'Purposive vagueness: an evaluative dimension of vague quantifying expressions', *Journal of Linguistics* 21: 31–50.

Powell, M. (1992) 'Semantic/pragmatic regularities in informal lexis: British speakers in spontaneous conversational settings', *Text* 12 (1): 19–58.

Prodromou, L. (2003a) 'In search of the successful user of English'. *Modern English Teacher* 12 (2): 5–14.

Prodromou, L. (2003b) 'Idiomaticity and the non-native speaker', *English Today* 19 (2): 42–8.

Prodromou, L. (2005) '"You see, it's sort of tricky for the L2-user": The puzzle of idiomaticity in English as a lingua franca'. Unpublished PhD dissertation, University of Nottingham, UK.

Roberts, P. (2005) 'Spoken English as a world language in international and intranational settings'. Unpublished dissertation, University of Nottingham, UK.

Simpson, R. and Mendis, D. (2003) 'A corpus-based study of idioms in academic speech', *TESOL Quarterly* 37 (3): 419–41.

Spöttl, C. and McCarthy, M.J. (2004) 'Comparing the knowledge of formulaic sequences across L1, L2, L3 and L4', in N. Schmitt (ed.) *Formulaic Sequences* (pp. 191–225). Amsterdam: John Benjamins.

Strässler, J. (1982) *Idioms in English: A Pragmatic Analysis*. Tübingen: Gunter Narr Verlag.

Tabossi, P. and Zardon, F. (1993) 'The activation of idiomatic meaning in spoken language comprehension', in C. Cacciari and P. Tabossi (eds) *Idioms: Processing, Structure and Interpretation* (pp. 145–62). Hillsdale, NJ: Erlbaum.

Volk, M. (1998) 'The automatic translation of idioms: machine translation vs. translation memory systems', in N. Weber (ed.) *Machine Translation: Theory, Applications, and Evaluation. An Assessment of the State of the Art*. St Augustin: Gardez-Verlag. Available at www.ling.su.se/DaLi/volk/publications.html.

Waring, R. (1997) 'A comparison of the receptive and productive vocabulary sizes of some second language learners', *Immaculata. The occasional papers at Notre Dame Seishin University*. Available online at: www1.harenet.ne.jp/~waring/papers/vocsize.html.

Weinert, R. (1995) 'The role of formulaic language in second language acquisition: a review', *Applied Linguistics* 16 (2): 180–205.

Wenger, E. (1998) *Communities of Practice: Learning, Meaning and Identity*. Cambridge: Cambridge University Press.

Wright, J. (1999) *Idioms Organiser*. Hove: Language Teaching Publications.

Yorio, C.A. (1980) 'Conventionalized language forms and the development of communicative competence', *TESOL Quarterly* 14 (4): 433–42.

Yorio, C.A. (1989) 'Idiomaticity as an indicator of second language proficiency', in K. Hyltenstam and Obler, L. (eds) *Bilingualism Across the Lifespan* (pp. 55–69). Cambridge: Cambridge University Press.

Chapter 17

Luke Prodromou

Bumping into creative idiomaticity

- 'How every fool doth play upon the word' – *The Merchant of Venice* 3:5
- 'I wanted to blend the two idioms and come up with something new and original and I was sort of punished for that!' – A Polish user of English

Jespersen (1904: 16–17) described phraseology as an 'indispensable' dimension of language competence, but in 1965 Chomsky banished idiomaticity to the fringes of linguistics, giving pride of place to syntax. It seems, however, that time has vindicated Jespersen's prioritizing of formulaic language. In recent years, the area of phraseology has evolved from its peripheral Chomskyan status to a fundamental role in language discussion, description, and acquisition that can be said to focus on 'creative idiomaticity'.

Introduction

In recent years, the concept of idiomaticity has been variously seen as 'pervasive' (Bolinger 1961: 366; Sinclair 1991: 111; Skehan 1998: 30), 'far from marginal' (Weinert 1995: 184), 'central' (McCarthy 1998: 122; Stubbs 2001: 73), and 'ubiquitous' (Carter 2004: 3). Indeed, Nattinger and DeCarrico have gone so far as to describe 'lexical phrases' as 'the very centre of language acquisition' (1992: xv), while, for Hopper, formulaic usage is so integral a feature of language that it is 'difficult or impossible to draw a line between a formulaic and a non-formulaic expression' (1998: 168).

Edited extracts from: Prodromou, L. 'Bumping into creative idiomaticity', in *English Today* 89 (23/1): 14–24, Cambridge University Press, 2007.

The importance of phraseology has also been highlighted by recent work in corpus linguistics. Indeed, one of the major insights of the corpus analysis of English has been the profoundly phraseological nature of much of what we say and write: 'the foundation of fluency, naturalness, idiomaticity, appropriateness' (Sinclair 1991: 496). In addition, Erman and Warren (2000), in their empirical study of 'the idiom principle', found that as much as 50 per cent of language may be explicable in idiomatic terms.

Ironically, however, it is often those linguists who insist on the *sine qua non* of phraseology in the achievement of fluency who have also noted the elusiveness of idiomaticity for the 'non-native speaker'. Its territory is described through such metaphors as:

'capricious' and 'tyrannical' (Jespersen 1894: 22)
'a jungle' (Bolinger 1976: 9; Sinclair 1985: 254)
'[a] dangerous minefield' (McCarthy and Carter 1994: 109)
'treacherous' (Altenberg and Granger 2001: 174)
'[a] stumbling block' and 'slippery' (Wray 2002: ix, 143)
both 'a scourge' and 'anarchic' (Sinclair 2004: 26, 27).

The conceptualization of idiomaticity as a difficult, even dangerous, area reflects the widespread view of this central feature of English as a particular challenge in L2 acquisition. The metaphors we use to describe idiomaticity in the learning context reflect the frequently observed phenomenon of L2-learners/users attempting to deploy idiomaticity in spoken language and ending up sounding *dys*fluent and *un*natural: '[C]olorful idioms, even when correctly produced, often sound strange and unnatural when spoken by "non-native speakers" of English' (Irujo 1986: 299).

Idiomaticity, then, 'sounds' different and comes with great effort in 'non-native' speech; it is where even highly competent L2-users 'are bound to make mistakes, even if [they have] mastered the grammar' (Coulmas 1981: 150).

Why should this be so? Sinclair describes the relationship of idiomaticity to a word meaning as 'mysterious' (2004: 27), and, comparably, Wray (2002: ix) describes the apparent conflict in the behaviour of idiomaticity in 'native' and 'non-native' speech as a 'mystery'. This mystery is the starting point for the present exploration of the 'puzzle' of idiomaticity in 'non-native-like' fluency.

Creative idiomaticity

Starting from the position that everyday conversation is essentially creative, I will focus here on the manipulation of 'opaque' idioms by L1- and L2-users of English, in order to throw light on the difficulty that idiomaticity presents for even fluent L2-speakers. In this I will draw on my own corpus of L2 spoken discourse (200,000 words) to illustrate the way in which successful L2-speakers share common features with their L1 counterparts while also diverging from them in significant ways, especially in how they use 'creative idiomaticity' for pragmatic purposes. The avowed difficulty of idiomaticity for L2-users is identified as a product of the contradictory nature of lexico-grammar and its deep roots in the sociocultural context of particular speech communities.

In the first 100,000 words of my L2-user corpus there are virtually no grammatical errors. There are, however, forty non-canonical versions of idiomatic phraseology: see Table 17.1. Why is creative idiomaticity such a rare occurrence in an L2 and why are colourful idioms error-prone in L2 discourse? [. . .]

Table 17.1 Non-canonical idiomaticity in the SUE Corpus

Type	L1 version	L2 version
Clichés and fixed expressions	(the) last time	in the last-time
	for some stupid reason	for one stupid reason
	by heart	from my heart
	it's a hassle	it's a bustle
	at the back of my mind	back in my head
	funnily enough	funny enough
	at the weekend	in the weekend
	in the long-run	on the long-run
	for the time being	by the time being
	A great advance on	a great advancement on
	side-effect	a side-product
Pragmatic idioms	what do we call	how do we call
	how should I know?	how could I know?
Collocations	the ordinary user of English	the pedestrian user of English
	a standard, regular question	a staple question
	got to the point/made a point	got into a point
	leaking oil	missing oil
	pre-empt problems	waylay problems
	do such a thing	make such a thing
Binomials and trinomials	in such and such a town	in this and this town
	wining and dining	dining and wining
Colourful idioms	I couldn't make head or tail of it	I couldn't make heads or tails of it
	a stroke of good luck	a streak of good luck
Proverbs and sayings	none	none
Quotations and allusions	none	none
Discourse markers	for my part	in my part
	in my (personal) opinion	on my personal opinion
Phrasal verbs	make their own mind up	make their own mind
	to hand in	to hand
Colligations	I couldn't care less	I could care less
	making mince-meat of	making a mince-meat of
	there's no going back on	there is no return from
	take a chance	take chance
	oriented towards	oriented for
	I'm not bothering you	I don't bother you
	established (that) rapport	made those rapports
	discuss	discuss about
	stick in their memory	stick to their memory
	I didn't think twice about it	I didn't think about it twice
	in a just manner	in a justice manner
Compounds	back-up copies	security copies

The 'poetry of everyday speech' (Gibbs 1994: 265; Hall 2001: 69) is the individual's capacity to be inventive, often on a one-off basis, by coming up, for pragmatic purposes, with a unique refashioning of a fixed phrase. Zili He (1989: 150) defines 'creative idiomaticity' as 'the ingenious manipulation of idiomatic expressions normally taken as fixed, which requires cultural or literary awareness and which effects all sorts of subtle variations and surprises.'

Thus, while it is true that much of phraseology is routine and repetitive (cf. Coulmas 1981; Aijmer 1996), there are significant areas of phraseology that are constantly reformed in original ways in everyday discourse (Carter 1997: 162). Conversational creativity extends beyond the ability to manipulate idiomatic language in inventive ways; creativity is an inherent quality in everyday speech, not the preserve of linguistically gifted individuals: '[I]t is not a capacity of special people but a special capacity of all people' (Carter and McCarthy 2004: 83).

This ordinary conversational creativity is manifested in the use of figures of speech and imagery (similes, metaphors), hyperbole, slang expressions, idioms, punning, and repetition, and is the outcome of both contextualized interaction and the co-construction of discourse, not a performance by a gifted individual (cf. Tannen 1989; Moon 1998; Hall 2001; Norrick 2001; Carter 2004).

Creativity in this broad sense is usually indicative of affective convergence and commonality of viewpoint on the part of the interlocutors, though it can also be a symptom of affective divergence from common ground. Carter and McCarthy make a useful distinction between the more overt manifestations of spoken creativity (metaphorical language, word-play) on the one hand and the more covert or subliminal creativity of repetition (parallelisms, echoes).

While the creativity of everyday speech – including 'creative idiomaticity' – extends the rhetorical capacity of the L1-user, it adds yet another layer of difficulty for the learner: there are variations on idioms, sayings, and proverbs which are created on the spur of the moment and quite unpredictable. Such moments of idiomatic creativity are invariably the product of interaction between the speakers and what is felt to be appropriate in a particular context. Though some individuals may be more inventive in producing such word-play than others, the creative utterance is a kind of co-construction between speaker and hearer.

In Bakhtin's terms (1981), the creative utterance anticipates the response of the addressee; it is a dialogic process constrained by social context, not a lone cognitive activity inside the head of the gifted individual: 'All understanding is constrained by borders' (Holquist, in Bakhtin, 1986: xix) and the L2-user often does not know where the borders begin and end.

The three examples that follow (author's data) were all uttered by L1-users. They depend on shared knowledge (both substantive and procedural) and are thus the outcome of co-operation between speaker and hearer, in which the conventional boundaries of phraseology are stretched or redefined:

It's raining kittens and puppies.
< *Common expression* 'It's raining cats and dogs.'

What seems to have got twisted is somebody's knickers.
< *Common informal, especially British, expression* 'She/He got her/his knickers in a twist.'

It's like putting the cat before the horse.
< *Common expression* 'putting the cart before the horse'.

Such language play and creativity often take the form of verbal duels, informal contests of wit and repartee, jokes, riddles, puns, repetitions and variations of previous language, and a whole range of ways of playing with formulaic expressions and especially idioms, all of which can be called *creative idiomaticity*. Sperber and Wilson (1981) have considered such usage in terms of 'echoic' speech and irony.

Language play is full of contradictions. It can serve the needs of collaboration and convergence between interlocutors and it can be aggressive and disruptive (cf. Beltz 2001). It involves the flouting of expectations of conventional regularities in language but depends on an intimate familiarity with those conventions. The disruptive function of language play is often humorous but is also often deployed to deflate official solemnity and even subvert authority (cf. Bakhtin 1984). Indeed, Beltz (2001:131) argues that the inversion of the established order, whether grammatical, semantic, or pragmatic, may be an appropriate interpretive frame for investigations of learner identity and agency in post-'native speaker' approaches to SLA, where learners are not necessarily conceptualized as 'defective communicators in pursuit of an idealized target language native speaker norm' (Beltz 2001: 131).

Exit L2-user, pursued by idiom

The participants in the following example are at an international conference in Brazil. It is the coffee break. Bill, Luke, Rob, and Jane are native speakers of English, and Ignatio is Brazilian. Bill is a professor of applied linguistics. Ignatio has been asking Bill about postgraduate study in the UK.

Bill: Well, I'll have to be going now.
Luke: Yes, 'We'll rise and go now . . .'
Bill: I should have gone some time ago.
Jane: [looking at a nearby tape-recorder] This is still working. . . . This is still running.
Luke: What's the use of running?
Rob: [from nearby] Your conversation may be recorded. Quality control.
Ignatio: [focused on his sole reason for being there] When will I know the outcome?
Bill: I'll just go and have a look at the bookstand
Luke: Make your stand there OK jolly good.
Rob: He's just got a suspicious mind.
Bill: Yes.
Luke: [sings] Caught in a trap . . .
Ignatio: Are you – Are you . . .?
Rob: When he sings there are some words he doesn't quite know and he glosses over them. [sings] 'We can't go on together with suspicious minds.'

Ignatio is present at a speech event where the L1-speakers co-construct the dialogue by drawing on a number of cultural allusions and then playing on the literal and metaphorical meanings of these lexical items. He looks on, like Romeo at the Capulets' ball, while the L1-users delight in echoic mention of poetry, pop-music, fixed expressions, quotations, and fragments from other genres.

The L1-users confirm the depth of what binds them both by drawing on the common store of idiomatic allusions and deploying a range of devices for reinforcing convergence. I will focus here on the 'dialogic' elements in the conversation, which are interwoven throughout the discourse, across different speaker turns, and act as a device for building discourse coherence. The relatively complex dialogue includes:

echoic mention (of a poem by Yeats, 'The Lake Isle of Innisfree')
fixed expressions ('to make a stand,' 'what's the use of running?')
a pop-song ('Suspicious Minds')
an allusion (to a more formal genre: 'your conversation may be recorded')
an ironic echo (of an informal and socially distinct genre: 'jolly good')

The L1-users' discourse is pieced together incrementally and held together, from turn to turn, through the manipulation of fixed expressions. Luke's poetic statement of intention, *we will arise and go now* initiates the sequence of dialogic wordplay. The allusion is taken up by Bill, who uses it to bring the conversation back to the prosaic here-and-now: *I should have gone some time ago.*

A second stretch of conversation is also given unity by creative wordplay across turns. Jane makes a literal, declarative statement about the fact that the tape-recorder is still 'running' (lines 4–5). Luke picks up this lexical item *running* and 'metaphoricizes' it, transforming a literal expression into an idiomatic allusion: *what's the use of running?* We see a similar process a few utterances later when the literal lexical item *stand* (as in *bookstand*) is idiomaticised into *make a stand* ('resist'). Rob takes Luke's play on *stand* as ironic and replies with *He's just got a suspicious mind.* Luke extends the allusion of *suspicious minds* to an Elvis Presley song by quoting a catchphrase from it: *(we're) caught in a trap.* Rob synthesizes the mock-conflict of the first two speakers by quoting a longer chunk from the same song: *we can't go on together with suspicious minds.*

Normal conversation has been taken over by a playful dialogue largely strung together with echoes of generic varieties, in which the L1-speakers dominate; the L2-user, Ignatio, hardly gets a word in and doesn't get involved in the dialogic wordplay. The reason for this peripheralization of the L2-user in such contexts might be that creativity with institutionalized phrases can only be indulged if exposed to a set of culturally familiar scenarios (cf. Tannen 1989: 43).

The echoes of diverse generic forms in conversation can be seen as a 'dialogue' between, on the one hand, the expected uses and connotations of a word or phrase and, on the other, the use actually selected (or invented) in a specific instance (cf. Louw 1993). The ironic humour is also a result of the difference between previous use and present mention (cf. Sperber & Wilson 1981), and the ironic effect of such prosodic features as stress, loudness, tone of voice, and snatches of old familiar tunes. Such informal conversation is dialogic in that the words the speakers use are 'saturated' by previous use, and engage in a 'verbal masquerade'; the words are 'shot through with shared thoughts, points of view, alien value judgments and accents' (Bakhtin 1981: 276, 293).

An intriguing suggestion here is that 'idiomaticity attracts idiomaticity': an idiomatic allusion does not occur in isolation but in the company of other such allusions: the idiomatic wordplay of one speaker stimulates a response in kind by other speakers. If L2-users are to take part in such diffuse interplay they must be able to sustain this kind of interaction across turns and across idiomatic types.

This dialogue of forms, meanings, intentions, and punning echoes of previous use constructs an interplay between constraint and creativity. Such creativity presupposes an important role for the speech community, the knowledge of speech genres, and the subliminal memory of frequent encounters with idiomatic strings in pragmatic contexts; the configuration of meanings and genres is the outcome of recurrent experience from an early age on into adulthood. Similarly, the knowledge of informal conversation and the place of idiomaticity in the sub-genre of friendly 'banter' is the fruit of long socio-historical processes and repeated encounters with the members of the speech community expressing themselves through such a repertoire.

The re-construction of such recurrent lifelong experience by EFL students – in the classroom, for short spurts of time, in a context poor in human interaction – is a formidable task requiring 'immense talent and dedication' (Sinclair 1992: 496). In the next section, we look at a SUE who seems to have achieved such idiomatic competence.

Re-enter L2-user

Dimitri (whose first languages are Greek and Spanish) is in conversation with a native-speaker of English, in which both speakers manipulate a shared knowledge of idioms to create both humour and speaker convergence.

Dimitri: There is this concept of work ethic, to do something because you want to do it and if you want to do it well; there's the old English saying 'If a job's worth doing it's worth doing well,' . . . er . . . er . . .

Luke: Now it seems the . . . er . . . motto is more like 'If you're going to do something, do it as profitably as possible'.

Dimitri: Which usually tends to be well.

Luke: It . . . It . . . It can help

Dimitri: Because of competition. Competition makes it that if you don't do it well, 'forget about it'.

Luke: You see another saying which I think the Americans have is 'if it ain't broke . . . '

Dimitri: '. . . don't fix it.'

In this exchange, notably, it is the L2-speaker who initiates the sequence of idiomatic expressions and indeed demonstrates a 'meta-idiomatic' awareness when he refers explicitly to the fact that he is resurrecting a somewhat 'musty' expression: *there's the old English saying*. The L1-user takes up the conscious 'mention' of idioms in his use of the word *motto* and initiates an example of the process McCarthy (1998) refers to as 're-lexicalisation'. In contrast to the idiomatic stereotype, it is the L1-user who responds to the L2-user's variation on a canonical formula: *if a job's worth doing, it's worth doing well.*

Convergence is clearly established between the two speakers through these idiomatic devices, and is intensified by Dimitri's relative clause *which usually tends to be well*, dovetailing neatly across turns with his interlocutor's utterance. At the same time, Dimitri's completion of Luke's variation on a well-known saying (line 7, '*which . . .*') constitutes a variation on a variation.

The idiomatic thread is taken up again in Dimitri's contributing yet another verbal echo of the original saying *if you don't do it well* followed by a syntactic variation: *forget about it*. The round of idiomatic one-upmanship is taken in another direction by the L1-user, who introduces an echoic and elliptical mention of another saying: *If it ain't broke (don't fix it)* – the rest of the fragment being completed by his L2 partner. Thus, the two speakers weave in and out of each other's utterances, co-constructing the dialogue, through their shared knowledge of both grammatical and idiomatic devices. It is English as a lingua franca in full flight, with the interlocutors in perfect dialogic counterpoint.

The idiomatic deficit

However, the course of verbal play does not always run so smooth, even for proficient L2-users. The persistence of the 'deficit' view of L2-user phraseology may cause the kind of fluent creative idiomaticity displayed by Dimitri to boomerang in pragmatic terms. The kind of resistance from 'native-speakers' that 'non-native' creative use of English may encounter is captured in the following description by a Polish SUE:

Greg: When you try and play with idioms, like those fixed ones . . . er . . . you know there was this . . . this party we had, you know, 'dine and wine' excessive, I would say, the . . . erm . . . next day I said that . . . something like . . . er . . . 'I was drinking like a horse' and . . . er . . . then I was told that you say 'drink like a fish' but 'eat like a horse' and . . . er . . . my intention was that there was so much to drink and to eat that I wanted to . . . I wanted to blend the two idioms and come up with something new and original and I was sort of 'punished' for that (*laughs*).

The speaker bemoans the fact that his fabrication of what he refers to as a 'fused formula' ('drinking like a horse') backfired (Tannen 1989: 41). It was perceived as an error by his native-speaker interlocutor. But as Tannen points out, the blending of two or more set expressions is normal and meaningful in native-speaker discourse: 'The language is mistake-proof' says Tannen (p. 42). I would add however that it is 'mistake-proof' *for the L1-user* but clearly not for the L2-user of English as a Lingua Franca (ELF), as the experience of the Polish user testifies. This may have something to do with the fact that L1-users make the pragmatics of 'mentioning' clear (through phonological features and gesture as well as the lexical choices made in the co-text as a whole), while L2-users may fail to signal the fact that they are 'mentioning' and are therefore heard only as 'using' (or 'misusing') an expression.

It is also possible, of course, that the speaker's attempt at being witty with idioms was infelicitous because the blend is simply not funny. It might be that it was not received by the 'native-speaker' interlocutor as either 'ingenious' or 'subtle' and the only 'surprise' element involved was that the speaker thought it witty in the first place. As Carter (1999) and Norrick (1984) both point out there is an element of risk in displays of wit in informal conversation and the embarrassing spectre of an attempted witticism falling flat is ever-present, for both L1- and L2-users (Carter 1999: 209).

It may well be that the risks involved when an L2-user undertakes to be playfully metaphorical in English are greater than when an L1-user does so, simply because of limited linguistic resources. There may also be sociocultural factors at work which influence the attitude of the interlocutor in terms of ownership of the language and questions of identity.

When a proficient user of ELF attempts to play this game of humorously unpacking idiomatic expressions the result is often pragmatic failure: the subliminal becomes conscious, the implicit becomes explicit, and the event is seen not as 'creative play' but an error:

Nick: (a Greek SUE): As a 'non-native speaker' I am not as free as native speakers to use the language creatively and idiomatically. For instance, yesterday I said something to a group of teachers and one of them commented 'You can say that again!' Humorously, I said 'OK, I'll say it again' and repeated myself more emphatically. Embarrassingly, she said, 'No, I actually meant that I agreed with you.' The assumption was, of course, that the meaning of the idiom had been lost on me!

It is ironic that a speaker's attempts at verbal play are misconstrued as linguistic incompetence, given a similar rhetorical ploy in the following excerpt from the popular British comedy television series, *Fawlty Towers*. In the following example, Basil Fawlty, 'unpacks' or literalizes the set expression *you can say that again* in an identical fashion to the proficient user of ELF in the extract above, but Fawlty, as is his wont, manipulates the idiom with aplomb:

Sybil: No, Polly doesn't forget things
Basil: Doesn't she?
Sybil: Can you remember the last time she did?
Basil: No, I can't but then my memory isn't very good.
Sybil: You can say that again.
Basil: Can I, dear? Oh, thank you . . . I've forgotten what it was.

(Cleese and Booth 1975)

Basil's playful literalizing of *you can say that again* does not establish commonality with his wife but creates ironic distance. Irony, sarcasm, and humour are some of the attitudinal effects available through the creative use of idiomaticity. The example from *Fawlty Towers* illustrates the way idiomatic creativity and phonological manipulation reinforce each other to create such effects: Basil's ironic response to Sybil depends on his ignoring the stress on *that* which the conventional idiomatic meaning of *you can say that again* requires. Instead, Basil responds as if Sybil had stressed *again*, which would be the expected nuclear stress if the string *you can say that* again were being selected on the open-choice principle. Basil also breaks a rule that fixed expressions are not normally followed by tags (Fernando and Flavell 1981).

Both players in this game of verbal pingpong also know the semantic and pragmatic effect of such bending of the rules; they also share an awareness of the (especially British) ironic tone of voice. Basil's 'Can I dear? Oh, thank you . . .' is in phonological quotation marks: 'Every word used "with conditions attached", every word enclosed in intonational quotation marks, is likewise an intentional hybrid' (Bakhtin 1981: 76).

Basil's response is 'double-accented' and the whole exchange is a good example of the dialogic nature of the utterance and even of individual lexical items (Bakhtin 1981: 304). The to-and-fro of meanings embodied in words, idiomatic phrases, and phonology is a constitutive feature of L1-speaker discourse; competence in manipulating the mesh of collocational and phonological potential for ironic or echoic effect is intimately bound up with what it means to be a fluent member of a speech community.

In my corpus, in contrast to the L1-user's subliminal phraseological competence, highly proficient L2-users often demonstrate a self-consciousness when producing collocations, which is not apparent on the grammatical level:

Tomas: I wouldn't lift – what is it, an eyebrow? What is it that you do?
Luke: 'Raise an eyebrow.'
Tomas: 'Raise an eyebrow.' I wouldn't raise an eyebrow.

The next example shows another SUE expressing hesitation and doubt in the context of creative collocations:

Tania: They just brought the whole conference down . . . er . . . the 'whole house', you would say. Is that the right idiom?
Luke: 'Brought the house down.'
Tania: 'Yeah, yeah. That's right.'

These examples suggest that the process of constructing idiomatic collocation, for the L2-user, may be more analytic than holistic (Wray 2002: 205–11).

Bumping into creativity

'Nursery rhymes and songs are very much the basis of my own English and allow me to understand and share things cultural that to a great extent surprise some natives: "You're not supposed to know things like Little Jack Horner and Little Miss Muffet, José!"' – José, a SUE and teacher trainer in Uruguay

What is considered creative in the mouth of the L1-user is often seen as a deviation in the mouth of even the most advanced successful bilingual user of the language. Thus, the acceptability or otherwise of creative collocations has very much to do with the perceived 'authenticity' of the utterance and the authority bestowed upon those who embody such 'authenticity' (Widdowson 1998).

It is ironic that the L2-speaker's attempts at verbal play are misconstrued as linguistic incompetence. The L2 speaker, as Thomas points out (1983: 96), does not seem to have the same right to break the rules as does the 'native speaker':

> [T]eachers and linguists fail to admit the possibility of a foreign student's flouting conventions in the same way as they fail to allow him/her to innovate linguistically – in fact, the foreign learner is usually expected to be hypercorrect, both grammatically and pragmatically.

This ability to transgress the shared system is a kind of creative versatility that marks out the speaker as a member of a cultural club to which access is limited.

Does the 'native-speaker' exist?

These assumptions about creativity in L1- and L2-speaker discourse were explored in a survey I conducted with 400 teachers of English. In this closing section, I will first report one more instance of collocational creativity by successful users of English as a Lingua Franca (ELF), then the results of the survey into how this creativity was received by L1- and L2-users from around the world. Here are examples of unusual collocations with the prepositional verb *bump into* produced by two different L2 speakers:

I'm always very glad when for example I bump into a new expression. . . . [T]his means that he or she is going to bump into 'although' at least thirteen times.

Sensing that something was not quite as one would have expected with these collocations, I looked up *bump into* in a corpus-based dictionary (Rundell 2002). According to this dictionary, *bump into* does not normally collocate with abstract nouns such as *a new expression* or a word like *although*. Here is part of the dictionary entry for this verb (Rundell 2002):

Bump into (sb) To meet someone unexpectedly: I bumped into your mother at the supermarket

Bump into (sth) To accidentally hit against something: As I turned round, I bumped into a filing cabinet

Turning, however, to the concordance lines for *bump into* in the British National Corpus, which is an L1-user corpus, I found these attested examples of *bump into*:

1   The way sound and vision copulate is what makes their music and ideas always a thrill to bump into.
2   Something tells me you may bump into a little politics on the way.

On the face of it, it seemed that what was possible for L1-users was 'out of bounds' for L2-users. In order to investigate this hypothesis, I conducted an e-mail survey of 400 teachers and other ELT professionals, both L1- and L2-users, from a wide range of countries, to gauge attitudes towards creativity in 'native' and 'non-native' speakers. The question I set was very simple (see Figure 17.1).

I sent out the question in two versions: 200 teachers were informed that the sentence had been produced by a 'native-speaker' and 200 were told it had been produced by a 'non-native speaker'. The aggregate responses to these questions are summed up in Figure 17.2.

This survey seems to confirm the existence of a contradiction in what is considered legitimate for 'native-speakers' and 'non-native speakers' to do with collocation. When my respondents thought the sample utterance belonged to a native-speaker they were overwhelmingly positive in their attitude, but the opposite was true in the case where the speaker was assumed to be a non-native speaker. Many respondents added comments explaining their choice of answer; some explicitly articulated a different attitude to creativity in English when the language is L1 from when it is L2. The following comment from an L1-user is typical: 'I must admit I'd be happier with this from a NS than a NNS!'

Would you say this sentence is 'acceptable' English?

I'm always very glad when for example I bump into a new expression . . .

Yes _____   No _____

Underline: I am a native/non-native speaker of English

Figure 17.1 The *bump into* questionnaire

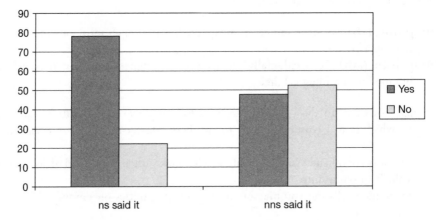

Figure 17.2 Native/non-native speakers' responses to the acceptability of *bump into* (% 400 responses)

It seems that *non-* can make a difference to people's attitudes towards creativity in language use.

The simultaneous existence of collocational norms and the potential for violating these norms is a defining feature of L1 competence and, at the same time (paradoxically) it seems to be – as Medgyes (1994) has argued – one of the defining features of the limits of 'non-native' competence, even at advanced levels. Many writers have identified the way idiomaticity is embedded in culture (for example, He 1989; Alexander 1992), which carries the conceptual knowledge that a child begins to acquire at school and at bedtime, through games and nursery rhymes. It is on this kind of knowledge that later more sophisticated creative play is built. The L1-speaker gains idiomatic competence (of which creative idiomaticity is the most sophisticated expression) after years of immersion, from childhood to adulthood, in the cultural context in which the language is embedded. Expressions of irony, sarcasm, or humour, packaged in their appropriate phonology and repeated countless times, become routinized in everyday discourse (cf. Coulmas 1981).

Conclusion: idiomaticity and an emerging ELF

In this chapter, I have identified what I see as a paradox at work in the relationship between ENL and ELF, whereby the same linguistic features produce opposite effects in L1- and L2-speakers. The difficulty of acquiring and implementing idiomatic shared knowledge is both linguistic and sociolinguistic – it has as much to do with attitudes and culture as it has to do with forms and meanings.

The subliminal command of thousands of phrases and sentences (Pawley and Syder 1983) is only the tip of the iceberg of 'native-like fluency'. Linguistic and cultural inference, lexical cohesion, an intuitive awareness of connotation, skilful use of repetition, quotative competence, and, finally, the weaving together of all these features in the co-production of on-line speech, are all part of the big picture of L1 fluency. Fluency in this framework involves an incremental co-construction of discourse by speakers who, rather than fulfilling a grand grammatical design, seem to be stitching together chunks of language as and when the need arises. This rhapsodic discourse is based on a dialogic orientation towards both language and the other speaker(s) in the dialogue, and is thus 'based on a here-and-now view of what the speaker is doing; and this perception co-operatively takes into account the listener's here-and-now point of view' (Brazil 1995: 222–3).

The challenge of the 'on-line' processing of creative language in spontaneous speech in the here-and-now intersubjectivity of dialogue may explain why word-play is not everybody's conversational cup-of-tea. The processing effort invested in interpreting the unusual combination of words and meanings is not always rewarded with a successful pragmatic outcome: for example, the pleasure found in achieving a humorous effect, in economically expressing complex ideas, or in yoking together heterogeneous ideas (cf. Norrick 1984). Disappointment and frustration are more likely in the case of L2-users looking in from the outside on L1 language games.

Of course, the task of acquiring idiomaticity is only a problem if one sets up L1 forms as the norm for English as a Lingua Franca. The question is whether L1-like idiomaticity is a valid strand in the tapestry of ELF. L1-users deploy their mother tongue from a position of deep commonality and, as a rule, L2-users of that language don't. This means that, as far as idiomaticity is concerned, L1-users are 'playing at home', with rules they can bend according to need. L2-users are 'playing away', and, if they break the rules, they are penalized. One begins to wonder just how fixed the rules governing language play are. After all, several of the SUEs in my corpus display undoubted skill in the manipulation of idiom, if not in the free-wheeling creativity that is the very stuff of common talk in L1 informal conversation. And they seem to have an intuition for where their limits are, as far as idiomaticity is concerned: they keep away from minefields.

References

Aijmer, K. (1986) 'Discourse variation and hedging', in J. Aarts and W. Meijs (eds) *Corpus Linguistics II: New Studies in the Analysis and Exploitation of Computer Corpora* (pp. 2–18). Amsterdam: Rodopi.

Aijmer, K. (1992) 'Fixed expressions, phraseology and language teaching: a sociosemiotic perspective', *Zeitschrift für Anglistik und Amerikanistik XL* 3 (3): 238–49.

Altenberg, B. and Granger, S. (2001) 'Grammatical and lexical patterning of *make* in student writing', *Applied Linguistics* 22 (2): 173–94.

Bakhtin, M. (1981) *The Dialogic Imagination*. Austin, TX: University of Texas Press.

Bakhtin, M. (1984) *Rabelais and his World*. Bloomington, IN: Indiana University Press.

Bakhtin, M. (1986) *Speech Genres and Other Late Essays*. Austin, TX: University of Texas Press.

Beltz, J.A. (2001) 'Review of language play, language learning', *Applied Linguistics* 22 (1): 129–32.

Bolinger, D. (1961) 'Syntactic blends and other matters', *Language* 37: 366–81.

Bolinger, D. (1976) 'Meaning and memory', *Forum Linguisticum* 1: 1–14.

Brazil, D. (1995) *A Grammar of Speech*. Oxford: Oxford University Press.

Carter, R. (1997) *Investigating English Discourse*. London: Routledge.

Carter, R. (1999) 'Common language: corpus, creativity and cognition', *Language and Literature* 8 (3): 195–216.

Carter, R. (2004) 'Creating, interacting: creative language, dialogue and social context', *Applied Linguistics* 25: 162–88.

Carter, R. (2004) *Language and Creativity: The Art of Common Talk*. London: Routledge.

Carter, R.A. and McCarthy, M.J. (2004) 'Talking, creating: interactional language, creativity and context', *Applied Linguistics* 25 (1): 62–88.

Chomsky, N. (1965) *Aspects of the Theory of Syntax*. Cambridge, MA: MIT Press.

Cleese, J. and Booth, C. (1975) 'The Anniversary'. In the *Fawlty Towers* series, *Radio Collection Vol. 3*. London: BBC.

Coulmas, F. (1981) 'Idiomaticity as a problem of pragmatics', in H. Parret, M. Sbisà and J. Verschuren (eds) *Possibilities and Limitations of Pragmatics: Proceedings of the Conference on Pragmatics* (pp. 139–51), Urbino 1979. Amsterdam: John Benjamins.

Erman, B. and Warren, B. (2000) 'The idiom principle and the open choice principle', *Text* 20 (1): 29–62.

Fernando, C. and Flavell, R. (1981) *On Idiom: Critical Views and Perspectives*. Exeter: University of Exeter.

Gibbs, R. (1994) *The Poetics of Mind: Figurative Thought, Language and Understanding*. Cambridge: Cambridge University Press.

Hall, G. (2001) 'The poetry of everyday language', in J. McRae (ed.) *Reading Beyond Text: Processes and Skills: CAUCE: Revista de Filologia su Didactica* 24 (pp. 69–86). Seville: University of Sevilla.

He, Z. (1989) 'Creative Idiomaticity', in H. Hall-Kira, M. Meacham and R. Shapiro (eds) *Proceedings of the 15th Annual Meeting of the Berkeley Linguistics Society*, 8–20 February 1989. Berkeley, CA: Berkeley Linguistics Society.

Hopper, P. (1998) 'Emergent grammar', in M. Tomasello (ed.) *The New Psychology of Language* (pp. 155–75). Hillsdale, NJ: Lawrence Erlbaum.

Irujo, S. (1986) 'Don't put your leg in your mouth: transfer in the acquisition of idioms in a foreign language', *TESOL Quarterly* 20: 287–304.

Jespersen, O. (1894) *Progress in Language, with Special Reference to English*. New York: Macmillan.

Jesperson, O. (1904) *How to Teach a Foreign Language*. London: Allen & Unwin.

Louw, B. (1993) 'Irony in the text or insecurity in the writer?' in M. Baker, G. Francis and E. Tognini-Bonelli (eds) *Text and Technology: In Honour of John Sinclair* (pp. 157–74). Amsterdam: John Benjamins.

McCarthy, M. (1998) *Spoken Language and Applied Linguistics*. Cambridge: Cambridge University Press.

McCarthy, M. and Carter, R. (1994) *Language as Discourse*. London: Longman.

Medgyes, P. (1994) *The Non-Native Teacher*. Basingstoke: Macmillan.

Moon, R. (1998) *Fixed Expressions and Idioms in English: A Corpus-Based Approach*. Oxford: The Clarendon Press.

Nattinger, J. and DeCarrico, J. (1992) *Lexical Phrases and Language Teaching*. Oxford: Oxford University Press.

Norrick, N. (1984) 'Stock conversational witticisms', *Journal of Pragmatics* 8: 195–209.

Norrick, N. (2001) 'Poetics and conversation', *Connotations* 10 (2–3): 241–67.

Pawley, A. and Syder, F.H. (1983) 'Two puzzles for linguistic theory: native-like selection and native-like fluency', in J.C. Richards and R.W. Schmidt (eds) *Language and Communication* (pp. 191–226). New York: Longman.

Rundell, M. (ed.) (2002) *Macmillan English Dictionary for Advanced Learners*. Oxford: Macmillan Education.

Sinclair, J. (1985) 'Selected issues', in R. Quirk and H. Widdowson (eds) *English in the World* (pp. 248–54). Cambridge: Cambridge University Press.

Sinclair, J. (1991) *Corpus, Concordance, Collocation*. Oxford: Oxford University Press.

Sinclair, J. (1992) 'Shared knowledge', in *Proceedings of the Georgetown University Round Table in Linguistics and Pedagogy: The State of the Art* (pp. 496–9). Georgetown, WA: Georgetown University Press.

Sinclair, J. (2004) *Trust the Text: Language, Corpus and Discourse*. London, Routledge.

Skehan, P. (1998) *A Cognitive Approach to Language Learning*. Oxford: Oxford University Press.

Sperber, D. and Wilson, D. (1981) 'Irony and the use-mention distinction', in P. Cole (ed.) *Radical Pragmatics* (pp. 295–318). New York: Academic Press.

Stubbs, M. (2001) *Words and Phrases: Corpus Studies of Lexical Semantics*. Oxford: Blackwell Publishers.

Tannen, D. (1989) *Talking Voices*. Cambridge: Cambridge University Press.

Thomas, J. (1983) 'Cross-cultural pragmatic failure', *Applied Linguistics* 4: 91–112.

Weinert, R. (1995) 'The role of formulaic language in second language acquisition: a review', *Applied Linguistics* 16 (2): 180–205.

Widdowson, H. (1998) 'Context, community and authentic language', *TESOL Quarterly* 32 (4): 705–16.

Wray, A. (2002) *Formulaic Language and the Lexicon*. Cambridge: Cambridge University Press.

Chapter 18

Philip Seargeant

Time, tense and perception in the narrative voice of Bret Easton Ellis's *Lunar Park*

Introduction

This chapter examines the way in which representations of the perception of time operate in narrative, and how such representations can be used to communicate the narrator's attitude towards the events being narrated. It offers a stylistic analysis of a short passage from Bret Easton Ellis's novel *Lunar Park* (2005) to illustrate the way in which the manipulation of linguistic features creates a distinctive narrative voice, and how, as part of this, the description of action and environment is used to index something of the narrator's state of mind. The contention is that the manipulation of tense and other means of expressing time will describe not only the sequence of events, but also the perspective and attitude that the narrator takes towards those events. Along with other stylistic features, this manipulation can thus be seen as a key component of narrative voice.

Tense and grammar

Tense is the grammaticalisation of time. That is to say, it is a concept that is used in linguistics as a means of categorising the way in which the grammatical construction of verbs denotes the time at which events take place. An event can happen in the past, the present, or the future, and this can be expressed in language by the manipulation of the form of the verb or verb phrase which is describing the event. So, for example, *I typed* the previous sentence a minute ago. *I am typing* this sentence now. *And in a moment I will start* a new paragraph. Standard English has two tenses that are inflectionally marked in the verb: a present (or non-past) tense (*I type*), and a past tense (*I typed*). In addition, the future may be marked by use of the auxiliary 'will' (*I will type*). In combination with aspect and mood, tense is one of the most powerful ways by which language is able to articulate the unfolding experience of lived reality.

The relationship between time and the grammatical concept of tense is not quite as straightforward as this synopsis suggests, however. As with most linguistic features, in actual use tense has more than one function (Fleischman 1990). And what I wish to focus upon in this article is how the manipulation of tense, as well as the various other resources provided by language for expressing relations of time, are able to express not only 'what happened when', but also something about the way in which the narrator views the world.

Time as tenseless

There is a strand of thought within philosophy that asserts that time itself is tenseless (e.g. Mellor 1998: ch. 2). That is to say, the categories of past, present, and future are not an inherent property of time. These categories are better understood as *relations* that are dependent on time, and so tense is a way of describing the relation between a person and an event. In other words, tense is not simply about when things happen, but rather about when things happen *in relation to* the person narrating them. According to this formula, the present is something that happens at the moment of speaking; the past is something that happens earlier than the moment of speaking; and the future is something that happens later than the moment of speaking. Each of the three categories, though, is relative to the person doing the speaking.

Viewing tense in these terms, we can see that the statement of an event also communicates something about the narrator's perception of that event. And thus, in a sense, the use of tense can tell us as much about the narrator as the event. Or at least, in combination with other stylistic features such as grammatical patterning, an evaluative vocabulary, and the blend of different voices, the textuality of discourse can both narrate events (tell us what happened) but also convey something of the narrator's perception and assessment of these events.

The text in context

To illustrate how this grammatical framing happens in practice, and how time, tense and perception are communicated by the manipulation of linguistic features, I will conduct a stylistic analysis of a short extract from Bret Easton Ellis's novel *Lunar Park* (2005: 107–8). *Lunar Park* is a ghost story about a successful writer haunted by the spectre of his late father and memories from his childhood. The passage below describes a conversation between the protagonist, his eleven-year-old son, Robby, and his six-year-old step-daughter, Sarah. The narrator's wife, Jayne, is a celebrated film actress, and at this juncture in the narrative their marriage is beginning to show signs of stress. Living now in the suburbs, the narrator is finding it difficult to adjust to domestic life, and recently he has begun to notice unnerving supernatural occurrences cropping up around him. In this passage he is taking the two children to the cinema when he has cause to remember an incident from a few weeks ago which he now interprets with added significance.

The passage has been chosen because it consists of two temporally separate episodes, one of which is embedded within the other in the form of a memory. It also includes the narrator's account of his engagement with his social circle and the portrait this presents of a certain section of modern American society. Both the structure of the act of memory and the perception of the social world he presently inhabits combine to convey something of the cast of the character's state of mind.

(1) I looked in the rearview mirror. (2) Robby was glaring at me through his orange-tinted wraparounds, one eyebrow raised, while tugging uncomfortably at his crewneck merino sweater, which I was certain Jayne had forced him to wear.

(3) "I can see that you're very cold and withdrawn today," I said.

(4) "I need my allowance upped" was his response.

(5) "I think if you were friendlier that wouldn't be a problem."

(6) "What's that supposed to mean?"

(7) "Doesn't your mom handle your allowance?"

(8) A huge sigh emanated from him.

(9) "Mommy doesn't let me sit in the front seat," Sarah said again.

(10) "Well, Daddy thinks it's okay. (11) Plus you look quite comfortable. (12) And will you please stop eating the Skittles that way?"

(13) We suddenly passed a three-story mock-colonial monstrosity on Voltemand Drive when Sarah sat up and pointed at the house and cried out, "That's where Ashleigh's birthday was!"

(14) The mention of that party in September caused a surge of panic, and I gripped the steering wheel tightly.

(15) I had taken Sarah to Ashleigh Wagner's birthday party as a favor to Jayne, and there was a sixty-foot stegosaurus balloon and a traveling animal show and an arch made up of Beanie Babies framing the entrance and a machine spewing a continuous stream of bubbles around the backyard. (16) Two weeks prior to the actual event there had been a "rehearsal" party in order to gauge which kids "worked" and which did not, who caused trouble and who seemed serene, who had the worst learning disability and who had heard of Mozart, who responded best to the face painting and who had the coolest SCO (special comfort object), and somehow Sarah had passed (though I suspected that being the daughter of Jayne Dennis was what got her the invite). (17) The Wagners were serving the lingering parents Valrhona hot chocolate that had been made without milk (other things excised that day: wheat, gluten, dairy, corn syrup) and when they offered me a cup I stayed and chatted. (18) I was being a dad and at the point at which I vowed that nothing would ever change that (plus

the Klonopin was good at reinforcing patience) and I appeared hopefully normal even though I was appalled by what I was witnessing. (19) The whole thing seemed harmless – just another gratuitously whimsical upscale birthday party – until I started noticing that all the kids were on meds (Zoloft, Luvox, Celexa, Paxil) that caused them to move lethargically and speak in affectless monotones. (20) And some bit their fingernails until they bled and a pediatrician was on hand "just in case." (21) The six-year-old daughter of an IBM executive was wearing a tube top and platform shoes. (22) Someone handed me a pet guinea pig while I watched the kids interact – a jealous tantrum over a parachute, a relay race, kicking a soccer ball through a glowing disc, the mild reprimands, the minimal vomiting, Sarah chewing on a shrimp tail ("*Une crevette!*" she squealed; yes, the Wagners were serving poached prawns) – and I just cradled the guinea pig until a caterer took it away from me when he noticed it writhing in my hands. (23) And that's when it hit: the desire to flee Elsinore Lane and Midland County. (24) I started craving cocaine so badly, it took all my willpower not to ask the Wagners for a drink and so I left after promising to pick Sarah up at the allotted time. (25) During those two hours I almost drove back to Manhattan but then calmed down enough that my desperate plan became a gentle afterthought, and when I picked up Sarah she was holding a goody bag filled with a Raffi CD and nothing edible and after telling me she'd learned her four least favorite words she announced, "Grandpa talked to me."

(26) I turned to look at her as she innocently nibbled a prawn. "Who did, honey?"

(27) "Grandpa."

(28) "Grandpa Dennis?" I asked. (29) "No. (30) The other grandpa."

(31) I knew that Mark Strauss (Sarah's father) had lost both parents before he met Jayne and that's when the anxiety hit. "What other grandpa?" I asked carefully.

Before moving to a detailed analysis of the passage, it is worth adding a word here about the genre of the book, as it is this that provides an interpretative framework for our reading. *Lunar Park* is a horror story concerning supernatural events (Ellis says that he was influenced by Stephen King in the conception and composition of the novel (Wyatt 2005)), but it is also a satire about a sector of contemporary American society. The expectations of both these genres are fulfilled in great part by the narrative voice and the presentation of the way in which the central character interacts with his environs. The horror genre relies often on a disconnect between perception and expectation (that's to say, on experiencing the supernatural with one's own senses), while the genre of satire requires a detached evaluation of the events surrounding the narrator. Both of these are managed by the manipulation of linguistic and discourse features, and specifically by the narrative voice.

A key structuring feature for the novel is that there is an I-narrator throughout, and thus the focalizing agent (the person from whose perspective the events are viewed) and the narrator (the person doing the telling) are one and the same. As such the narrative voice is able to represent directly the way that the protagonist perceives events, and when other voices or perspectives are introduced, it is nearly always via the mediating presence of this I-narrator. This allows for the mixture of evaluation and perturbed self-reflection that drives the two genres.

There is, however, one significant way in which this impression is undermined, and that is in the use of certain intertextual references that appear within the fictional world of the novel. The names of two of the streets that are mentioned in this passage – Voltemand Drive (line 13) and Elsinore Lane (line 23) – are both allusions to *Hamlet* (the former being the name of one of the Danish ambassadors to Norway; and the latter, of course, being the place where the action of the play predominantly takes place). The significance of these references is clear enough in a story in which the protagonist feels that he is being haunted by the ghost of his father, and thus the intertextuality here is operating at a different narrative scale to the rest of the description, revealing the pre-meditated artifice of the author behind the narrator.

Time and the ordering of events

The theme that provides the intertextual references with significance is also the main structuring frame for this particular passage, which ends with the revelation that the daughter, Sarah, has talked to a man whom she describes as her 'grandpa'. One point that is not explicit in this passage alone is the issue of the order of events. Of great significance within the context of the story is that the man who apparently talked to Sarah is already dead (a fact that has been established earlier in the novel). The events as they unfold – and as they are perceived by the narrator – appear to contravene the common sense understanding of the order of events. If Sarah can have talked to the narrator's father just a few weeks ago, and yet much earlier in the story this same father has already died, there seems to be a breach in the natural flow of events. And this breach causes the narrator significant psychological disquiet. What in effect is happening, therefore, is that the narrator's perception of the past (that his father is dead) creates the way he now perceives the present (as an uncanny incident). The event of Sarah's encounter with the 'grandfather' (or more specifically the event of Sarah telling the narrator of this encounter) is only significant *in relation to* the narrator's experience of other events, and his perception of it is therefore expressed by means of a complex of layered temporal episodes in which past and present confront each other with the antagonism of illogicality.

We can begin looking at how this is achieved in the text by examining the way in which time is organised in this passage. The following table lists the events narrated in the passage according to their chronology. This list indicates the 'event structure' (Brewer 1985) of the action, which stretches back to the death of Sarah's paternal grandparents, and brings us up to the point of the car journey to the cinema. In the right hand column are the line numbers at which these events occur within the narrative. This column shows us the 'discourse structure' employed by the text in the narration of these events.

The death of Sarah's paternal grandparents	31
Mark Strauss and Jayne meet	31
The practice party	16
Narrator takes Sarah to the party	15
Narrator leaves for a two-hour drive	24
Sarah talks to her 'grandfather'	25
Narrator picks Sarah up from party	25
Jayne forces Robby to wear a sweater	2
Narrator driving Robby and Sarah to the cinema	1
Sarah points out the Wagner house	13

As is immediately apparent from this table, discourse structure and event structure are markedly different in this passage (the line numbers in the right hand column are far from being in any sequential order), thus accommodating the dramatic juxtaposition of different time periods, with the significance of the passage as a whole coming from this juxtaposition. Early influential work in the analysis of narrative that was conducted by the Russian Formalists identified a key distinction between the *fabula* (the chronological series of events as they happen) and the *sjuzhet* (the narrative organisation of those events in a plot). As we can see, in this passage it is the organisation (the *sjuzhet*) that produces the dramatic dynamic of the narrative. In the events that directly precede this passage the narrator has experienced other sightings and episodes related to his apparently deceased father, and it is within the context of these that the memory of what Sarah said at the end of the party assumes a new significance. As was noted above, it is the narrator's act of remembering the past event *now* that is important, not just the past event itself. And the structure of this act of memory is created by grammatical and discoursal structuring.

The narrative is broadly divided into two discrete periods of time: the first fourteen lines are predominantly about the 'now' in which the narrative is unfolding, which acts as the 'implicit present' for the story. Lines 16 to 31 recount an event that happened some weeks earlier, and which is now being recalled as a memory which has been triggered by an action in the present. In the discourse structure the two episodes have their chronology reversed, so that the narration of the past event is causally triggered by the present event, and the substance of the past event can now be interpreted in the light of what is happening in the present.

The death of Sarah's paternal grandparents *Mark Strauss and Jayne meet* *The practice party*	} *Background for the memory*
Narrator takes Sarah to the party Narrator leaves for a two-hour drive Sarah talks to her 'grandfather' Narrator picks Sarah up from party	} Memory
Jayne forces Robby to wear a sweater	*Background to the present*
Narrator driving Robby and Sarah to the cinema Sarah points out the Wagner house	} Present

How, then, is this layering of temporal episodes achieved in terms of the linguistic features that are used within the passage? The novel as a whole is told in the simple past, which is by far the most common tense used in narrative in fiction. Its habitual use in the context of fiction means that 'it is best interpreted not as a temporal or deictic marker, but as a generic marker' (Black 2006: 6); that's to say, within the context of a piece of fiction it is taken by the reader as an implicit present rather than a marker of the actual past. (This can be seen in the way that the simple past is often used even in narratives that are set in the future.) With the simple past established as the base line against which the unfolding of narrated events takes place, the use of other temporal markers including tense and aspect can then create a hierarchal temporal system. If we look at the first two sentences of this passage we can see this happening quite clearly.

> I (a) **looked** in the rearview mirror. Robby (b) **was glaring** at me through his orange-tinted wraparounds, one eyebrow raised, while tugging uncomfortably at his crewneck merino sweater, which I was certain Jayne (c) **had forced** him to wear.

The narration begins with a simple past tense (a) expressing a distinct action, which we take to be one that is happening at the point of narration; the passage then uses the past progressive (b) for an ongoing action with which the distinct action of (a) intersects; and finally it switches to the past perfect (c) to refer to something that happened prior to the 'now' of the unfolding action. There is no sense of *when* these various actions happen, other than the relation they have with each other.

The shift from the implicit present to the events recalled in the memory is also managed by means of a shift from simple past to past perfect (line 15: "I had taken Sarah"). A further shift back to the "'rehearsal' party" (16) is managed by the past perfect ("there had been") plus an adjectival phrase indicating relational time ("two weeks prior to"). Once the shift has been made, however, the narrative returns to the use of simple past (in combination with past progressive), which once again becomes the base line for this particular part of the narrative (17 onwards). It is not until the contextualising background information about the death of Sarah's paternal grandparents that the past perfect is again used (line 31: "Mark Strauss . . . had lost both parents"), which provides a deictic marker indicating that the loss of Mark Strauss's parents prefigured his union with Jayne (which resulted in the birth of Sarah). Of importance in this narration is simply this sequence of events, but nothing more about their location within the flow of time.

To plot the various events on a time line, therefore, would be impossible with any exactness because almost without exception the time at which events happened is indicated simply by their relation to other events. These relations are the salient facts for the narrator, and they form his perception of the action. What we have in his narration is the importance of one event happening before another, which conforms to the elementary understanding of time as it is normally experienced. The conundrum of the man that Sarah spoke to then threatens to disrupt this simple sequential patterning of events, and provides the dynamic for the narrator's sense of disquiet.

Sentence and phrase structure

Manipulation of tense within the narrative is not simply a matter of juxtaposing different time periods in such a way as to create a particular cognitive experience for the main character, however. The way that the events that occur within these time periods are presented is also part of the representation of the narrator's perception of the action. In line 13, for example, the approach to the transition from one time period to another is marked by a sentence which combines four dynamic verbs each in the simple past, and, in the case of the last three of these, each indicating a discrete action related to the same act of perception: "We suddenly **passed** a three-story mock-colonial monstrosity on Voltemand Drive when Sarah **sat up** and **pointed** at the house and **cried** out". The combination of multiple verbs (where one would probably have sufficed for purely descriptive purposes) acts to emphatically stress this one particular moment, which proves to be the trigger for the memory.

This example also involves an 'and' coordinated sentence construction ("Sarah sat up **and** pointed at the house **and** cried out"), which is another key stylistic feature used throughout the text. In the long central paragraph (lines 15–25) the dominant syntactic pattern is one of a series of main clauses coordinated together (either by conjunctions such as 'and', or by commas), interspersed with lists of nouns or noun phrases. However, whereas the sentence quoted above (line 13) stresses a single event which is marked by dynamic verbs indicating the agency of a particular character (Sarah), the lists that describe the party itself are comprised of discrete and anonymous events. These lists string together salient details or vignettes which the narrator notices during his time at the party, but which he rarely, if ever, interacts with in a causal way. In line 15, for example, there is an inventory of the elaborate decorations at the party, all of which are governed by a single stative verb ("there **was** a sixty-foot stegosaurus. . .") and coordinated by successive uses of 'and'. Line 22 likewise itemises a series of discrete incidents ("a jealous tantrum over a parachute, a relay race" etc) by means of a long, comma-coordinated list construction which noticeably lacks a final 'and' (the conventional stylistic means of rounding off such a list). In both cases, the details that are listed are indicative of the social world which the narrator inhabits, and they describe by means of select detail rather than generic evaluation of the elaborate indulgence that characterises the party. The effect throughout is one of disengaged observation, where tense (mostly past progressive for the phenomena he witnesses, and simple past for his own actions) is used in conjunction with this serial juxtaposition of clauses to mark the recursive nature of the eccentric details, rather than to articulate relations of cause and effect. Events are perceived, one after another after another, with the narrator mostly a peripheral figure merely observing them as he drifts through the day.

When the syntax diverges from this pattern it is all the more conspicuous for doing so. The most noticeable disruption comes at the end of the passage where the long paragraph of description gives way to reported speech. This is a form of 'internal deviation', that is to say 'deviation against a norm set up by *the text itself*' (Short 1996: 59). In other words, there is a noticeable shift in style between the expectations that have been built up in the central paragraph with its long, coordinated sentence structures, and the staccato paragraphing which follows, with the most dramatic change coming in line 27, which comprises a paragraph of a single word.

The effect is to foreground this one word ("Grandpa") which, in the development of the narrative, is, of course, the punchline of this particular incident. This word is then further foregrounded by being repeated five times in seven lines. From drifting through the party listlessly recording a catalogue of slightly grotesque incidents, perception is suddenly focused insistently on this one notion.

Before moving to look at the use of other stylistic techniques which also manage the representation of perception in this passage, it is worth pointing to one other interesting use of tense and aspect which provides a telling moment within the narrative. Midway through the description of the party the narrator reports that "I was being a dad" (line 18). Thematically, this statement touches upon a central concern for the book, as the developing narrative dwells not only upon the central character's relationship with his father, but also on the relationship he has with his own children. Indeed, part of the emotional journey that the narrator takes throughout the story is to reconcile anxieties about fatherhood with his own ambivalent emotions to his experience of being a son. And again, the grammatical construction of this one statement works to draw attention to some of these themes by subtly subverting expectations. In this clause a stative verb is used, unusually, with the progressive aspect, giving it a dynamic sense. The result is that the verb changes from representing a particular state of being ('I was a dad') to representing an action ('I was being a dad'). As being a father is more commonly understood as something that one is rather than does, the tinkering with basic grammatical constructions here foregrounds the narrator's attitude towards his situation.

Multiple voices

The patterning of tense and sentence structure is one aspect of the linguistic basis for the impressions of satirical detachment and emotional disconnection within this passage. Another is voice. I have mentioned already how intertextual references to canonical literature introduce intimations of an authorial presence which operates at a different scale to that of the autobiographical narrator. I suggested also, however, that with the exception of this, all the other voices in the text are introduced via the mediating presence of the I-narrator. The treatment of these other voices works to position the narrator within a range of specific discourses (related to the speech and preoccupations of the other parents at the party). This is another key aspect of the satirical nature of the text, and the effects produced by it complement those achieved by the manipulation of time and tense. Two specific ways in which this positioning of the narrator is managed are through the use of punctuation, and in the employment of a varied lexis.

In terms of punctuation, a number of lexical items within the narrative description are placed in what are known as scare quotes, which indicate that the phrase thus highlighted is part of the discourse of someone other than the narrator, though is not meant as a quotation from anyone in particular. The use of scare quotes thus allows for an explicit double-voicing (Bakhtin [1929] 1984), with both a phenomenon and the narrator's ironic or ambivalent attitude to that phenomenon being recorded in the same phrase. Line 16, which recalls the "'rehearsal' party" with its remit of gauging "which kids 'worked' and which did not", contains two such examples. In both cases the scare quotes foreground particular words from which the narrator appears to wish to disassociate himself, and which are thus highlighted as being, in his view, incongruent for the given circumstances. The effect then is to distance the narrator from the attitudes of the social circle with which he is interacting.

The passage also includes a high proportion of items from specialised lexicons, which are used to index either social position or a particular lifestyle. Most salient are the pharmaceutical terms (Klonopin, Zoloft, Luvox, Celexa and Paxil), which suggest a social class for which a specialist knowledge of anti-depressant medication appears to be an essential aspect of the paraphernalia of everyday life. The use of such brand names in the context not of a clinical setting but of a children's party is particularly disconcerting, and the effect is extended with reference to items such as the "SCO (special comfort object)", which is an everyday concept but described here in the register of popular psychology.

Social class is also indexed in the use of other types of brand names, such as that of the French luxury chocolate manufacturer Valrhona, and in the use of specialised registers such as the French "*une crevette*". These are metonyms – that's to say they are discrete details which stand as representatives of a larger complex of behaviours. The detail of the *crevette*, for example, works on two different levels as a metonymy for the privileged and rarefied social world which the people attending the party inhabit. Firstly, it is used to indicate the fact that this type of cuisine is being served at a children's party, and this particular dish is thus representative of the elaborate menu on offer to the child attendees. And secondly, Sarah's actual utterance makes the point that within this community not only is a six-year-old girl able to recognise and appreciate such cuisine, but she also knows how to refer to it in French, which likely operates as a symbol of cosmopolitan sophistication for this particular social group.

Often in the construction of narrative, choices over lexis can also provide an evaluative aspect to the description of events or environments, as, for example, when the Wagner's house is referred to as a "three-story mock-colonial **monstrosity**" (line 13). This technique is not a particularly frequent feature of the narrative voice in this passage, however, and the majority of details are listed without direct narratorial comment. In fact, the lack of any direct evaluation of the various details can be seen as a notable feature of the overall style, especially given the content of some of the description. Approximately half way through the long paragraph (at the end of line 18) the satire turns more sinister. The details that are listed after the narrator has confessed to being "appalled by what I was witnessing" (the bleeding fingernails, the medicated and lethargic behaviour, the minimal vomiting) are distinctly more perverse than they were in the earlier part of the paragraph where they were simply excessive (the sixty-foot stegosaurus balloon, the travelling animal show). Yet even here the vocabulary is not evaluative, and instead the satire comes by means of the disinterested list of increasingly unsettling metonymic details.

Conclusion

In conclusion, then, we can say that it is the relationships between events and the narrator – relationships that are expressed by various different grammatical, discoursal and lexical means – that create the representation of perception. Specifically it is the sense of distance that produces these effects: the use of different voices distances the description from the narrator, even though he himself is doing the narrating; and likewise the use of tense and other temporal markers manipulates the distance between events and narrator. To perceive something is to be causally affected by it, and within a written text that causal effect is expressed in the framing of events that grammar manages, which operates to convey the relationship between a narrator and an event. And when the expression of that relationship develops a particular pattern we can call it narrative voice.

References

Bakhtin, M. ([1929] 1984) *Problems in Dostoevsky's Poetics* (ed. and trans. C. Emerson). Minneapolis, MN: University of Minnesota Press.

Black, E. (2006) *Pragmatic Stylistics*. Edinburgh: Edinburgh University Press.

Brewer, W. (1985) 'The story schema: universal and culture-specific properties', in D.R. Olson, N. Torrance and A. Hildyard (eds) *Literacy, Language, and Learning: The Nature and Consequences of Reading and Writing*. Cambridge: Cambridge University Press.

Ellis, B.E. (2005) *Lunar Park*. New York: Alfred A Knopf.

Fleischman, S. (1990) *Tense and Narrativity: From Medieval Performance to Modern Fiction*. London: Routledge.

Mellor, D.H. (1998) *Real Time II*. London: Routledge.

Short, M. (1996) *Exploring the Language of Poems, Plays and Prose*. Essex: Longman.

Wyatt, E. (2005) 'Bret Easton Ellis: the man in the mirror', *New York Times*, 7 August. Available at: www.nytimes.com/2005/08/07/arts/07wyat.html (accessed 26 April 2008).

Chapter 19

Greg Myers

Applied linguists and institutions of opinion

Introduction

Christopher Brumfit has defined applied linguistics as 'the theoretical and empirical investigation of real-world problems in which language is a central issue' (Brumfit 1995: 27). In this definition, the scope of the field is much wider than would be suggested by the already broad range of its traditional applications to language learning, education, lexicography, and language policy. It is hard to think of any 'real-world' problems – from global warming to refugees to genetic counselling to outsourced call centres to AIDS/HIV to military intelligence – that do not have a crucial component of language use.

One important area of language practice in real-world problems that has led to an enormous amount of social science research activity, but has not attracted much involvement from linguists, is the work of the commercial, government, and academic organizations that I have called institutions of opinion (Myers 2004). Measures of public opinion are used by politicians on one side or the other; constant polling for example fed back into the 2004 US Presidential election, and the debates were followed instantly by focus groups assessing who won. Phone-ins fill radio time, and many web pages (such as that of CNN) have a QuickVote(tm) feature allowing anyone to express an opinion on the day's topic. The UK Labour Party held a 'Big Conversation' on the future of the country, and my local government conducted a survey on whether the big new road should go to the north or the west of the city (although they did not follow its outcome). It is important to be able to challenge institutions that have such an influence on our political lives.

From: Myers, G. 'Applied linguists and institutions of opinion', in *Applied Linguistics* 26 (4): 527–45, Oxford University Press, 2005.

Institutions of opinion are based on language practices, because questionnaires, interviews, focus groups, and even web page surveys all have at their basis some kind of interaction involving talk, reading, or writing. However much we dismiss reports of opinions as just opinions, as showing the superficiality and malleability of the public, or the narrowing of public discourse, we are often eager to seize on them when they support our own views. And it could be argued that we are right to seize on such evidence: some sense of the will of the public underpins representative democracy. The questions for us, as linguists and as citizens, are how the signs of opinion are elicited and packaged, and what differences these processes make.

Opinion is big business, and it has attracted a great deal of academic and commercial research in political science, sociology, and social policy studies. Most of this research assumes that opinion is something already out there to be measured, like the average temperature in Antarctica or the number of owls in Oregon. Academic public opinion research examines the instruments, the questionnaires and questions, and the ways they are analysed, and asks how to make the procedures more reliable. But there is another approach to these processes that does not take the act of giving an opinion for granted, that starts with the interactions of questioners and respondents, and asks what opinions are, and how they are transformed between contexts; it is in this approach that I think linguists (and conversation analysts, rhetoricians, and social psychologists) have something to offer.

It is only fair, when criticizing public opinion research, to acknowledge that these institutions have had some impressive successes in prediction (I will return to one of these later). It is also fair to note that academic researchers in this area have from the very beginning pointed out possible limitations and distorting factors in surveys (Lazarsfeld 1944; Payne 1951; Schuman and Presser 1981; Schuman 1986; Schaeffer and Presser 2003; Bulmer 2004). Some of the most interesting findings have been on cognitive processes studied through think-aloud protocols of respondents answering questions (DeMaio and Rothgeb 1996) or post-questionnaire debriefing (Belson 1981). Graham Low has applied these methodologies to the kind of evaluation questionnaires often used in applied linguistics (Low 1996, 1999).

As public opinion researchers have noted, people do talk about some public issues (though not all such issues) in pubs and at the dinner table and on the bus. For the researchers, the parallels between everyday conversation and professional survey validate the opinions found, because people are just having the kind of talk that they usually have, even if institutional modifications are necessary to produce reliable results (Gallup and Rae 1940; Schuman 1986). Public opinion polls often present the interactional aspects of the process, such as audience design, multiplicity of interpretations, and indexical meanings, as technical problems to be dealt with by testing of the wording of questions and standardization of interviewer procedures, for instance by changing the order of questions.

But there is an alternative view of the talk involved in the elicitation of opinions. Suchman and Jordan (1990a and 1990b) argue that 'interactional troubles' cannot be so easily eliminated or set aside as the public opinion researchers would have it. In the survey interviews they videotaped, features of everyday conversation that are problematic for standardization of survey questions included: recipient design, signals of what kind of answer is required, establishment of relevance, repair, and clarification of meaning. Schaeffer and Maynard (1996) provide detailed transcripts of how questioners and respondents work out problematic aspects of the questionnaire. Their work is part of a line of research that focuses on the encounter that produces the data, treating it as an interaction, a conversation like other talk in institutions (Antaki and Rapley 1996; Maynard and Schaeffer 1997; Houtkoop-Steenstra 2000; Maynard and Schaeffer 2000; Maynard *et al.* 2002). This line of critique can indeed be used to improve survey and focus group techniques by making responses more reliable (see for instance the work of Yuling Pan for the US Bureau of the Census (Pan 2004)).

But even analyses aimed at improving existing techniques (such as Houtkoop-Steenstra 2000) pose a challenge to the whole idea of public opinion research, by seeing opinion not as a unitary entity inside an individual, to be elicited and aggregated, but as something two or more talkers produce in a particular situation. For any given statement of opinion, we need to ask whom the respondent thinks they are talking to, who they are talking as, why are they saying this just now, how this issue fits in the conversation. Traditional public opinion research tells us what the people say; this line of research is equally interested in how they say it. And in studying how they say it, this research leads us to questions about the way people think of themselves and present themselves to others.

I will present three fragments of public opinion research on one heavily researched topic: public attitudes to nuclear power and nuclear waste. The topic is heavily researched because it matters both to the public, worried about safety and about energy supplies, and to the industries that build and operate nuclear plants, and need to find ways of persuading the reluctant public (see for instance, the Nuclear Energy Institute at www.nei.org). My textual examples are from a national survey series (in the USA, where there have been surveys asking the same questions over long periods), a single local survey (done in my region of the UK), and a focus group transcript (also in the UK, where there have been extensive efforts at public consultation on the topic). I will consider possible questions about the words in these texts, the interactions, the role of commonplaces, and the models of public discourse they suggest.

Example 1: A national survey series

Eugene Rosa and Riley E. Dunlap (1994) have reviewed three decades of polling on public attitudes towards nuclear power in the USA, for the main US journal of public opinion research. One of the many items they consider is a question asked in October of each year by the Roper organization, concerning the safety of power plants.

Example 1

'There are some differences in opinion about how safe nuclear power plants are. Some people say they are completely safe, while others say they present dangers and hazards. How do you feel – that it would be safe to have a nuclear energy plant *someplace near here* or that it would present dangers?' (Emphasis added [by Rosa and Dunlap])

	10/75%	9/79%	9/89%	9/90%
Safe	42	27	22	25
Would present dangers	43	64	70	67
Don't know	15	9	8	8

$N = 2000$. *Source*: Roper (Rosa and Dunlap 1994).

I should note that I have simplified the presentation and argument given by Rosa and Dunlap; they give the full series for each year 1973–90, and compare the results to those from other, more detailed questions, in which respondents compare the risks posed by various means of producing power, and estimate the risks associated with nuclear plants in comparison to other risks they might face. Their response to many of the criticisms one might make of specific question items might be that they are pointing to the *change* of opinion over time, not some essentialist snapshot, and that they are referring to risk in relative terms, not asking respondents to arrive at absolute figures. The years I have chosen are those noted by Rosa and Dunlap to show shifts in opinion after the accidents at Three Mile Island (1979) and Chernobyl (1986).

Example 2: A survey report

We can compare this national series to a smaller-scale study in the UK conducted in 1995 by North East Market Surveys on people living in West Cumbria, a beautiful and rather sparsely populated area of England in which the main employer is the largest nuclear installation in the UK, the nuclear fuel reprocessing plant at Sellafield. The results were used by Copeland Borough Council (the unit of local government for the area around the plant) in their submission to an inquiry on the proposed use of Sellafield as a nuclear waste site in addition to its other functions. Respondents were asked to agree or disagree with four statements, with the results given in the following table.

Example 2

	Agree strongly/ Agree	Disagree/ Disagree strongly
I think it is safe living near Sellafield	79%	17%
I believe the nuclear industry is a safe industry	71%	23%
I am apprehensive about the safety assurances given by the nuclear industry	41%	55%
I am concerned about the health risks posed by the activities of the nuclear industry at Sellafield	40%	58%

Source: North East Market Surveys (Waterton and Wynne 1999).

The report also noted that those who lived in Seascale (the nearest village to the plant) and those who worked in the plant were more likely to agree with the reassurances in the first two statements, and disagree with the criticisms in the third and fourth. I am taking this example from a paper by Waterton and Wynne (1999), who use it to criticize some of the assumptions made in surveys on risk; I will return to some of their comments.

Words and interpretations

Most of the research and guidance on both surveys and focus groups is concerned with the planning and wording; for instance, Stanley Payne's classic *The Art of Asking*

Questions (1951) is a witty demonstration of some unexpected ambiguities and associations in apparently straightforward questions. We can find some issues of wording in Examples 1 and 2, even though the items were undoubtedly well designed for their purposes:

- *You* and *I*: Payne starts his list of problem words with 'you', because it can be both singular and collective; the 'you' in Example 1 could mean 'you personally' or (less probably) 'you around here'. In Example 2 the researchers avoid this ambiguity by phrasing the question as 'I think . . .' – although they may still have respondents who answer for others around them rather than themselves.

- *Think, believe,* and *feel*: Payne also warns against 'believe' as a questionnaire word. For some respondents, 'I think' may imply knowledge and reflection, and be stronger, while for others 'I believe' may imply deeper conviction. So in Example 2, some could have taken the issue in statements 1 and 2 to be, not the difference between 'safe living near Sellafield' and 'a safe industry', but the difference between 'think' and 'believe'. In Example 1, some people 'say' one thing and some people 'say' another, but you are asked what you 'feel', a word that is not always used with embedded propositions; this use could imply stronger conviction than what people merely say, or less certainty than what people think.

- *Safe* and *danger*: In both Example 1 and Example 2, we might look for instance at how people interpret 'safe' – as completely safe, safe enough, provided with appropriate protections, comparatively safe. In Example 1, 'safe' contrasts with 'would present dangers', with the implication that only something without any dangers is safe. People have more complex views of risk. For instance, one could evaluate the safety of a plant in terms of statistics on possible failure, or knowledge of its design, or trust (or lack of trust) in those who work there, or one's sense of agency in doing something about any dangers. In the context of other questions in the Roper Survey (Example 1), 'safety' is to be evaluated in comparative terms, considering other dangers. But comparison is also problematic, requiring some uniform standard of measurement between risks that pose different kinds of uncertainty, different levels of control, and different kinds of effects. (For difficulties in evaluating public perception of risk, see Slovic (2001) and Lupton (1999); for a study of risk in cultural terms see Douglas and Wildavsky (1982).)

- *Someplace near here* and *near Sellafield*: 'Someplace near here' must be deliberately vague, to fit all the possible local geographies of the respondents in a national survey. But 'here' has all sorts of meanings not only in geographical scope (five miles? the whole valley? the whole county?), but also in geographical meanings: it could be 'in this area that already has toxic waste dumps' or 'here in Nevada that has had a disproportionate part of radiation risk' or 'here in Michigan where there is high unemployment' or 'here where I look out on my view of the Pacific'. In Example 2 the researchers can be more specific than in a national survey. But asking about living 'near Sellafield' is different from asking about living 'in West Cumbria', 'on the sea', 'near the Lake District', or 'far from cities', all of which are equally true descriptions of the place the survey was administered. 'Near Sellafield' emphasizes that this plant defines the identity of the place, that others think there is good reason not to feel safe there.

Professionals in public opinion research might point out that all these issues are potential problems, but not necessarily real problems for a given purpose. The survey researcher can test out different wordings, and use different wordings on different but related questions; the problems will wash out over the whole survey, or the series over time, and the results will be reliable. So if there are ambiguities of interpretation of 'safe', they are the same ambiguities year after year, and the series shows reliable changes even if the percentage responses on one year's results might be questioned.

But the reliable result may still be the aggregation of very different interactions, people presenting themselves in different ways for what they see as different purposes. These interactions are lost to us as readers of the report of public opinion. They may matter to us if we are just interested in predicting how people will vote (polls are demonstrably effective at predicting that). But they do matter to us if we are interested in the tensions and contradictions within people's views, the ways they use opinions to present themselves to others, and to relate to friends and family, the ways they use taken-for-granted and familiar opinions, the ways opinions relate to other kinds of talk, and crucially, the way talk about everyday practices such as shopping, travel, or taking the kids to school might relate to actions (Billig 1987; Shotter 1993; Billig 1995; Antaki et al. 1996; Puchta and Potter 2002). For insights into these aspects of opinion, we might turn to less structured interviews, or to focus groups, where the interactions around key terms would be treated as interesting, rather than as problematic.

Example 3: A focus group extract

The following extract is from one of a series of focus groups conducted by Jane Hunt and Peter Simmons, in a study commissioned by Nirex, the organization created by the UK government to deal with nuclear waste. It is worth noting that Nirex was conducting research on how best to open up preliminary public discussion of waste disposal sites (Hunt and Simmons 2001), that is, the client was interested in how people said things (and how they might say more) as well as what they said. Traditional survey methods and official inquiries had failed to give any clear insight into what to do with nuclear waste; not surprisingly, people seem to want something done with it, but not near them. The following excerpt is from a group of people living near a conventional nuclear power plant now being decommissioned; they are talking about the official procedures in case of an accident. One participant has just said she thinks local officials are supposed to have iodine ready.

Example 3

| 1 | F1 | I think there are plenty of . supplies for the locals= |
| 2 | F2 | =for the locals ((laughter)) |

3	M1	probably need to get a prescription for it though . that's gonna take three weeks ((laughter))
4	F2	being as they've got five little bottles over there ((laughter))
5		(6)
6	Mod1	so . you seem to be saying you're you're pretty confident about the levels of . regulation the levels of control
7	M2	well let's put it this way . we haven't been told anything . to the contrary have we
8	M	mm
9	M2	if we were told something then you'd worry about it . but it's kept quiet . if anything has happened it's . pushed under the carpet

Even with twenty-two focus groups (in eleven sites), the study of which this transcript is a part cannot give us the scope of the surveys in Example 2, much less the huge scope over space and time of the series in Example 1. But focus groups can tell us about what people do in expressing an opinion, and that can be particularly important in sensitive issues such as those around risk and local identities.

Interaction

The issues about multiple interpretations of wording that I raised with the survey questions apply as well to the questions a focus group moderator might introduce into the discussion, but in a focus group we can also see which interpretations the participants are taking this time, for their purposes. In line 6 of Example 3, the moderator formulates the discussion up to this point as saying that they are 'pretty confident' about the levels of regulation and control at the plant. But the response is not a simple matter of agreeing or disagreeing, or of placing a response on a scale from 'very confident' to 'very sceptical'. A participant begins (7) with a marker of a dispreferred turn, 'well', and 'let's put it this way', suggesting that his response is not going to confirm this formulation, and then he gives three different responses, that 'we haven't been told anything to the contrary', that 'if we were told something you'd worry', that 'if anything has happened it's pushed under the carpet'. This response unpacks the formulation in a way that is not possible with a questionnaire, drawing out the different contingencies that might affect an answer, and emphasizing the contradictory feelings between the need for the public to believe in the plant management, and the unspoken doubts that remain.

Some of the other issues of wording, of 'you' and 'I', and 'around here', also depend on interaction, on who is talking to whom for what purpose. In Example 2, the report compares responses from people living close to Sellafield to responses from other locations in the region, to make a point about the attitudes of those who should, presumably, know the plant best and have most cause to worry about it. But it can be argued that the people living close to Sellafield were answering a different question. Waterton and Wynne (1999) point out some of the issues of recipient design here: an outsider is asking about the area's largest employer, perhaps one's own employer, in questions that assume one can simply agree or disagree. There are also more subtle cultural issues in any response; one might feel pride in one's work and that of one's work colleagues, guilt about the risks some say nuclear workers bring to their families (even if one doubts the risks exist), fatalism about any possibility of changing the plant or organization, disgust at different kinds of pollution, isolation in living in a region that is out of sight for most people in the country (and therefore a possible site for nuclear plants), or anger at outsiders who know none of this and joke about Sellafield workers glowing in the dark. If one lives in a community that is stigmatized as polluted and dangerous, and one is talking to someone from outside, one might assert agreement with the safety of the plant, or disagreement with the implied criticism, as a form of solidarity with one's community (Wynne 1982; Zonabend 1993; Bolter 1996; Myers 2005). The reported feeling of safety is worth recording, but the utterances indicate particular interactions, not necessarily an underlying attitude that exists independent of who is talking to whom.

I have already noted that an aggregation of these 'around heres' is not a generalized response to the abstraction of the local, but a confused summation of many concrete localities. And in each of these places, the assertion that one would feel safe with a plant near here could be made with different meanings, as a way of displaying scepticism about claims of environmentalists, or showing common sense in the face of pressure group campaigns, or comparing these dangers to others, or denying the implication that one is a hypocritical NIMBY who accepts the need for nuclear power but says 'Not In My Back Yard'. Bronislaw Szerszynski has drawn on speech act theory to argue that statements of trust are in part performative, that to say 'I trust you' is a commitment that is meant to make you more likely to be worthy of that trust (Szerszynski 1999). In this perspective, when people say that a plant is safe, it could be that they are not describing a situation, but trying to bring it about.

As we see in Example 3, a focus group transcript can suggest some (though not all) of the interaction going on in eliciting an opinion. The joking about the iodine, for instance, serves several functions: showing knowledge of what preparations for an accident might involve, giving the sense that these preparations are inadequate, and that 'outsiders' would be excluded, and that bureaucratic procedures and inefficiency would undermine any procedure. And the laughter suggests that this view of the situation is shared by some or all of the group, and that the group also shares a way of dealing with this anxiety. (See Waterton and Wynne (1999) for discussion of laughter in focus group discussions of risk.) In a focus group, it is exactly the community sense of shared norms that is at issue (Bloor *et al.* 2001), not the aggregation of individual levels of knowledge, trust, or anxiety.

So far I have been praising focus groups because they are more accessible than surveys for interpretation of interaction. But focus groups are not a form of open discussion; they have their own institutional form. The obvious constraints are the moderator's control and topic guide; a more subtle constraint is the participants' emerging sense of what the group is for. As they look around the room and see who else is there, they may talk as locals, or farmers, or mothers, or retired people. Kitzinger (1994) has noted that the ongoing interaction makes some responses possible and closes off others. Claudia Puchta and Jonathan Potter (1999, 2004) have shown in a series of studies the way the moderator provides slots for responses that will be easily detached and used in reports. Greg Matoesian and Chip Coldren (2002) have analysed part of an evaluation group discussion of community policing, and have argued that we miss the response of participants if we look only at their words, missing their full performance using gaze and gestures. My own research has looked at agreement and disagreement, topic shifts, and reported speech, and has considered different styles of moderation (Myers 1998, 1999; Myers and Macnaghten 1999; Macnaghten and Myers 2003; Myers 2004). For most public opinion researchers, these variations in the nature of interaction are trouble, because they make it impossible to abstract any underlying entity, much less a quantity, for 'public opinion'.

Commonplaces

Circularity is built into public opinion research: the big survey organizations ask questions about the issues that are news, and their results then become news (Bourdieu 1990, 1993; Herbst 1993; Schudson 1998). Surveys assume a shared repertoire of issues that people talk about; that is why they can use standard questions (and why phone-in callers can name their topic in a word or two, and opinions can fit on a placard or bumper sticker). They rely on commonplaces, *koinos topoi*, *loci communes*. These are the rhetorician's terms for short evocations of standard arguments that will work in many situations (Myers and Macnaghten 1998). Although people who are not rhetoricians typically use the term 'commonplace' to demean a statement, John Shotter (1993), following Vico (1988 [1710]), argues that they are worth attention, that 'sensory topics' can carry the 'socially shared identities of feeling' of a community. References to 9/11, our children's future, the need to take care of one's own family or local group first, or the necessity of the daily drive to work could all be commonplaces; one does not need to spell out one's argument. Ellen Barton (1999) looks at the use of formulaic phrases and commonplaces in a support group for parents of disabled children; they draw on an existing repertoire, while also signalling a solidarity and shared experience among members of the group.

Commonplaces, pools of shared ways of arguing, are both an opportunity and a problem for opinion research; an opportunity because they are textual instances of shared identities, and a problem because these instances are unstable in meaning. When speakers use commonplaces, they say something on the current topic, but they also invoke a sense of shared experience and perspective, or ironic predictability, or scepticism. In Example 3, M2's 'let's put it this way' signals that what follows is to be taken as one phrasing, that there are alternative, perhaps more direct ways of saying this. He says: 'it's . pushed under the carpet', bringing out the commonplace after a pause. The use of the commonplace conveys not just that any accidents there might have been concealed, but that they all recognize and share this suspicion of such organizations and the ways they might act. The lack of knowledge and the suspicion are both offered as shared, not as just the opinion of this speaker: 'we haven't been told anything . to the contrary have we'. Or consider a phrase that comes up, not in this passage, but in many focus groups: people (or sheep) who live near nuclear installations are said to 'glow in the dark' (or to have extra limbs). The phrase usually raises a laugh, even when used by people who live near a nuclear installation, but it also conveys vividly the sense of stigmatization that may underlie the answers in Example 2, the survey near Sellafield.

Commonplaces are at the heart of legitimate public opinion – they are one way of referring to shared experiences and points of view, and affirming or questioning what we, as this group here and now, take for granted. There is a long history, from Plato to Bourdieu, of critique of what people take for granted, of 'judgment without reflection' to use Vico's phrase (for background on Vico, see Grassi 1990; for background on Bourdieu, see Myles 2004). What distinguishes commonplaces from the taken-for-granted *doxa* is that they are by no means unchallengeable; people use commonplaces as commonplaces, and happily invoke a commonplace and its opposite for the same argument, or the same commonplace for opposite arguments (Billig 1987); pro- and anti-nuclear lobbies can both appeal to the need to protect the environment. Commonplaces such as 'Political correctness gone mad' or 'Think globally act locally' come (or should come) with scare quotes around them. They do not just express an opinion, they are a way of talking about expressions of opinion as familiar, everyday conversational acts. Participants in focus groups may not just express the group norm; they may report views of other people who are not in the group, or take up devil's advocate positions. Commonplaces can be ways of opening and acknowledging dialogue.

Commonplaces are at the heart of public opinion, but they are a problem for institutions of opinion if they mean people repeat back to researchers the same phrases people have been offered as encapsulating public opinion. This circularity is particularly apparent in the web surveys provided for instance by 'QuickVote(tm)'; when one comes across the page, one reads a list of colloquial statements on an issue, clicks one, and then immediately compares one's own 'vote' to those of others who have clicked on the site. These surveys usually have a disclaimer about the obviously biased sample: 'This QuickVote is not scientific and reflects the opinions of only those Internet users who have chosen to participate. The results cannot be assumed to represent the opinions of Internet users in general, nor the public as a whole'. But the problem is not just with the sample, but with the choices as well: we are offered what we will think (on the basis of the news on the rest of the page) is an issue on which we must have an opinion, and we are offered the sorts of words in which we might express this opinion. And then, instantly, these words are given back to us as an aggregate opinion. Snapshot public opinion surveys work more slowly and with a more careful sample, but with the same circularity.

Deliberation and discourse

Critics of polling have long worried about a 'bandwagon effect' in which polls would bias public opinion by leading people to join the most popular opinion; polling researchers have long argued that such an effect does not exist (Gallup and Rae 1940). But the omnipresence of institutions of opinion may have other, more subtle effects, reifying public opinion as something out there, already formed and ready to be elicited. Some political theorists have argued that the sum of such individual opinions does not constitute public opinion, whatever Gallup, MORI, *USA Today* and the *Daily Mail* might say. They argue for 'deliberative democracy', and argue that truly public opinion begins to emerge when one individual opinion has to encounter another, and engage with it in dialogue (Dryzek 1990; Benhabib 1996;

Elster 1998; Kim *et al.* 1999). These theorists argue that decisions based on dialogue are not just more legitimate, they are better, because they have more experiences to draw on, and they are more likely to be accepted.

Critical discourse analysts have argued that there is a gap between the existing public sphere and the ideal, and that gap is certainly there. Fairclough (2000: 182), for instance, calls for democratic dialogue that 'is accessible to anyone . . . is sensitive to difference . . . gives space for disagreement, dissent, and polemic . . . gives space for new positions . . . to emerge . . . [and] can lead to action'. A typical poll, focus group, or radio phone-in does not begin to meet these criteria.

But we need to ask what sort of forum could provide something like the ideal of dialogue. It is interesting that with all the ink spilled in the last two decades on deliberative democracy (in political theory) and dialogicality (in discourse analysis), there has been so little academic study of actual public dialogues (but see Goodin and Niemeyer 2003). Experiments initiated by government agencies, whether Oregon Health Decisions (see www.cpn.org/topics/health/commoregon.html) or the UK government's debate on genetically modified organisms, GM Nation (see www.gmnation.org.uk/), are useful exercises in broadening consultation, but remain uncritical about what constitutes opinion. There have been some interesting prescriptions from counsellors, political scientists, and activists, for instance from the Public Conversations Project (www.publicconversations.org) (Becker *et al.* 1995), and the Deliberative Democracy Consortium (www.deliberative-democracy. net). What sorts of forums open out discussions to a wider range of participants and views, more engagement between conflicting views, more commitment to and examination of what one says? And one might reasonably ask, of such ideal debates, who would then participate, and why. People enjoy polemics, slogans, repetition of what they already know, playful abuse. Rants, it seems, are entertaining. If there was to be an open and rational discussion of nuclear waste on the television at 8 o'clock tonight, with detailed presentation of all the arguments, would you turn it on? Really?

Applied linguists and 'the real world'

I would like to draw from this particular case – institutions of opinion – some more general observations about how applied linguists approach real-world problems. Such contacts may lead us to questions about our discipline, our framing of problems, our assumptions about language, the scope and scale of research, our own disciplinary biases, and our relation to wider audiences. In all these issues, as in earlier applications to language learning, education, or lexicography, we have to reconsider our relation to practitioners, and be cautious about presenting ourselves as experts.

1 *Most of the studies of language in institutions of opinion are not by applied linguists.* Public opinion researchers are, of course, already familiar with *wh*-questions, presuppositions, connotations, and polysemy, and their studies of question wording provide empirical tests of interpretations that go beyond most of our work in semantics and pragmatics. Focus group moderators know more than I do about group dynamics, and those who write reports on focus groups have an effective,

if implicit, system for analysing them. There have indeed been important studies by linguists (Low (1996, 1999) on questionnaires; Matoesian and Coldren (2002) on focus groups), but we are just as likely to learn about language use from public opinion researchers who have accumulated years of hard-won experience with ambiguity and interpretation. This rather humbling situation is a consequence of a definition of applied linguistics in terms of real-world problems – given a problem involving language, it is not necessarily the case that our rather small academic discipline will get there first, or that it will have all the necessary tools.

2   *We bring our own disciplinary biases to new areas.* I have criticized the view of opinions as cognitive entities located in individuals, to be elicited by survey questions and analysed statistically. But large parts of applied linguistics take just such an approach to cognitive entities in language learning, as if they could be considered apart from the situated interactions in which they are elicited. For instance, questionnaire studies of attitudes towards language learning have the same basic problem of reifying cognitive entities. I think we have a lot to learn from sociologists and social psychologists who look at cognitive entities in terms of situated interactions (e.g. Billig 1987; Middleton and Edwards 1990; Suchman and Jordan 1990a, 1990b; Edwards and Potter 1992; Antaki and Rapley 1996; Edwards 1997).

3   *Practitioners and academics may not conceptualize the 'real-world problem' in the same way.* Public opinion researchers conceive of opinions as measurable outputs related to real underlying cognitive entities, attitudes. Discourse analysts and linguists more generally are likely to see them as forms of interaction, tokens in our exchanges with other people. They develop ways of making their studies faster, more reliable, and more easily represented, while we may be making their work slower, more difficult, and more complicated. It would not be surprising if they did not queue up to benefit from our insights.

4   *Practitioners and academics may not conceptualize 'language' in the same way, either.* For practitioners in this field, language seems to be an opaque screen between them and their object, a potential source of distortion to be repaired by attention to grammar and word choice (Payne 1951; Sudman and Bradburn 1982). For discourse analysts, language brings with it the historical conditions, cultural value systems, ambivalences, interrelations of participants, and conceptions of the speech event. We see language use as constituting and shaping organizations, identities, social changes, and agency, not as providing a more or less transparent medium for the real entities.

5   *As a practical matter, academic timescales are radically different from those of non-academics.* Academics plan their projects over years, and since we are generally part-time researchers, even small projects spread out. We tend to focus on aspects of problems that can be studied intensively and in general terms. Consultations on nuclear waste, GMOs, mobile phones, or even a proposal for speed bumps in a residential street cannot wait until we arrive at what would be an ideal design of a discussion. There are also issues of scale. Even relatively small exercises in consultation and public opinion research, exercises perhaps smaller than they should be, take place on a grand scale, requiring a large organization. There are many insights to be had from the kind of small-scale academic study that characterizes my own work, but by definition public opinion is something broader.

Making a difference

Despite the problems in adapting applied linguistics to this new area, public opinion is too important to leave to commercial polling organizations, academic public opinion specialists, newspapers, and television networks. These institutions claim to speak for 'the people', and their results can be powerful, as they recirculate and define the terms of political and practical possibility, on nuclear power, gun control, war, genetically modified foods, vaccinations, trade agreements, or on issues that are not even recognized as issues because opinions are not surveyed and do not circulate in this way. If applied linguists who study language and interaction want to intervene, we might consider how these institutions got to be so powerful (Herbst 1993; Schudson 1998).

George Gallup offered an origin myth for public opinion research when he traced the success of his commercial polling organization to the failure of a previously trusted way of packaging opinions, the provision of a superior technology, and the enlistment of media organizations, because his results were comprehensible to the public as news (Gallup and Rae 1940). We too may be witnessing a failure of current institutions of opinion, even if it is not as spectacular as the case Gallup uses, the failure of the *Literary Digest* poll to predict the 1936 US Presidential election. Gallup's technical innovation was the use of a small but carefully designed representative sample (which enabled him to predict the 1936 election more or less accurately). Gallup's method—systematizing what had been left to unsystematic straw poll and crowd counts, quantifying it, and commodifying it—fitted a model of modernity. Readers of polls could recognize the man or woman with the clipboard, the reporting forms, the central calculation office, the statistical results, as signs of a new and improved public opinion.

Polls are now much better at predicting voting behaviour, within their stated limits. But often organizations and people are interested in something much more complicated than predicting an election, that is, understanding what people treat as an issue, what it means to them in their relations with others, what links they make between it and other issues, how much they care about it, how it relates to their daily round of work, commuting, shopping, cooking, getting the children to school. That is why clients who need to know more about response to a policy or decision commission focus groups, citizen juries, inquiries, and other qualitative techniques for researching public opinion (the Nirex study cited here is one such example (Hunt and Simmons 2001)). But if these rich qualitative studies are then framed in terms of clients' expectations, and reported back to them in catchphrases, they are still not getting a sense of how people are talking.

We may be able to show, as Gallup did, that there is a crisis in public opinion research; we may have more trouble in showing that we have a solution. Applied linguists are unlikely to sign up hundreds of newspapers to carry their reports of public opinion, the way Gallup did. Conversation analysis may provide insights but it does not provide headlines; there is no news in bringing out what everyone knows but no one notices. The problem is not just that we in applied linguistics lack a big crossover bestseller that tells the public what we do, like those of Stephen Pinker on language acquisition and psychology (Pinker 1995). There are good writers of potentially popular books in our field (e.g. Agar 1994; Cameron 2000). But the popular books by academics that sell in airport bookshops and are talked about in radio programmes, the books with subtitles beginning 'How . . .' or 'Why . . .', appeal by offering hidden and complete knowledge in an authoritative tone.

What we can offer is an appreciation of what is there on the surface, the intricate way people interact, and the difference these little intricacies make in social action and change. Such detailed studies of talk about opinions have shown ambivalences in attitudes to people with AIDS (Miller *et al.* 1998), shared anxieties about inner-city community policing (Matoesian and Coldren 2002), evaluation of claims of experts (Myers 2004), and hope, guilt, and defensiveness about environmental sustainability (Hinchliffe 1996; Myers and Macnaghten 1998). The ways people talk connect to the ways they see their world and the ways they act in it and on it. If there is a crisis in public opinion research, it is not a technical problem of sampling, calculation, or prediction, it is that people no longer recognize their own talk and actions in the slogans and the numbers attached to them in surveys. That is where we come in.

References

Agar, M. (1994) *Language Shock: Understanding the Culture of Conversation*. New York: William Morrow and Company.

Antaki, C. and Rapley, M. (1996) '"Quality of life" talk: the liberal paradox of psychological testing', *Discourse & Society* 7 (3): 293–316.

Antaki, C., Condor, S. *et al.* (1996) 'Social identities in talk: speakers' own orientations', *British Journal of Social Psychology* 35: 473–92.

Barton, E.L. (1999) 'Informational and interactional functions of slogans and sayings in the discourse of a support group', *Discourse & Society* 10 (4): 461–86.

Becker, C., Chasin, L. *et al.* (1995) 'From stuck debate to new conversation: a report from the Public Conversations Project', *Journal of Feminist Family Therapy* 7: 143–63.

Belson, W.A. (1981) *The Design and Understanding of Survey Questions*. Aldershot, Hampshire: Gower.

Benhabib, S. (ed.) (1996) *Democracy and Difference: Contesting the Boundaries of the Political*. Princeton, NJ: Princeton University Press.

Billig, M. (1987) *Arguing and Thinking: A Rhetorical Approach to Social Psychology*. Cambridge: Cambridge University Press; Paris: Editions de la Maison de l'Homme.

Billig, M. (1995) *Banal Nationalism*. London; Thousand Oaks, CA: Sage.

Bloor, M., Frankland, J. *et al.* (2001) *Focus Groups in Social Research*. London: Sage.

Bolter, H. (1996) *Inside Sellafield*. London: Quartet.

Bourdieu, P. (1990) 'Opinion polls: a "science" without a scientist', in P. Bourdieu (ed.) *In Other Words: Essays Towards a Reflexive Sociology* (pp. 168–75). Cambridge: Polity.

Bourdieu, P. (1993) 'Public opinion does not exist', in P. Bourdieu (ed.) *Sociology in Question* (pp. 149–57). London: Sage.

Brumfit, C.J. (1995) 'Teacher professionalism and research', in G. Cook and B. Seidlhofer (eds) *Principle and Practice in Applied Linguistics* (pp. 27–41). Oxford: Oxford University Press.

Bulmer, M. (ed.) (2004) *Questionnaires. Sage Benchmarks in Social Research Methods*. London: Sage.

Cameron, D. (2000) *Good to Talk?* London: Sage.

DeMaio, T.T. and Rothgeb, J. (1996) 'Cognitive interview techniques: in the lab and in the field', in S. Sudman (ed.) *Answering Questions: Methodology for Determining*

Cognitive and Communicative Processes in Survey Research (pp. 177–95). San Francisco, CA: Jossey-Bass.

Douglas, M. and Wildavsky, A. (1982) *Risk and Culture: An Essay on the Selection of Technological and Environmental Dangers*. Berkeley, CA: University of California Press.

Dryzek, M. (1990) *Discursive Democracy: Politics, Policy, and Political Science*. Cambridge: Cambridge University Press.

Edwards, D. (1997) *Discourse and Cognition*. London: Sage.

Edwards, D. and Potter, J. (1992) *Discursive Psychology*. London; Newbury Park, CA: Sage Publications.

Elster, J. (ed.) (1998) *Deliberative Democracy*. Cambridge: Cambridge University Press.

Fairclough, N. (2000) 'Dialogue in the public sphere', in M. Coulthard (ed.) *Discourse and Social Life* (pp. 170–84). Harlow: Longman.

Gallup, G.H. and Rae, S.F. (1940) *The Pulse of Democracy: The Public Opinion Poll and How It Works*. New York: Simon and Schuster.

Goodin, R.E. and Niemeyer, S.J. (2003) 'When does deliberation begin? Internal reflection versus public discussion in Deliberative Democracy', *Political Studies* 51 (4): 621–700.

Grassi, E. (1990) *Vico and Humanism: Essays on Vico, Heidegger, and Rhetoric*. New York: Peter Lang.

Herbst, S. (1993) *Numbered Voices: How Opinion Polling Has Shaped American Politics*. Chicago, IL: University of Chicago Press.

Hinchliffe, S. (1996) 'Helping the earth begins in the home: the social construction of environmental responsibilities', *Global Environmental Change* 6: 53–62.

Houtkoop-Steenstra, H. (2000) *Interaction and the Standardized Survey Interview: The Living Questionnaire*. Cambridge: Cambridge University Press.

Hunt, J. and Simmons, P. (2001) *The Front of the Front End: Mapping Public Concerns about Radioactive Waste Management Issues*. Lancaster: Institute for Environment, Philosophy, and Public Policy, Lancaster University.

Kim, J. and Wyatt, R.O. *et al*. (1999) 'News, talk, opinion, participation: the part played by conversation in deliberative democracy', *Political Communication* 16 (4): 361–86.

Kitzinger, J. (1994) 'The methodology of focus groups – the importance of interaction between research participants', *Sociology of Health and Illness* 16 (1): 103–21.

Lazarsfeld, P. (1944) 'The controversy over detailed interviews – an offer for negotiation', *Public Opinion Quarterly* 8: 38–60.

Low, G. (1996) 'Intensifiers and hedges in questionnaire items and the lexical invisibility hypothesis', *Applied Linguistics* 17 (1): 1–37.

Low, G. (1999) 'What respondents do with questionnaires: accounting for incongruity and fluidity', *Applied Linguistics* 20 (4): 503–33.

Lupton, D. (1999) *Risk*. London: Routledge.

Macnaghten, P. and Myers, G. (2003) 'Focus groups', in J.G. Giampietro Gobo, C. Seale and D. Silverman (eds) *Qualitative Research Practice*. London: Sage.

Matoesian, G.M. and Coldren, J.R.C., Jr. (2002) 'Language and bodily conduct in focus groups evaluations of legal policy', *Discourse and Society* 13 (4): 469–93.

Maynard, D. and Schaeffer, N. (1997) 'Keeping the gate – declinations of the request to participate in a telephone survey interview', *Sociological Methods & Research* 26 (1): 34–79.

Maynard, D. and Schaeffer, N. (2000) 'Toward a sociology of social scientific knowledge: survey research and ethnomethodology's asymmetric alternates', *Social Studies of Science* 30 (3): 323–70.

Maynard, D.W., H. Houtkoop-Steenstra *et al*. (eds) (2002) *Standardization and Tacit Knowledge: Interaction and Practice in the Research Interview*. New York: Wiley.

Middleton, D. and Edwards, D. (eds) (1990) *Collective Remembering*. London: Sage.

Miller, D., Kitzinger, J. *et al*. (1998) *The Circuit of Mass Communication*. London: Sage.

Myers, G. (1998) 'Displaying opinions: topics and disagreement in focus groups', *Language in Society* 27 (1): 85–111.

Myers, G. (1999) 'Functions of reported speech in group discussions', *Applied Linguistics* 20 (3): 376–401.

Myers, G. (2004) *Matters of Opinion: Dynamics of Talk about Public Issues*. Cambridge: Cambridge University Press.

Myers, G. (2005) 'Communities of practice, risk, and Sellafield', in K. Tusting (ed.) *Beyond Communities of Practice*. Cambridge: Cambridge University Press.

Myers, G. and Macnaghten, P. (1998) 'Rhetorics of environmental sustainability: commonplaces and places', *Environment and Planning* A 30 (2): 333–53.

Myers, G. and Macnaghten, P. (1999) 'Can focus groups be analysed as talk?' in J. Kitzinger (ed.) *Developing Focus Group Research: Politics, Theory and Practice* (pp. 173–85). London: Sage.

Myles, J.F. (2004) 'From Doxa to experience: issues in Bourdieu's adoption of Husserlian phenomenology', *Theory Culture & Society* 21: 91–107.

Pan, Y. (2004) 'Opening the circumference of census-taking: a nexus analysis'. *American Association for Applied Linguistics Conference*, May 2004, Portland, OR.

Payne, S.L. (1951) *The Art of Asking Questions*. Princeton, NJ: Princeton University Press.

Pinker, S. (1995) *The Language Instinct: The New Science of Language and Mind*. London: Penguin.

Puchta, C. and Potter, J. (1999) 'Asking elaborate questions: focus groups and the management of spontaneity', *Journal of Sociolinguistics* 3: 314–35.

Puchta, C. and Potter, J. (2002) 'Manufacturing individual opinions: market research focus groups and the discursive psychology of evaluation', *British Journal of Social Psychology* 41: 345–63.

Puchta, C. and Potter, J. (2004) *Focus Group Practice*. London: Sage.

Rosa, E.A. and Dunlap, R.E. (1994) 'Poll trends: nuclear power: three decades of public opinion', *Public Opinion Quarterly* 58: 295–325.

Schaeffer, N.C. and Maynard, D.W. (1996) 'From paradigm to prototype and back again', in S. Sudman (ed.) *Answering Questions: Methodology for Determining Cognitive and Communicative Processes in Survey Research* (pp. 65–88). San Francisco, CA: Jossey-Bass.

Schaeffer, N.C. and Presser, S. (2003) 'The science of asking questions', *Annual Review of Sociology* 29: 65–88.

Schudson, M. (1998) *The Good Citizen: A History of American Civic Life*. Cambridge, MA: Harvard University Press.

Schuman, H. (1986) 'Ordinary questions, survey questions, and policy questions', *Public Opinion Quarterly* 50: 432–42.

Schuman, H. and Presser, S. (1981) *Questions and Answers in Attitude Surveys: Experiments on Question Form, Wording, and Content*. New York: Academic Press.

Shotter, J. (1993) *Conversational Realities: Constructing Life Through Language*. Thousand Oaks, CA: Sage.

Slovic, P. (2001) *The Perception of Risk*. London: Earthscan.

Suchman, L. and Jordan, B. (1990a) 'Interactional troubles in face-to-face survey interviews', *Journal of the American Statistical Association* 85 (409): 232–41.

Suchman, L. and Jordan, B. (1990b) 'Interactional troubles in face-to-face survey interviews – Rejoinder', *Journal of the American Statistical Association* 85 (409): 252–3.

Sudman, S. and Bradburn, N. (1982) *Asking Questions*. San Francisco, CA: Jossey-Bass.

Szerszynski, B. (1999) 'Risk and trust: the performative dimension', *Environmental Values* 8 (2): 239–52.

Vico, G. (1988 [1710]) *On the Most Ancient Wisdom of the Italians*. Ithaca, NY: Cornell University Press.

Waterton, C. and Wynne, B. (1999) 'Can focus groups access community views?' in J. Kitzinger (ed.) *Developing Focus Group Research* (pp. 127–43). London: Sage.

Wynne, B. (1982) *Rationality and Ritual: The Windscale Inquiry and Nuclear Decision in Britain.* Chalfont St. Giles, Berks: British Society for the History of Science.

Zonabend, F. (1993) *The Nuclear Peninsula.* Cambridge: Cambridge University Press.

Index

In the following index, British English spelling conventions have been used, which may differ slightly from those in the text. Unless stated otherwise, entries relate primarily to the English language.